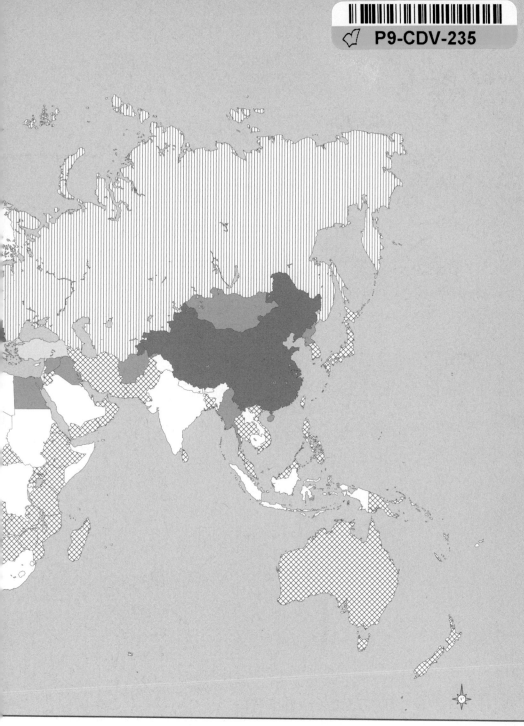

Map 1. With the decolonization of Europe's former empires, the Cold War spread from Europe to large parts of the globe.

COLD
WAR

AN INTERNATIONAL HISTORY

CAROLE K. FINK

THE OHIO STATE UNIVERSITY

WESTVIEW
PRESS

A MEMBER OF THE PERSEUS BOOKS GROUP

Westview Press was founded in 1975 in Boulder, Colorado, by notable publisher and intellectual Fred Praeger. Westview Press continues to publish scholarly titles and high-quality undergraduate- and graduate-level textbooks in core social science disciplines. With books developed, written, and edited with the needs of serious nonfiction readers, professors, and students in mind, Westview Press honors its long history of publishing books that matter.

Westview Press books are available at special discounts for bulk purchases in the United States by corporations, institutions, and other organizations. For more information, please contact the Special Markets Department at the Perseus Books Group, 2300 Chestnut Street, Suite 200, Philadelphia, PA 19103, or call (800) 810-4145, ext. 5000, or e-mail special.markets@perseusbooks.com.

Designed by Jack Lenzo

Library of Congress Cataloging-in-Publication Data

Fink, Carole, 1940-
  Cold War : an international history / Carole K. Fink, The Ohio State University.
    pages cm
  Includes bibliographical references and index.
  ISBN 978-0-8133-4795-0 (pbk.) — ISBN 978-0-8133-4796-7 (ebook) 1. Cold War. 2. World politics—1945-1989. 3. Cold War—Influence. I. Title.
  D843.F456 2014
  909.82'5--dc23
                          2013029847

10 9 8 7 6 5 4 3 2

To my students

CONTENTS

Preface, xiii
List of Photographs, xv
List of Maps, xvi
List of Abbreviations and Acronyms, xvii
Chronology, xx

INTRODUCTION · 1

CHAPTER ONE PRELUDE: SOVIET RUSSIA
AND THE WEST, 1917–1941 · 5
War and Revolution, 5
A Contested Peace, 8
The Soviet Entry into World Politics, 10
The Dark Decade, 1931–1939, 15
The Aggressors Triumphant, 1939–1941, 19
Suggestions for Further Study, 23

CHAPTER TWO THE GRAND ALLIANCE, 1941–1945 · 27
Disparate Partners, 28
Turning the Tide While Tensions Mount, 33
Moving Apart, 37
Yalta, 40
The End of World War II, 43
Suggestions for Further Study, 48

CHAPTER THREE   COLD WAR, 1949–1952 · 53
                Two Rivals Emerge, 54
                Nuremberg: The Final Collaboration, 55
                The Rupture, 56
                1947: The Division of Europe, 62
                The World Outside Europe, 64
                Prague and Berlin, 68
                1949, 72
                War in Korea, 79
                Suggestions for Further Study, 84

CHAPTER FOUR   THE WIDENING CONFLICT, 1953–1963 · 90
                A Global Cold War, 93
                Hungary, 98
                Suez, 100
                The Nuclear Question, 105
                Building Europe, 106
                Peaceful Coexistence? 107
                Cuba and Berlin, 111
                Exit Kennedy and Khrushchev, 115
                Suggestions for Further Study, 116

CHAPTER FIVE   THE SIXTIES · 122
                The Cold War in Vietnam, 124
                June 1967: The Arab-Israeli War, 131
                Prague: August 1968, 137
                1968: International Human Rights Year, 141
                Suggestions for Further Study, 145

CHAPTER SIX   DÉTENTE, 1969–1975 · 149
                Reducing the Nuclear Threat, 150
                Ostpolitik, 153
                Ping-Pong Diplomacy, 156
                Testing Détente, 1970–1974, 159
                    The Middle East, 159
                    South Asia, 162
                    Vietnam, 163
                    The October War in the Middle East, 164
                Helsinki, 168
                Suggestions for Further Study, 170

CHAPTER SEVEN DÉTENTE COLLAPSES, 1975–1980 · 174
Human Rights, 175
The Cold War in Africa, 181
SS-20 Missiles and SALT II, 185
The Middle East: 1979, 188
Solidarność, 197
Suggestions for Further Study, 200

CHAPTER EIGHT THE SECOND COLD WAR, 1981–1985 · 204
The Deterioration of US-Soviet Relations, 206
Martial Law in Poland, 206
Reagan's Strategic Defense Initiative (SDI), 207
The Downing of KAL 007, 209
"White Hot, Thoroughly White Hot," 211
Human Rights, 212
Central and South America, 213
Asia, 218
Africa, 220
The Middle East, 221
Suggestions for Further Study, 226

CHAPTER NINE THE END OF THE COLD WAR, 1985–1991 · 229
The Gorbachev Revolution in International Affairs, 230
1989: The Transformation of Eastern Europe, 236
1990: German Reunification, 243
1991: The Collapse of the Soviet Union, 247
Suggestions for Further Study, 254

CHAPTER TEN AFTERMATH, 1992–2001 · 260
The 1990s: A Global View, 261
Asia, 265
Africa, 267
The Middle East, 269
Latin America, 272
Europe, 274
The Wars in Yugoslavia, 274
The European Union, 280
The United States and 9/11, 281
Suggestions for Further Study, 285

CONCLUSION · 290

List of Individuals, 293
Bibliography, 299
Index, 306

PREFACE

Almost three years ago I decided to transform my many years of teaching and writing on the Cold War into an accessible book for twenty-first-century readers. It has been a fascinating task to revisit the rivalry between the world's first communist state and the Western powers, one that consumed a major portion of the twentieth century and altered its politics and economy along with its physical, social, and cultural environment.

Although the Cold War's unexpected end led to an unprecedented opening of archival sources and the publication of numerous memoirs and books, there have been few efforts up to now to view this conflict in a broad international perspective. Based on new evidence along with the observations and analyses of contemporaries and two generations of scholarship, this book is an attempt to comprehend the Cold War as a dynamic rivalry, one in which large and small powers and diverse groups of people maneuvered in a militarized and divided world.

I thank my original editor, Priscilla McGeehon, and her successor, Ada Fung, and their able assistant, Stephen Pinto, for their generous support, and Annie Lenth, Carolyn Sobczak, and Beth Wright for bringing this book to completion. I thank David Lincove, History, Political Science, and Philosophy Librarian at The Ohio State University, and Sue Ann Cody, Associate University Librarian for Public Services Emerita, University of North Carolina at Wilmington, for helping me obtain research materials. The late Terry Benjey, a devoted friend and computer mentor, provided superb technical assistance. I thank family and friends who have given unstinting support to this project: Renate Bridenthal, Nan Cameron, Sandi Cooper, Emily Davidson, Muriel Dimen, Hilda Godwin,

John Haley, Dorothy Kahn, Joyce Kuhn, Marjorie Madigan, Richard Nochimson, Peter Schuck, Ben Steelman, and Juanita Winner. My son, Stefan Harold Fink, has made my move to Wilmington, North Carolina, a joy.

Thanks also to the reviewers who provided such thoughtful feedback on this project: John Chambers (Rutgers University), David Messenger (University of Wyoming), Thomas Maulucci (American International College), Cristofer Scarboro (King's College), and Michael Slattery (Campbell University).

I am grateful to all my students (including the recent Cold War class in OLLI, the Osher Lifelong Learning Institute, at the University of North Carolina at Wilmington) for their inspiration and especially to Stuart J. Hilwig (1968–2012), who will long be remembered as a wise, witty, and extraordinarily dedicated scholar and teacher.

Wilmington, North Carolina
March 2013

PHOTOGRAPHS

1.1 Lenin · 12

2.1 Yalta · 41

3.1 The Berlin Airlift · 71

4.1 The Bandung Conference · 97

4.2 Budapest, 1956 · 99

4.3 Eisenhower and Khrushchev at Camp David · 109

4.4 The Berlin Wall · 113

4.5 Kennedy and the Cuban Missile Crisis · 115

6.1 Mao and Nixon · 156

6.2 Brezhnev and Nixon · 165

7.1 Sandinista Soldiers · 180

7.2 Sadat, Carter, and Begin · 190

7.3 Poster of Ayatollah Khomeini · 192

7.4 Anti-Soviet Mujahedeen · 197

8.1 US Antinuclear Demonstration · 208

9.1 Reagan and Gorbachev in Geneva · 232

9.2 Demonstrators in Tiananmen Square · 239

9.3 The Berlin Wall, 1989 · 241

MAPS

1 The Cold War Division of the World, 1961 · Frontispiece

2 Europe After World War I · 9

3 Southeastern Europe and the Middle East After World War II · 59

4 The Partition of British India · 65

5 The Establishment of the State of Israel · 66

6 Europe After World War II · 69

7 Germany Divided · 74

8 East Asia After World War II · 80

9 The Suez Crisis · 103

10 The United States in Vietnam · 127

11 The Middle East After the June 1967 War · 133

12 Africa in the 1970s · 182

13 The Soviet Invasion of Afghanistan · 195

14 The Flight of KAL 007 · 210

15 The United States, Central America, and the Caribbean · 215

16 The Falklands War · 217

17 The Middle East and the Horn of Africa · 222

18 The Disintegration of the Communist Bloc and the Soviet Union · 251

19 The Breakup of Yugoslavia · 275

20 The World in 2000 · Endpiece

ABBREVIATIONS AND ACRONYMS

ABM	Antiballistic Missiles
AK	Armia Krajowa—Home Army (Poland)
ANC	African National Congress (South Africa)
APEC	Asia-Pacific Economic Cooperation
ASEAN	Association of Southeastern Asian Nations
Benelux	Belgium, the Netherlands, and Luxembourg
CCP	Chinese Communist Party
CDU	Christlich Demokratische Union Deutschlands—Christian Democratic Union (Germany)
CFM	Council of Foreign Ministers (Britain, China, France, United States, USSR)
CHR	Commission on Human Rights (UN)
CGDK	Coalition Government of Democratic Kampuchea (Cambodia)
CIA	Central Intelligence Agency (United States)
Comecon	Council for Mutual Economic Assistance (USSR-directed, sometimes referred to as CMEA)
Cominform	Communist Information Bureau
Comintern	Communist International
CSCE	Conference on Security and Cooperation in Europe
EEC	European Economic Community
ETIM	East Turkestan Islamic Movement
EU	European Union

FDP   Freie Demokratische Partei—Free Democratic Party (Germany)

FLN   Front de Libération Nationale—National Liberation Front (Algeria)

FNLA   Frente Nacional de Libertação de Angola—Front for the National Liberation of Angola

FRELIMO Frente de Libertação de Moçambique—Mozambique Liberation Front

FRG   Federal Republic of Germany (West Germany)

GATT   General Agreement on Tariffs and Trade

GDP   Gross Domestic Product

GDR   German Democratic Republic (East Germany)

ICBM   Intercontinental Ballistic Missile

IMF   International Monetary Fund

INF   Intermediate-Range Nuclear Forces

KAL   Korean Air Lines

KFOR   Kosovo Force (NATO)

KGB   Komitet Gosudarstvennoy Bezopasnosti—Committee for State Security (USSR)

KLA   Kosovo Liberation Army

KOR   Komitet Obrony Robotników—The Workers' Defense Committee (Poland)

MAD   Mutual Assured Destruction

Mercosur Mercado Común del Sur—Common Market of the South (South America)

MPLA   Movimento Popular de Libertação de Angola—Popular Movement for the Liberation of Angola

NATO   North Atlantic Treaty Organization

NPT   Treaty on Non-Proliferation of Nuclear Weapons

NSC-68 National Security Council paper number 68

OAS   Organization of American States

OPEC   Organization of the Petroleum Exporting Countries

OSCE   Organization for Security and Cooperation in Europe (Successor to CSCE)

PCNL   Polish Committee of National Liberation (Polish: Polski Komitet Wyzwolenia Narodowego, PKWN) also known as Lublin Committee

PFLP   Popular Front for the Liberation of Palestine

PLO Palestine Liberation Organization
PRC People's Republic of China
PRK People's Republic of Kampuchea (Cambodia)
RENAMO Resistência Nacional Moçambicana—Mozambican National Resistance
SAC South African Communist Party
SALT Strategic Arms Limitation Treaty
SAM Surface-to-Air Missile
SDI Strategic Defense Initiative
SDP Social Democratic Party (German: Sozialdemokratische Partei Deutschlands, SPD), Germany
SEATO Southeast Asia Treaty Organization
SORT Strategic Offensive Reductions Treaty
START Strategic Arms Reduction Treaty
Stasi Ministerium für Staatssicherheit—Ministry for State Security (GDR)
SWAPO Southwest Africa People's Organization (Namibia) (Afri-kaans: Suidwes-Afrikaanse Volk-Organisasie, SWAVO)
UDHR Universal Declaration of Human Rights
UK United Kingdom
UN United Nations
UNITA União Nacional para a Independência Total de Angola—National Union for the Total Independence of Angola
UNPROFOR United Nations Protection Force (Croatia, Bosnia-Herzegovina)
USSR Union of Soviet Socialist Republics

CHRONOLOGY

1917	**April**	US entry into World War I
	November	Bolshevik Revolution in Russia
1918	**January**	Wilson's Fourteen Points
	March	Treaty of Brest Litovsk
	November	Armistice with Germany
1919	**January**	Opening of Paris Peace Conference
	March	Establishment of Comintern (Communist International)
	June	Treaty of Versailles
1922	**April**	Stalin named general secretary of the Communist Party
		Genoa Conference opens (–May 1922)
		Treaty of Rapallo between Germany and Soviet Russia
	December	Establishment of Union of Soviet Socialist Republics (USSR)
1924	**January**	Death of Lenin
1929	**October**	Beginning of the Great Depression
1931	**September**	Japan invades Manchuria
1932	**November**	Franklin Roosevelt elected US president
1933	**January**	Hitler assumes power in Germany

1935	**March**	German rearmament
	June	Anglo-German naval agreement
	August	US Neutrality Act (extended in 1936, 1937, and 1939)
	October	Italy invades Abyssinia (Ethiopia)
1936	**March**	Germany reoccupies the Rhineland
	July	Outbreak of Spanish civil war (–April 1939)
	October	Rome-Berlin Axis
	November	Anti-Comintern Pact (Germany-Japan)
1937	**July**	Japan invades China
	November	Italy joins Anti-Comintern Pact
1938	**September**	Munich Conference
1939	**August**	Nazi-Soviet Pact
	September	Outbreak of World War II in Europe
	November	USSR war with Finland (–March 1940)
1940	**June**	Fall of France
	July	Battle of Britain begins (–October 1940)
	November	Roosevelt reelected to unprecedented third term
1941	**March**	US Lend Lease Act ends neutrality policy
	June	German invasion of Soviet Union
	August	Atlantic Charter
	December	Japanese attack on Pearl Harbor; Germany declares war on United States
1942	**January**	Declaration of the United Nations
1943	**January**	Casablanca Conference
	May	Stalin dissolves Comintern
	October	Moscow Conference of Foreign Ministers
	November	Cairo Conference; Tehran Conference
	December	Second Cairo Conference
1944	**July**	Bretton Woods Conference
	August	Dumbarton Oaks Conference
	October	Churchill-Stalin meeting in Moscow
	December	Civil war erupts in Greece (–October 1949)

1945	January	Stalin recognizes Polish Committee of National Liberation (PCNL) as the provisional government of Poland
	February	Yalta Conference
	April	Death of Roosevelt
	May	World War II ends in Europe
	June	San Francisco Conference approves UN Charter
	July	First successful atomic bomb test in New Mexico
		Potsdam Conference opens (–August)
	August	Atomic bombs dropped on Hiroshima and Nagasaki
		Red Army moves into Manchuria
		World War II ends in Asia
	November	Nuremberg trials begin (–October 1946)
	December	Bretton Woods agreement signed by twenty-seven governments; USSR withdraws
1946	February	Stalin election address to USSR
		Kennan "Long Telegram"
	March	Churchill "Iron Curtain" speech, Fulton, Missouri
		Iran crisis (–May 1946)
	July	Civil war in China (–October 1949)
	September	Byrnes speech affirming US commitment to Germany's revival
1947	February	Peace treaties signed with Bulgaria, Finland, Italy, and Romania
	March	Truman doctrine: aid to Greece and Turkey
	June	Marshall Plan announced
	July	"Mr. X" (George Kennan) article in *Foreign Affairs*
		Soviet withdrawal from Marshall Plan
	August	India declares independence
	September	Cominform (Communist Information Bureau) established
	November	UN partition of Palestine
		London Conference of Foreign Ministers fails to agree on peace treaties with Germany and Austria (–December 1947)
1948	February	Coup in Czechoslovakia brings communist government to power
	April	Soviet Union withdraws from Allied Control Council for Germany
	May	Israel declares independence
	June	US Selective Service Act reinstates draft
		Berlin blockade (–May 1949)
		Stalin expels Tito from Cominform
	December	Universal Declaration of Human Rights adopted by UN General Assembly

1949	April	North Atlantic Treaty Organization (NATO) founded
	May	Federal Republic of Germany (FRG) established in West Germany
	September	Truman announces successful Soviet atomic bomb test
	October	People's Republic of China established
		German Democratic Republic (GDR) established in East Germany
1950	January	Dean Acheson excludes Korea and Taiwan from US defense perimeter in Asia
	February	Sino-Soviet Treaty
	April	NSC-68 defines US Cold War policy
	June	North Korea invades South Korea; UN resolution calls for an international force
	September	UN troops cross thirty-eighth parallel in Korea
	November	Chinese troops enter Korean War
1952	November	Dwight David Eisenhower elected US president
1953	March	Death of Stalin
	June	Soviet troops crush uprising in East Germany
	July	Armistice signed ending Korean War
	August	CIA-led coup in Iran
	September	Nikita Khrushchev becomes first secretary of the Communist Party of the Soviet Union
1954	May	French defeat at Diên Biên Phu
		Geneva Conference on Indochina (–July 1954)
	June	CIA-sponsored coup in Guatemala
	September	Formation of Southeast Asia Treaty Organization (SEATO)
1955	April	Bandung Conference
	May	West Germany joins NATO
		Warsaw Pact established
		Austrian State Treaty
	July	Geneva summit meeting
1956	February	Khrushchev speech before Twentieth Party Congress denouncing Stalin
	April	Cominform dissolved
	June	Anti-Soviet protests in Poland (–October 1956)
	October	Revolt in Hungary and Soviet suppression (–November 1956)
		Suez crisis (–November 1956)
	November	Eisenhower reelected

1957	**January**	Eisenhower doctrine to defend Middle East against communism
	March	Treaty of Rome creating European Economic Community
	October	Soviet Union launches *Sputnik*, the first earth satellite
1958	**November**	Berlin crisis (–August 1959)
1959	**January**	Fidel Castro overthrows Batista regime in Cuba
	September	Khrushchev visits United States
1960	**May**	Paris summit meeting collapses over U-2 incident
	November	John F. Kennedy elected US president
	December	UN Declaration on the Granting of Independence to Colonial Countries and Peoples
1961	**April**	Soviet astronaut Yuri Gagarin becomes first man to fly in space
		Bay of Pigs invasion of Cuba
	June	Kennedy-Khrushchev meeting in Vienna
	August	Berlin Wall erected
	October	Sino-Soviet split becomes public at Twenty-Second Soviet Communist Party Congress
1962	**October**	Cuban missile crisis
		Sino-Indian war
1963	**June**	US-Soviet hotline established
	August	Nuclear test-ban treaty
	November	Coup in South Vietnam; assassination of Ngô Đình Diệm
		Assassination of Kennedy; succeeded by Lyndon B. Johnson
1964	**August**	Gulf of Tonkin resolution
	October	Khrushchev replaced by Leonid Brezhnev as general secretary of Communist Party of USSR
		China explodes its first atomic weapon
	November	Lyndon Johnson elected US president
1965	**March**	3,500 US marines dispatched to South Vietnam
	April	Indo-Pakistan War (–September 1965)
	December	US forces in Vietnam reach 180,000
1966	**March**	President Charles de Gaulle orders removal of NATO headquarters and US and Canadian military bases from France
	May	Cultural Revolution begins in China (–September 1971)

1967	**June**	Arab-Israeli War
	November	UN Security Council Resolution 242
1968	**January**	Tet offensive in Vietnam (–August 1968)
	March	Johnson withdraws his candidacy for reelection
	April	UN International Conference on Human Rights (–May 1968)
	July	Great Britain, United States, and USSR sign Nuclear Non-Proliferation Treaty
	August	Warsaw Pact invasion of Czechoslovakia
	November	Richard Nixon elected US president
		Brezhnev doctrine announced
1969	**March**	Chinese unit ambushes Soviet forces on Ussuri River
	September	Willy Brandt elected chancellor of West Germany and launches *Ostpolitik*
	November	Strategic Arms Limitation Talks (SALT) begin in Helsinki
1970	**January**	USSR sends assistance to Egypt against Israel
	April	US forces attack communist bases in Cambodia (–May 1970)
	August	Moscow Treaty between West Germany and Soviet Union
	September	Jordanian crisis
		Socialist candidate Salvador Allende wins presidency of Chile
	December	Treaty between West Germany and Poland
1971	**July**	Kissinger visits China
	August	Quadripartite Pact on Berlin
	October	UN General Assembly votes to seat China
	December	Indo-Pakistan War ends in formation of Bangladesh
1972	**February**	Nixon visits China
	May	Nixon visits USSR, signing of SALT I and ABM treaties
	June	Break-in at Democratic National Committee Headquarters in the Watergate building in Washington, DC
	November	Nixon reelected
	December	West Germany and East Germany sign Basic Treaty
1973	**January**	Great Britain joins European Community
		Paris Peace Accords signed, ending US war in Vietnam
	July	Conference on Security and Cooperation in Europe opened in Helsinki
	September	Allende overthrown in military coup and dies
	October	War between Israel and Egypt and Syria; Arab oil boycott against Western powers

1974	**August**	Nixon resigns as US president; succeeded by Gerald Ford
	September	Ethiopia emperor Haile Selassie overthrown in military coup; Ethiopia then gravitates toward USSR
1975	**August**	Signing of Helsinki Accords by thirty-five governments
	November	Outbreak of Angola civil war
1976	**June**	South African police attack unarmed student protesters in Soweto
	November	Jimmy Carter elected US president
1977	**July**	War between Somalia and Ethiopia (–March 1978)
	October	CSCE meeting (follow-up of Helsinki) in Belgrade
1978	**November**	Egyptian president Sadat visits Jerusalem
	December	Vietnam invades Cambodia, establishes puppet government PRK (People's Republic of Kampuchea)
1979	**January**	United States and China establish full diplomatic relations
		Shah of Iran flees the country
	February	Ayatollah Ruhollah Khomeini returns to Iran from exile
	March	Egyptian-Israeli peace treaty signed in Washington, DC
	June	Carter and Brezhnev sign SALT II treaty
	November	Iranian militants invade US embassy, taking seventy hostages
	December	Soviet troops invade Afghanistan
1980	**September**	Polish trade union Solidarność established
		Iran-Iraq War (–September 1988)
	November	Ronald Reagan elected US president
1981	**December**	General Wojciech Jaruzelski declares martial law in Poland
1982	**April**	Falklands War between Great Britain and Argentina (–June 1982)
	June	Israel invades Lebanon
	November	Death of Brezhnev; succeeded by former KGB chief Yuri Andropov as general secretary of Communist Party of USSR
1983	**March**	Reagan announces development of Strategic Defense Initiative (SDI)
	April	Attacks on US forces in Lebanon (–October 1983)
	September	Soviet Union shoots down Korean Air Lines Flight 007
	October	United States invades Grenada

1984	**January**	Reagan calls for renewed negotiations with USSR
	February	Death of Andropov; succeeded by Konstantin Chernenko as general secretary of Communist Party of USSR
	November	Reagan reelected as US president
1985	**March**	Death of Chernenko; succeeded by Mikhail Gorbachev as general secretary of Communist Party of USSR
	November	US-Soviet summit in Geneva
1986	**February**	Gorbachev introduces perestroika (reconstruction) and glasnost (openness)
	April	Explosion at Soviet nuclear power plant in Chernobyl
	October	Reagan-Gorbachev meeting in Reykjavik
1987	**June**	Reagan in Berlin urges Gorbachev to "tear down this Wall"
	December	Outbreak of Palestinian Intifada (uprising) on the West Bank and in Gaza
		Gorbachev in Washington, signs Intermediate-Range Nuclear Forces (INF) Treaty
1988	**February**	Gorbachev announces withdrawal of Soviet troops from Afghanistan within two years
	November	George H. W. Bush elected US president
	December	Gorbachev address to UN General Assembly announcing end of Cold War
		Angola-Namibia Accords signed in New York
1989	**April**	Roundtable talks in Poland leading to legalization of Solidarność and national elections
	May	Hungary opens border with Austria
	June	Suppression of protest movement in China
	August	Citizens in Estonia, Latvia, and Lithuania protest fifty-year Soviet occupation
	September	Apartheid ends in South Africa; Nelson Mandela released after twenty-seven years in prison
	November	Berlin Wall falls
	December	Bush and Gorbachev meet in Malta
		United States invades Panama, removes Manuel Noriega
		Romanian leader Nicolae Ceauşescu overthrown and executed
		Václav Havel elected president of Czechoslovakia
1990	**July**	NATO summit declares USSR no longer an enemy
	August	Iraq invades Kuwait
	October	German reunification
		Gorbachev awarded Nobel Peace Prize

Chronology

1991	March	Gorbachev proposes new union treaty for USSR
	June	Civil war erupts in Yugoslavia (–November 1995)
	August	Coup in USSR
		Baltic states declare independence
	October	Opening of Madrid Conference on the Middle East
	December	Dissolution of USSR, Gorbachev resigns
1992	February	Maastricht Treaty lays basis for European Union
	November	Bill Clinton elected US president
1993	January	Czechoslovakia divided into Czech Republic and Slovakia
	September	Oslo Accords between Israel and Palestinian Authority
1994	April	Mandela elected president of South Africa
	June	Carter visits North Korea to negotiate on nuclear weapons
	September	US occupation of Haiti
1995	November	Assassination of Yitzhak Rabin
		Dayton Peace Agreement ends war in Bosnia
1996	May	Osama bin Laden returns to Afghanistan from Sudan, issues fatwa against United States
	November	Bill Clinton reelected US president
1997	June	Britain returns Hong Kong to China
	December	Kyoto Protocol on reducing greenhouse gas emissions
1998	July	Rome Statute establishes International Criminal Court
	August	Al Qaeda militants bomb US embassies in Kenya and Tanzania, killing 224 people
1999	March	NATO bombing campaign against Yugoslavia (–June 1999)
2000	July	Camp David meeting between Ehud Barak and Yasser Arafat fails to reach agreement
	September	Outbreak of Second Intifada
	October	Al Qaeda attacks the USS *Cole* in Yemen, killing seventeen US sailors
	November	George W. Bush elected US president
2001	September	Using four hijacked planes Al Qaeda terrorists bring down twin towers of World Trade Center in New York and crash into the Pentagon and into a field in Pennsylvania, killing over three thousand people
	October	US and NATO troops invade Afghanistan to capture bin Laden

INTRODUCTION

History does not long entrust the care of freedom to the weak or the timid.

—Dwight David Eisenhower

Whether you like it or not, history is on our side.

—Nikita Khrushchev

For readers in the twenty-first century, even those who experienced some of the events described in this book, the Cold War has taken on a patina of antiquity. Scarcely had the Berlin Wall collapsed and the Soviet Empire headed toward dissolution when the world faced new challenges in the Middle East, the Balkans, and Africa, culminating in the shock of September 11, 2001. Suddenly the Cold War was transformed from the dynamic reality of everyday life during almost five decades into a closed episode with a seemingly definitive outcome.

This short book brings a new perspective to the history of the Cold War. I examine the US-Soviet rivalry as part of a global contest that began with the Bolshevik Revolution of 1917 and ended seventy-four years later when the world's first communist state collapsed. Although the conflict between the two Superpowers was the Cold War's principal element, this study also includes the crucial role of allies, rivals, and bystanders, and it stresses the linkage between personalities, ideas, and events around the globe.

In earlier cold wars, among them the Anglo-Spanish conflict in the sixteenth century, the Anglo-French contest in the seventeenth and eighteenth centuries, and the Anglo-Russian clash in the nineteenth century (labeled the Great

Game), the chief combatants faced each other directly on the battlefield but also indirectly, using espionage, propaganda, economic pressure, political subversion, and proxy wars. What made the twentieth-century Cold War unique were three key elements: the enormous nuclear arsenals accumulated by both sides; the role of political ideology,* which permeated almost every aspect of the combatants' policies toward the other; and the solidification of Cold War institutions that provided leaders with unprecedented power but also limited their options.

Although the use of lethal weaponry predated the Cold War—in Europe's imperial wars and in World Wars I and II there was mass killing of civilians and warriors—the advent of the atomic bomb utterly transformed international relations. Once both sides possessed weapons capable of not only destroying the other's territory and population but also contaminating large parts of the earth, the Cold War developed into a rigid struggle driven by fear and a costly arms race. While nuclear weapons intensified several major Cold War crises, the threat of atomic warfare also served as a brake on the Superpowers.

The ideological chasm separating the USSR from the capitalist world was substantial. The Cold War began as a messianic contest. One side presented itself as a regime dedicated to removing economic and political exploitation and ushering in an era of international peace and brotherhood. The other side presented itself as dedicated to individual freedom, political democracy, and unfettered national and international markets. And both sides claimed that the other was a menace to their security and way of life. However, when the Cold War spread to the former colonial world in Africa, the Middle East, and Asia and to Latin America, these core ideological principles became blurred. Vying for influence over near and far away clients, all with their own distinctive histories, political goals, and ancient quarrels, the Superpower rivalry was transformed into a conventional military struggle. And even in Europe—the Cold War's heartland—the ideological Iron Curtain was permeable: orthodox socialism and capitalism continuously faced the challenges of religion and ethnic nationalism.

Although individual leaders' decisions ultimately molded the course of the Cold War, these were subject to several internal and external factors. In the Soviet Union the Communist Party was the motor for political and international action, and in the United States there were two national political parties, but in both capitals economic interests exerted considerable influence. The leadership on both sides was also affected by a burgeoning military and intelligence

---

* To be sure, the sixteenth-century Anglo-Spanish conflict, pitting a Protestant against a Catholic power, may be considered a forerunner in this respect.

apparatus as well as by the press and the intellectual elite. On the other hand, both sides were constrained by a web of sometimes competing domestic pressures and by their mounting international obligations.

Historical memories also played an important role in shaping Cold War decision making. The leaders of large and small states were intent on replicating past triumphs and avoiding (or undoing) earlier setbacks, and not unexpectedly these memories diverged sharply. For Western leaders the "lessons of Munich"* reinforced their reluctance to appease the Soviet Union, but for Moscow, Munich was a reminder of Western betrayal. Similarly, the early events of the Cold War, like the 1948–1949 Berlin blockade, handed down mixed messages to the next generation over the virtues of assertiveness over conciliation.

Studying the history of the Cold War offers us broader historical insights. Despite its unique characteristics this period was replete with instances of *continuity* in human affairs. For example, Russia's rivalry with the Western powers dates back to the eighteenth century, America's dominant relationship toward Latin America started at the beginning of the nineteenth century, and the policy of forming coalitions against heavily armed rivals was practiced by Britain in the decades before World War I.

Cold War history also teaches us the importance of unanticipated events. Mao's victory in China, Castro's ascension in Cuba, and North Vietnam's victory over the United States remind us of the powerful role of human agency in political affairs, as do the fierce resistance to the Soviet invasion in Afghanistan, the rise of a national trade union in Poland, and the fall of the Berlin Wall. Moreover, these events reveal the limits of wealth and military power, and even of the most sophisticated intelligence gathering.

Finally, the Cold War left its mark on global culture. Some of its political iconography, rhetoric, and practice had historical roots—for example, the embalmed communist leaders in Moscow, Beijing, and Hanoi. But there were also new words, sounds, images, and occurrences—ranging from "hawks" and "doves," to the beeps of the Soviet space-satellite *Sputnik* in 1957 and the wondrous earth photograph taken by an *Apollo 8* astronaut on December 24, 1968, to the massacre in Tiananmen Square in June 1989 and the euphoria of Czechoslovakia's peaceful "Velvet Revolution" later that year. In this way the Cold War produced its own legacy for the twenty-first century, one still to be understood from new perspectives.

---

* The September 1938 four-power conference, in which Britain and France, capitulating to Hitler's threats, ceded strategic areas of Czechoslovakia to the Third Reich.

Underlying this work is the old-fashioned conviction that history still greatly matters. Although we lack the ability to replicate yesterday's events or fully comprehend the conditions under which our forerunners operated, historians have the obligation and the capacity to interrogate the past in order to increase our understanding of the world we inhabit today. In the case of the Cold War, our challenge is to sift a welter of testimonies and analyses in complete awareness that this effort will reap only preliminary conclusions but may nonetheless bring a measure of clarity.

Chapter 1

PRELUDE

SOVIET RUSSIA AND THE WEST, 1917–1941

It is easier to make war than peace.

—Georges Clemenceau

We can't solve problems by using the same kind of thinking we used when we created them.

—Albert Einstein

The starting point for our study of the Cold War is the year 1917, when the Bolshevik leadership established a communist regime in Russia and defied the international order by preaching world revolution and challenging conventional diplomatic practices. The Western powers (Britain, France, and the United States) responded with military intervention and ostracism. During the next twenty-four years the estrangement between Russia and the West was overshadowed by the challenges of Italy, Japan, and Germany, but the capitalist world continued to regard the Soviet Union with fear, mistrust, and repugnance—sentiments that Moscow duly reciprocated.

WAR AND REVOLUTION

The Bolsheviks' seizure of power in November 1917 not only shaped the outcome of World War I but also changed the history of the twentieth century. For more than three years tsarist Russia had been an indispensable member of the Triple

5

Entente with France and Great Britain. It had pinned down vast numbers of German and Austro-Hungarian troops in the East by launching several valuable, if ruinous, offensives and also kept pressure on the Ottoman Empire. It had nonetheless been a difficult partner with the West: repressive at home, suspicious of its allies and their clients' territorial designs in southeastern Europe and the Middle East, and insistent on annexations in Poland and Constantinople.

The March 1917* Revolution created Russia's first constitutional government, kindling hopes of freedom among its subject peoples, salving its allies' consciences, and facilitating the US entry into the war on the side of the Entente. But one month later, the charismatic Bolshevik leader Vladimir Lenin returned from his ten-year exile in a sealed train provided by the German government and was determined to seize power. When Prime Minister Alexander Kerensky chose to continue Russia's disastrous combat against the Central Powers, the Bolsheviks—appealing to the population's widespread war weariness and land hunger—led an insurrection of workers, soldiers, and sailors and toppled the provisional government on November 7.

Like the French revolutionaries of 1789, the Bolsheviks were imbued with messianic fervor. In his 1916 expansion of classic Marxism, Lenin had characterized Russia as "the weakest link in the imperialist chain" but also as the potential spearhead of a global uprising against the imperialist powers that had ravaged the earth with their greed and militarism. Accordingly, the Bolsheviks' first acts were to call for an immediate end to the fighting (the Decree on Peace), to publish all the secret wartime treaties over the disposition of enemy territories, to denounce annexations and indemnities, and to proclaim the right of all nationalities to secede from foreign rulers.

Western leaders denounced the revolution as a German-Bolshevik conspiracy and feared the spread of strikes, mutinies, and rebellions across their borders. Russia's erstwhile partners were also irate over Lenin's repudiation of tsarist war debts, which wiped out some 25 percent of France's foreign investments, as well as the Bolsheviks' seizure of private property. For European socialists, many of whom had sacrificed the principle of class solidarity for the defense of their homelands, the Bolsheviks' ascendancy, the dictatorship of the proletariat, and the call for armed revolution had violated their patriotic and democratic creed. Consequently, after November 1917 the hostility between democratic and

---

* The March 1917 Revolution occurred in February according to the old Julian calendar, which remained in use in Russia until 1918.

revolutionary Marxists became almost as strong as the enmity between capitalists and communists.

Russia's former allies moved swiftly to counter Bolshevik propaganda. In January 1918 British premier David Lloyd George and US president Woodrow Wilson each enunciated their nations' war aims in ringing and idealistic terms. In particular, Wilson's Fourteen Points provided a democratic and capitalist alternative to Lenin's dramatic appeal to the world by calling for open diplomacy, global disarmament, freedom of the seas, border adjustments based on national claims, and an international organization to secure the peace.

The Central Powers' reaction was harsher. In March 1918, having driven deeper into a devastated Russia and impervious to Leon Trotsky's audacious "no war—no peace" stratagem, the German military extracted a punitive peace at Brest Litovsk. The treaty eliminated Russian power from Europe, creating a string of puppet states in the western part of the former tsarist empire and establishing German control over vast amounts of its agricultural and mineral resources. A jubilant German Reichstag (parliament), ignoring its 1917 Peace Resolution and the Bolsheviks' protests over a dictated treaty, ratified Brest Litovsk by an overwhelming majority, with the opposition Social Democrats merely abstaining.

The Bolsheviks' diplomatic debut at Brest Litovsk established important precedents for future relations between Soviet Russia and the West. Among them was the introduction of Lenin's concept of a "breathing space," a temporary coexistence with a more powerful enemy. Overcoming the hard-liners' protests, Lenin insisted on the necessity of this retreat in order to save the Bolshevik Revolution. With stunning pragmatism, he also appreciated the value of dividing the capitalist world by establishing contact with the still-powerful Germans.

The West regarded Brest Litovsk as evidence of Moscow's treachery, which enabled Germany to break the Allied blockade and opened the way for its new offensive on the Western front. On the pretext of preventing a German seizure of their military supplies stacked up in Russian ports as well as rescuing stranded Czech and Slovak prisoners of war and reopening an eastern front, the Allies in March 1918 sent troops to the east. After landing in Murmansk, Archangel, and Vladivostok, their forces collaborated with anti-Bolshevik factions and were briefly embroiled in Russia's civil war, stirring bitterness among the Soviet population.

In another major surprise, Germany's western offensive failed in July 1918. When the Allies' counterattack created panic within the imperial command, the

German leadership appealed to Wilson for an armistice based on the Fourteen Points. Faced with Germany's unexpected collapse and revolution in 1918, the victors made the momentous decision to convene a major peace conference—the first in a century—to rebuild the postwar world. For the first time in history, a US president traveled to Europe to attend the conference. Thousands of supplicants from all over the globe along with a huge press corps thronged to Paris expecting the peace of justice that Wilson had promised.

A CONTESTED PEACE

Peacemaking between January and June 1919 was dominated by the leaders of the three democracies—which were also the world's largest empires. Their deliberations took place in the shadows of their clients' expansive territorial claims, German recalcitrance, and communist uprisings in Berlin, Munich, and Budapest. Moreover, the Big Three had fundamental differences over the postwar order, with France demanding maximum security against Germany and Russia, Great Britain seeking to revive the old balance of power, and the United States promoting democracy and open markets, the end of colonialism, and a League of Nations to preserve the peace. As they plunged into a series of complex economic and territorial issues, the victors excluded their ex-enemies, Germany and Russia, from their often fraught deliberations.

Predictably, there were awkward political compromises. Poland, a state resurrected after a century of partitions by its neighbors, was a prime test case. Out of Franco-British wrangling over its western border came the improvisations of the "Corridor" (giving Poland access to the sea, but also separating the main part of Germany from East Prussia), the Free City of Danzig (a German city placed under international control to serve as Poland's port), and the plebiscite in Upper Silesia that would eventually divide the coal-rich province between Germany and Poland. Over Polish protests, the Allies forced the Warsaw government to sign the world's first minority treaty to protect the rights of non-Poles, numbering some 33 percent of the population, and proceeded to impose similar arrangements on several other unwilling Eastern European governments.

The League of Nations was created at the peace conference but had several major impediments as a global body. Against the will of their populations, the former Arab territories of the Ottoman Empire, designated as League mandates, were divided between Britain and France, and Germany's colonies in Africa, Asia, and the Pacific were handed over to Britain, France, South Africa, Japan,

EUROPE AFTER WORLD WAR I

FINLAND

NORWAY

SWEDEN

Baltic Sea

ESTONIA

North Sea

LATVIA

DENMARK

MEMEL
LITHUANIA

SOVIET
UNION

NORTH
SCHLESWIG

Danzig
EAST
PRUSSIA

NETHERLANDS

CORRIDOR

POLAND

BELGIUM

GERMANY

ALSACE-
LORRAINE

UPPER
SILESIA

GALICIA

FRANCE

CZECHOSLOVAKIA

SWITZER-
LAND

AUSTRIA

BESSARABIA

SOUTH
TYROL

HUNGARY

TRANSYLVANIA

ISTRIA

ROMANIA

Black
Sea

YUGOSLAVIA

ITALY

BULGARIA

ALBANIA

GREECE

TURKEY

Mediterranean

Sea

0   200 mi

0   200 km

Formerly German

Formerly Russian

Formerly Bulgarian

Formerly Austro-Hungarian Empire

Map 2. The territorial changes between 1919 and 1923 created volatile political conditions in central and Eastern Europe.

Australia, and New Zealand. There were other anomalies: US and British opposition blocked Japan's efforts to insert a clause guaranteeing racial equality in the League Covenant. The League's membership excluded Germany and Soviet Russia, two former great powers whose cooperation would be essential to creating peace. And the world's first international organization left out most of the colonial world, whose populations would view the peace settlement as an old-fashioned distribution of the spoils of victory.

The official end of World War I took place on June 28, 1919, with the formal treaty signing in the Palace of Versailles. Germany was now a republic whose population was stunned by its unexpected defeat and whose leaders, determined to resist the Allies' harsh territorial, military, and economic terms by any means possible, created a propaganda machine to denounce them. The Treaty of Versailles, which indeed fell far short of the victors' promises, was almost universally criticized. Lenin termed it "a treaty of robbers and plunderers . . . which has made slaves of tens of millions of people." British economist John Maynard Keynes decried the reparations clauses, which would thwart Europe's recovery. French marshal Ferdinand Foch termed it a "twenty-year truce." And the US Senate refused to ratify it, removing the major architect from either the enforcement or the modification of the peace settlement.[*]

THE SOVIET ENTRY INTO WORLD POLITICS

At the end of almost every major war, coalitions have dissolved and old rivalries erupted. What was unique in 1919 was the emergence of an ideological struggle between Lenin's Russia and the West that sowed the seeds for the future Cold War. The immense popularity of the American communist John Reed's chronicle, *Ten Days That Shook the World*, spread the story of the Bolshevik Revolution. In March 1919 the new Soviet regime founded the Communist International (Comintern) to wage a global struggle against capitalism and imperialism and deploy propaganda, espionage, and recruitment to subvert its enemies, the foremost of which was the British Empire.[†] At home, the Bolsheviks unleashed a

---

[*] In a joint resolution in July 1921 the US Congress declared the war at an end, and one month later the new president, Warren G. Harding, concluded separate treaties with Germany, Austria, and Hungary that omitted the League of Nations.

[†] At the 1920 Congress of the Peoples of the East held in Baku, Comintern leaders—breaking the long silence of their Western socialist rivals toward European imperialism—pledged their solidarity with the global anticolonial struggle.

wave of terror against the church and also drove hundreds of thousands of anti-Bolsheviks into exile, forcing the League of Nations to cope with its first major refugee crisis. Western governments, terrified by the postwar Red Scare within their countries,* were intent on isolating, weakening, and even undermining the nascent Bolshevik regime.

Soviet Russia's first years of existence were indeed tumultuous. Instead of inciting war against its enemies, as had France in 1791, it found itself under an Allied blockade, fighting foreign troops, and defending itself against a band of opponents, from tsarist reactionaries on the right to Menshevik and socialist revolutionaries on the left. Thanks to Leon Trotsky's military leadership and their enemies' disorganization, the Bolsheviks were victorious in the civil war and reconquered Ukraine (as well as the Caucasus and Siberia) but they were forced to acknowledge the other new states created by the Treaty of Brest Litovsk—Estonia, Finland, Latvia, and Lithuania—and also a greatly expanded Poland that had defeated the Red Army. By 1920 the revolution had survived in Russia, but with greatly reduced frontiers in Europe and appalling material and human conditions at home.

Lenin, ever the realist, dramatically changed course in 1921. In that year of pervasive drought, crop failures, epidemics, and anti-Bolshevik rebellions, he launched the New Economic Policy (NEP) and announced a temporary retreat from orthodox communism. Convinced that the West needed Russia to survive the postwar economic crisis, Lenin for the next three years pursued the dual path of advertising his country as the vanguard of world revolution while appealing for normal relations with the advanced capitalist world. From Moscow came the call for "peaceful coexistence" and an appeal for Western capital, loans, trade, and recognition along with hints of concessions to prospective Western partners.

The Soviet initiative was received by a wary Western audience. Lenin's regime, which the United States had excluded from the Washington Naval Conference of 1921–1922, had become a political blank space on the map of Eurasia.

---

* In the United States in particular, where there had been a wave of strikes during World War I, the Bolshevik Revolution heightened the government's fears of foreign agents stirring political unrest. The Red Scare intensified in 1919, when more than 3,600 separate strikes erupted, and there were explosions, fires, and race riots in several cities. In 1920 the Federal Bureau of Investigation, newly created within the Justice Department, placed thousands of individuals under surveillance and launched raids across the nation but never discovered evidence of a foreign plot against the United States. After the September 16, 1920, Wall Street bombing, in which 38 people were killed and 141 wounded, the Red Scare gradually diminished.

Photo 1.1. Vladimir Il'ich Lenin, the leader of Soviet Russia, leaning over a balcony, May 1920. *Courtesy of Library of Congress.*

But the capitalist world was also sorely divided. The United States and France were resolutely anti-Soviet, but Britain sought to revive contacts with Moscow in order to restore its own and Europe's economy. The small states wedged between Germany and Russia were a feeble, disunited force against their still-powerful neighbors: at odds over their territorial disputes and weakened by discontented minorities, lack of investment capital, high tariff barriers, and the cost of their excessively large armies.

Western society was also in ferment. Artists and intellectuals bemoaned the crushed illusions, bodies, and landscapes, destroyed by four years of mechanized warfare, and one historian predicted the decline of the West.* When the postwar period brought inflation and high unemployment, the public protested against a peaceless world and frightened their leaders with the threat of revolution.

One tantalizing diplomatic byway was the Genoa Conference, an unprecedented gathering of thirty-four states in April–May 1922 that included Germany and Russia. Its purpose was to quell public discontent by reintegrating the two outcast states, revitalizing the European economy, and forging a new world order based on neither victor nor vanquished. However, this brainchild of the mercurial Lloyd George faced too many obstacles, among them America's refusal to participate, France's obstruction, and the panic of the divided small powers. The denouement occurred within a week of the meeting. On Easter Sunday the German and Soviet foreign ministers signed the Treaty of Rapallo, establishing full diplomatic relations and paving the way for close military and economic cooperation.

Rapallo was a triumph for Lenin's pragmatic foreign policy. It not only cemented relations between his revolutionary regime and a major capitalist government† but also ruptured the possibility of a unified Western stance against Russia and stiffened Moscow's resistance to making any concessions on debts or nationalized property. Seven months later, the ailing Soviet leader achieved his last major triumph with the formation of the Union of Soviet Socialist Republics (USSR), which survived until Christmas Day 1991.

The failure of the Genoa Conference brought an end to Lloyd George's conciliation project and was followed by a cascade of ominous events. In Europe the fascist seizure of power in Italy (October 1922) and Adolf Hitler's first putsch (November 1923) warned of the frailty of liberal democracy in Central and Southern Europe; the stirring of anticolonialism from Egypt to India threatened the future of European imperialism; and the League of Nations, the scene of Anglo-French bickering, drew back from both developing a robust collective security system and guiding Europe and the world toward economic cooperation and disarmament.

Lenin's death at age fifty-four in January 1924 marked the close of the world-revolutionary phase of Soviet politics. Proclaiming the doctrine of

---

* Among them, Vincente Blasco-Ibanez, *Four Horsemen of the Apocalypse* (1918); Paul Nash, *We Are Making a New World* (1918); Fernand Léger, *The City* (1918); Igor Stravinsky, *The Soldier's Tale* (1918); George Bernard Shaw, *Heartbreak House* (1921); T. S. Eliot, *The Wasteland* (1922); and Oswald Spengler, *The Decline of the West* (1918).

† Much to the chagrin of German Marxists and Bolshevik hard-liners.

"socialism in one country," his successor, Joseph Stalin, set out to build up the USSR's economic and military strength as the best means of promoting the ultimate victory of global communism. While maintaining Moscow's stance as a major critic of the peace settlement, Stalin also exerted greater control over the Comintern's activities throughout the world.

By the mid-1920s, thanks to US financial assistance, a tenuous European peace was established that essentially excluded the Soviet Union. The Locarno Treaties (1925), signed by Britain, France, Italy, and Germany, paved the way for Germany's entry into the League of Nations with a permanent council seat. During the next years Berlin, Moscow's principal partner, maintained a delicate balancing act between the West and the Soviet Union, with which it had clandestine military ties and a shared aversion toward Poland.

France and Britain, on the other hand, remained hostile toward the Soviet Union, insisting on full debt repayment, restoration of private property, and cessation of the Comintern's intrigues. Tensions heated up in 1927, when the British government severed relations with the USSR over Moscow's machinations during Britain's general strike and its intervention in China. Franco-Soviet relations also reached a nadir at that time.

Stalin, ever cautious, drew back from a confrontation with the West. The Anglo-Soviet dispute was defused but not forgotten. As part of his "great turn" in 1928–1929, Stalin launched the first Five-Year Plan to create a powerful and self-sufficient military-industrial complex. He also moved to destroy his domestic rivals (foremost among them the followers of Leon Trotsky) and to coerce the peasantry and expand the police and terror apparatus. Abroad, Stalin's roving ambassador, Maxim Litvinov, exhibited the friendly face of the USSR. Despite the USSR's hostility toward the League of Nations, it engaged in multilateral peace efforts, such as the Kellogg-Briand Pact and the Preparatory Commission on Disarmament in Geneva. It also concluded security arrangements with neighboring countries and improved trade relations with the United States. Nonetheless Stalin remained inherently suspicious of the capitalist governments, which had excluded and threatened the world's only communist regime and knew no other way of settling their rivalries except by recourse to war.

Soviet and American abstention from a leading role in world affairs had left a dangerous power vacuum. Britain and France continued to squabble over enforcing a contested peace, and Germany prepared for its overturn. The illusory calm of the late 1920s ended abruptly in 1929 with the outbreak of the global Depression, followed by the Japanese occupation of Manchuria in 1931 and Hitler's ascent to power two years later.

THE DARK DECADE, 1931–1939

In 1931 Japan, which had been a permanent League Council member and had enjoyed amicable relations with the West, suddenly altered its domestic and foreign policies. Spurred by the collapse of Japan's export markets and the revival of an expansionist form of nationalism, the military seized control and on September 18 launched an invasion of Manchuria.

The ensuing crisis set the pattern for the Western powers' feeble response to aggression. The League of Nations was unprepared either to halt the Japanese conquest or to respond to pleas for assistance from China, one of its members. The two most interested governments, Britain and the United States, reeling from the Depression, shrank from risking war with Japan, and the USSR, despite its considerable interest in Manchuria, also wished to avoid offending Japan. The League's mild sanction—nonrecognition of the puppet state of Manchukuo—prompted Japan's withdrawal from the Geneva organization and kindled widespread alarm among the League's smaller members over their vulnerability to attack.

The advent of the Third Reich in January 1933 posed an even greater danger to the international order. In his book *Mein Kampf* (published in 1925–1926) the Nazi leader and new German chancellor Adolf Hitler had made clear that his goals were not merely to overturn the Versailles treaty but also to vanquish communism and achieve German racial and political domination in Europe and the larger world. When the Nazis' persecution of German Jews created a flood of refugees and the Third Reich peremptorily exited Geneva, the League issued only a mild censure. The West was unready to meet the threat of the Nazi dictatorship.

The Soviet Union, no longer Berlin's partner, had become potential prey. Stalin's government made another crucial turn, ceasing to vilify the post–World War I peace settlement, preaching collective security, and joining the previously reviled League of Nations in 1934. In 1935 the Comintern reversed its long-standing refusal to cooperate with reformist socialists and bourgeois parties and ordered its members to pursue a Popular Front strategy to resist the spread of fascism.

Stalin's about-face created ripples abroad. The United States, under its new president, Franklin D. Roosevelt, was mired in the Depression and swept by strong waves of isolationist and anticommunist sentiments, but to stimulate trade, Roosevelt established relations with the USSR in 1933 and sent a corps of wary diplomats to Moscow. The French government made even stronger overtures to the Soviet Union, proposing to create a barrier against Nazi expansion in Eastern Europe and concluding a Treaty of Mutual Assistance in May 1935.

However, almost two decades of anti-Sovietism prevented the resurrection of the 1894 French-Russian alliance, which had saved Paris in World War I. Not only were France's small allies, Poland and Romania, terrified of the price of Soviet "protection," but France's own political and military leadership was unwilling to forge an alliance with Stalin's Russia. In addition, France's aloof partner Britain was suspicious of Stalin's goals and preferred to deal directly with Nazi Germany. Thus when Hitler in March 1935 scrapped Versailles and announced full German rearmament, Britain responded three months later with a bombshell— the Anglo-German naval agreement—that torpedoed the treaty's last disarmament clauses and wiped out Paris's last independent initiative.

With the failure of organized resistance, the aggressors moved quickly. Italy invaded Abyssinia (Ethiopia) in 1935, and in 1936 dispatched "volunteers" in support of the Nationalist leader Francisco Franco's insurrection against the Spanish Republic, where he was joined by a special German air force unit.* In February 1936 Hitler, claiming that the largely innocuous French-Soviet pact had created a "red menace," renounced the Locarno Treaties and reoccupied the demilitarized zone of the Rhineland. And in July 1937 Japanese military forces, moving south from Manchuria, captured the principal cities and ports of northern and central China. The three formed offensive alliances: the Rome-Berlin Axis (1936) and the Anti-Comintern Pact (1937) linking Italy, Germany, and Japan.

World reaction was muted. The League failed to enforce sanctions against Italy, to condemn Germany's violation of the Versailles and Locarno agreements, or to offer assistance to China, and the French-British–sponsored Non-Intervention Agreement, signed by twenty-seven governments in August 1936, did not halt the flow of arms and manpower to Franco's forces in Spain. Despite efforts by liberals and socialists to mobilize an antifascist resistance, pacifism was widespread in Western Europe, epitomized by the powerful 1937 antiwar French film *The Grand Illusion*.

The United States was conspicuously silent. The Roosevelt administration, facing another severe economic downturn in 1937, resisted British pleas for a joint diplomatic initiative against the fascists' aggression. Congress in 1935 and 1937 passed Neutrality Acts banning sales or loans to belligerents in wars and in civil wars, harming the victims more than the aggressors. And although distressed over the Nazis' racism and sympathetic to China's plight, the American

---

* Pablo Picasso's graphic depiction of the bombing of Guernica, displayed at the Paris World Exhibition in 1937, brought world attention to the atrocities against Spanish civilians.

public—in a strongly isolationist mood—was determined to avoid being dragged by the British Empire into another world war.

Stalin, who in 1936 had launched a major wave of purges against his political, military, and intellectual enemies, now faced major threats in Europe and in Asia. In line with his Popular Front strategy against fascism, the Soviet Union became the major outside supporter of the Spanish Republic, furnishing military supplies and advisers, directing the Comintern to mobilize an international army of volunteers, and producing a global propaganda campaign on behalf of the Madrid government. Not surprisingly, post–Cold War documents have revealed that Stalin's principal goals in Spain were to purge the local communists of Trotskyites, to create a Soviet satellite in Western Europe, and also, like Hitler, to prolong the conflict and divert attention from his domestic policies.

Britain, faced with powerful rivals and restive colonial populations in Palestine and India, pursued an active policy of appeasement toward Germany and Japan. This approach, promoted in 1937 by Prime Minister Neville Chamberlain, had historic and practical roots as well as a strongly ideological flavor. Deeply suspicious of US designs on the empire, Chamberlain was also appalled at the prospect of collaborating with Soviet Russia, a sworn enemy of Britain that had been stigmatized by the purges and by its self-seeking policies in Spain. Lacking reliable partners—France was divided internally and Italy now firmly in the Nazi camp—Britain sought to thwart Hitler's aggressiveness by encouraging him to fulfill his territorial designs in the East.

British appeasement reached its apogee in September 1938 at the Munich Conference, convened to devise a peaceful solution to Hitler's saber-rattling against Czechoslovakia, which threatened to plunge Europe into war. Britain, France, Italy, and Germany, ignoring the League and excluding both Czechoslovakia and its Soviet ally, agreed to a substantial cession of Czechoslovak territory to the Third Reich. The Munich agreement averted war and bought time for British and French rearmament, but it also represented a moral and political defeat for the West—the betrayal of a small democratic ally—that simply whetted Hitler's appetite for armed conquest. It also had a jarring effect on Stalin.

Scholars have long debated whether Stalin had ever seriously intended to honor his treaty obligation to defend Czechoslovakia (with which he had no contiguous border and would have involved the transit of Soviet troops and air power through Poland and Romania). One group, although acknowledging the dictator's ruthless realism, views Soviet diplomacy between 1933 and 1938 as both a genuine quest for collective security and an attempt to stave off war against Nazi Germany and Japan. According to this perspective, Stalin, convinced by Munich that the appeasement-obsessed Western powers hoped to direct German aggression eastward, moved defensively into the Nazi camp.

The opposite argument, which has grown since the end of the Cold War, insists that Stalin had always been bluffing and that Moscow's collective security strategy was simply a ruse to bait Hitler into a joint revisionist project against the new order in Eastern Europe. Thus Stalin's infamous warning to the "instigators of war" (Britain and France) during the Eighteenth Party Congress on March 10, 1939, that he had no intention of "pulling their chestnuts out of the fire."

There is evidence for both interpretations, which bring together Stalin's growing conviction that another world war was imminent and his overall strategy for protecting the Soviet state. In the wake of the German seizures of Prague and Memel in March 1939, the Soviet dictator suddenly launched two seemingly contradictory initiatives. On March 18 he proposed to resurrect the Triple Entente of 1914 in the form of a military alliance with France and Great Britain for the purpose of protecting the nations of Eastern Europe against further Nazi aggression, but that same day he also informed Berlin of his interest in suspending their ideological conflict and negotiating a Soviet-German rapprochement. Unlike the Russian leadership in 1914, Stalin was appealing to the highest bidder over his response to Hitler's anticipated attack on Poland.

Britain and France's reluctance to negotiate an equal partnership with Moscow became quickly apparent. The Allies recognized that Soviet support would require politically undesirable concessions to a dangerous and longtime ideological opponent and necessitate territorial sacrifices by their clients, Poland and Romania. They also had considerable doubts over Moscow's military value, because of Stalin's liquidation of almost the entire high command of his armed forces in the 1937–1938 purges and the Soviet Union's inadequate transportation network. Thus, instead of immediately sending a high-level delegation (as had France twenty-five years earlier during the July 1914 crisis), London and Paris waited four full months to appoint a mission of low-ranking military officers, then postponed their departure for eleven days, and finally sent them to Moscow via a very slow form of sea transport, instead of by air. Upon their arrival on August 10, 1939, these hapless Allied envoys at once revealed their governments' unwillingness to coordinate military operations with Moscow or to put pressure on the Poles or Romanians to permit the passage of Soviet troops. During these five crucial months the alliance that might have prevented the outbreak of World War II failed to materialize because of Anglo-French unwillingness but also because of the Soviets' loss of interest.

By May 1939, the German option had become increasingly attractive to the Kremlin. Through a Soviet agent in Tokyo, Stalin had learned that Hitler was determined to turn westward after crushing Poland, thereby diminishing the threat to Russia and the value of joining a new entente with Britain and France. An accommodation with the Third Reich would enable the Soviet Union to expand its military and economic forces while the capitalist powers exhausted themselves in a slugfest. In an important signal, Stalin replaced Litvinov (the apostle of collective security) as foreign minister with his crony, Vyacheslav Molotov, who not only guided the German discussions but also taunted Berlin over the prospect of a Soviet deal with the West. By August Hitler, impatient to launch his Polish campaign and ready to placate Stalin, sent his foreign minister, Joachim von Ribbentrop, to the Kremlin.

The Nazi-Soviet pact, signed on August 23, 1939, was a blatant license for aggression. The public document pledged both sides to observe strict neutrality should either become involved in a military conflict, and the secret protocol (known in full detail only after the Cold War) gave Stalin an impressive payment in kind: the annexation of eastern Poland; the assignment of Finland, Estonia, and Latvia* to the Soviet sphere of influence; and the recovery of Bessarabia from Romania, thus restoring all of Russia's losses after World War I. In an equally stunning coup, one month later Stalin ended hostilities with Japan, which Soviet troops had battled, on and off, over the previous two years, thus freeing his country from the immediate threat of a two-front war (and enabling Japan to focus on China, Southeast Asia, and the Pacific).

The news from Moscow shocked the world's Marxists and crushed their resistance to fascism. Britain and France, disconcerted by Stalin's defection, continued to seek a peaceful solution to the Polish crisis, but Hitler, refusing to return to the conference table, used a fictitious border incident as the pretext for his attack on Poland on September 1, 1939. When he ignored their ultimatum to withdraw, Britain and France reluctantly declared war two days later.

THE AGGRESSORS TRIUMPHANT, 1939–1941

The outbreak of World War II in Europe—it had already erupted in Asia—pitted only four official combatants: the British Empire, France, Poland, and Nazi Germany. Mussolini, pleading unpreparedness, stayed out. On September 17, 1939,

---

* Lithuania was added one month later in another agreement, in which Stalin relinquished territory in Eastern Poland and the German-Soviet border was established on the River Bug.

two days after concluding an accord with Japan, the USSR, without a declaration of war, sent troops across the Polish border, sealing the fate of its western neighbor, which collapsed at the end of the month and once more disappeared from the map of Europe.

The United States was jolted into action. Labeling Nazi aggression a threat to the Western Hemisphere, President Roosevelt urged the modification of the Neutrality Acts. On November 4 Congress, while still banning American ships and civilians from entering the war zone, voted to allow "cash and carry" purchases of arms and goods by France and Great Britain, which had as yet made no significant military moves against the Third Reich.

Indeed, the period between the autumn of 1939 and the spring of 1940 has been dubbed the "phony war," with French troops languishing on the Maginot Line along its border with Germany and a few Anglo-German naval skirmishes around the British Isles. Yet in northeastern Europe a very real war exploded on November 30. After Finland had refused to follow the Baltic states and allow the Red Army to build bases on its soil, Stalin, ostensibly to protect Leningrad (only twenty miles from the border), now committed one of his greatest blunders. Again, without a declaration of war he ordered an invasion of his small neighbor, whom he suspected of German sympathies. Although three times larger and far better equipped, the Soviet forces were poorly prepared to face an unexpectedly strong Finnish resistance and initially suffered high casualties. On March 12, 1940, Stalin, after a string of Soviet counterattacks (and perhaps fearing Allied intervention), ended the brutal 105-day war with the Moscow Treaty, which allowed Finland to preserve its independence but forced it to cede 11 percent of its territory, including a large swath of land on Lake Ladoga that would later shield Leningrad, and to allow a Soviet military base on the Hanko peninsula.

The war with Finland had important consequences. Soviet-US relations plummeted after Stalin rebuffed Roosevelt's mediation offer. The moribund League of Nations, which had been helpless against Japanese, Italian, and German treaty violations, was suddenly aroused by the attack on a neutral member. For the very first time in its history the League Council (with some notable abstentions and absences) voted to support the victim and expel the Soviet Union—too late, however, to save Finland. The principal victor of the Winter War was Nazi Germany. Watching from the sidelines, Hitler had noted the Red Army's weakness and the West's ill-coordinated and feeble responses, including the stillborn threat to punish Soviet Russia by bombing the Baku oil fields. Berlin also reaped the bonus of closer relations with Finland, which would be an important partner a year later.

The phony war finally ended on April 8, 1940. Britain and France, now facing two powerful opponents as well as an irate citizenry, opted to take the war to neutral Scandinavia and block the delivery of Sweden's iron ore crucial to Nazi Germany. In a highly risky operation British naval units laid mines in Norwegian waters, and Allied troops were sent to the Norwegian coast. But the next day the well-prepared Germans seized Norway's capital and major ports and also occupied Denmark, thus securing not only their northern flank but also a string of indispensable naval and air bases for future combat. Then on May 10 the Reich's long-awaited Western offensive brought the collapse of the neutral Netherlands and Belgium, the audacious sweep through the Ardennes, and, on June 22, the capitulation of France.

Stalin, now the observer, had anticipated a lengthy struggle in the West and was startled by France's sudden collapse. He was still building up his military force and also consolidating his newly expanded realm, extending the Soviet political system from the Baltic to the Black Sea. To ensure Poland's permanent subjugation, in March and April 1940 Stalin ordered the mass killing of some twenty-two thousand captured Polish officers, which took place in Soviet prisons and in the Katyn Forest. In July, he ordered the incorporation of the three Baltic Republics into the USSR along with the murder and deportation of thousands of their leading figures. That month, to secure his southwestern border, Stalin formally annexed the two former Romanian provinces of Bessarabia and northern Bukovina. After the Nazi victory over France, the Soviet Union also expanded its diplomatic contacts with Persia, Turkey, Bulgaria, and Yugoslavia, much to the annoyance of Berlin.

By the summer of 1940 the Third Reich dominated the entire European continent with its string of annexed territories, satellites, allies, and compliant neutrals, including the Soviet Union, which supplied the grain and oil to fuel the Nazi Empire.* Only Britain, now led by the tenaciously anti-Nazi prime minister Winston Churchill, held out. Thanks to the quality of its air power, radar, and code breaking as well as Churchill's indomitable grit and optimism, Britain in the fall of 1940 withstood the Nazis' massive air offensive. It was also saved by Hitler's indecisiveness and blunders, and by Germany's naval weakness.

In November 1940 Europe's flagging anti-Nazi resistance was stirred by Roosevelt's reelection to an unprecedented third term. The next month, the US president

---

* In September 1939 Stalin had announced: "The USSR is interested in a strong Germany and will not let it be beaten."

urged Congress to adopt his Lend-Lease program, which held out the prospect of substantially increased aid and supplies to a beleaguered and nearly bankrupt Great Britain. In the meantime Mussolini, who had entered the war against France and Britain, had forced Hitler to salvage Italy's failed adventures in the Balkans and North Africa, temporarily diverting the Reich from turning eastward.

Stalin during this critical period gravitated between overconfidence and fear. Discounting the numerous warnings of a German attack from credible US, British, and even Soviet intelligence sources, he insisted that Hitler would not risk a two-front war until Britain was vanquished. Thus Stalin failed to construct defenses along the new border with the Reich or to relocate military and industrial plants into the interior, boasting that the Red Army would repel any invader and then "crush" him on his own territory. Nonetheless, having witnessed the wages of the German blitzkrieg (lightning war) and the bombing of civilians and well aware of Hitler's racist and anti-Bolshevik views, the Soviet leader knew that the calendar and Russia's snows could not indefinitely protect his vast and vulnerable realm.

At 3:15 A.M. on June 22, 1941 (the 129th anniversary of Napoleon's ill-fated attack on Russia), the Wehrmacht crossed the Bug River, and Operation Barbarossa began. Hitler had assembled the largest invasion force in human history—approximately 3.5 million troops (including a half million non-German soldiers), 2,700 aircraft, 3,000 tanks, and 7,000 artillery pieces—which were hurled against the Soviet Union over a two-thousand-mile front from Finland to Romania. By the autumn of 1941, the Nazi offensive threatened to destroy the Red Army and overthrow Stalin's regime: Kiev had fallen, Leningrad was under siege, and Moscow was within reach. Accompanying the attack were the SS Einsatzgruppen, the mobile killing units that not only targeted Soviet partisans but also massacred 1.5 million Soviet Jews.

At this calamitous moment the antifascist alliance, unachievable in peacetime, suddenly materialized. On June 22 Churchill, characterizing Hitler as a "monster of wickedness" spreading desolation in Russia, swallowed his longtime anti-Bolshevism and pledged to aid the Soviet Union.* One day later, US secretary of state Cordell Hull, speaking on behalf of the US president, announced that his country would give Russia "all aid to the hilt." Stalin's reply on a grim July 18 was a masterpiece of arrogance and desperation. While defending the

---

* Because defeating the Third Reich had become his foremost objective, the prime minister famously announced: "If Hitler invaded Hell, I should at least make a favorable reference to the Devil in the House of Commons."

terms of the Nazi-Soviet pact, he urged his new partners to launch offensives in France, Norway, and Finland to relieve the struggling Red Army.

Almost a quarter of a century after the Bolshevik Revolution, the Soviet Union and its two principal capitalist enemies had been drawn together by Axis aggression, but the habits of exclusion, rivalry, and suspicion remained.

SUGGESTIONS FOR FURTHER STUDY

Primary Sources

"Agreement Between the United Kingdom and the Union of Soviet Socialist Republics, July 12, 1941." Yale Law School Avalon Project: Documents in Law, History and Diplomacy. http://avalon.law.yale.edu/wwii/brsov41.asp.

Auswärtiges Amt (German Foreign Ministry). *Documents and Materials Relating to the Eve of the Second World War.* 2 vols. New York: International Publishers, 1948.

"Comintern Electronic Archives." Russian State Archives for Social and Political History. Accessed February 24, 2013. http://www.comintern-online.com.

Foreign Office of Great Britain. *Documents Illustrating the Hostile Activities of the Soviet Government and the Third International Against Great Britain.* London: H. M. Stationery Office, 1927.

"Foreign Relations 1918—The Conclusion of the Peace of Brest Litovsk." Yale Law School Avalon Project: Documents in Law, History and Diplomacy. http://avalon.law.yale.edu/subject_menus/blmenu.asp.

Gromkyo, A. A., ed. *Soviet Peace Efforts on the Eve of World War II.* Moscow: Progress Publishers, 1973.

Hitler, Adolf. *Mein Kampf.* Originally published in German as two volumes, 1925–1926. New York: Reynal & Hitchcock, 1939.

Lenin, Vladimir Ilyich. *The Foundations of the Communist International.* New York: International Publishers, 1934.

Nazi-Soviet Relations, 1939–1941: Documents from the Archives of the German Foreign Office. Edited by Raymond Sontag and James Beddie. Washington, DC: US Department of State, 1948.

Roosevelt, Franklin Delano. "Quarantine Speech, October 5, 1937." Miller Center, University of Virginia. http://millercenter.org/president/speeches/detail/3310.

Wilson, Woodrow. "President Woodrow Wilson's Fourteen Points, 8 January, 1918." Yale Law School Avalon Project: Documents in Law, History and Diplomacy. http://avalon.law.yale.edu/20th_century/wilson14.asp.

Contemporary Writing

Borkenau, Franz. *The Communist International.* London: Faber and Faber, 1938.

Eastman, Max. *The End of Socialism in Russia.* Boston: Little, Brown, 1937.

Trotsky, Leon. *The First Five Years of the Communist International.* New York: Pioneer Publishers, 1945.

Films

Alexander Nevsky. Directed by Sergei M. Eisenstein and Dmitri Vasilyev. Moscow: Mosfilm, 1938.

The Czar Wants to Sleep (Poruchik Kizhe). Directed by Aleksandr Faintsimmer. Moscow: Belgoskino, 1934.

Five Cartridges (Fünf Patronenhülsen). Directed by Frank Beyer. East Berlin: Deutsche Film (DEFA), 1960.

The Flowers of War. Directed by Yimou Zhang. Beijing: Beijing New Picture Film, 2011.

The Grand Illusion (La Grande Illusion). Directed by Jean Renoir. Paris: RAC, 1937.

Land and Freedom. Directed by Ken Loach. London: British Broadcasting Corporation, 1995.

The Last Train from Madrid. Directed by James P. Hogan. Los Angeles: Paramount Pictures, 1937.

Ninotschka. Directed by Ernst Lubitsch. Los Angeles: Metro-Goldwyn-Mayer, 1939.

October (Ten Days That Shook the World). Directed by Grigori Aleksandrov and Sergei M. Eisenstein. Moscow: Sovkino, 1928.

Reds. Directed by Warren Beatty. Los Angeles: JRS Productions, 1981.

Triumph of the Will. Directed by Leni Riefenstahl. Berlin: Leni Riefenstahl Produktion, 1935.

The Winter War. Directed by Pekka Parikka. Helsinki: National Filmi Oy See, 1989.

Fiction

Bulgakov, Mikhail. *The Master and Margarita.* Translated by Diana Burgin and Katherine Tiernan O'Connor. New York: Vintage, 1995.

Koestler, Arthur. *Darkness at Noon.* New York: Macmillan, 1941.

Malraux, André. *Man's Fate.* Translated by Haakon M. Chevalier. New York: Random House, 1934.

Orwell, George. *Animal Farm: A Fairy Story.* London: Secker and Warburg, 1945.

Platonov, Andrei. *Soul.* Translated by Robert and Elizabeth Chandler et al. London: Harvill, 2003.

Sartre, Jean-Paul. *Troubled Sleep.* Translated by Gerard Hopkins. New York: Vintage, 1950.

Poetry

Auden, W. H. "September 1, 1939." In *The Collected Poems.* Edited by Edward Mendelson. 2007 Modern Library Edition. New York: Modern Library, 2007.

Diaries, Memoirs, and Journals

Dimitrov, Georgi. *The Diary of Georgi Dimitrov.* Edited by Ivo Banac. New Haven, CT: Yale University Press, 2003.

Djilas, Milovan. *Memoir of a Revolutionary.* New York: Harcourt Brace Jovanovich, 1973.

Fischer, Louis. *Men and Politics: An Autobiography.* London: Cape, 1941.

Kennan, George F. *Memoirs.* Vol. 1: 1925–1950. Boston: Little, Brown, 1967.

Litvinov, M. M. *Notes for a Journal.* New York: Morrow, 1955.

Orwell, George. *Homage to Catalonia.* New York: Harcourt Brace, 1952.

Secondary Sources

Caballero, Manuel. *Latin America and the Comintern, 1919–1943.* Cambridge: Cambridge University Press, 1986.

Carley, Michael Jabara. *1939: The Alliance That Never Was and the Coming of World War II.* Chicago: I. R. Dee, 1999.

———. *The Silent Conflict: A Hidden History of Early Soviet-Western Relations.* Lanham, MD: Rowman and Littlefield, 2014.

D'Agostino, Anthony. *The Rise of Global Powers: International Politics in the Era of the World Wars.* Cambridge: Cambridge University Press, 2012.

Davis, Donald E., and Eugene P. Trani. *The First Cold War: The Legacy of Woodrow Wilson in U.S.-Soviet Relations.* Columbia: University of Missouri Press, 2002.

Ericson, Edward E. *Feeding the German Eagle: Soviet Economic Aid to Nazi Germany, 1933–1941.* Westport, CT: Praeger, 1999.

Fink, Carole. *The Genoa Conference: European Diplomacy, 1921–1922.* Rev. ed. Syracuse, NY: Syracuse University Press, 1993.

Gorodetsky, Gabriel. *Grand Delusion: Stalin and the German Invasion of Russia.* New Haven, CT: Yale University Press, 1999.

———. *The Precarious Truce: Anglo-Soviet Relations, 1924–1927.* Cambridge: Cambridge University Press, 1976.

Haslam, Jonathan. *The Soviet Union and the Struggle for Collective Security in Europe, 1933–39.* New York: St. Martin's, 1984.

———. *The Soviet Union and the Threat from the East, 1933–1941: Moscow, Tokyo, and the Prelude to the Pacific War.* Pittsburgh: University of Pittsburgh Press, 1992.

Imlay, Talbot. *Facing the Second World War: Strategy, Politics, and Economics in Britain and France, 1938–1940.* Oxford: Oxford University Press, 2003.

Iriye, Akira. *The Origins of the Second World War in Asia and the Pacific.* London: Longman, 1987.

Jacobson, Jon. *When the Soviet Union Entered World Politics.* Berkeley: University of California Press, 1994.

Knox, MacGregor. *Mussolini Unleashed, 1939–1941: Politics and Strategy in Fascist Italy's Last War.* Cambridge: Cambridge University Press, 1982.

Leonhard, Wolfgang. *Betrayal: The Hitler-Stalin Pact of 1939.* New York: St. Martin's, 1989.

Louis, William Roger. *British Strategy in the Far East, 1919–1939.* Oxford: Clarendon, 1971.

Manela, Erez. *The Wilsonian Moment: Self-Determination and the International Origins of Anticolonial Nationalism.* Oxford: Oxford University Press, 2007.

Marks, Sally. *The Ebbing of European Ascendancy: An International History of the World, 1914–1945*. London: Arnold, 2002.

Mayer, Arno J. *Political Origins of the New Diplomacy, 1917–1918*. New Haven, CT: Yale University Press, 1959.

———. *Politics and Diplomacy of Peacemaking: Containment and Counterrevolution at Versailles, 1918–1919*. New York: Knopf, 1967.

McDonough, Frank. *Hitler, Chamberlain and Appeasement*. Cambridge: Cambridge University Press, 2002.

McKenzie, Kermit. *Comintern and World Revolution, 1928–1943: The Shaping of Doctrine*. New York: Columbia University Press, 1964.

Medvedev, Roy. *Let History Judge: The Origins and Consequences of Stalinism*. Translated by George Shriver. New York: Columbia University Press, 1989.

Miner, Steven Merritt. *Between Churchill and Stalin: The Soviet Union, Great Britain, and the Origins of the Grand Alliance*. Chapel Hill: University of North Carolina Press, 1988.

Ogata, Sadako N. *Defiance in Manchuria: The Making of Japanese Foreign Policy, 1931–1932*. Berkeley: University of California Press, 1964.

Parker, Robert. *Chamberlain and Appeasement*. New York: St. Martin's, 1993.

Pons, Silvio. *Stalin and the Inevitable War, 1936–1941*. London: Frank Cass, 2002.

Ragsdale, Hugh. *The Soviets, the Munich Crisis, and the Coming of World War II*. Cambridge: Cambridge University Press, 2004.

Roberts, Geoffrey. *The Soviet Union and the Origins of the Second World War: Russo-German Relations and the Road to War, 1933–1941*. Houndmills, UK: Macmillan, 1995.

Saul, Norman E. *War and Revolution: The United States and Russia, 1914–1921*. Lawrence: University Press of Kansas, 2001.

Steiner, Zara. *The Lights That Failed: European International History, 1919–1933*. Oxford: Oxford University Press, 2005.

———. *The Triumph of the Dark: European International History, 1933–1939*. Oxford: Oxford University Press, 2010.

Thornton, Richard C. *The Comintern and the Chinese Communists, 1928–1931*. Seattle: University of Washington Press, 1969.

Volkogonov, Dmitri. *Stalin: Triumph and Tragedy*. New York: Grove Weidenfeld, 1991.

Watt, Donald C. *How War Came: The Immediate Origins of the Second World War, 1938–1939*. New York: Pantheon, 1989.

Weinberg, Gerhard L. *A World at Arms: A Global History of World War II*. Cambridge: Cambridge University Press, 1994.

Chapter 2
THE GRAND ALLIANCE, 1941–1945

We have learned that we cannot live alone, at peace; that
our own well-being is dependent on the well-being of
other nations far away.

—Franklin D. Roosevelt, Fourth
Inaugural Address, January 20, 1945

Hell is—other people!

—Jean-Paul Sartre, *Huit-Clos* (*No Exit*), 1944

World War II created powerful patriotic myths among the three victors of the Battle of Britain, Stalingrad, and Iwo Jima, but there is no shared public remembrance of the coalition that finally, and at very great cost, defeated the Axis powers in 1945. What Winston Churchill grandiosely dubbed the Grand Alliance was in fact a coalition of three highly disparate partners that dissolved almost immediately when the fighting was over. Even in wartime, the alliance was unstable, often lacking cohesion and mutual confidence and buffeted by alarming intelligence reports and bad news from the battlefield. A reexamination of the Grand Alliance thus requires us to peel away almost a half century of Cold War memoirs and accounts, amalgamate three separate national narratives— of America's "Good War," the Soviet Union's "Great Patriotic War," and Great Britain's heroic defense of its homeland and empire—and reappraise this brittle, ephemeral, but also indispensable partnership.

DISPARATE PARTNERS

There were, of course, considerable differences among the three. The Soviet Union, extending 8.6 million square miles between the Baltic and the Pacific, was the world's largest country, with nearly 200 million people, vast mineral deposits, and an economy that had made spectacular gains in heavy industry during the three Five-Year Plans between 1928 and 1941.* The United States, although one-third smaller, had a population of 132 million, extensive mineral reserves, and a giant manufacturing and agricultural base that could be rapidly mobilized for war production. By contrast, Great Britain, a relatively small, industrialized island state off the northwestern coast of Europe, comprised only 92,000 square miles and a population of 48 million people. Heavily dependent on trade and raw material supplies from its far-flung global empire (encompassing almost 25 percent of the world's land area and population), Britain also carried the huge burden of its defense.

The three had markedly different political orders. The USSR was a highly centralized communist dictatorship ruled under the terms of the 1936 Stalinist constitution; Great Britain was a constitutional monarchy with power centered in Parliament and its dominant party; and the United States, one of the world's oldest republics, was a government in which power was divided among the executive, legislative, and judiciary branches. The foreign policies of these three states reflected compromises among different interests. In the Soviet Union agreement had to be forged between the party and the military and in Great Britain between the government, permanent civil servants, and the services; but in the United States there was the widest range of contenders: business and academic leaders as well as the press and the armed forces vied with the State Department and the administration, and America's biennial congressional elections, dominated by two national parties, contributed to the irregular course of its diplomacy.

Moreover, their leaders were a study in contrasts. Secretive and suspicious, Josef Stalin, the former Orthodox seminarian and Bolshevik functionary, had clamped his sole rule over the USSR after 1926 through purges and terror. Winston Churchill, the longtime political outsider and passionate anti-appeaser, had become prime minister in May 1940 in Britain's grimmest hour. And Franklin Roosevelt, although stricken with polio, was an exceptionally shrewd politician

---

* Accompanied by the forced collectivization of over 90 percent of the country's agriculture (producing famine and millions of deaths) as well as a drastic fall in consumer goods.

who had mobilized the United States during the Depression through his eloquence and dynamism. As a war organizer the Soviet autocrat would be unre-
strained by the political, institutional, and public pressures that restricted his
partners, but Churchill and Roosevelt, although sharing a common language
and political eloquence, were often at odds over military strategy and the future
of European empires. Finally, Stalin, despite his lack of worldliness, would pose
a formidable diplomatic challenge to his interlocutors because of his remarkable
memory and tenacity.

Nonetheless, a four-year partnership did commence in June 1941 that included
economic and military cooperation as well as the cultivation of positive popular
images of the others. Dramatically reversing course, the two Western powers extended their security interests to building up the Red Army and provisioning the
Soviet Union in its struggle against Hitler, and Stalin, without ever overcoming
his fears and aversion toward the West dating back to World War I, traded isolation for a wary engagement with his distant allies. Limited and imperfect as
it was, the Grand Alliance changed the history of all three countries and of the
world.

Things started off badly in the summer of 1941 with Churchill's dismissal of
Stalin's plea for a second front, raising Soviet suspicions of an imminent Anglo-
German deal (fueled by the still-mysterious Rudolf Hess mission to Britain in
May). In late July Roosevelt dispatched his close adviser, Harry Hopkins, to Moscow to sound out Stalin on the Soviets' needs, but Allied aid began slowly, im-
peded by distance, inadequate coordination, and lingering qualms over working
with communists along with Washington and London's well-grounded fears of
a Soviet collapse.

In August 1941 Churchill and Roosevelt, in their first wartime encounter,
met off the coast of Newfoundland and drew up the Atlantic Charter. Echoing
Wilson's Fourteen Points, this key World War II document banned annexations
that violated "the freely expressed wishes of the peoples concerned," guaranteed
"the right of all peoples to choose the form of government under which they will
live," called for free and open markets, and anticipated a "wider and more permanent system of general security" to replace the moribund League of Nations.

Essentially dictated by the noncombatant United States, the Atlantic Charter was aimed at stirring resistance among millions of captive peoples and mobilizing outside support against the Axis powers—Germany, Italy, and Japan.
Churchill grumbled at this "poor substitute for a US declaration of war" that
threatened the British Empire, but he was intent on placating the American

colossus that had become indispensable to its survival, and grudgingly acquiesced. The absent Stalin, dismissing the charter's pious generalities and demanding specific terms to be imposed on the Third Reich, refused to sign. Until
battlefield conditions changed, the charter's virtuous language papered over
three separate war aims: Britain to preserve its global status, the Soviet Union
to achieve territorial security, and the United States—as in 1918—to reorder a
volatile, leaderless world.

Beneath the surface, the three began to cooperate in practical ways. In the
fall of 1941 a joint Anglo-Soviet action toppled the pro-German government in
Iran, divided the country into northern and southern occupation zones, and set
up a crucial military supply route to the USSR from the Persian Gulf; the British
and Soviet navies began working together; and the first Moscow supply protocol
facilitated the expansion of trilateral economic and military contacts. Strong
intelligence sharing between London and Washington, especially at the height of
the German blitzkrieg in 1941–1942, provided Moscow with crucial information
obtained from decoding Enigma* transmissions, supplemented by the Soviets'
own sources in Switzerland.

Stalin at once revealed himself as a difficult partner. In mid-December, just
after the Red Army's first successful counteroffensive near Moscow, the Soviet
ruler set the tone for future encounters. Flouting the Atlantic Charter and alarming Churchill, Stalin demanded recognition of the USSR's 1941 borders with
Finland, the Baltic States and Romania, although he did not mention Poland.

A few days earlier, Japan's unexpected and devastating attack on the American fleet at Pearl Harbor had expanded the Anglo-American struggle into Asia
and the Pacific.[†] The Nationalist government of China, which had lost control
over the coastal cities but was holding out in the mountains against Mao Zedong's communist forces and the Japanese invaders, now formally became an
American ally. Japan easily captured the West's colonies in Asia and the Pacific—with the remnants of French Indochina falling in July 1941, the port of
Singapore in February 1942, and the Philippines, Malaya, most of the Dutch
East Indies, and Burma in the spring of 1942—leaving almost all of East Asia
under Japanese domination and India and Australia vulnerable to attack.

---

* On the eve of World War II the Polish government had passed on to Britain its techniques for
decrypting messages transmitted by Germany's Enigma machines. Throughout the war, British
code breakers at Bletchley Park were able to track most of the Third Reich's secret communications. The intelligence they gathered was called "Ultra."

† The Soviet Union, preferring to focus its forces on repelling the Nazi invasion, rebuffed its allies'
entreaties to declare war on Japan.

After Hitler, in one of his most self-destructive acts, declared war on the United States on December 11, 1941. Churchill raced to Washington to confirm Roosevelt's commitment to defeating the Third Reich. Again, the United States stamped its creed on the conflict. On January 1, 1942, America and Britain, joined by the Soviet Union and twenty-three other countries (including the representatives of six European governments in exile), issued "A Declaration of the United Nations," reiterating their support for the Atlantic Charter and foreswearing a separate peace. Bowing to Moscow's reluctance to open a second front against Japan, Roosevelt allowed the signatories to pledge their full economic military resources against "those . . . with which they were at war," and agreed to defer the actual details of this new world organization.

Churchill and Roosevelt also made major decisions to coordinate their efforts. These included a combined Anglo-American Joint Chiefs of Staff to direct global operations, with the United States leading in the Pacific, Britain the Middle East and India, and a joint responsibility for the Atlantic-European theater. Equally significant, they announced a "Europe-First" strategy involving the buildup of Allied power against Germany and a largely defensive posture against Japan until the Third Reich was defeated.

Europe-First raised highly delicate political questions. Churchill, seeking to strike at an Axis weak point, restore British power in the Mediterranean, and gain a base to attack Nazi Europe through its southern back door, convinced Roosevelt to launch a joint campaign in North Africa. The president's military commanders were cool to this imperialist "diversion," but also divided between two larger offensives: a cross-Channel attack to relieve pressure on the Soviet Union and an immensely popular Pacific operation against Japan.

Roosevelt, skilled at mollifying rivals, crafted a crucial compromise in the spring of 1942. He countenanced the costly but ultimately successful naval engagements in the Coral Sea and Midway as well as the Guadalcanal and Papuan campaigns, which halted Japan's threat to Australia and New Zealand and gave the initiative to US forces in the Pacific. But the political price was high: the abandonment of Sledgehammer, the direct cross-Channel operation that he had offered Stalin as a quid pro quo for removing the Soviets' territorial claims in Eastern Europe from the May 1942 Anglo-Soviet treaty of alliance. Instead, the president opted for Torch, an Allied landing in a lightly defended French North Africa that, according to Churchill's scenario, would coordinate with British troops in Egypt as a first step in removing Italy from the war.

This Anglo-American version of "Europe-First" infuriated Stalin. While the Battle of Stalingrad raged that summer, the Allies suddenly halted their

Lend-Lease convoys to Murmansk and Archangel because of mounting losses from air attacks during the almost twenty-four hours of Arctic daylight. Stalin suspected that the Western powers intended to watch from the sidelines while Nazi Germany and the Soviet Union fought each other to exhaustion and would then arrive to dictate peace. Soviet citizens, despite their gratitude for Allied foodstuffs and war supplies, complained over the West's inactivity.* But Britons bitterly recalled that only two years earlier, during their own desperate hours, Stalin had been aligned with Hitler.

To be sure, there was some validity to Stalin's fears. Churchill, scarred by the bloodbath in the Great War and the disastrous Dieppe raid in August 1942, was undoubtedly keen on preserving British troops and allowing the Red Army to bear the brunt of Hitler's might. Allied planners certainly believed that the attrition of Nazi forces on the eastern front would ease a cross-Channel invasion. But there were also objective reasons for delaying a headlong attack on Fortress Europa in 1942, including the formidable German emplacements along the French coast, the absence of sufficient landing craft, and, above all, the danger of transporting large numbers of US troops to Britain until the Battle of the Atlantic was won.

The delay in opening a second front not only contributed to heightened tensions among the three, to the extreme disparity between Western and Soviet casualties in World War II, and to a half century of Cold War debate. It was also during this two-year period that the West learned of the Nazis' deportations of millions of European Jews to their deaths in the gas chambers in Poland and did not respond.

In the wake of the British victory at El Alamein and the success of Torch, Churchill and Roosevelt met in Casablanca in January 1943 to plan future operations. Stalin, engaged in combat and fearful of air travel, passed up an opportunity to threaten and cajole his partners. Churchill, in probably his last major victory, won Roosevelt's support to continue his indirect strategy for regaining control over the North Atlantic and the Mediterranean and coordinating their bombing offensive against Germany.

Then the president dropped his bombshell. Alarmed over Stalin's peace feelers to Hitler, and determined to stave off any decision on the specifics of a postwar

---

* In September 1942 the journalist Ilya Ehrenburg wrote: "It's high time. . . . Fifty divisions on the Atlantic coast would have made a greater contribution to the fight for the Volga and the Caucasus than all the supplies," and by 1943 Soviet soldiers were calling US canned meat "the Second Front."

settlement, Roosevelt announced the Allied goal of unconditional surrender. Stalin was unimpressed with US bravado and Churchill annoyed by Roosevelt's denunciation of "the conquest and subjugation of other peoples." Moreover, the doctrine of unconditional surrender may also have prolonged the European war by stiffening the German army's resistance, disheartening the anti-Hitler opposition, and feeding the Nazi propaganda machine's calls for national solidarity.

TURNING THE TIDE WHILE TENSIONS MOUNT

For the Grand Alliance, 1943 was a year of major but still separate military successes. The Red Army's heroic victories at Stalingrad, Kursk, and Orel set the stage for the removal of 90 percent of German troops from Soviet soil by the end of the year. The Allies had achieved smaller but significant gains. By May, Anglo-American forces had quelled the German submarine menace in the Atlantic and vanquished the Axis in North Africa. Two months later they landed in Sicily, bringing down Mussolini but also commencing a brutal year-and-a-half-long fight with Wehrmacht troops up the rugged Italian peninsula,* which exasperated Stalin but also reduced Nazi forces in France. In the Pacific, Admiral Chester W. Nimitz's westward island hopping achieved a costly victory in November in the Gilbert Islands, and American submarines were crippling Japanese sea communications with the empire. Although the war in China continued to drain US resources and show little progress, it tied down more than half of Japan's army and refuted the Tokyo government's claims that it was conducting an anticolonial, antiracist crusade.

But for most of that year the Grand Alliance was not functioning well. On the Soviet side there were mounting complaints over delays and shortages of Lend-Lease deliveries and bitter comments on the delayed second front. On the Allied side there was frequent grumbling over Soviet secretiveness around its war production, weapons, and troop deployments, Stalin's scolding, and his callousness toward potential Allied casualties. Despite extensive written communication and intelligence sharing, it remained essentially a "two plus one" arrangement in which London and Washington maintained closer ties with each other than with Moscow, to which they simply conveyed their decisions. Moreover, there

---

* During which the German occupiers rounded up and shot or deported tens of thousands of partisans and Jews.

were widespread interceptions of internal communications among all three parties as well as active espionage. For example, Anglo-American efforts to hide information from Stalin about the Manhattan Project to develop an atomic bomb were easily overcome by well-placed Soviet agents.

With the demonstration of Soviet military power in 1943, the United States and Britain could no longer ignore Stalin's demands, particularly under the threat of a separate peace between Moscow and Berlin. In March Stalin added Eastern Poland to his list of territorial claims, deftly suggesting compensation for the Poles in the West at the expense of Germany. Although British and US leaders were amenable, they could not overcome the opposition of the exile Polish government in London. Nor could they silence their misgivings over a repeat of the Munich agreement, which mutilated a small ally, and over violating the Atlantic Charter.

One month later the Polish issue became explosive when Radio Berlin reported the discovery of mass graves in the Katyn Forest containing the remains of some four thousand of the twenty-two thousand missing Polish prisoners of war. Citing the report by a foreign investigation team, Germany hoped to shake the Grand Alliance. Moscow refused an independent medical investigation and blamed the Germans for the atrocity, and Washington and London withheld public criticism of the Soviets. Stalin, ignoring his allies' pleas, took the opportunity to sever relations with the London Poles over their "hostile propaganda" and to cultivate candidates for an alternative Polish government among the communist exiles in Moscow.

In the wake of Katyn, on May 15, 1943, Stalin issued the startling announcement of the dissolution of the Comintern (Communist International), which was widely interpreted as abandoning the goal of world revolution.[*] According to the official Soviet announcement the abolition of this "obsolete" form of international communist mobilization would promote the struggle of all freedom loving peoples against Nazi Germany and lay the basis for a new form of international cooperation, but this ostensibly conciliatory gesture also served Stalin's purposes. By unfettering the world's communist parties from their Moscow master, Stalin not only removed an institutional rival and strengthened his own control over the Marxist movement but also lay claim to a dominant role in a new postwar political order by enabling small and hitherto suspect communist

---

* The president of the British Trade Union Congress insisted that Moscow would continue to finance subversion throughout the globe, which, in fact, was the case.

groups, such as those in Poland, to reinvent themselves as patriotic antifascists and enter national coalitions.

Roosevelt, convinced that the Soviet Union had become decisive for the defeat of Germany and Japan, went behind Churchill's back and requested a private meeting with Stalin. Undeterred by the Kremlin's rebuff, the president pressed Churchill to set a firm date—the spring of 1944—for the long-delayed cross-Channel invasion, only to receive a caustic response to this news from Stalin. By August, however, after the Red Army had stopped the German offensive at Kursk and Kharkov and Stalin had abandoned his efforts for a separate peace, he was ready to end his passive role in Anglo-American decision making. Beginning with his unfilled demand for Soviet participation in the occupation regime in Italy, Stalin set in motion an extraordinary two-year period of thorny tripartite deliberations over the conduct of the war and the world's future.

The new nature of the Grand Alliance was manifest at the three secret meetings in late 1943. In October, the Moscow Conference of Foreign Ministers (the first gathering of the Big Three's top diplomats) tackled an ambitious agenda under the watchful eyes of Stalin and the very deft chairmanship of Vyacheslav Molotov. Once reassured on the date of the second front, the Soviet side was surprisingly accommodating toward Allied proposals regarding Turkey, France, and the restoration of Austria as well as on the establishment of two new agencies, a European Advisory Commission in London to deal with postwar problems and a trilateral commission to lay the groundwork for the United Nations. There was also general agreement on Germany and the need to "disarm, denazify, democratize, and dismember" Hitler's Reich and to try the major leaders as war criminals. But much to the discomfort of British foreign secretary Anthony Eden, Secretary of State Cordell Hull not only failed to support the full restoration of Polish independence but also stepped up America's anticolonial rhetoric.

One month later, at the first face-to-face meeting of Churchill, Roosevelt, and Stalin in Tehran, the new dynamics were all the more evident. Stalin's choice of location forced Roosevelt to fly almost seven thousand miles, which included a stopover each way in Cairo that provided an opportunity to meet with the British envoys. The Tehran proceedings, dominated by the US and Soviet leaders, saw the eclipse of Churchill, who up till then had enjoyed an exclusive relationship with Washington and had served as the essential go-between with Moscow. Now outnumbered—wedged between the "Russian bear" and the "US buffalo"—the British leader's Mediterranean strategy would be decisively rebuffed by his partners.

Roosevelt and Stalin appeared to hit it off at Tehran. Although less loquacious than the president and noticeably tough, Stalin displayed an affable demeanor that convinced Roosevelt of his reasonableness and willingness to negotiate. Indeed, the two struck a powerful bargain in the Iranian capital: in exchange for a cross-Channel offensive in six months (and, to appease Churchill, an operation in southern France), Stalin offered not only a simultaneous assault on the eastern front but also to enter the war in Asia once Germany was defeated.

Yet underneath the amity of Tehran lay the seeds of future conflict. Unconvinced by Anglo-American bickering and Roosevelt's caustic private remarks about British and French imperialism, Stalin recognized the fundamental differences between Moscow and the West. Rejecting the principles of the Atlantic Charter, he was determined to impose territorial changes and pro-Soviet governments on his neighbors. While paying lip service to Roosevelt's vaguely sketched notion of "Four Policemen" operating under the aegis of the United Nations, Stalin preferred old-fashioned spheres of influence.

At Tehran, Roosevelt, ignoring his own doctrines, tried to win Stalin's confidence by acquiescing in his demands, including the dismemberment of Germany, establishing the borders of a resurrected Poland,[*] and Soviet acquisition of "warm-water" outlets[*†] and concessions in Manchuria. Yet contrary to his critics' charges, the president's conduct at Tehran was a display neither of naïveté nor excessive self-confidence. Wartime conditions dictated many of Roosevelt's decisions. The United States and Britain, despite their greater material resources, had a weak political hand. Until they attained a major foothold on the European continent and turned the tide in Asia, they still required Soviet support.

On a more fundamental level, the US president was clearly looking toward the future. Noticeably cooler toward Churchill and his imperialist worldview, Roosevelt intended to engage the chief of the looming military power whose voice would be essential for the peaceful world he envisaged once hostilities ceased. And finally, Roosevelt was indeed an improviser, which may have confirmed Stalin's suspicions that once military and political conditions had changed, his partners might well contest his successes at Tehran.

The shadow of Tehran hung over the two adjacent meetings in Cairo on November 22–26 and December 4–6, 1943, which Stalin declined to attend. On

---

[*] In the East the Curzon Line (the 1797 border between Prussia and tsarist Russia proposed in December 1919 by the British foreign secretary but rejected by both Poland and Soviet Russia) and in the West the Oder River, with lands taken from Germany.

[†] Königsberg and Memel in the Baltic, Port Arthur (Lushun) and Dairen (Dalian) in the Far East.

both occasions, Anglo-American relations were frosty. On the eve of the first Big Three meeting, Roosevelt, aiming to allay Stalin's suspicions, avoided any semblance of an Anglo-American alignment. Moreover, dismissing Churchill's objections, Roosevelt invited Chiang Kai-shek to Cairo and tried to rouse the Chinese Nationalist leader's weak war spirit by proposing an amphibious campaign in the Bay of Bengal and pledging to restore all of China's territory, only to backtrack on both pledges after his meetings with Stalin just days later.

After Tehran, it was Turkey's turn to stir Anglo-American discord. At Churchill's initiative, President Ismet Inönü, a seasoned veteran of the four-year bidding contest between the Axis and the Allies over Turkey's neutrality, was invited to Cairo. Because Turkey figured prominently in his Balkan designs, Churchill had hoped for US support in persuading Inönü to declare war or at least to provide air bases for the Allies. But after Stalin had reversed the Soviets' friendly stance toward Turkey and vetoed Western military operations in the Balkans, Roosevelt's own lack of enthusiasm—combined with Turkey's exorbitant demands—doomed this British project.

MOVING APART

Fifteen months would elapse until the next Big Three meeting, and in the meantime the course of World War II changed dramatically. By May 1944 the Soviet army had reached the 1941 borders. In June the Allies mounted a spectacular amphibious campaign on the coast of France and began their arduous march toward Germany. By the end of the year the troops of the Soviet Union, Britain, and the United States were for the first time all fighting in Germany.

Nevertheless, political cooperation among the three countries remained tenuous.* In May 1944 Stalin had for the first time publicly acknowledged the extent and generosity of Allied supplies and the valuable Anglo-American military contributions to the common struggle. One month later the Soviets, in coordination with D-Day (the Allies' June 1944 invasion of Normandy), launched Operation Bagration, a major offensive that dealt a lethal blow to the Wehrmacht. But in August a new crisis erupted when the Soviet advance on Warsaw halted, and the Germans proceeded to crush the uprising of the Polish Home Army (AK) in the capital. For two months London and Washington bristled over Stalin's refusal to allow their planes, bringing arms and supplies to the Polish partisans,

---

* In June and September Stalin declined invitations for another summit.

to refuel at Soviet airfields, his unwillingness to provide aid to the Poles, and his dismissal of the AK as "adventurers" and criminal elements.

At stake that summer was the very future of Poland, long the martyr of Europe, which had been resurrected in 1919 and become the victim of Nazi-Soviet aggression in 1939. Poland's political fate, already compromised by the Anglo-American territorial concessions at Tehran, now hinged on the Red Army's advance and on the contest between the communist Polish Committee of National Liberation (PCNL) that Stalin had installed on August 1 in Lublin and the London exile government that had launched the last-ditch Warsaw revolt. To achieve the expanded Soviet frontiers to block a resurgent Germany, Stalin needed a compliant Polish partner. But unlike former Czechoslovak president Eduard Beneš, who (ignoring British cautions) had scurried to Moscow after the Tehran summit and concluded a lopsided treaty with Stalin,* Polish prime minister Stanisław Mikołajczyk had defied the Kremlin, rejecting border adjustments in the east and a merger with the PCNL and thus creating an insoluble predicament for Roosevelt and Churchill.

The Red Army's smashing victories over Romania and Bulgaria in September 1944 and its imminent entry into Yugoslavia and Hungary underlined the urgency of Great Power consultation. With Roosevelt occupied by his fourth presidential campaign, Churchill journeyed alone to Moscow, where he offered to Stalin the infamous percentages agreement defining their respective interests in East Central and Southern Europe.† Stalin coolly responded with figures of his own, raising Soviet influence in Hungary and Bulgaria. The ostensible purpose of this bilateral transaction was to set up the Allied control commissions to oversee the transformation from military occupation to civilian rule. In reality, as the Italian precedent had established one year earlier, political control over each vanquished country would ultimately depend on the occupying army.‡

The ensuing outrage over the Churchill-Stalin deal misses the point. Churchill, faced with the Red Army's triumphs, made a traditional balance-of-power

---

* In which Stalin countenanced the expulsion of three million Germans from Czechoslovakia in return for the cession of Carpathian Ukraine to the USSR and Beneš's assurance that he would work amicably with the Czech and Slovak communists.

† The details were as follows: Romania: 90 percent Russia, 10 percent others; Bulgaria: 75 percent Russia, 25 percent others; Yugoslavia: 50–50; Hungary: 50–50; and Greece: Great Britain (in accord with the United States) 90 percent, Russia 10 percent. Poland, already largely in Soviet hands, was not included in the offer.

‡ In his famous statement to the Yugoslav partisan Milovan Djilas in April 1945, Stalin announced: "Everyone imposes his own system as far as his army can reach. It cannot be otherwise."

offer. In return for a Soviet guarantee of Britain's interests in Greece and the eastern Mediterranean, the prime minister was prepared to make substantial concessions: to acknowledge Soviet predominance in the rest of the Balkans, preach moderation to the London Poles, accept Soviet demands over access to the Turkish Straits, acquiesce in Stalin's veto of any form of federation among the restored East Central European states, and agree to Stalin's punitive plans for Germany. Stalin was more than willing to concede Greece, because he still needed his partners' cooperation on more essential issues closer to home.* Machiavellian as it was, the Churchill-Stalin discussions brought the prospect of order to a region that had been brutalized by Nazi rule and internecine warfare, even under two entirely different political systems. However, second thoughts by the British, belated expressions of indignation from Washington, and the later outcry from the parties involved consigned this old-fashioned, informal transaction into a nasty Cold War footnote.

The United States was pursuing a different course, a Wilsonian quest for a postwar order to ensure economic stability and global security. Shortly after D-Day Roosevelt's Treasury secretary, Henry Morgenthau, convened a meeting of financial representatives from the forty-four UN allies at a lavish rural resort in Bretton Woods, New Hampshire. To avoid the revival of the ruinous economic nationalism of the Great Depression, the Roosevelt administration presented a plan to promote free trade, ensure capital movement, and provide investment loans to devastated economies. At the center of its proposal was a return to the stability of the gold standard, with the US dollar to become the world's reserve currency, as well as the creation of an International Monetary Fund to pool members' resources and facilitate trade by correcting temporary imbalances (thus avoiding the extreme currency swings and the weapons of exchange controls and devaluation of the 1930s) and a linked International Bank for Reconstruction and Development (the future World Bank) to lend funds to governments, businesses, and individuals.

Its partners greeted the US initiative warily, anticipating that the now booming US economy would dominate the postwar world. British representatives, led by the economist John Maynard Keynes, challenged the revival of the gold standard and the supremacy of the dollar and fought futilely for parity in managing the postwar economic structure and also to salvage their system of imperial

---

* Stalin also vaguely agreed to Churchill's request to rein in the Italian and French communists, thus conceding Western dominance in these two countries.

preference.* London was ultimately bought off with promises of debt relief, loans, and trade concessions. The Soviet Union, more interested in future credits than international monetary stabilization and a multilateral trading system, was loath to expose its internal economic affairs to outside scrutiny. Soviet negotiators used their strong political bargaining position to demand a reduced contribution to the fund and higher lending rights, which the United States—to bring Bretton Woods to life—obligingly granted.

One month later, on August 21, 1944, US undersecretary of state Edward Stettinius convened a diplomatic gathering of UN representatives at the Dumbarton Oaks estate in Washington, DC, to lay the foundation for the United Nations. Remnants of the League of Nations were to be preserved in the revival of a secretariat, council, and assembly, the formation of a Social and Economic Council, and the maintenance of an affiliated Court of International Justice. But there was this Rooseveltian change: in dealing with threats to peace, the new UN Security Council would be dominated by a group of five permanent members (the United States, Great Britain, and Soviet Russia, with the addition of China and France), whose decisions had to be unanimous.

Here agreement ended, because this scenario envisaged a council that would halt aggression only by powers outside the five. The Soviets, recalling their expulsion from the League and wary of the council's four to one majority, demanded a veto on all decisions. The United States, although inclined to go along, suspended the discussion. Similarly, the Soviets' startling demand for sixteen votes in the General Assembly (to match the votes the United States and Britain would command) was tabled. Other unresolved issues were also deferred, including the specifications for UN membership, the disposition of Japanese and European colonies, and the jurisdiction of the International Court. The transformation of the wartime alliance into a stable international structure would require risky commitments, but Stalin, after his meetings with Churchill, announced reassuringly that the Big Three's differences did not exceed "the bounds of what is tolerable."

YALTA

The next summit had been delayed first by Stalin's refusals and then by Roosevelt's fourth inauguration. By the time the three finally met in February 1945, US forces

---

* Long an object of US opposition, the system of imperial preference (negotiated at the 1932 Imperial Economic Conference in Ottawa) established special tariff rates, subsidies, and other forms of official trade support to members of the British Empire and Commonwealth.

Photo 2.1. Winston Churchill, Franklin Roosevelt, and Joseph Stalin at the Yalta Conference, February 1945. *Courtesy of National Archives.*

had recaptured the Philippines but were still a long way from Japan. In Europe both sides had encountered fierce German resistance, the Red Army in East Prussia and Pomerania, the Anglo-American forces in the Ardennes. There was thus a pressing need for military as well as political coordination among the Big Three.

In the Western public mind, the Yalta Conference has joined Munich in a special position of historical notoriety, the site of another craven and possibly avoidable capitulation to a dictator's demands. Yalta's detractors differ only between the realists who acknowledge the West's strategic weakness and Roosevelt's physical debility and the moralists who accuse the West of betrayal. Although the decisions at Yalta were less definitive than those made at Tehran, the timing—close to the end of the war and to the rupture of the Grand Alliance—raised the proceedings in the Crimea into a preview of the Cold War.

In retrospect, it is easy to emphasize the tensions leading up to the Yalta meeting. Despite a marked improvement in battlefield conditions on all fronts at the beginning of 1945 and a growing level of coordination among Soviet and Western forces in Europe, there was indeed a rising distrust among the three that

Roosevelt was determined to end. Having tacitly accepted the Anglo-Soviet percentages deal, the president was disconcerted over two of its abrupt repercussions: Britain's intervention in the Greek civil war in December 1944 and Stalin's recognition of the PCNL as the provisional government of Poland in January 1945, both contravening the principles of the Atlantic Charter. Like Wilson twenty-seven years earlier, a visibly frail president undertook an arduous journey to a place even harder to reach than Tehran on a highly ambitious venture: to settle outstanding wartime disputes and reach agreement on the postwar world.

Despite later judgments, the Yalta Conference was an exceptionally harmonious and productive gathering. Repeating his conduct at Tehran, Roosevelt, at his preliminary meeting with Churchill in Malta, rejected an Anglo-American bloc. In Yalta he courted Stalin by stressing his differences with the British; negotiating directly over such key issues as Germany, Poland, the war against Japan, the treatment of China, and the United Nations; and making plain his intention to withdraw US troops from Europe within two years, thus conceding a major role on that continent to the USSR. Stalin, firm but affable, agreed to include France in the occupation of Germany* and assented to the Declaration on Liberated Europe calling for free elections, which, to be sure, was unenforceable.

The problem with the Yalta agreements lay in three crucial elements: the prior commitments made at Tehran, the imbalance in the three bargaining positions, and, especially, the participants' recognition of the incompatibility of their future interests. On Germany—echoing the debate between France and its allies after World War I—Stalin's desire for a punitive peace of dismemberment and high reparations clashed with Anglo-American fears of creating a power vacuum in Central Europe and of Soviet dominance. Thus the implementation of the Yalta arrangements for the defeated Reich—establishing four-power rule and providing the USSR with the lion's share of damages—would greatly depend on the survival of the Grand Alliance. Similarly in regard to Poland, Stalin's unilateral border changes and his insistence on installing a pro-Soviet regime in Warsaw stirred strong protests by the Western Allies, which also recognized the weakness of their position.† Nonetheless, the vagueness of the Yalta terms for expanding the Polish government with representatives from London (and the anticipated domestic backlash in the United States and Britain if this

---

* But insisted that its territory be carved from the US and British zones.
† Particularly in light of Stalin's acquiescence in British control of Greece and US and British predominance in Italy, France, and the Low Countries.

failed) reinforced the potential for future quarrels between the Soviet Union and the West.

Things were easier elsewhere. To gain Soviet entry into the Asian war, the West agreed to generous concessions at Japan's and China's expense. To breathe life into the United Nations, Roosevelt accepted a full Soviet veto in the Security Council and accorded three seats to the USSR in the General Assembly (the additional two went to Ukraine and Belorussia, the republics that had borne a large part of the brunt of the Nazi invasion and had been expanded by land seized from Poland). But with British help, Roosevelt stopped Stalin from dictating the terms of UN membership and excluding wartime neutrals such as Turkey and Argentina. And at Yalta Roosevelt was also noticeably silent on deciding the fate of European empires.

Indeed, the Yalta conference may well have stirred controversy precisely because its civilized and amicable façade had obscured a series of momentous improvisations. With World War II not yet over the three strongest powers—with rival goals and forms of behavior—sketched out a postwar world. Yet none of the participants considered the decisions to be definitive, and indeed, despite their overwhelming military might, none was entirely in control of the local scene in Europe, where events, particularly in the Balkans, were occurring at a dizzying speed, or in Asia.

Yet each expected the alliance to continue. The alternatives—a separate deal with Germany and a reprise of East-West antagonism—were politically unthinkable in 1945. Each also expected his partners to keep their Tehran and Yalta commitments while retaining the maximum flexibility on his and his clients' parts. Thus, the United States and Britain were quick to criticize the Kremlin's role in the coup in Romania in February 1945, and in March Stalin fumed over the revival of secret contacts between US intelligence and the Germans. By April both sides were trading barbs over their post-Yalta disagreements, particularly the political impasse in Poland and the fierce dissension within the Control Councils in Hungary, Romania, and Bulgaria.

THE END OF WORLD WAR II

Complicating the war's final year were also the revelations of its horrors. Starting with the Red Army's capture of the death camp in Majdenak in August 1944 and its liberation of Auschwitz (Oświęcim), Bełzec, Chełmno, Sobibór, and Treblinka, Soviet correspondents reported to the world the gruesome details of the mechanized slaughter of millions of Jews, Slavs, Roma, homosexuals, and prisoners of war by the Nazis and their accomplices.* Later there were revelations of Japan's mistreatment of prisoners of war and of female civilians in China, Korea, and the Philippines. To be sure, there were atrocities by the Allies. After crossing the Soviet borders, the once greatly admired Red Army unleashed a wave of looting and rapes that compromised the USSR's image among the liberated peoples and created an embarrassing political dilemma for Stalin. Although the US, British, and French invading forces committed fewer acts of theft and violence, the Allied bombing campaign—particularly of urban areas such as Berlin, Cologne, Hamburg, and Dresden, and with casualties estimated at between three hundred thousand and six hundred thousand civilians—tarnished their image as well. In his Buchenwald cell in December 1944, the former French premier Léon Blum accused his Nazi captors and presciently predicted: "I tremble at the thought that you are already conquerors in this sense: You have breathed such terror all about that to master you, to prevent the return of your fury, we shall have no other way of fashioning the world save in your image, your laws, the law of Force."

The death of Franklin Roosevelt on April 12, 1945, undoubtedly contributed to the deterioration of relations among the Big Three. Gone was the subtle politician and negotiator. Roosevelt's successor, Vice President Harry Truman, a World War I veteran, two-term senator, and passionate reader of history, was unprepared for global leadership and suddenly forced to direct two theaters of war and work with two fractious allies. Out of temperament and political necessity Truman, instead of papering over disagreements with Stalin, sought clarification, and an increasingly combative Churchill, fresh from his triumph in Greece, stood by his side.

The Big Three began to spar openly over their Yalta decisions. Using Poland as a test case, the British and Americans demanded the replacement of the minority communist regime with an entirely new and more representative government, but Stalin, recalling their Tehran agreement on a pro-Soviet Poland and questioning the democratic character of the governments the United States and Britain had installed in France, Belgium, and Greece, refused. On the eve of the April 25 opening of the founding UN conference in San Francisco, Stalin's new coolness toward this organization raised alarms in the West.

---

* In January 2013 researchers at the US Holocaust Memorial Museum in Washington, DC, announced that they had catalogued some 42,500 Nazi ghettoes and camps from France to the Soviet Union in which an estimated fifteen to twenty million people were imprisoned or perished.

Yet contrary to the views of some Cold War historians, the Grand Alliance did not immediately collapse with Truman's accession to the presidency. In early May 1945 the armies of the Big Three, coordinating their efforts, vanquished the Third Reich, and shortly afterward, Truman turned down Churchill's dramatic plea for a showdown with Stalin over the fate of Eastern Europe. Although a jarring note was struck on May 12, when the United States announced the termination of Lend-Lease to the USSR, Truman soon dispatched Roosevelt's old confidant, Harry Hopkins, to Moscow. Four years after their first encounter in the gloomy summer of 1941, the ailing US envoy and the victorious Soviet dictator tried to revive a frayed bond.

It was a successful mission. Hopkins, applying Roosevelt's stratagems, blamed the British for their misunderstandings and encouraged Stalin to vent his grievances. Stalin acknowledged America's global power and conceded its legitimate interests in Central and Eastern Europe. Much to the consternation of British envoys in Moscow, the two arranged a series of deals, setting up an Allied Control Council for Germany, a Polish government that included four pro-Western ministers and was almost immediately recognized by the United States and Britain, the next Big Three meeting in July, and the specific date (August 8) for Soviet entry into the war against Japan as well as achieving a more conciliatory stance by Molotov in San Francisco and the signing of the UN Charter on June 25.

The last and longest wartime meeting of the Grand Alliance took place in Potsdam from July 17 through August 2, 1945. The meeting was punctuated by Churchill's abrupt departure on July 25 after his overwhelming electoral defeat and his replacement by British Labour leader Clement Atlee. This was not an unexpected event but one that shocked Stalin, who had suddenly lost another familiar sparring partner, and perhaps confirmed his suspicions toward the electoral process. Potsdam was overshadowed by two even more important elements: the Red Army's imposing presence in Eastern Europe and the dawn of the atomic age. Less than twenty miles from Hitler's ruined capital, around the famous round table brought especially from Moscow, the new masters of Europe tackled a wide and very difficult agenda.

Truman, clearly the dominant figure, had chosen the Potsdam dates.* As chair of the conference, assisted vigorously by Secretary of State James Byrnes, he faced a tough and triumphant Stalin, who was nonetheless still intent on

---

* In the hope of facing Stalin from a position of strength, the new president had delayed the summit until the testing of the atomic bomb.

gaining his partners' acquiescence in his territorial and economic claims, and British partners suddenly without force or direction. The sheer length of the Potsdam meeting enabled American diplomats to test the Soviets' mettle. Moreover, unlike Wilson's thorny situation in 1919, the United Nations had already been brought to life, the German Reich was under complete Allied control, and the victors had no intention of convening an international gathering to conclude a European or global peace.

The Big Three's decisions on Germany were far-reaching and harsh. When the United States, despite its Yalta commitment, now refused to set a total reparations sum, the stage was set for an eventual partition. Although the Allied Control Council was still to treat Germany as a unified economic entity, the occupying powers would extract restitution from their assigned zones and thus dominate their respective areas. The German military was dissolved, the fleet and merchant marine divided among the Big Three, and the major war criminals to be brought before an Allied tribunal. The occupiers would have almost unlimited jurisdiction over Germany's administration as well as its educational, judicial, financial, economic, and transport systems. Moreover, Germany's 1937 territory was reduced by 25 percent, with East Prussia carved up between the USSR and Poland, and Poland's western border expanded to the Oder and western Neisse Rivers.* With ethnic Germans flooding the western zones in flight from the Red Army and their vengeful neighbors, the Big Three agreed on the "orderly and humane" transfer of the remaining Germans out of Poland, Czechoslovakia, and Hungary, eventually some twelve million in all, thereby ethnically cleansing the East, burdening the West with the refugees' sustenance, and creating an enduring rift between communist and noncommunist Central Europe.

Behind the scenes at Potsdam were two crucial compromises. To obtain Stalin's assent to abandoning a fixed sum, the United States offered to supplement the Soviets' share of reparations with industrial equipment from the three western zones according to negotiations to be held within six months. In addition, the British and Americans withdrew their earlier objections to Poland's acquisition of the Silesian coal fields that lay between the eastern and western Neisse River pending a final German peace treaty. Stalin on his part agreed to replace the European Advisory Commission in London with a more permanent institution, a Council of Foreign Ministers (CFM), to draw up peace treaties with Italy,

---

* Poland also gained full control over the former Free City of Danzig.

Romania, Bulgaria, Hungary, and Finland and pave their way to membership in the United Nations.

The Potsdam deliberations over the war in Asia took a far different turn. On July 16, 1945, the US delegation received word of the successful test of an atomic bomb in New Mexico. With this new weapon and the growing signs of Japan's imminent collapse, the long-sought Soviet entry into the war in Asia now appeared unnecessary, and even inconvenient for the United States, given Stalin's expansive territorial claims and the undesirable prospect of a joint occupation of Japan.

Stalin, surprised only by the timing of the atomic test, reacted coolly to the president's disclosure of a "powerful new weapon." He encouraged Truman to use it and reiterated the Soviets' readiness to attack Japan by mid-August. Yet on July 26 the still-neutral USSR was not asked to sign the Potsdam declaration calling for unconditional surrender by Japan, signifying that the Grand Alliance did not extend to Asia.

Nor indeed did it extend much beyond Europe. The United States and Britain curbed Stalin's ambition to acquire Italy's North African colonies and establish Soviet naval bases in the Mediterranean, deferring his claim for a UN trusteeship in Libya until the conclusion of a peace treaty with Italy.* On Turkey, the United States and Britain, reversing their earlier signs of acceptance, rebuffed Stalin's proposal to pressure the Ankara government to revise the 1936 Montreux Convention and grant the Soviets a permanent military presence and joint control over the Bosporus Straits and the Dardanelles, which connect the Black Sea with the Mediterranean. On Iran, the three, while agreeing on an immediate military withdrawal from Tehran, came to no final decision on the total evacuation of the country.

The atomic age began on August 6, 1945, when the United States dropped its first nuclear bomb on Hiroshima, killing more than seventy thousand people, injuring an equal number, and destroying four square miles of Japan's eighth-largest city. Three days later the United States dropped an equally destructive bomb on Nagasaki. At the time Truman's decision to use nuclear weapons to end the war quickly was scarcely questioned. Yet almost immediately afterward, the world public recognized a quantum change in modern warfare: a device threatening human life and the earth itself. Truman's supporters insisted that the bomb had saved the hundreds of thousands of American lives that would have

---

* Stalin's proposal for Soviet participation in the international regime in Tangier was similarly delayed.

been lost in an amphibious invasion of the Japanese mainland and pointed to the even worse bombing atrocities during the war. His critics have protested the callous and even unnecessary destruction of an enemy about to collapse, when either a demonstration test or a blockade could have convinced Japan to capitulate. Some also suspected that this US show of force was designed to intimidate Stalin and check Soviet designs in Europe, Asia, and the rest of the world.

Stalin, duly shocked by the attack, sped up the Soviets' military schedule. On August 8, the Red Army swept into Manchuria and down to the thirty-eighth parallel in Korea and also moved on to the Kurile Islands and the southern half of Sakhalin Island, thus gaining direct access to the Pacific. This swift and tenacious Soviet campaign eliminated any Japanese hope of a negotiated peace and—combined with the two atomic bombs—forced Japan to accept an unconditional surrender. By the end of August 1945 Stalin had regained the territories and privileges lost to Japan by tsarist Russia forty years earlier, dictated a lopsided treaty with Chiang Kai-shek, and captured more than a half million Japanese prisoners of war, who were summarily dispatched to Soviet labor camps. Yet a major prize eluded him when Truman vetoed his request to occupy the northern half of Hokkaido and to take part in Japan's surrender and the occupation regime. World War II ended officially on August 15, 1945, with Japan's acceptance of US terms.

Only three months earlier the leaders and peoples of the Grand Alliance had exulted together—but not on the same day—over their victory against Nazism.[*] "V-J" Day on the other hand was an almost exclusively US triumph, symbolized by the iconic Times Square photo and the Japanese surrender on the USS *Missouri* on September 2.[†] Nine days later, with the convocation of the new Council of Foreign Ministers in London on September 11, 1945, a now frayed Grand Alliance confronted the challenges of peace.

SUGGESTIONS FOR FURTHER STUDY

Documents

"The Atlantic Conference, August 9–12, 1941." Yale Law School Avalon Project: Documents in Law, History and Diplomacy. http://avalon.law.yale.edu/subject _menus/atmenu.asp.
"Atomic Bomb and the End of World War II: A Collection of Primary Sources."

---

[*] Because of the time difference when official word of the German surrender reached Moscow, the Soviets declared victory on May 9, the Western Allies May 8.
[†] The Japanese did surrender to the Soviets in Manchuria and Korea.

National Security Archive. Last modified April 27, 2007. http://www.gwu.edu /~nsarchiv/NSAEBB/NSAEBB162/index.htm.

"The Bretton Woods Agreements." July 22, 1944. Yale Law School Avalon Project: Documents in Law, History and Diplomacy. http://avalon.law.yale.edu/20th _century/decad047.asp.

Churchill, Winston, and Franklin D. Roosevelt. *Churchill and Roosevelt: The Complete Correspondence.* Edited by Warren F. Kimball. Princeton, NJ: Princeton University Press, 1984.

"Declaration by the United Nations, Jan. 1, 1942." Yale Law School Avalon Project: Documents in Law, History and Diplomacy. http://avalon.law.yale.edu/20th _century/decade03.asp.

International Tracking Service. Accessed February 25, 2013. http://www.its-arolsen .org/index.php?id=2&L=1.

The MAGIC Documents: Summaries and Transcripts of the Top Secret Diplomatic Communications of Japan, 1938–1945. Washington: University Publications of America, 1980.

"The Tehran Conference, November 28–December 1, 1943." Yale Law School Avalon Project: Documents in Law, History and Diplomacy. http://avalon.law.yale.edu /wwii/tehran.asp.

"United Nations Charter." June 26, 1945. United Nations. http://www.un.org/en /documents/charter/intro.shtml.

"The Yalta Conference, February, 1945." Yale Law School Avalon Project: Documents in Law, History and Diplomacy. http://avalon.law.yale.edu/wwii/yalta.asp.

Memoirs

Cripps, Richard Stafford. *Stafford Cripps in Moscow, 1940–1942: Diaries and Papers.* London: Valentine Mitchell, 2007.

Djilas, Milovan. *Wartime.* Translated by Michael B. Petrovich. New York: Harcourt Brace Jovanovich, 1977.

Harriman, W. Averell. *Special Envoy to Churchill and Stalin, 1941–1946.* New York: Random House, 1975.

Levi, Primo. *Survival in Auschwitz: The Nazi Assault on Humanity.* Translated by Stuart Woolf. New York: Simon and Schuster, 1996.

———. *The Truce: A Survivor's Journey Home from Auschwitz.* Translated by Stuart Woolf. London: Bodley Head, 1965.

Molotov, Vyacheslav Mikhaylovich, and Feliks Ivanovich Chuev. *Molotov Remembers: Inside Kremlin Politics: Conversations with Felix Chuev.* Edited by Albert Resis. Chicago: I. R. Dee, 1991.

Snow, Edgar. *Red Star over China.* New York: Grove, 1968.

Speer, Albert. *Inside the Third Reich: Memoirs.* New York: Macmillan, 1970.

Szpilman, Władysław. *The Pianist: The Extraordinary Story of One Man's Survival in Warsaw, 1939–45.* Translated by Anthea Bell. New York: Picador USA, 1999.

Fiction

Benioff, David. *City of Thieves: A Novel.* New York: Viking, 2008.

Grass, Günter. *The Tin Drum.* Translated by Ralph Manheim. New York: Pantheon Books, 1963.

Grossman, Vasily. *Life and Fate: A Novel.* Translated by Robert Chandler. New York: Harper and Row, 1985.

Heller, Joseph. *Catch-22: A Novel.* New York: Simon and Schuster, 1961.

Malaparte, Curzio. *Kaputt.* Translated by Cesare Foligno. New York: E. P. Dutton, 1946.

Mann, Thomas. *Doctor Faustus: The Life of the German Composer, Adrian Leverkühn.* Translated by H. T. Lowe-Porter. New York: Knopf, 1948.

Mo, Yan. *Red Sorghum: A Novel of China.* Translated by Howard Goldblatt. New York: Viking, 1993.

Semyonov, Julian. *Seventeen Moments of Spring: A Novel.* Translated by Katherine Judelson. London: John Calder, 1988.

Films

Black Rain. Directed by Shôhei Imamura. Tokyo: Tohokashinsha Film Company, 1989.

Come and See. Directed by Elem Klimov. Moscow: Mosfilm and Belarusfilm, 1985.

Dark Blue World. Directed by Jan Sverák. Prague: Biograf Jan Sverák, 2001.

The Downfall of Berlin: Anonyma. Directed by Max Färberböck. Munich: Constantin Film Produktion, 2008.

Hope and Glory. Directed by John Boorman. Los Angeles: Columbia Pictures, 1987.

Ivan's Childhood. Directed by Andrei Tarkovsky. Moscow: Mosfilm, 1962.

Kanal. Directed by Andrzej Wajda. Warsaw: Studio Filmowe Kadr, 1957.

Katyn. Directed by Andrzej Wajda. Warsaw: Polish Film Institute, 2007.

Letters from Iwo Jima. Directed by Clint Eastwood. Los Angeles: Warner Brothers, 2006.

Mission to Moscow. Directed by Michael Curtiz. Los Angeles: Warner Brothers, 1943.

Mrs. Miniver. Directed by William Wyler. Los Angeles: Metro-Goldwyn-Mayer, 1942.

The North Star. Directed by Lewi Milestone. Los Angeles: Samuel Goldwyn, 1943.

Open City. Directed by Roberto Rossellini. Rome: Excelsa Film, 1945.

Schindler's List. Directed by Steven Spielberg. Los Angeles: Universal Pictures, 1993.

Stalingrad. Directed by Yuri Ozerov. East Berlin: Deutsche Film (DEFA), 1989.

Stalingrad. Directed by Joseph Vilsmaier. Grünwald: Bavaria Filmstudios, 1993.

World War II: When Lions Roared. Directed by Joseph Sargent. Los Angeles: Kushner-Locke, 1994.

Music

Blitzstein, Marc. *Airborne Symphony.* 1946.

Britten, Benjamin. *War Requiem* (op. 66). 1962.

Copland, Aaron. *Fanfare for the Common Man.* 1942.

Górecki, Henryk Mikołaj. *Symphony No. 3* (op. 36, "Symphony of Sorrowful Songs"). 1976.

Nono, Luigi. *Il Canto Sospeso.* 1956.

Penderecki, Krzysztof. *Dies Irae.* 1967.

———. *Threnody to the Victims of Hiroshima.* 1960.

Schnittke, Alfred. *Historia von D. Johann Fausten.* 1995.

Schoenberg, Arnold. *A Survivor from Warsaw.* 1947.

Shostakovich, Dmitri. *Symphony No. 7 in C Major* (op. 60, "Leningrad"). 1941.

———. *Symphony No. 13 in B Flat Minor* (op. 113, "Babi Yar"). 1962.

Secondary Sources

Alvarez, David J. *Secret Messages: Codebreaking and American Diplomacy, 1930–1945.* Lawrence: University Press of Kansas, 2000.

Breitman, Richard, et al. *U.S. Intelligence and the Nazis.* Cambridge: Cambridge University Press, 2005.

Churchill, Winston. *The Second World War.* 6 vols. Boston: Houghton Mifflin, 1948–1953.

Costigliola, Frank. *Roosevelt's Lost Alliances: How Personal Politics Helped Start the Cold War.* Princeton, NJ: Princeton University Press, 2012.

Dobbs, Michael. *Six Months in 1945: FDR, Stalin, Churchill, Truman, and the Birth of the Modern World.* New York: Knopf, 2012.

Edmonds, Robin. *The Big Three: Churchill, Roosevelt, and Stalin in Peace and War.* New York: Norton, 1991.

Folly, Martin H. *Churchill, Whitehall and the Soviet Union: 1940–45.* Basingstoke, UK: Macmillan, 2000.

Gardner, Lloyd C. *Architects of Illusion: Men and Ideas in American Foreign Policy, 1941–1949.* Chicago: Quadrangle Books, 1970.

Harbutt, Fraser J. *Yalta 1945: Europe and America at the Crossroads.* New York: Cambridge University Press, 2010.

Hasegawa, Tsuyoshi. *Racing the Enemy: Stalin, Truman, and the Surrender of Japan.* Cambridge, MA: Belknap Press of Harvard University Press, 2005.

Heinrichs, Waldo H. *Threshold of War: Franklin D. Roosevelt and American Entry into World War II.* New York: Oxford University Press, 1988.

Iriye, Akira. *Power and Culture: The Japanese-American War, 1941–1945.* Cambridge: Harvard University Press, 1981.

Levering, Ralph B. *American Opinion and the Russian Alliance, 1939–1945.* Chapel Hill: University of North Carolina Press, 1976.

Louis, William Roger. *Imperialism at Bay: The United States and the Decolonization of the British Empire, 1941–1945.* New York: Oxford University Press, 1978.

Mastny, Vojtech. *Russia's Road to the Cold War: Diplomacy, Warfare, and the Politics of Communism, 1941–1945.* New York: Columbia University Press, 1979.

Miner, Steven Merritt. *Between Churchill and Stalin: The Soviet Union, Great Britain, and the Origins of the Grand Alliance.* Chapel Hill: University of North Carolina Press, 1988.

Miscamble, Wilson D. *From Roosevelt to Truman: Potsdam, Hiroshima, and the Cold War.* Cambridge: Cambridge University Press, 2007.

Plokhy, Serhii. *Yalta: The Price of Peace.* New York: Viking, 2010.

Reynolds, David. *From World War to Cold War: Churchill, Roosevelt, and the International History of the 1940s.* Oxford: Oxford University Press, 2006.

———. *In Command of History: Churchill Fighting and Writing the Second World War.* New York: Random House, 2005.

Roberts, Geoffrey. *Stalin's Wars: From World War to Cold War, 1939–1953.* New Haven, CT: Yale University Press, 2006.

Ryan, Henry Butterfield. *The Vision of Anglo-America: The US-UK Alliance and the Emerging Cold War, 1943–1946.* Cambridge: Cambridge University Press, 1987.

Sainsbury, Keith. *The Turning Point: Roosevelt, Stalin, Churchill, and Chiang Kai-Shek, 1943: The Moscow, Cairo, and Teheran Conferences.* Oxford: Oxford University Press, 1985.

Schild, Georg. *Bretton Woods and Dumbarton Oaks: American Economic and Political Postwar Planning in the Summer of 1944.* New York: St. Martin's, 1995.

Sherry, Michael S. *Preparing for the Next War: American Plans for Postwar Defense, 1941–45.* New Haven, CT: Yale University Press, 1977.

Sherwin, Martin J. *A World Destroyed: The Atomic Bomb and the Grand Alliance.* New York: Knopf, 1975.

Stoler, Mark A. *Allies in War: Britain and America Against the Axis Powers, 1940–1945.* London: Hodder Arnold, 2005.

Tamkin, Nicholas. *Britain, Turkey and the Soviet Union, 1940–1945: Strategy, Diplomacy and Intelligence in the Eastern Mediterranean.* Basingstoke, UK: Palgrave Macmillan, 2009.

Thorne, Christopher G. *Allies of a Kind: The United States, Britain, and the War Against Japan, 1941–1945.* New York: Oxford University Press, 1978.

Weinberg, Gerhard L. *A World at Arms: A Global History of World War II.* Cambridge: Cambridge University Press, 1994.

———. *Visions of Victory: The Hopes of Eight World War II Leaders.* Cambridge: Cambridge University Press, 2005.

Chapter 3

COLD WAR, 1945–1952

Tyranny over the mind is the most complete and most brutal type of tyranny.

—Milovan Djilas

We should rid our ranks of all impotent thinking. All views that overestimate the strength of the enemy and underestimate the strength of the people are wrong.

—Mao Zedong[*]

After almost a quarter of a century of distant rivalry followed by a successful, if prickly, four-year partnership during World War II, the West and the Soviet Union came face to face in 1945 and over the next seven years developed into resolute enemies. This antagonism was accentuated by the presence of nuclear weapons, forceful ideological competition, and an unparalleled mobilization of civilians imbued with the fear of an imminent World War III. By 1949, the Big Three's wartime practices of direct consultation and compromise had ceased, and for the next three years the United States and the USSR became locked in a Cold War.

---

[*] Mao Zedong, "The Present Situation and Our Tasks (December 25, 1947)," in *Selected Works*, 5 vols. (New York: Pergamon, 1961), 4:173.

TWO RIVALS EMERGE

The rupture did not occur at once. Indeed, there has been an ongoing—and ultimately unresolvable—debate among historians over when the Grand Alliance dissolved, when the Cold War began, and who was responsible. This origins debate, heated for a half century by partisan positions, has now been tempered by the collapse of the Soviet Union and the opening of its archives and also by the passage of time and the challenge of new global problems, all of which may obscure the Great Powers' actual situation, decisions, and interactions after 1945.

The rupture in the Grand Alliance occurred in the wake of the immense human and material devastation in World War II. Some sixty million people had died, and the combatants' bombs had left a swath of destruction from London to Tokyo. Moreover, the losses were uneven. While large parts of Europe and Asia faced enormous human and physical losses along with a flood of wounded soldiers, hungry and diseased civilians, and fleeing refugees, the United States emerged from the war with no physical damage to its mainland, a death toll (400,000) that was only a fraction of the USSR's loss of 30 million people, and a booming economy with a $211 billion gross national product.

There was also no "zero hour" in 1945. The total defeat of the Axis powers had given the victors not only a heady sense of power but also a new realization of their vulnerability. The Soviet and US responses of "Never again!" to the attacks on June 22 and December 7 necessitated an active defense of their national interests, clothed in the garb of "security." Each expected its partners to comply with its expansive desires for maintaining this security, and each was irate at every demonstration of the other's bad faith and aggressiveness, sentiments augmented by both sides' vigorous intelligence gathering and their less frequent personal encounters.

Consequently, along with the immense tasks of postwar reconstruction came the perhaps inevitable clash of interests among the Grand Alliance. Inevitable too was the expansion of the victors' rivalry. Although Europe was the source and the core of the Cold War, the rest of the world was inevitably drawn in. Because the struggle with the Axis had been a global one and Europe's empires had been disrupted, Asia and the Middle East, and later Africa and South America, would all be engulfed by the US-Soviet struggle.

Leading personalities still counted, but in a different way than in wartime. President Truman and Prime Minister Atlee headed vast political, diplomatic, and military establishments weighed down by global burdens over which they could never exert complete control. In choosing their diplomatic paths the novice US and British chiefs navigated among rival advisers, bureaucracies, legislators, and publicists at home and beleaguered and tough foreign governments abroad. Even Stalin, who formulated Soviet foreign policy almost singlehandedly, received conflicting advice from his colleagues and often faced intractable client states outside his borders.

The Great Power rivalry that followed World War II was fueled by a resurgence of ideological competition between communism and capitalism, which had been restrained in wartime. The East-West clash also became *systemic*, rooted in almost every institution—economic, military, political, diplomatic, religious, and even cultural. For a world newly freed from war, the prospects were menacing. Contemplating the dire prospect of "two or three monstrous superstates, each possessed of a weapon by which millions of people can be wiped out in a few seconds, dividing the world between them," George Orwell in October 1945 used the term "Cold War" to describe "a peace that is no peace" and grimly predicted that pressures would develop within both sides to ensure conformity and stifle dissent.* The first seven postwar years thus had the semblance of a global compression chamber, but one that was also porous and short-lived—and unavoidably so.

NUREMBERG: THE FINAL COLLABORATION

Shortly after the Potsdam meeting, on August 8, 1945, British, French, Soviet, and US jurists adopted a detailed charter governing the international military tribunal that would conduct the trial of the major German war criminals. This momentous undertaking—first agreed upon in Moscow in 1943 and confirmed at Tehran, Yalta, and Potsdam but requiring six weeks of laborious negotiations in the summer of 1945—opened on November 21 in Nuremberg, the site of spectacular annual Nazi rallies and where their notorious 1935 racial laws were adopted. Before its ending on October 1, 1946, the four-nation tribunal heard hundreds of witnesses, scrutinized thousands of pages of captured Reich documents, meted out sentences to twenty-four individuals and seven organizations, and produced an unprecedented and voluminous historical record of aggressive war, state violence against combatants and civilians, and crimes against humanity.

---

* George Orwell, "You and the Atomic Bomb," *Tribune* (London), October 19, 1945.

The Cold War dimension of the trials is surprisingly unexplored. One of the final acts of the Grand Alliance, the Nuremberg trials were immediately controversial: defended for giving voice to the Nazis' victims and replacing vengeance with justice, but also criticized for their faulty legal practices and politically motivated judgments toward particular defendants. The preparations for the trials by the four nations had been largely harmonious, but by early 1946 the growing East-West tension entered the courtroom. Much to the Soviets' chagrin, the defense attorneys raised the sensitive issues of the Nazi-Soviet pact and the Katyn massacre. In contrast, the United States, Britain, and France were able to block any discussion of the Allied bombing of German cities and the atomic attacks on Hiroshima and Nagasaki, and they prevailed in the meting out of lenient sentences to German bankers and industrialists as well as to submarine captains.[*]

Nonetheless, the Nuremberg collaboration among the three Western governments and the USSR survived quietly for four decades, enacted through the formalities of four-power control over the Spandau prison in Berlin, where seven Nazi prisoners were incarcerated, and ending only with the death of the last inmate, Rudolf Hess, in 1987. The international tribunal was dissolved in 1946, followed by separate trials in Europe and by the US-dominated proceedings against Japanese war criminals, all raising more accusations of legal lapses and political expediency. As the Grand Alliance unraveled and the Cold War expanded, the principles and practice of international jurisdiction over war crimes and crimes of aggression disappeared from the world for almost a half century.[†]

THE RUPTURE

On the eve of the Nuremberg trials, the first foreign ministers' conference in London had ended abruptly on October 2, 1945, demonstrating the widening gap among the victors. Not only had they failed to reach agreement over the future of Europe, Asia, and the Middle East, but they had also clashed over the control of atomic weapons. Secretary of State Byrnes, although annoyed by Foreign Minister Molotov's audacity, was also fearful of a permanent rupture and thus persuaded Stalin to convene another foreign ministers' meeting. In a reprise of Tehran and Yalta, Byrnes arrived in Moscow in December 1945 brimming

---

[*] Submarine warfare against Japan had played a major role in the US war in Asia.

[†] In 1998 the United Nations established the International Criminal Court, a permanent tribunal to prosecute genocide, crimes against humanity, war crimes, and the crime of aggression.

with confidence that US power would enable him to break the stalemate with the USSR, and he held two long meetings with Stalin. Ignoring British grumbling, US and Soviet diplomats seemed poised to work together.

The result was a series of US-Soviet arrangements bolstering their respective interests and crafting compromises to bridge their differences. In return for the West's tacit acknowledgment of the communist-dominated governments in Romania and Bulgaria and the Soviets' occupation and looting of Manchuria (as well as the transfer of Japanese arms to the Chinese communists), Stalin grudgingly recognized America's leading role in Japan and the temporary presence of its troops and bases in the rest of China. The agreement on Korea—far more strategically vital to the USSR than to the United States (which was nonetheless fearful of a communist takeover, à la Poland)—was a masterpiece of Great Power improvisation. Ignoring strong local sentiments for the country's unity and independence, the diplomats superimposed an ultimately unworkable four-power trusteeship on the Soviet-US military partition at the thirty-eighth parallel, paving the way for Korea's eventual division.

Disagreements were quietly papered over in Moscow. Although Great Britain, the USSR, and the United States had agreed to create a UN Commission on Atomic Energy, they differed fundamentally over information sharing, surveillance, and existing stocks of atomic weapons.* There was also no resolution of their conflicting policies on Turkey and Iran. Shortly after the Moscow meeting, on the last day of 1945, the Soviet Union firmly detached itself from the postwar US-led international economic system by announcing its withdrawal from the Bretton Woods agreements, which were signed in Washington by twenty-seven governments on December 27, 1945.

Whereas the international press greeted the Moscow accords as a new and positive step toward world peace, the reality was grimmer. In stark contrast to the aftermath of World War I, by January 1946—five months after an even more ruinous war and the total defeat of their enemies—the victors had neither convened a peace conference nor produced separate peace treaties with Germany and its five European allies.† In Germany the occupying powers were pursuing competing strategies. While proclaiming their conciliatory intentions, their leaders began recoiling from a thorny and increasingly unpopular relationship.

---

* The prospect of US-Soviet cooperation was halted at the first meeting of the UN Atomic Energy Commission in June 1946, when the Soviet delegate rejected the so-called Baruch Plan as a US attempt to control the development of nuclear energy.

† Bulgaria, Finland, Hungary, Italy, and Romania.

Britain and the United States blamed the Soviet Union for the unsettled world. Taking the lead was Foreign Secretary Ernest Bevin, the novice but tough diplomat and former member of Churchill's wartime cabinet who espoused Labour's traditional antipathy toward Moscow. Truman, increasingly irritated by US inability to alter Soviet positions, immediately scolded the returning Byrnes for appeasing Stalin. The US press began to fan anti-Sovietism with reports of the USSR's suppression of the anticommunist opposition in Eastern Europe, Soviet vetoes in the new United Nations, and the sensational discovery of a communist spy network in North America.*

The first postwar elections for the Supreme Soviet provided a platform for Stalin's reply. In his much noted, often misinterpreted speech to the communist faithful on February 9, 1946, the Soviet dictator sent a mixed message, praising the wartime achievements of the Grand Alliance but also underscoring capitalism's bellicose tendencies, announcing the expansion of Soviet civilian production and warning of the rapid buildup of its industrial and military power to protect the Motherland "against all contingencies." Party hard-liners G. M. Malenkov and L. M. Kaganovich went further, proposing that the Soviet Union go its own way in world affairs.

The West escalated the rhetoric. In Fulton, Missouri, on March 5, 1946, with Truman at his side, Churchill warned that an "Iron Curtain" had descended across the center of Europe. Although rejecting the idea that war was either imminent or inevitable and advocating continued dialogue with Moscow, Britain's opposition leader insisted on the indispensability of Anglo-American unity and an increase of the West's armed might. Stalin's retort, an unprecedented, scripted interview published in the official Soviet newspaper *Pravda*, characterized his old partner as a "racist" and "warmonger," in a sly reference to Hitler.

Behind the scenes, disgruntled diplomats also weighed in. From Moscow in February and March 1946 came detailed dissections of the Soviets' nationalist and Marxist mind-set and their aggressive behavior toward their neighbors by the US and British envoys George Kennan and Frank Roberts, who also revived prewar historical and racial stereotypes about Russia itself. Six months later the Soviet ambassador in Washington, Nikolai Novikov, delivered his critique of US "striving for world supremacy" as witnessed by its thirst to control the world's

---

* Set off by the September 1945 defection of Igor Gouzenko, a cipher clerk in the Soviet embassy in Ottawa, Canada, who delivered extensive evidence of Soviet espionage.

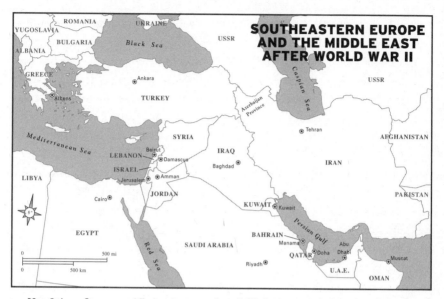

Map 3. Iran, Greece, and Turkey became sites of US-Soviet confrontation between 1946 and 1948.

economic resources and its atomic saber rattling against the Soviet Union. All three diplomats came to the identical conclusion: the prospects for further collaboration with an aggressive power were dismal.

There were also dissenting voices to the emerging US-Soviet confrontation. In September 1946 the US secretary of commerce and former vice president Henry Wallace advocated peaceful cooperation with the USSR but also urged Stalin to maintain an open door to US trade with Eastern Europe. Thereupon some Americans criticized Wallace for his naïve idealism, while others took him to task for upholding US economic imperialism.

It is thus not surprising that 1946 witnessed the first direct clashes between the West and the Soviet Union. The area of contestation was Iran, and at issue was the Soviet refusal to withdraw troops from its northern zone by the March 2, 1946, deadline.* Stalin had decided to exploit separatist movements in Iran to force oil concessions from the Tehran government. Observers also suspected another motive: to hinder US and British oil companies from prospecting in the

---

* According to the January 29, 1942, tripartite treaty, Iran agreed to extend nonmilitary assistance to the war effort, and Great Britain and Russia agreed to respect its independence and territorial integrity and to withdraw their troops from Iran within six months of the end of hostilities.

north. At the last minute Stalin summoned the Iranian prime minister to Moscow and, with the threat of Soviet troop movements toward Tehran, demanded an oil concession.

Once the deadline had passed without a Soviet withdrawal, the United States and Britain went into high diplomatic gear in defense of the sanctity of international treaties and their oil interests. After instigating an Iranian appeal to the United Nations, Byrnes publicly condemned Moscow's "imperialism" before the Security Council, causing a dramatic walkout by Andrei Gromyko, the Soviet Union's permanent UN representative. The old diplomatic niceties among the three had ended. Stalin, surprised by the furor and fearing US retaliation elsewhere, backed off. Prudently, he removed his troops on May 9 but secured the oil concession (which the Iranian parliament refused to ratify). He also withheld support from his Iranian clients, who were crushed by the government later that year.

The Iranian episode was the first chilling lesson in Cold War brinkmanship. Instead of a bargain struck by the three foreign ministers, a seemingly minor episode at the periphery (complicated, to be sure, by oil and ethnic tensions) had developed into a full-blown international crisis with distinct winners and losers. Later that year, a US show of naval force along with intelligence reports of US combat scenarios convinced Stalin to withdraw his demands on Turkey to establish Soviet naval bases along the Straits. But while some Westerners exulted in their easy victories, these confrontations also had consequences: not only bolstering hard-liners on both sides but also diminishing Stalin's confidence in an equal treatment by his partners and reinforcing his obsession with building an atomic bomb.

The German question remained the center of dispute. Unlike the single-power control that had been established in Japan and the Balkans or the dual control over Korea, in Germany four states had inherited the awkward Potsdam arrangement of joint governance of Germany through a polarized Allied Control Council combined with almost total political, economic, and judicial control over their respective zones. In addition, the occupying powers faced the day-to-day complications of ruling a hungry and sullen conquered people.

Stalin, looking back to the post–World War I period, had hoped for another rapid US withdrawal from Europe and the reestablishment of a unified and neutral but also smaller Germany from which he would extract substantial reparations. Siding with Kremlin pragmatists, he restrained the ideological fervor of the German communists, ended wholesale looting and food requisitions, and launched a "charm offensive" in 1946, calling for a "united and peaceful" Germany on the model of Austria.[*]

The Americans and British parried the Soviet challenge by moving further toward partition; as occupiers of Germany's largest, richest, and most populous regions, they held the upper hand. On May 3, 1946, the United States suspended reparations deliveries to the Soviets to protect the economic well-being of its zone, and that month Britain, citing Soviet obstruction, assailed the continuation of four-power control. On September 6, 1946, Byrnes, in a major speech to German dignitaries in Stuttgart, announced two key facets of the new US policy: the amalgamation of the US and British zones (Bizonia) and an American commitment "to stay" and to restore freedom, self-government, and a robust capitalism to the German people. In another, quite clever repudiation of the Potsdam accords, Byrnes challenged the permanence of the Oder-Neisse border separating Poland from Germany, forcing Stalin to take the side of his Polish comrades against the Germans he was trying to court.

The remainder of 1946 was consumed by acrimonious negotiations over the peace treaties with Nazi Germany's former allies, with the terms for Italy drawing the most heated discussion. Harking back to their wartime strategy, the British were intent on defending their vital interests in the Mediterranean against Soviet claims, specifically in regard to Libya and the port of Trieste.[†]

The United States was the crucial mediator. Earlier in the year it had tipped decisively toward London, granting a huge (and controversial) $3.75 billion loan to Britain but denying a similar Soviet request. Two civil wars were now raging, in China and in Greece, and although the Soviet hand was not evident in either of these, the United States had become increasingly committed to halting left-wing revolutionary movements. Thus, in dealing with the question of Libya, Washington blocked Moscow's bid for a presence in North Africa; swallowing its long-standing resistance to European imperialism, it countenanced a four-year Franco-British trusteeship under UN supervision. On Trieste, the United States strongly supported the British, and a still-cautious Stalin (much to the fury of his Yugoslav ally) backed down. The United States authored a compromise solution that kept the Adriatic port out of communist hands and eight years later awarded the city to Italy.

---

[*] Which had been restored to sovereignty in 1945 under a moderate left-wing government and four-power occupation.

[†] Trieste had been liberated in 1945 by Tito's communist partisan forces, who had refused to withdraw in the face of Anglo-American demands but were persuaded by Stalin to do so.

1947: THE DIVISION OF EUROPE

The signing of the peace treaties with Bulgaria, Finland, Hungary, Italy, and Romania on February 10, 1947, marked the culmination of the Great Power arrangement that Roosevelt had envisaged. Truman, facing the first Republican-dominated US Congress since 1932, was assuming a less conciliatory and tougher stance toward the Soviet Union. Stalin, through his intelligence sources, studied the details of Washington's growing estrangement and pondered America's economic and military might, its growing string of bases throughout the world, and its emerging alignment with Great Britain. The Soviet leader remained committed to his forward strategy, bolstered by the terms of the wartime agreements but also tempered with caution and pragmatism. However, by 1947 an increasingly edgy West was preparing initiatives of its own.

That year an overburdened Britain essentially turned the mantle of its global leadership over to Washington. Faced with insurgencies throughout the empire, it announced its withdrawal from the Indian subcontinent and the referral of its Palestine mandate to the United Nations. On February 21 London informed the State Department of its intention to terminate aid to Greece and Turkey in fourteen months.

Truman, his new secretary of state, George Marshall, and undersecretary Dean Acheson were determined to fill the gap created by Britain's departure. With great speed, the State Department prepared a $400 million package of economic and military support for the beleaguered Greek and Turkish governments. In order to rally a skeptical and parsimonious Congress, the president warned on March 12 that the world had become divided into two ways of life, "democracy and totalitarianism," and in the so-called Truman doctrine called on the United States "to support free peoples who are resisting attempted subjugation by armed minorities or by outside pressure."

Although Acheson had quietly assured Congress that the administration contemplated no military corollary to the Truman doctrine, this startling and expansive commitment reverberated throughout US public life. In April 1947 the venerable financier and presidential adviser Bernard Baruch used the term "Cold War" to urge Americans to unite in the face of a dire internal as well as external threat. In July "Mr. X" (later revealed to be George Kennan), in a much-noted *Foreign Affairs* article, called for a policy of "long-term, patient but firm and vigilant containment of Russian expansive tendencies" through the "adroit and vigilant application of counter-force at a series of constantly shifting geographical and political points, corresponding to the shifts and maneuvers of Soviet policy," an approach that would eventually result "either in the break-up or the gradual mellowing of Soviet power."*

On June 5, 1947, Marshall focused the Truman doctrine on the economic rehabilitation of Europe. In his famous Harvard commencement speech the secretary of state issued an invitation to every nation on the continent, including the USSR, to coordinate their recovery efforts as a condition of receiving substantial US aid. Among the goals of the Marshall Plan were not only to alleviate postwar Europe's dire economic condition and reduce the attraction of communism but also to open the door broadly to US commerce.

Stalin decided to test Washington's initiative. Harking back to the 1920s and to Lenin's belief in Russia's indispensability to the West's economic recovery, the Soviet leader sent a large delegation to the conference in Paris to explore direct and unconditional US aid to the USSR and also to offer an alternative to Washington's domination. To their surprise and alarm, his delegates encountered strong West European endorsement of the Marshall Plan as well as a potential threat to the Soviet Union's East European realm. Stalin backed away, recalling Molotov on July 2 and pointedly counseling the governments of Poland, Hungary, and Czechoslovakia also to withdraw.

The Soviets' exit created little surprise and was, in fact, a relief to Washington. It not only removed an obstacle to rapid agreement but also shifted the blame for Europe's growing division onto the USSR. In Western Europe the prospect of Marshall Plan aid strengthened the anticommunist political forces, which were easily able to quash their leftist opponents by the end of the year. Moscow's departure also facilitated Washington's major goal: the inclusion of the western zones of Germany in the Marshall Plan, providing the indispensable labor and mineral resources for Europe's revival.

Soviet historiography has asserted that the proclamation of the Truman doctrine and the Marshall Plan laid the foundation for Stalin's decisive break with the West in 1947. Faced with the threat of an anti-Soviet bloc, Stalin abandoned his efforts at cooperation and moved to consolidate the communist position in

---

* Kennan's call for a global containment of the Soviet Union immediately drew two major criticisms: The famed columnist Walter Lippmann presciently warned that a worldwide struggle with the USSR would condemn the United States to align itself with "dubious and unnatural allies," neglect Europe, cripple the UN by attempting to turn it into "an anti-Soviet coalition," and end the search for an enduring peace settlement. Kennan's State Department colleague Paul Nitze deplored the reactive aspects of this policy and urged a significant buildup of US military power to thwart Soviet advances, a position that gained support two years later.

Eastern Europe. The new Soviet stance was announced by the creation of the Communist Information Bureau (Cominform) in September 1947 as the successor to the Comintern. In his address to the new organization, Stalin's ideological spokesman, A. A. Zhdanov, parodied the Truman doctrine, blaming US aggressiveness for dividing the world into two distinct camps—imperialist and anti-imperialist. Whatever the exact motive or moment of his retreat from multilateralism (which the Soviet archives may someday reveal), Stalin still recognized his country's unpreparedness for another armed conflict. He thus continued to proceed cautiously, responding to as much as creating events, although now taking more risks in order to chip away at Western power.

THE WORLD OUTSIDE EUROPE

Events outside Europe greatly complicated the quest for a peaceful postwar order. In China, despite lavish US aid and notable Soviet restraint, the feeble Chiang Kai-shek government was collapsing before the resilient revolutionary forces led by Mao Zedong. The anticolonial struggles in the Dutch East Indies, British Malaya, and French Indochina also provided opportunities for communist penetration, weakening Western Europe and kindling alarm in Washington.

Moreover, the British Labour government's decision to hastily withdraw from empire brought ethnic and religious violence to South Asia and the Middle East. The partition of the Indian subcontinent was followed by a ruinous civil war between Hindus and Muslims, creating millions of casualties and refugees and two rival successor states with ongoing border disputes: India and Pakistan (see Map 4).

The UN division of Palestine in November 1947 was also followed by an internecine struggle between Jews and Arabs. The communist bloc, perceiving an ally in the Zionist movement, provided crucial military supplies to the Jewish forces, but the United States, fearing to antagonize the Arabs, declared an official arms embargo. Israel's declaration of independence in May 1948 and its subsequent military victory over four Arab states brought about the revival of Jewish statehood, but it also created an uneasy truce in the region. The United Nations assumed responsibility for some 750,000 Palestinian refugees, whose national aspirations had been crushed by the division of Palestine among Israel, Jordan, and Egypt (see Map 5).

The impact of decolonization and these civil wars was not fully understood by the Great Powers. Nonetheless, Truman and Stalin, although lacking global perspectives, recognized that the collapse of European empires would affect

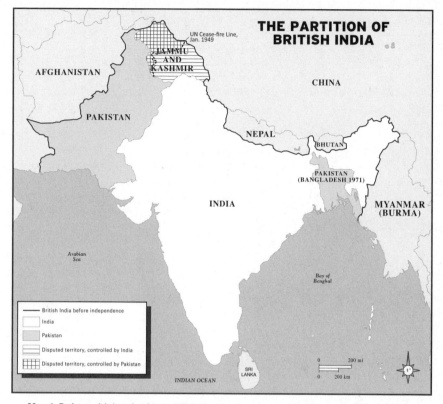

THE PARTITION OF BRITISH INDIA

UN Cease-fire Line, Jan. 1949

AFGHANISTAN

JAMMU AND KASHMIR

CHINA

PAKISTAN

NEPAL

BHUTAN

PAKISTAN (BANGLADESH 1971)

INDIA

MYANMAR (BURMA)

Arabian Sea

Bay of Benghal

British India before independence

India

Pakistan

Disputed territory, controlled by India

Disputed territory, controlled by Pakistan

0   200 mi
0   200 km

SRI LANKA

INDIAN OCEAN

Map 4. Before withdrawing in 1947, Britain drew the boundaries of India and Pakistan, producing the largest exodus of refugees in the twentieth century.

strategically important regions from North Africa to the Pacific and inevitably draw them in as rivals. Thus the United States moved to bolster stability in the Western Hemisphere with the Rio Pact in 1947 and the restructuring of the Organization of American States a year later. On the other hand, India's proclamation of neutrality in the emerging Cold War offered newly independent states an alternative to joining the communist or capitalist blocs and even a means of provoking a bidding rivalry between the two.

Another unforeseen consequence of the changing postwar world was the attempt by nongovernmental organizations and small and medium-sized powers to transform the United Nations from a US-Soviet battleground into a site of human progress. One major focus—emanating from the promises in the Atlantic Charter and the atrocities of World War II—was the defense of human rights. These not always complementary goals—promoting freedom and self-determination for subject peoples on the one hand and shielding individuals

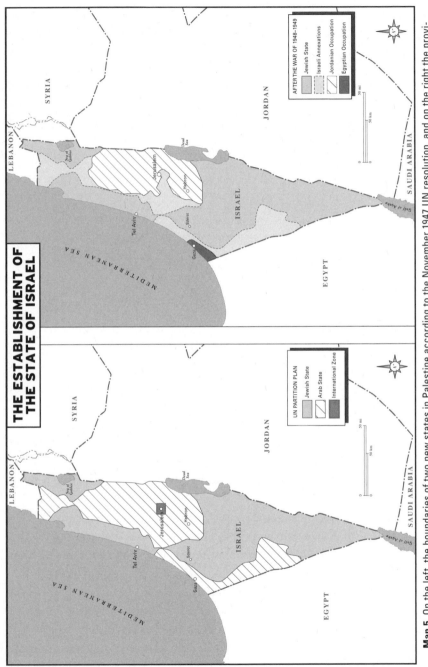

Map 5. On the left, the boundaries of two new states in Palestine according to the November 1947 UN resolution, and on the right the provisional borders of Israel and its neighbors established by a UN mediator in 1949.

and groups from arbitrary state power on the other—held little attraction for the Great Powers. At the Nuremberg trials the victors had been more intent on punishing the Nazis' aggression than siding with their victims, and the same held true at the Tokyo tribunals. Although the UN Charter contained several references to human rights, the United States, Great Britain, and the Soviet Union had frustrated human rights activists by blocking the inclusion of a universal bill of rights. Nonetheless, in 1946 the fifty-one-member General Assembly flexed its muscle, creating the Commission on Human Rights (CHR).

Despite the high expectations that attended its birth, the eighteen-member CHR was immediately dominated by Cold War realities. Its chair, Eleanor Roosevelt, was kept on a tight leash by the US government, which was intent on thwarting any binding obligations that interfered with "the internal problems of nations" and on using the commission's forum mainly to castigate the Soviets' misdeeds. The US and Soviet delegates both rejected the right to petition an international institution for redress of human rights violations by his or her government. The two Superpowers were also behind the CHR's momentous decision to split its task into three separate components: the drafting of a nonbinding declaration of principles, followed—at some indeterminate interval—by the conclusion of a human rights convention, and, finally, the creation of a means of enforcement. The first task was completed within two years, but the second took twenty more, and the third still another year to come to life. By 1948 the Superpowers had effectively blocked the aspirations of human rights activists and smaller countries to derail the international order they intended to lead.

The Universal Declaration of Human Rights (UDHR), the product of the lopsided power relations in the CHR, was nonetheless a historic document graced with ringing language and high aspirations. It was not, however, a "universal" statement but based heavily on Western liberal philosophical and legal traditions. The UDHR not only placed the Soviets' insistence on economic, social, and cultural rights in a secondary position but also omitted Asian and African claims to self-determination and rejected recognition of minority rights. Moreover, for over two decades it was a pledge without a means of enforcement.

Yet even as a nonbinding gesture, the UDHR gained worldwide currency. Its text permeated constitutions, treaties, and regional agreements and infused political language throughout the globe. Its principles buttressed the work of the UN agencies that protected labor, women, children, and refugees and stirred the General Assembly to annually reaffirm its commitment to human rights. And while Washington and Moscow considered the UDHR a minor weapon in their

Cold War arsenals, other countries began to invoke its moral authority to protest racism and colonialism throughout the world.

PRAGUE AND BERLIN

For the United States and the Soviet Union, the prize was still in Europe, and in 1948 Europe's East-West division hardened. In the Balkans, Albania, Bulgaria, Romania, and Yugoslavia had already fallen under communist control, but the Greek government, with US aid, was forcibly resisting a communist insurgency. Poland and Hungary had ended their brief periods of political pluralism with communist takeovers, although Finland and Austria were able to maintain non-communist governments through prudent neutrality.* Czechoslovakia, the last surviving quasi-independent government east of Germany fell on February 28, 1948, almost ten years after the Munich agreement. The Prague coup—a brief, chilling, and largely bloodless episode of veiled Soviet threats, treachery by the local communists, and miscalculation by the anticommunists—destroyed the last remnant of Czechoslovakia's sovereignty.

In stark contrast with the outcry in the media, Western leaders had already conceded Czechoslovakia (unlike Greece, Turkey, Italy, and Iran) to the Soviet sphere. Although Britain and France protested the communists' seizure of power, there was no repeat of the Iran crisis, no urgent appeal to the UN Security Council.† Instead, public attention was focused on the danger of a Soviet military strike on the West. Asserting their will to defend themselves, Britain, France, Belgium, Luxembourg, and the Netherlands met in Brussels in March 1948 and, with Washington's endorsement but no precise US commitment, signed a pact pledging mutual aid against foreign aggression.

Cooler Western observers construed the Prague events as a defensive move by Stalin. After the foreign ministers meeting in London (November–December 1947) had deadlocked over concluding a German or an Austrian peace treaty, the Western powers had decided to exclude the USSR from their decision making on Germany's future. Indeed, two days before the Prague coup, the foreign ministers of Britain, France, and the United States had met in London and announced plans to raise coal and steel production in the Ruhr, create a separate

---

* In June 1948 the Finnish communists suffered a decisive electoral defeat, and thereafter the Helsinki government toed a strictly neutral line. Austria, still under four-power occupation, also escaped the Soviet yoke by accepting neutralism.

† When the Prague events finally came up in the Security Council on May 24, 1948, the Soviet delegate quashed the discussion with a veto.

Map 6. By 1948 Europe was divided between East and West and would remain so for forty-one years.

West German state, and incorporate it into the Marshall Plan. The Soviets' loud protests were ignored.

Stalin also faced problems within his own camp. Fearing independent voices in Eastern Europe, the Kremlin removed Władysław Gomułka, an advocate of a "Polish path to socialism" and outspoken critic of the Cominform. A more formidable rival was Josip Broz Tito, the Yugoslav resistance leader whose wartime exploits and independent postwar policies had long frustrated the Kremlin. In June 1948 Stalin decided to punish Tito's "nationalist deviationism"—particularly his alleged efforts to dominate the Balkans—by expelling Yugoslavia from the Cominform. Once more the Soviet leader miscalculated, not only failing to topple the Yugoslav chief but also—despite the heavy Soviet hand in the "anti-Titoist" purges and trials throughout Eastern Europe between 1948 and 1953—failing to stifle the genie of nationalism that would forever threaten communist unity. Moreover, after a cautious response to the Stalin-Tito rupture, the United States moved into the breach, offering aid to Yugoslavia in 1949 as a means of encouraging other communist dissident leaders.*

Moscow also suffered political setbacks in Western Europe, where the Cominform had encouraged widespread strikes in France and Italy that threatened two fragile governments but also stirred the ambitions of two highly independent communist parties. When Washington in late 1947 determined to use economic and political pressure to counter a perceived Soviet conspiracy, Stalin prudently backed off. In France, he stood by while the Americans orchestrated the secession of noncommunist labor leaders from the communist (CGT) union, the consequent reduction of the latter's power and influence, and the stabilization of the Fourth Republic. In Italy Stalin reined in his most militant comrades, who were roundly defeated by the CIA-financed Christian Democrats in the April 1948 elections.

Not unexpectedly, 1948's second crisis occurred in Berlin, the thorny relic of the Big Three's wartime collaboration that lay one hundred miles inside the Soviet sector. Incensed by the introduction of the new Western currency (the deutsche mark) that would further separate the occupation zones, the Soviets angrily withdrew from the Allied Control Council in March. The announcement of the West's intention to introduce the new currency in Berlin threatened to

---

* Poland's leader, Władysław Gomułka, met a different fate. At the first signs of his support for Tito, Moscow encouraged Gomułka's rival Bolesław Bierut to remove him from his post as party secretary general and from the politburo, and he was imprisoned between 1951 and 1954.

Photo 3.1. US transport plane landing in West Berlin during the 1948–1949 blockade. *Courtesy of Library of Congress.*

immensely increase the cost of the Soviet occupation that heretofore had been financed by inflated Reich marks. In response, on June 24, 1948, Soviet authorities cut off food, gas, electricity, and other supplies from the Western sectors and announced the closing of all road, rail, and water routes to and from Berlin.

Stalin, balancing the easy takeover in Prague with the communists' setbacks in France and Italy, had made an imprudent gamble. By closing land access to the Western sectors, he had hoped to convince his ex-partners to return to the conference table or lose their place in Berlin. However, the British and Americans took up the challenge by instituting an extraordinary airlift, flying 278,000 sorties over the next eleven months that delivered some two million tons of food and fuel to the isolated outpost. They also instituted a punishing counterblockade against the entire Soviet zone.

The Berlin crisis occupies a special place in Cold War historiography, as an emblem of Soviet aggressiveness and Anglo-American resistance. It was nonetheless an extraordinarily calibrated confrontation. Truman, determined to avoid a military showdown, rebuffed advice to send in armed convoys, and Stalin refrained from attacking the Allied aircraft. Even when Truman announced the dispatch of sixty B-29s to Great Britain in July—aircraft capable but still not fitted to deliver an atomic bomb—the United States issued no direct threat against Moscow. Cold War mythology has also stressed the privations and stoicism of the West Berliners, who nonetheless received ample food and fuel from the local black market and from their eastern neighbors.

The crisis ended on May 12, 1949, when Stalin finally lifted the botched blockade, using the face-saving excuse of a foreign ministers' conference, which, predictably, accomplished nothing. For eleven months Stalin had insisted on Moscow's peaceful intentions and its fidelity to the Grand Alliance, but he lost the propaganda war. The West European press castigated the Soviet Union as an inept bully and praised the United States for its resolute defense of a beleaguered outpost.

Few at the time or since have questioned the costs or the risks associated with Berlin in 1948–1949. From that time until the end of the Cold War, the Allies' presence in West Berlin remained the embodiment of Soviet frustration and, despite the city's real vulnerability, of America's commitment to halt aggression. Moreover, less than four years after World War II, two million West Berliners—and, by extension, the entire population of western Germany—were suddenly transformed into America's democratic protégés. Truman's actions in 1948–1949 replaced appeasement with firmness and selective engagement with an expansive definition of US interests and prestige. The Berlin airlift also redefined America's view of its Cold War partnerships to include populations unwilling or incapable of defending themselves from aggression that would be rescued by decisive US action. In real as well as symbolic terms, the "Berlin syndrome" wiped out the Munich nightmare that had haunted the West for a decade.

1949

Beyond a simple scorecard of political winners and losers, the Berlin crisis also had larger consequences. Both sides, after three years of demobilization, now began a vast and rapid buildup of their arms and military forces, including the reintroduction of the US military draft in June 1948. Second was the creation of the North Atlantic Treaty Organization (NATO). According to the treaty signed in Washington, DC, in April 1949, the Brussels Pact was expanded to twelve members, including the United States and Canada, who committed themselves to mutual defense against "aggressor(s) . . . with such action as [they] deem[ed] necessary."* Despite the vagueness over its members' actual military commitments, the birth of NATO—which, like the Rio Treaty, conformed to the UN Charter's authorization of regional self-defense measures—demonstrated the West's ultimate abandonment of the Grand Alliance. Unworried by Stalin's protests (particularly over Italy's membership), the West reminded Moscow of the mutual defense pacts that the Soviets had imposed on their small neighbors. If the Berlin crisis had demonstrated the Superpowers' reluctance to go to war, it had also thickened the structures of their rivalry.

Many writers cite Stalin's threat to Berlin as the catalyst for the division of Germany. The West's resolve to end the fruitless haggling and create a German ally against the Soviets was undoubtedly facilitated by the blockade. However, the path to the creation of a West Germany involved more than simply detaching their zones from the Soviets. Germany's western neighbors feared an entity that, with only 50 percent of the Reich's prewar territory, would still outnumber France by fourteen million people and possess enormous industrial and military potential.

Thus there were political compromises in the creation of West Germany. Under Western tutelage the Basic Law, a preliminary constitution adopted by German officials on May 8, 1949 (the fourth anniversary of V-E Day), announced a total break with the Nazi past, creating a parliamentary democracy with strong human rights protection and the potential to collaborate closely with other governments as well as ensuring Allied occupation rights. France, which had failed to obtain the Ruhr industrial region or to suppress Germany's economic revival, was mollified by the integrative conditions that gave extensive powers to the new German state governments (*Länder*), brought the western zones into the Marshall Plan, and maintained the US commitment to NATO. To assuage German nationalism (and neutralize Soviet propaganda), the Allies did not foreclose the possibility of future unification through free national elections and in the meantime allowed the new state to proclaim itself the sole legitimate representative of the entire German people (including the inhabitants of the eastern sector), to legislate on their behalf, and even to include Berlin within its jurisdiction.

On September 21, 1949, Stalin appeared to suffer a major political setback when the Federal Republic of Germany (FRG, or West Germany) was officially

---

* The original NATO members were France, Great Britain, the Netherlands, Belgium, Luxembourg, the United States, Canada, Portugal, Italy, Denmark, Norway, and Iceland. Significantly, one of the foremost critics of NATO's establishment was George Kennan, who feared it would freeze the division of Europe and thwart the goal of containment: to bring about a peaceful reform and rollback of the Soviet Empire.

Map 7. The two German states between 1949 and 1990.

established. The Allies, ignoring Moscow's loud protests over the violation of the Potsdam accords, recognized the new state, comprising ninety-six thousand square miles and a population of some fifty-six million. Two weeks later, on October 8, the Soviets set up the nominally independent German Democratic Republic (GDR, or East Germany), a state with almost nineteen million people and occupying territory of about 44 percent the size of its western neighbor. Stalin's blunders, combined with deft Allied leadership and the cooperation of West German politicians, had enabled a potential colossus to arise in the FRG's new capital in Bonn and West Berlin to remain free.

Yet Germany's division in 1949 also offered advantages for Stalin, who as usual had a prepared fallback position. The two-state solution not only ended the uneven four-power negotiations, but also gave the Soviet Union a small but solid base from which it could exploit German labor, resources (particularly uranium), and chemical industries, and to station a half million troops in Central Europe without any constraints from the West. Some scholars believe that Stalin appreciated the symbolic value of achieving a communist domain in Germany, something that had eluded Lenin and one that would keep guard over Poland and Czechoslovakia. Although Stalin until his death never dropped his demand for a neutral, unified Germany,* the prospect of a military withdrawal from Central Europe may well have become less attractive than staying. If Soviet threats to West Berlin had failed miserably, other forms of pressure could still be applied.

The creation of two German states, an event unforeseen at Tehran, Yalta, or even at Potsdam, was a signal Cold War phenomenon. Foreshadowed by the dual occupation of Korea, Germany's partition in 1949 combined both real and symbolic elements as a means of stabilizing Central Europe as well as a punishment for the Nazis' crimes. Four-power occupation had worked in Austria—thanks to the smaller strategic stakes, a moderate socialist government, and the Allies' Tehran decision to treat this country gently as "Hitler's first victim"—and the country remained intact. In the more populous, resource-rich Germany, which lacked a central government, the occupiers were able to dominate the revival of local politics. East Germany became the first "workers' and peasants' state on German soil," and West Germany a liberal, robustly capitalist state. Both regimes represented not only a renunciation of the Nazi past but also the revitalization of two opposing political traditions—Marxism and liberalism—each claiming redemptive power over Germany and Europe's future and each mirroring the Cold War itself.

Whatever satisfaction the West reaped from its pragmatic solution to the German problem—and from the end of the bloody Greek civil war and Tito's escape from Stalin's grip into a US-supported Cold War neutrality—was undermined by two grave developments in 1949: the explosion of the first Soviet atomic bomb and the victory of Mao Zedong's communist forces in China. Both, unexpected only in their speed, not only challenged America's nuclear monopoly and its position in China but also appeared to strengthen the global revolutionary camp.

On September 23, 1949, Truman shocked the world with his announcement that the Soviet Union had secretly tested its first atomic weapon one month earlier.† Although the United States already had sufficient bases, aircraft, and bombs to

---

* In 1952, ignoring the GDR, Stalin floated another proposal for unified neutral Germany, which was rebuffed by the West.

† Thanks to Soviet espionage, an almost complete copy of the bomb dropped on Nagasaki was replicated by the USSR.

inflict considerable damage on the Soviet Union, Moscow's incipient nuclear arsenal stirred Western fears of political blackmail. Having long abandoned the effort for international control over nuclear weapons, Truman in January 1950 launched a large-scale program to develop the even more powerful hydrogen bomb, which was matched by an equally ambitious program by the Soviets.

The birth of the nuclear arms race in 1949 was imprinted in the history of the Cold War when both sides began committing vast resources to the production of arms capable of destroying not only the enemy's military capacity but also the entire planet. The specter of preventive war that had loomed over the Soviet Union after 1945 was now matched by both sides' hope that deterrence—backed by ever-growing stocks of nuclear weapons—would compel prudent behavior by their adversaries. Yet both sides also recognized that even the most powerful delivery systems might not be decisive in managing local conflicts and that armies still counted, especially in Europe. Moreover, the genies unleashed by nuclear testing and proliferation and by madman scenarios and civilian terror had the paradoxical effect of eroding the ideological distinction between the two Superpower rivals and kindling a global peace movement focusing specifically on the eradication of nuclear weapons.

Only eight days after Truman's announcement another momentous event occurred: the formal establishment of the People's Republic of China on October 1, 1949. The world's most populous country had come under the rule of Mao Zedong's communist forces. The US-supported Nationalist government of Chiang Kai-shek, which Roosevelt had envisaged as the fourth pillar of the postwar world, fled into exile on the island of Taiwan on December 8. From Washington's perspective, the Soviets had greatly expanded their power and now threatened Japan and Southeast Asia.

The revolutionary dimensions of Mao's victory were not well understood at the time and are still contested. Neither a grievous political defeat for the United States nor a great victory for the USSR, the establishment of communist rule in China exposed the limits of the Superpowers' agility and skill. Locked in their rivalry over Europe in 1947–1948, both had failed to deal adroitly with the rapid deterioration of the Nationalist (Kuomintang) government and with the communists' determination to prevail. In Washington, which was caught up in the close presidential campaign of 1948, the debate between the ardent proponents of military support for Chiang and the equally passionate decriers of his government's corruption and ineptitude produced a $400 million aid appropriation but also a paralyzing fatalism over the US role in China's future, particularly given the political impossibility of armed intervention. Similarly, in Moscow, the fears of US intervention and of a feisty Chinese Tito as well as the advantages of a weak and divided China that would preserve the Yalta gains had to be weighed against the ideological benefits of obtaining a huge Asian satellite. Stalin's capricious gestures in 1948 were the result: a mediation offer that annoyed Washington and infuriated Mao and the delay in inviting the communist leader to Moscow, but also the intense communications between the two parties, the pro-communist pronouncements later that year, and the stepped-up arms deliveries and diplomatic contacts in 1949.

The aftereffects of Mao's victory were equally misread at the time. In Moscow on February 14, 1950, the Soviet Union and China signed a treaty linking 50 percent of the world's land mass in a pact of friendship, alliance, and mutual assistance if either were involved in hostilities with Japan or its allies. China obtained significant concessions, including the retrocession within two years of the Chang-chun railway,* the return of Port Arthur (Lushun) and Dairen (Dalian), and the removal of Soviet extraterritorial privileges. Mao had to recognize the independence of Soviet-dominated Outer Mongolia, but he obtained Stalin's permission to occupy Tibet, which he proceeded to do in the next year. Moreover, Stalin encouraged Mao to demand China's seat on the UN Security Council and put pressure on the West by boycotting council meetings until this claim was fulfilled.

The 1950 pact between the two communist regimes reflected their unequal power and divergent national interests even more than their ideological solidarity. Despite the semblance of generosity and largesse, Soviet terms were tough. Moscow's low-interest but modest $300 million credit for the purchase of Soviet industrial goods, to be granted in five installments, had to be fully repaid within ten years. Along with its agreement to create joint stock companies to exploit Chinese mineral resources, the Kremlin obliged Beijing to exclude other foreign investors. Finally, Stalin asserted his predominance over a regime he had neither anticipated nor energetically promoted by assigning to Mao the task of promoting anticolonial revolutions in Asia.

Cold War scholars disagree over whether the United States lost an opportunity in 1949–1950 to establish relations with the People's Republic of China, particularly when its closest ally risked its ire and hastened to do so. The Atlee government, concerned over Hong Kong's future, spurred by realist sentiment in

---

* A T-shaped, 2,400-kilometer rail system running through China from Manzhouli in the west to Suifenhe in the east and connecting Harbin with the port of Dalian on the Yellow Sea.

the Commonwealth, and wishing to have a "foot in the door" when Sino-Soviet tensions would inevitably escalate, announced on January 6, 1950, its willingness to grant de jure recognition. Although France held back out of fear of Beijing's threat to Indochina, two other NATO allies (Denmark and Norway) and three European neutrals (Sweden, Switzerland, and Finland) joined India, Indonesia, and Burma and ten communist governments in recognizing the People's Republic of China (PRC) in 1950.

The United States stood back because of powerful political reasons—the widespread support for the exiled Nationalist leader Chiang Kai-shek in Congress, the press, and the churches—but also as a result of conflicting signals from Beijing. In May 1949, a few months before the communists' victory, Zhou Enlai, Mao's chief aide and one of the leading members of the Chinese Communist Party, had sent a conciliatory message through a third party that drew a suspicious response from Truman, who was peremptorily rebuffed by Beijing. One month later came an unofficial invitation to US ambassador John Leighton Stuart to hold talks with Zhou and Mao. But while this offer hung in the air, the Chinese were detaining the US consul general in Mukden on trumped-up charges of espionage.

Both sides, wary of the other and divided within, could not move forward until the verdict of Mao's victory was delivered. The Chinese leadership was still distrustful of American imperialism and hamstrung by its pro-Soviet faction. America's leaders, skeptical over uncovering a new Tito, feared manipulation by Beijing and were concerned over the actions of the third very interested player, the Soviet Union. Moscow, with good reason to fear another heretic, put extreme pressure on Mao to declare his solidarity.* The Chinese communist leader, whose exact sentiments cannot be known, undoubtedly bristled at the Kremlin's behavior, but he could not ignore Stalin's stranglehold over Manchuria or his own ideological commitment to Marxist unity. On June 30, 1949, Mao announced that China was "Leaning to One Side" and intended to ally itself with "the Soviet Union, with the People's Democracies, and with the proletariat and the broad masses of the people in all other countries and form an international united front." One day later, Secretary of State Acheson vetoed Stuart's trip to Beijing.

Once the People's Republic of China (PRC) was established, Washington chose a pragmatic policy between the two extremes of open hostility and

---

* Indeed, Mao claimed equal status with Soviet leaders because of his original contribution to Marxist-Leninist ideology: the revolutionary potential of the peasantry.

conciliation. Combining balance-of-power concerns, ideological aversion, and fears for the safety of Chiang's exile government in Taiwan, the United States refused recognition of the PRC and blocked its seating in the United Nations, but Washington did not stop others from opening embassies in Beijing or from breaking relations with Chiang Kai-shek.

Nonetheless, the Chinese revolution (following close after the explosion of the Soviet atomic bomb) intensified the Truman administration's fears of communist expansion in Asia. Alarmed over the Vietnamese communist leader Ho Chi Minh's February 1950 mission to Moscow, the Soviet decision to recognize his government, and Chinese support for the Viet Minh insurgency against French colonial rule, the United States swallowed its anti-imperialist sentiments and cast its lot with the Paris-backed puppet emperor Bao Dai.

Equally significant was the appearance in April 1950 of the National Security Council document NSC-68. This top-secret paper prepared by the State Department's Policy Planning Staff, called for a major buildup of US military forces to counter the Kremlin's threats to America's interests in Europe and in Asia.* NSC-68 aimed at reassuring America's allies of its resolve to halt the spread of communism, but it also channeled US Cold War diplomacy away from pragmatism and patience toward fear and frustration, and from Kennan's watchful containment of the Soviet Union to an open-ended crusade against global communism.

WAR IN KOREA

The Cold War's first hot war began on June 25, 1950. Following almost two years of armed skirmishes between North and South Korea, that day ninety thousand North Korean troops crossed the thirty-eighth parallel, easily captured Seoul two days later, and threatened to overrun the southern part of the peninsula. During the two preceding months, the North Korean communist leader Kim Il Sung had obtained Stalin's assent and the Kremlin's promises of military support for the invasion as well as an endorsement from Mao.† But the timing was the North Korean's alone, and the invasion created a cascade of surprises for all the major parties.

---

* NSC-68's principal author was Paul Nitze, who had replaced Kennan in late 1949 as head of the State Department's policy-planning staff.
† Still facing pockets of armed Nationalist opposition on the mainland, Mao would probably have preferred Soviet support for an attack on Taiwan, but he bowed to Moscow's decision and to the pleas of Kim Il Sung, who had been an ally in the Chinese civil war.

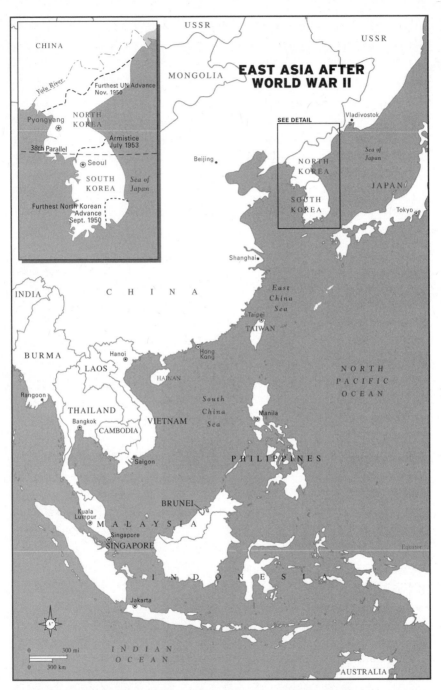

Map 8. The establishment of the People's Republic of China in 1949 created a major change in power relations in East Asia.

In echoes of the 1930s, the United Nations now faced its first test of repelling military aggression against one of its members. Although dominated by a Western majority, the Security Council until then had been paralyzed by Moscow's vetoes. But because of the six-month Soviet boycott over the UN failure to seat Communist China, the council on June 27 was able to adopt a US-sponsored resolution to provide South Korea (ROK) "with all necessary aid to repel the aggressors" and then to establish a UN expeditionary force under the command of US general Douglas MacArthur, to which sixteen nations ultimately contributed.*

Until June 1950 the defense of South Korea had not been part of America's Asian strategy. Now the Truman administration, using the language of NSC-68, made it a symbol of the West's "strength and determination" to resist Soviet aggression. Even before the UN resolution, Truman had hastily sent Japan-based US ground, naval, and air forces to South Korea. Washington, viewing the Korean crisis as an opportunity to protect the rest of Asia from falling as dominoes to communist expansion, also opted to support the French war in Indochina and moved the Seventh Fleet to the Taiwan Straits to shield the exiled Nationalists against a communist attack.† In Europe, the United States used the North Korean attack to urge its NATO allies to build a stronger barrier against Soviet aggression, one that would include West German rearmament.

Over the next three months the Korean War shifted dramatically. By early September the North Korean offensive had halted after a South Korean uprising never materialized, and UN soldiers, tanks, and aircraft began pouring in. After their spectacular landing behind enemy lines at Inchon on September 15, the UN troops went on the offensive, liberating Seoul and reaching the thirty-eighth parallel. At this decisive moment the Truman administration pressed the UN to approve a crossing into North Korea. With the announced aim of punishing the aggressors, US-led forces in the beginning of October moved northward toward the Yalu River, Korea's border with China. Ignoring Beijing's warnings, the United States aimed to solve the Korean problem by unifying the entire peninsula under a pro-Western government.

Stalin, although startled by Washington's strong response, had initially refrained from intervening. Only after UN troops crossed the thirty-eighth parallel and North Korea appeared doomed did Stalin take action, urging Mao to aid their comrades and offering military support and Soviet air support (which did not, however, materialize until the summer of 1951). A resolute Mao fended

---

* The United States provided half the ground troops and most of the air and sea power.
† Both moves raised alarm in Beijing, which feared encirclement by the United States.

off his politburo colleagues' objections to launching a war with the world's most powerful country, proclaiming his own domino theory of communist solidarity* and insisting that Korea was the most favorable terrain for China's inevitable clash with the imperialist United States.

The Korean War again changed dramatically on October 19, 1950, when nearly three hundred thousand Chinese People's Volunteers (CPV) crossed the Yalu River and drove the US Eighth Army southward. Seoul fell again in January 1951 but was recaptured by UN troops in March. Mao's momentous decision to cross the thirty-eighth parallel (which Stalin strongly endorsed) led to a bloody two-year war of attrition until the July 1953 armistice agreement, which reset the two Koreas' boundaries in a diagonal line extending only slightly north of the thirty-eighth parallel.

The Korean War also witnessed the first direct (if camouflaged) US-Soviet combat.† Beginning in late 1950, Soviet MiG-15s, based in Chinese air fields, joined their Chinese comrades in dogfights against US pilots accompanying B-29 bombing missions over North Korea. Also, some seventy thousand Soviet troops were stationed along the Yalu to provide air defense.

The costs of the Korean War were horrific. The country was devastated by massive US air strikes using bombs and napalm as well as by the three years of fierce fighting. Roughly three million (10 percent) of the Korean population were killed, wounded, or missing, including a very high number of civilians; thirty-seven thousand Americans lost their lives, along with three thousand other UN members; and some nine hundred thousand Chinese soldiers died. The casualty figures might have been worse had Truman acted on his initial impulse to use an atomic weapon.‡

The war's political balance sheet was largely negative for all sides.§ The United States had repelled communist aggression but had succeeded in neither reunifying Korea nor ending South Korea's vulnerability without a permanent UN occupation force. At home the Korean War created an inflationary spiral and a

---

* "If China stood by when North Korea was in peril, then the Soviet Union could also stand by when China was in peril, and Internationalism would be empty talk."

† Initially Soviet planes were marked with North Korean insignia, and their pilots wore North Korean uniforms; although this cumbersome practice soon ended, Soviet pilots were under strict orders to avoid capture.

‡ On August 1950 nine B-29s arrived in Guam loaded with unarmed atomic bombs, and at a press conference on November 30, Truman confirmed that he had been actively considering their use since the beginning of the war, only to assure a panicked Atlee that the United States had "no intention" of doing so except to prevent a "major military disaster."

§ One of the sole gainers was Japan, the new US ally in East Asia, which reindustrialized, increased its military capacity, and obtained extensive economic benefits from the Korean War.

wave of anticommunist hysteria, and abroad it not only froze US relations with China for almost two decades but also expanded the Berlin syndrome and militarized American foreign policy in Asia. Moreover, by linking US policy with French colonialism in Indochina, the defeated Chinese Nationalists, and the highly unpopular South Korean president Syngman Rhee, Washington damaged its prestige among the newly emerging countries in Africa and Asia.

Stalin also had miscalculated. Having failed to anticipate Truman's response and having goaded the Chinese to engage the United States, he now faced a major buildup of US military power, including the quadrupling of America's defense budget and the doubling of its draft quota as well as the establishment of permanent US bases in Japan and South Korea, the increase in aid to anticommunist governments in Southeast Asia, and the strengthening of NATO with the addition of West German forces. The Korean War had seriously drained Soviet resources, and Moscow and its allies' $220 million contribution to North Korea's postwar reconstruction burdened their economies and created domestic discontent. Moreover, the aging and increasingly rigid Soviet leader failed to recognize that his callous exploitation of an impoverished and dependent China during the Korean War would sow the seeds of a Sino-Soviet split. China, although suffering enormous losses, deterred from capturing Taiwan, and forced to postpone its Five-Year Plan, had emerged from the Korean War with its international prestige greatly enhanced and as a potential rival to Moscow in the colonial world.

By the time the Korean armistice was signed on July 27, 1953, Joseph Stalin was dead, Harry Truman had been replaced by Dwight David Eisenhower, and a diplomatic revolution had occurred. The three former Axis states were now firmly in the Western camp, and the entire mainland of China had fallen within the Soviet orbit. Germany and Europe had become divided, and Asia and the Middle East were seething with anticolonial revolts.

The Korean War represented the gory culmination of seven years of Superpower probes of the other side's aspirations, strength, and resolve. Each new test had led not to the provisional compromises that had sustained the Grand Alliance but to deepening their mutual suspicions, elevating their hostile rhetoric, and reinforcing their resolve to strengthen their respective camps. The near collisions in Berlin and the Korean War had added a military dimension, and the escalating nuclear arms race lent an element of rigidity and terror to US-Soviet encounters.

Nonetheless, the Korean War belied both sides' hopes of attaining a preponderance of power: whether in wealth, military might, or ideological truth. The birth of a second communist state in China was a major challenge to their aim of dividing the world. Given the scale of political and social upheaval in Asia, Africa, and the Middle East, neither the United States nor the Soviet Union could hope to impose its will everywhere on its own terms. Having gone almost to the atomic brink, the new leaders in Moscow and Washington in 1953 faced the challenge of building a less perilous, more orderly Cold War world that now extended beyond its original European borders.

SUGGESTIONS FOR FURTHER STUDY

Documents

Churchill, Winston. "The Sinews of Peace," The Iron Curtain Speech, March 5, 1946. National Churchill Museum. http://www.nationalchurchillmuseum.org/sinews -of-peace-iron-curtain-speech.html.

Dedijer, Vladimir. *Tito Speaks: His Self-Portrait and Struggle with Stalin*. London: Weidenfeld and Nicolson, 1953.

"Marshall Plan." 1948. National Archives and Records Administration Featured Documents. http://www.archives.gov/exhibits/featured_documents/marshall_plan.

"NATO Treaty, Washington, April 4, 1949." Yale Law School Avalon Project: Documents in Law, History and Diplomacy. http://avalon.law.yale.edu/20th_century /nato.asp.

Parrish, Scott D., and M. M. Narinskii. *New Evidence on the Soviet Rejection of the Marshall Plan, 1947: Two Reports*. Washington, DC: Woodrow Wilson International Center for Scholars, 1994.

Stokes, Gale. *From Stalinism to Pluralism: A Documentary History of Eastern Europe Since 1945*. New York: Oxford University Press, 1995.

"Trial of the Major War Criminals Before the International Military Tribunal, Nuremberg, 14 November 1945–1 October 1946." Library of Congress Military Legal Resources. http://www.loc.gov/rr/frd/Military_Law/NT_major-war-criminals.html.

Truman, Harry. "Atomic Explosion in the USSR." September 23, 1949. Yale Law School Avalon Project: Documents in Law, History and Diplomacy. http://avalon .law.yale.edu/20th_century/decad244.asp.

Truman, Harry S., and Winston Churchill. *Defending the West: The Truman-Churchill Correspondence, 1945–1960*. Edited by G. W. Sand. Westport, CT: Praeger, 2004.

"The Universal Declaration of Human Rights, Adopted by the General Assembly in December 1948." United Nations. http://www.un.org/en/documents/udhr/index .shtml.

Woodrow Wilson International Center for Scholars and Cold War International History Project. *New Evidence on North Korea*. Cold War International History Project Bulletin, Issue 14/15. Washington, DC: Woodrow Wilson International Center for Scholars, 2004. http://www.wilsoncenter.org/sites/default/files /CWIHP_Bulletin_14–15.pdf.

Contemporary Writing

Lippmann, Walter. *The Cold War: A Study in U.S. Foreign Policy.* New York: Harper, 1947.

Miłosz, Czesław. *The Captive Mind.* New York: Knopf, 1953.

Niebuhr, Reinhold. *The Irony of American History.* New York: Scribner, 1952.

Stone, I. F. *The Hidden History of the Korean War.* New York: Monthly Review Press, 1952.

X [George Kennan]. "The Sources of Soviet Conduct." *Foreign Affairs* 25, no. 4 (July 1947): 566–582.

Memoirs

Acheson, Dean. *Present at the Creation: My Years in the State Department.* New York: Norton, 1969.

Dimitrov, Georgi. *The Diary of Georgi Dimitrov, 1933–1949.* Edited by Ivo Banac. New Haven, CT: Yale University Press, 2003.

Djilas, Milovan. *Conversations with Stalin.* Translated by Michael B. Petrovich. New York: Harcourt Brace, 1962.

Kennan, George F. *Memoirs.* Vol. 2: 1950–1963. Boston: Little, Brown, 1972.

Philbrick, Herbert A. *I Led Three Lives: Citizen, "Communist," Counterspy.* New York: McGraw-Hill, 1952.

Truman, Harry S. *Memoirs.* 2 vols. Garden City, NY: Doubleday, 1955–1956.

Films

The Day the Earth Stood Still. Directed by Robert Wise. Los Angeles: Twentieth Century Fox, 1951.

Exodus. Directed by Otto Preminger. Los Angeles: Carlyle Productions, 1960.

The 49th Man. Directed by Fred F. Sears. Los Angeles: Katzman Corporation, 1953.

Gandhi. Directed by Richard Attenborough. Los Angeles: International Film Investors, 1982.

High Noon. Directed by Fred Zinneman. Los Angeles: Stanley Kramer Productions, 1952.

The Iron Curtain. Directed by William A. Wellman. Los Angeles: Twentieth Century Fox, 1948.

M*A*S*H*. Directed by Robert Altman. Los Angeles: Twentieth Century Fox, 1970.

On the Waterfront. Directed by Elia Kazan. Los Angeles: Columbia Pictures, 1952.

Pickup on South Street. Directed by Samuel Fuller. Los Angeles: Twentieth Century Fox, 1953.

The Red Menace. Directed by R. G. Springsteen. Los Angeles: Republic Pictures, 1949.

The Steel Helmet. Directed by Samuel Fuller. Los Angeles: Deputy Corporation, 1951.

The Third Man. Directed by Carol Reed. London: Carol Reed's Production/London Film Productions, 1949.

Fiction

Gouzenko, Igor. *The Fall of a Titan*. New York: Norton, 1954.

Ḥabībī, Imīl. *The Secret Life of Saeed, the Ill-Fated Pessoptimist: A Palestinian Who Became a Citizen of Israel*. Translated by Salma Khadra Jayyusi and Trevor Le Gassick. New York: Vantage, 1982.

Jin, Ha. *War Trash*. New York: Pantheon, 2004.

Rushdie, Salman. *Midnight's Children*. London: Jonathan Cape, 1980.

Singh, Khushwant. *Train to Pakistan*. New York: Grove, 1956.

Secondary Sources

Banac, Ivo. *With Stalin Against Tito: Cominformist Splits in Yugoslav Communism*. Ithaca, NY: Cornell University Press, 1988.

Baylis, John. *The Diplomacy of Pragmatism: Britain and the Formation of NATO, 1942–1949*. Kent, OH: Kent State University Press, 1993.

Bostdorff, Denise M. *Proclaiming the Truman Doctrine: The Cold War Call to Arms*. College Station: Texas A&M University Press, 2008.

Brogi, Alessandro. *A Question of Self-Esteem: The United States and the Cold War Choices in France and Italy, 1944–1958*. Westport, CT: Praeger, 2002.

Cardwell, Curt. *NSC-68 and the Political Economy of the Early Cold War*. New York: Cambridge University Press, 2011.

Chen, Jian. *China's Road to the Korean War: The Making of the Sino-American Confrontation*. New York: Columbia University Press, 1994.

——. *Mao's China and the Cold War*. Chapel Hill: University of North Carolina Press, 2001.

Cohen, Michael Joseph. *Fighting World War Three from the Middle East: Allied Contingency Plans, 1945–1954*. London: Frank Cass, 1997.

Corke, Sarah-Jane. *US Covert Operations and Cold War Strategy: Truman, Secret Warfare, and the CIA, 1945–1953*. New York: Routledge, 2008.

Craig, Campbell, and Sergey Radchenko. *The Atomic Bomb and the Origins of the Cold War*. New Haven, CT: Yale University Press, 2008.

Creswell, Michael. *A Question of Balance: How France and the United States Created Cold War Europe*. Cambridge, MA: Harvard University Press, 2006.

Dallas, Gregor. *1945: The War That Never Ended*. New Haven, CT: Yale University Press, 2005.

Dallek, Robert. *The Lost Peace: Leadership in a Time of Horror and Hope, 1945–1953*. New York: Harper, 2010.

Deighton, Anne. *The Impossible Peace: Britain, the Division of Germany and the Origins of the Cold War*. Oxford: Clarendon, 1990.

Dower, John W. *Embracing Defeat: Japan in the Wake of World War II*. New York: Norton, 1999.

Eisenberg, Carolyn Woods. *Drawing the Line: The American Decision to Divide Germany, 1944–1949*. Cambridge: Cambridge University Press, 1996.

Fawcett, Louise L'Estrange. *Iran and the Cold War: The Azerbaijan Crisis of 1946.* Cambridge: Cambridge University Press, 1992.

Foot, Rosemary. *The Wrong War: American Policy and the Dimensions of the Korean Conflict, 1950–1953.* Ithaca, NY: Cornell University Press, 1985.

Glendon, Mary Ann. *A World Made New: Eleanor Roosevelt and the Universal Declaration of Human Rights.* New York: Random House, 2001.

Goda, Norman J. W. *Tales from Spandau: Nazi Criminals and the Cold War.* Cambridge: Cambridge University Press, 2007.

Goncharov, S. N., John Wilson Lewis, and Litai Xue. *Uncertain Partners: Stalin, Mao, and the Korean War.* Stanford, CA: Stanford University Press, 1993.

Gorlizki, Yoram, and O. V. Khlevniuk. *Cold Peace: Stalin and the Soviet Ruling Circle, 1945–1953.* Oxford: Oxford University Press, 2004.

Gormly, James L. *The Collapse of the Grand Alliance, 1945–1948.* Baton Rouge: Louisiana State University Press, 1987.

Grose, Peter. *Operation Rollback: America's Secret War Behind the Iron Curtain.* Boston: Houghton Mifflin, 2000.

Harbutt, Fraser J. *The Iron Curtain: Churchill, America, and the Origins of the Cold War.* New York: Oxford University Press, 1986.

Hewison, Robert. *In Anger: Culture in the Cold War, 1945–1960.* London: Weidenfeld and Nicolson, 1981.

Hogan, Michael J. *A Cross of Iron: Harry S. Truman and the Origins of the National Security State, 1945–1954.* Cambridge: Cambridge University Press, 1998.

———. *The Marshall Plan: America, Britain, and the Reconstruction of Western Europe, 1947–1952.* Cambridge: Cambridge University Press, 1987.

Holloway, David. *Stalin and the Bomb: The Soviet Union and Atomic Energy, 1939–1956.* New Haven, CT: Yale University Press, 1994.

Kaplan, Karel. *The Short March: The Communist Takeover in Czechoslovakia, 1945–1948.* New York: St. Martin's Press, 1987.

Kent, John. *British Imperial Strategy and the Origins of the Cold War, 1944–49.* Leicester, UK: Leicester University Press, 1993.

Klein, Christina. *Cold War Orientalism: Asia in the Middlebrow Imagination, 1945–1961.* Berkeley: University of California Press, 2003.

Kuniholm, Bruce Robellet. *The Origins of the Cold War in the Near East: Great Power Conflict and Diplomacy in Iran, Turkey, and Greece.* Princeton, NJ: Princeton University Press, 1980.

Lee, Steven Hugh. *Outposts of Empire: Korea, Vietnam and the Origins of the Cold War in Asia, 1949–1954.* Montréal: McGill-Queen's University Press, 1995.

Lees, Lorraine M. *Keeping Tito Afloat: The United States, Yugoslavia, and the Cold War.* University Park: Pennsylvania State University Press, 1997.

Leffler, Melvyn P. *A Preponderance of Power: National Security, the Truman Administration, and the Cold War.* Stanford, CA: Stanford University Press, 1992.

Lewkowicz, Nicolas. *The German Question and the International Order, 1943–48.* Basingstoke, UK: Palgrave Macmillan, 2010.

Lingen, Kerstin von. *Kesselring's Last Battle: War Crimes Trials and Cold War Politics, 1945–1960*. Lawrence: University Press of Kansas, 2009.

Loth, Wilfried. *Stalin's Unwanted Child: The Soviet Union, the German Question, and the Founding of the GDR*. Translated by Robert F. Hogg. New York: St. Martin's, 1998.

Louis, William Roger. *The British Empire in the Middle East, 1945–1951: Arab Nationalism, the United States, and Postwar Imperialism*. Oxford: Clarendon, 1984.

Lucas, Scott. *Freedom's War: The US Crusade Against the Soviet Union, 1945–56*. Manchester, UK: Manchester University Press, 1999.

MacShane, Denis. *International Labour and the Origins of the Cold War*. Oxford: Clarendon Press, 1992.

Mastny, Vojtech. *The Cold War and Soviet Insecurity: The Stalin Years*. New York: Oxford University Press, 1996.

McMahon, Robert J. *Colonialism and Cold War: The United States and the Struggle for Indonesian Independence, 1945–49*. Ithaca, NY: Cornell University Press, 1981.

Mitrovich, Gregory. *Undermining the Kremlin: America's Strategy to Subvert the Soviet Bloc, 1947–1956*. Ithaca, NY: Cornell University Press, 2000.

Monod, David. *Settling Scores: German Music, Denazification, and the Americans, 1945–1953*. Chapel Hill: University of North Carolina Press, 2005.

Morris, Benny. *The Birth of the Palestinian Refugee Problem, 1947–1949*. Cambridge: Cambridge University Press, 1987.

———. *1948: A History of the First Arab-Israeli War*. New Haven, CT: Yale University Press, 2008.

Murray, Brian. *Stalin, the Cold War, and the Division of China: A Multiarchival Mystery*. Cold War International History Project Working Paper, No. 12. Washington, DC: Woodrow Wilson International Center for Scholars, 1995. http://wilsoncenter.org/sites/default/files/ACFB69.PDF.

Naimark, Norman M. *The Russians in Germany: A History of the Soviet Zone of Occupation, 1945–1949*. Cambridge, MA: Belknap Press of Harvard University Press, 1995.

Ninkovich, Frank Anthony. *The Diplomacy of Ideas: US Foreign Policy and Cultural Relations, 1938–1950*. Cambridge: Cambridge University Press, 1981.

Offner, Arnold A. *Another Such Victory: President Truman and the Cold War, 1945–1953*. Stanford, CA: Stanford University Press, 2002.

Qing, Simei. *From Allies to Enemies: Visions of Modernity, Identity, and U.S.-China Diplomacy, 1945–1960*. Cambridge, MA: Harvard University Press, 2007.

Roberts, Geoffrey. *Stalin's Wars: From World War to Cold War, 1939–1953*. New Haven, CT: Yale University Press, 2006.

Rucker, Laurent. *Moscow's Surprise: The Soviet-Israeli Alliance of 1947–1949*. Cold War International History Project Working Paper, No. 46. Washington, DC: Woodrow Wilson International Center for Scholars, 2005. http://wilsoncenter.org/sites/default/files/CWIHP_WP_461.pdf.

Schwartz, Lowell. *Political Warfare Against the Kremlin: US and British Propaganda Policy at the Beginning of the Cold War*. Basingstoke: Palgrave Macmillan, 2009.

Selverstone, Marc J. *Constructing the Monolith: The United States, Great Britain, and International Communism, 1945–1950*. Cambridge, MA: Harvard University Press, 2009.

Shlaim, Avi. *Collusion Across the Jordan: King Abdullah, the Zionist Movement, and the Partition of Palestine*. New York: Columbia University Press, 1988.

——. *The United States and the Berlin Blockade, 1948–1949: A Study in Crisis Decision-Making*. Berkeley: University of California Press, 1983.

Siracusa, Joseph M. *Into the Dark House: American Diplomacy and the Ideological Origins of the Cold War*. Claremont, CA: Regina Books, 1998.

Spalding, Elizabeth Edwards. *The First Cold Warrior: Harry Truman, Containment, and the Remaking of Liberal Internationalism*. Lexington: University Press of Kentucky, 2006.

Steininger, Rolf, and Mark Cioc. *The German Question: The Stalin Note of 1952 and the Problem of Reunification*. New York: Columbia University Press, 1990.

Stueck, William Whitney. *Rethinking the Korean War: A New Diplomatic and Strategic History*. Princeton, NJ: Princeton University Press, 2002.

Tarling, Nicholas. *Britain, Southeast Asia and the Onset of the Cold War, 1945–1950*. Cambridge: Cambridge University Press, 1998.

Taylor, Peter J. *Britain and the Cold War: 1945 as Geopolitical Transition*. London: Pinter, 1990.

Trachtenberg, Marc. *A Constructed Peace: The Making of the European Settlement, 1945–1963*. Princeton, NJ: Princeton University Press, 1999.

Tucker, Nancy Bernkopf. *Patterns in the Dust: Chinese-American Relations and the Recognition Controversy, 1949–1950*. New York: Columbia University Press, 1983.

Wagnleitner, Reinhold. *Coca-Colonization and the Cold War: The Cultural Mission of the United States in Austria After the Second World War*. Chapel Hill: University of North Carolina Press, 1994.

Westad, Odd Arne. *Brothers in Arms: The Rise and Fall of the Sino-Soviet Alliance, 1945–1963*. Stanford, CA: Stanford University Press, 1998.

——. *Cold War and Revolution: Soviet-American Rivalry and the Origins of the Chinese Civil War, 1944–1946*. New York: Columbia University Press, 1993.

Wettig, Gerhard. *Stalin and the Cold War in Europe: The Emergence and Development of East-West Conflict, 1939–1953*. Lanham, MD: Rowman and Littlefield, 2008.

Yergin, Daniel. *Shattered Peace: The Origins of the Cold War and the National Security State*. Boston: Houghton Mifflin, 1977.

Young, John W. *France, the Cold War, and the Western Alliance, 1944–49: French Foreign Policy and Post-War Europe*. New York: St. Martin's, 1990.

Zubkova, Elena. *Russia After the War: Hopes, Illusions, and Disappointments, 1945–1957*. Translated by Hugh Ragsdale. Armonk, NY: M. E. Sharpe, 1998.

Zubok, V. M., and Konstantin Pleshakov. *Inside the Kremlin's Cold War: From Stalin to Khrushchev*. Cambridge, MA: Harvard University Press, 1996.

Chapter 4
THE WIDENING CONFLICT, 1953–1963

To govern is always to choose among disadvantages.

—Charles de Gaulle

Events are not a matter of choice.

—Gamal Abdel Nasser

In the decade following the carnage of World War II and Korea, most of the world experienced an extraordinary economic recovery as well as a striking diffusion of ideas and technology and record rates of population and GDP growth. In the noncommunist countries the Bretton Woods system created stable currencies and exchange rates, the General Agreement on Tariffs and Trade (GATT) smoothed international commerce, and the IMF and World Bank began pouring resources into Africa, Asia, and Latin America, which provided the West with cheap and crucial raw materials. The Soviet Union, with the exception of its ties to China and North Korea, was slower than the United States to engage in trade outside its borders.

Europe's revival was spectacular. In Western Europe, where the Marshall Plan had poured $13 billion into its recipients' economies, a neo-Keynesian economic order was established in which governments used public spending and monetary policies to maintain strong and balanced economic growth. The Soviet Union and Eastern Europe, although constrained by tight financial, trade, and currency regulations, also made remarkable technological, industrial, and infrastructural gains.

Postwar Europe was nonetheless split by an Iron Curtain not only with barbed wire, mines, guard dogs, and machine guns but also with substantial political, material, and spiritual barriers. In communist Eastern Europe, up to Stalin's death there had been major efforts to "engineer human souls" by emulating Soviet models promoting a socialist language, education, science, and aesthetics and rejecting decadent Western ways. The United States parried Moscow's utopian message by exporting its consumer products, popular culture, and liberal political ideals. The most striking site of East-West cultural competition was in the rebuilding of Berlin. On one side of Hitler's former capital rose the Stalinallee, a two-kilometer long, eighty-nine-meter wide boulevard with its monumental eight-story structures in the socialist-classicist style, and on the other the Hansaviertel, a neighborhood of brightly colored residential buildings designed by the world's foremost architects in the international style.*

Both Superpowers used propaganda to penetrate their enemy's territory. From the Kremlin came torrents of upbeat economic reports and antifascist diatribes as well as attacks on Western racism, capitalism, warmongering, and imperialism, which were echoed by Communist Party leaders and adherents in the West. The other side sent radio broadcasts in the national languages of Eastern Europe from the Voice of America, Radio Free Europe, and the BBC with news from the outside world; these encouraged the "captive populations" to seek freedom from Moscow's domination.

The Iron Curtain was porous in other ways. Not only did Western and communist diplomats, businessmen, church groups, and labor unions maintain regular contacts, but by the mid-1950s a number of cross-border cultural, scientific, and university exchanges as well as sports competitions, although never removed from politics, established solid networks between East and West. Images and personalities also counted. Despite a decade of intense Cold War rivalry between their two governments, Soviet and American citizens were equally delirious over the twenty-three-year-old Texan Van Cliburn's triumph in Moscow's first Tchaikovsky piano competition, held in April 1958.

Two new leaders appeared on the scene. The new US president, Dwight David Eisenhower, was a veteran of two world wars, the architect of D-Day, and

---

* The international chain of Hilton hotels built in the 1950s also conveyed a cultural message. Conrad Hilton, whom the US State and Commerce Departments had encouraged to build his chain of grandiose pleasure palaces in the major cities of the world as "Little Americas," called his modernist structure in West Berlin in 1958 "a new weapon with which to fight communism, a new team of owner, manager, and labor to confront the class conscious Mr. Marx."

NATO supreme commander between 1950 and 1952; he came to office in 1953 promising a tougher stance toward the Soviet Union. The new Soviet chief Nikita Khrushchev was a Ukrainian-born metalworker who had served as a political commissar in the Red Army during the civil war, had risen rapidly through Communist Party ranks, and was again a commissar on the Ukrainian front in World War II. As party first secretary after Stalin's death he deftly outmaneuvered his rivals Malenkov and Beria to attain almost complete power over the Soviet Union by 1955.

The other Cold War players fell into two camps. Whereas most European leaders* had been born in the nineteenth century, almost all the non-Europeans† had come to political maturity during World War II and had imbibed the promises of freedom and independence in the Atlantic Charter. The generational split was also evident in the cultural sphere. In both parts of Europe young writers and musicians began challenging their elders' political and moral evasions under Hitler and Stalin and attempted to escape the Cold War straitjacket by embracing the romanticism and spirituality of the hero of Boris Pasternak's novel *Dr. Zhivago* (1958) or the gruff unruly individualism of Oskar Matzerath in Günter Grass's novel *The Tin Drum* (1959). Outside Europe, a new generation espoused the proud rebelliousness of Chinua Achebe's protagonist Okonkwo in *Things Fall Apart* (1959), which shattered the image of "primitive" Africa and of its elders' submission to imperialism.

The world of the 1950s drew closer through radio, via the new medium of television, and especially in the movie houses. The filmmakers of that decade produced striking universal narratives of love and violence, death and heroism, memory and forgetfulness, the strength of family bonds, the struggle against consumerism, and the power of myth and music.‡ Regional and foreign travel

---

* Among them FRG Chancellor Konrad Adenauer (born in 1876), the GDR party chief Walter Ulbricht (born in 1893), French president Charles de Gaulle (born in 1890), British prime ministers Anthony Eden (born in 1897) and Harold Macmillan (born in 1894), and Yugoslav prime minister Josip Broz Tito (born in 1892).

† Among them Ahmed Sukarno (born in 1901) of Indonesia, Habib Bourguiba (born in 1903) of Tunisia, Kwame Nkrumah (born in 1909) of Ghana, Gamal Abdel Nasser (born in 1918) of Egypt, Nelson Mandela (born in 1918) of South Africa, and Fidel Castro (born in 1926) of Cuba. Important exceptions included Indian prime minister Jawaharal Nehru (born in 1889), Iranian prime minister Mohammad Mossadeq (born in 1882), and Kenyan revolutionary and first prime minister Jomo Kenyatta (born in 1894).

‡ These references are to the films *La Strada*, directed by Federico Fellini (Rome: Ponti-De Laurentiis Cinematografica, 1954); *The Seventh Seal*, directed by Ingmar Bergman (Stockholm: Svesnk Filmindustri, 1957); *Hiroshima, mon amour*, directed by Alain Resnais (Paris: Argos Films, 1959); *Pather Panchali*, directed by Satyajit Ray (Kolkata: Government of West Bengal,

brought people together and created lasting bonds. From the glittering Sixth World Festival of Youth and Students in Moscow, held in July 1957 and attended by thirty-four thousand young people from all over the globe, came the prize-winning song "Moscow Nights" ("Podmoskovnye Vechera"), which transcended its Soviet origins to become a worldwide romantic anthem.

Popular movements spread throughout the globe. The United States in the 1950s gave the world rock and roll and blue jeans, the Beatnik lifestyle and the impudent figure of the Cat in the Hat, as well as the brave spirit and voices of its civil rights movement. Humanitarianism also connected rival nations. From Great Britain in 1959 emerged World Refugee Year, an international effort sponsored by the UN and joined by fifty-four countries in an effort to end the refugee problem through widespread publicity and innovative fundraising, political mobilization and private charitable efforts.

But the Cold War also intruded into popular culture. Some of the most striking moments occurred during the 1956 Sixteenth Summer Olympic Games in Melbourne, Australia. Not only were these the first televised games and the first to be held outside Europe and North America, but they also stood in the shadow of the Suez crisis and the Soviet invasion of Hungary (described later in this chapter).[*]

A GLOBAL COLD WAR

It was inevitable that the Superpower rivalry would spread beyond Europe, where the Cold War had reached a stalemate. Neither Washington's "New Look"—the increased production of nuclear weapons and B-52 bombers to provide greater military capability at reduced cost—nor the extensive covert activities of the CIA were capable of rolling back the Soviet Empire in Eastern Europe. Indeed, the United States could only watch passively on June 17, 1953, when Soviet tanks crushed the East German protesters whom American propaganda had encouraged to break their chains. Similarly, Khrushchev, despite the Soviet Union's

---

1955); *Mon Oncle*, directed by Jacques Tati (Paris: Specta Films, 1958); and *Black Orpheus*, directed by Marcel Camus (Rio de Janeiro: Dispat Films, 1959).

[*] The Suez crisis in October–November delayed the torch relay from Greece to Australia, and the International Olympic Committee turned back calls by several Arab nations to bar Israel, France, and Britain from participating in the games.

Even more dramatic was the response to the Soviet invasion of Hungary. Spain, Switzerland, and the Netherlands boycotted the games. And at the notorious foul-ridden Soviet-Hungarian water polo match on December 6 the Hungarians won four goals to nil; the photograph of a blood-covered Hungarian athlete became a worldwide sensation.

increasingly impressive nuclear accomplishments, quickly recognized Moscow's inability to dislodge the United States from Western Europe or to thwart the resurrection of an economically and politically strong West Germany, its entry into NATO, and its rearmament.

The former colonial world was a more promising arena for US-Soviet competition. With their large populations, crucial raw materials, and strategically important locations, Third World* countries represented a prime arena to launch a global contest between capitalism and communism. Beginning in 1953 Washington and Moscow, eager to supplant European control while advertising their own anti-imperialist credentials, formulated two rival economic development models accompanied by generous military and civilian aid packages and goodwill gestures (from student scholarships to high-level government visits) to attract the elites in the colonial and semicolonial states of Asia, the Middle East, Africa, and Latin America. Both deployed their overseas intelligence agencies, the Central Intelligence Agency (CIA) and the KGB, to enlist allies and informants in the Third World, monitor political movements and foreign governments, and penetrate their rivals' activities.

Both sides entered this global competition with assets and liabilities, and both approached the Third World with a combination of ambition, altruism, and fear of the other's gains. The United States, brimming with confidence over its role in rebuilding Western Europe and Japan, sought to extend its political influence by supporting the expansion of free markets and elected governments. The Soviet Union, which had revived spectacularly after World War II as a major military and industrial power, countered the West's appeal with its call for centralized planning and a regime that promoted social and economic justice.

The United States embarked on this contest with a mixed record. Observers were distressed by the wave of virulent anticommunism that swept the country in the early 1950s and the bleak condition of its African American citizens. Abroad, America's "pactomania,"† its hostility toward nonalignment, and its tendency to intervene in the affairs of its neighbors far and near raised alarm among

---

* This term, evoking the underrepresented Third Estate in the French political order on the eve of the revolution in 1789, was first used in 1952 by the radical French economist Alfred Sauvy to characterize the aspirations of the world's less powerful, more populous states to achieve the recognition and respect of the dominant minority. But by the 1960s the expression "Third World" also came to represent a group of states distinct from the capitalist West and the communist bloc.

† The name given to the Eisenhower administration's efforts to link the United States with strategic areas of the world, forming alliances with forty-two states and treaty relations with nearly one hundred.

Third World leaders. Particularly damaging to Washington's reputation were the coups engineered by the Central Intelligence Agency against two elected foreign governments: in Iran in 1953, toppling a prime minister who had nationalized the country's oil industry and returning Shah Mohammad Reza Pahlavi to power, and in Guatemala in 1954, replacing the popular left-wing president Jacobo Árbenz Guzmán, who had advocated extensive land reform and the expropriation of undeveloped foreign property, with a more compliant regime. The stereotype of the "Ugly American" was made famous by the 1958 novel and 1963 film depicting the US government's clumsy efforts to outdo the communists in the rural hamlets of Southeast Asia.

The Soviet Union's forays outside its borders were also fraught with problems. Echoing Lenin's call for a global struggle against Western colonialism and neocolonialism, the USSR in the mid-1950s launched an ambitious foreign aid program in the Third World.* But at home, this initiative created problems, straining Moscow's economic and financial resources at a time when Khrushchev was vowing to raise living standards and expand the Soviets' military and nuclear capacity. Abroad, Khrushchev's courtship of noncommunist Third World governments and his endorsement of a "hybrid" form of noncapitalist development (integrating state and private initiatives) weakened and disheartened Marxist militants in Egypt, Iran, Burma, India, and Indonesia. But above all, Khrushchev's initiative left the Kremlin vulnerable to manipulation by ambitious Third World leaders and to a bidding contest with the wealthier West.

By the 1950s European imperialism was in full retreat in Asia, the Middle East, and North Africa. A spectacular note was sounded on May 7, 1954, when, after an almost two-month siege, the communist-led Vietnamese forces, backed by China, defeated the US-supported French army at Diên Biên Phu.† On July 21 the Geneva Accords ended more than six decades of French rule in Indochina. Laos and Cambodia became independent, and Vietnam, temporarily partitioned along the seventeenth parallel, was to hold national elections two years hence.‡

---

* Over the next fifteen years, Moscow extended some $4 billion in military and economic assistance to thirty-five countries, which included the dispatch of thousands of Soviet technicians, the granting of low-interest loans, and support for three giant development projects: the Bhilai steel complex in India, transport facilities and power plants in Afghanistan, and the construction of the Aswan High Dam in Egypt.

† By 1954, the United States was supplying 78 percent of France's war materiel, but Eisenhower refused French pleas to use US air power, including tactical nuclear weapons, to lift the siege.

‡ Recent research in the Vietnamese archives has modified earlier accounts of Ho Chi Minh's reluctant acceptance of partition because of Chinese and Russian pressure (neither wishing

France's disaster at Diên Biên Phu reverberated throughout the colonial world, particularly in French Algeria, where a nationalist insurrection erupted on November 1, 1954. Unlike Morocco and Tunisia (which it would grant independence in 1956), the French government was determined to maintain control over its largest possession, which had a million European inhabitants, immense natural resources, and more than a century of political, economic, and cultural ties with France. After the Soviet Union and China in 1955 endorsed the FLN (the Front de Libération Nationale, or National Liberation Front), the union of Algeria's revolutionary factions, France, brandishing the specter of communism in North Africa, appealed for Washington's aid. But the Eisenhower administration responded cautiously, wavering between support for its NATO ally and fears of alienating the Muslim world, between America's decade-long Cold War reflexes and its growing recognition of a new world of emerging nations that were determined to avoid falling into either the communist or the Western camp.*

At the 1955 Bandung Conference, delegates representing twenty-nine states in Africa and Asia (one-fourth of the world's land surface and 1.5 billion people) had declared their "common detestation of colonialism" and their adherence to the principles of nonalignment.† The ten-point Bandung declaration reaffirmed the charter of the United Nations, in all of whose agencies Asian and African members were now playing a major role, and also the Universal Declaration of Human Rights. The Bandung meeting was a pivotal moment in the creation of a Third World identity. It drew an immediate endorsement from the Soviet Union, but one of its principal participants was communist China, which under its own revolutionary, anticolonial banner, was now vying with Moscow in the former colonial world.

Faced with rising Third World self-confidence, the United States began to reduce its hostility toward nonalignment (which Secretary of State John Foster Dulles had earlier denounced as "morally bankrupt"). Washington began to recognize the

---

to prolong the fighting and reignite Cold War tensions with the United States). Because of his heavy losses, the need to consolidate his rule over the north, and the favorable prospects of winning the 1956 elections and unifying the entire country peacefully, Ho (perhaps making the best of a difficult political situation) claimed he had gained a "big victory" (*thang loi lon*) with the Geneva Accords.

* Significantly, the USSR was also cautious over Algeria. Khrushchev, who was attempting to woo France away from NATO, tempered his military support for the FLN with assurances of nonintervention in the "internal affairs of the French Union" and held off political recognition of the Algerian nationalists for several years.

† Despite the participants' claims of their inclusiveness, several countries were excluded from Bandung because their presence would have been divisive: Israel, South Africa, and Taiwan as well as North and South Korea.

Photo 4.1. India's future leader, Indira Gandhi, and her father, Prime Minister Jawaharlal Nehru, returning from the meeting hall of the Asian-African Conference in Bandung, Indonesia, April 1955. *Courtesy of Corbis.*

diminishing appeal of its multilateral security pacts, which had become tainted with a neocolonial label. In line with its earlier acceptance of Tito's socialist form of neutralism, the United States—in order to compete effectively with the Soviets in Asia and Africa—began to woo independent Third World leaders.

Vietnam was an exception. The Eisenhower administration, which had refused to sign the Geneva Accords, feared a communist victory in the national elections and a domino effect throughout Southeast Asia. After the French withdrawal, the United States proceeded to build up a client state in the south, allowing President Ngô Đình Diệm to cancel the 1956 elections and to clamp down on his opponents. Contrary to the Geneva Accords, which had forbidden the Vietnamese from entering foreign alliances or allowing foreign troops, Dulles mobilized the US-led Southeast Asia Treaty Organization to agree to protect South Vietnam against communist aggression. When a popular insurgency, which Diệm contemptuously labeled Viet Cong (Vietnamese communists), erupted in the south two years later and received support from the north, Eisenhower expanded US economic and military aid and personnel on the ground.*

---

* Between 1955 and 1961 the United States poured more than $1 billion in economic and military aid to the Diệm regime, and by the time Eisenhower left office there were approximately one thousand US military advisers in South Vietnam.

HUNGARY

Nikita Khrushchev appeared to be a new Soviet boss. Seeking to counteract West Germany's entry into NATO, the Soviet Union in May 1955 concluded the Warsaw Pact with its seven East European satellites, tying them tightly to the Kremlin and expanding Moscow's voice in European affairs. But in that same year, Khrushchev also emitted conciliatory signals, reestablishing relations with renegade Yugoslavia, withdrawing Soviet forces from Austria, returning Soviet captured bases to China and Finland, and establishing diplomatic relations with the Federal Republic of Germany, including the repatriation of the remaining ten thousand German prisoners of war still held in the Soviet Union. At the Geneva Big Four meeting of Britain, France, the United States, and the USSR, ten years after the last Allied summit in 1945, Khrushchev uttered the words "peaceful coexistence."

There were more surprises. Shortly after midnight on February 25, 1956, Khrushchev shook the communist faithful with his four-hour-long secret speech to the Twentieth Party Congress of the Soviet Union, in which he denounced Stalin's crimes: the self-glorification and the cult of the individual that violated Leninist principles of collective leadership, the terror tactics against his enemies, the ruinous errors during the Great Patriotic War, the hideous postwar purges, and Stalin's "suspicion and haughtiness [toward] whole parties and nations."

Khrushchev's secret speech, accompanied by the dissolution of the Cominform in April, and Tito's visit to Moscow in June 1956 seemed to point to major reforms in the Soviet empire, but the new Soviet leader had no such intention. In response to nationwide anti-Soviet demonstrations in Poland between June and October and the return of the renegade Władysław Gomułka, Khrushchev planned a Soviet military strike, backtracking only in return for Polish assurances that the existing communist power structure would remain intact and the country would remain in the Warsaw Pact.

The Hungarian revolution posed an even greater challenge. By mid-October Hungary's massive anti-Soviet demonstrations led by students, soldiers, writers, and workers had led to the disintegration of communist control. The newly appointed prime minister, Imre Nagy, a moderate party man who lacked Gomułka's political agility, was swept along by the revolutionaries, suddenly announcing a multiparty system and Hungary's withdrawal from the communist bloc.

The danger to Moscow was clear. An independent Hungary threatened to create a physical wedge in the Soviet Union's East European empire, encourage

Photo 4.2. Street scene in Budapest after a battle between Soviet tanks and Hungarian protesters, November 1, 1956. *Courtesy of Corbis.*

imitators, and create a domino effect that would menace the homeland. Khrushchev, after a period of hesitation on the night of October 31 at the height of the Suez crisis (see the next section), gave the order to intervene militarily and reestablish reliable communist rule in Budapest.

The cost was substantial. Some 640 Soviet soldiers were killed and 1,251 wounded; on the Hungarian side were 2,000 dead, tens of thousands wounded, some 35,000 arrested, 22,000 incarcerated, 200 executed (among them Imre Nagy in 1958), and over 200,000 people who fled the country. Not only was Khrushchev's stature at home and abroad greatly diminished, but he forced his country to assume the economic and political burdens of pacifying millions of resentful East European subjects through military occupation and with a less austere, more consumer-oriented ("goulash") communism.

The Western public reacted strongly to the images of Soviet tanks crushing a popular uprising. Their governments promptly accepted thousands of refugees, and in a taunt to diehard Western leftists, the French political philosopher Raymond Aron declared in October 1956 that the Soviet Union was merely a "long-term despotism" that was doomed to fail.

Yet the United States, whose secretary of state John Foster Dulles for several years had preached the rollback of communism in Eastern Europe, had also suffered a moral defeat. Until the last moment, its paid radio broadcasters had imprudently encouraged the revolutionaries' belief that outside support was imminent. Eisenhower, in the final days of his second presidential campaign and absorbed by the Suez crisis, was unwilling to risk a nuclear war over Hungary. Indeed, prior to the invasion Washington had sent reassuring signals to Moscow and declined to raise a protest in the United Nations. After the revolt was crushed and his reelection sealed, Eisenhower combined expressions of sympathy for the Hungarians' plight with open acceptance of a divided and stable Europe, thus dispelling the myth of liberation and taking the first step toward détente in Europe.

Indeed, after 1956 the Cold War in Europe did change its face. The ideological confrontation became less aggressive. The doctrine of peaceful coexistence, repeated by Khrushchev at the Twentieth Party Congress, facilitated cultural exchanges between East and West. Westerners gradually discovered the films, literature, music, art, and scholarship from behind the Iron Curtain, while Soviet and East European citizens, increasingly exposed to Western visitors and ideas, continued to hope for less repressive, more humane socialism.

Although Moscow had secured its East European empire in 1956, its control over the world communist movement was diminishing. There were still loyalists to Stalin, such as the eighty-eight-year-old African American political philosopher W. E. B. Du Bois, who pronounced Khrushchev's criticisms "irresponsible and muddled" and blamed the upheavals in Eastern Europe on US meddling. There were also new renegades, such as the Comintern veteran Palmiro Togliatti, leader of Italy's second-largest party, who coined the term "polycentrism" to distance himself from the Kremlin's dictates, and the Yugoslav dictator Tito, who again escaped Moscow's clutches by embracing nonalignment.

The strongest response came from Beijing. Not only were Mao Zedong and Khrushchev mistrustful comrades, but the Chinese leader was appalled by the general secretary's de-Stalinization campaign that had led to the tumult in Poland and Hungary. Stung by Moscow's arrogance, tough economic terms, and lack of enthusiasm for liberating Taiwan, Mao also decided to pursue a more independent path.

SUEZ

By 1956, only four years after toppling the corrupt and ineffective King Farouk, Egypt's second president and virtual dictator, the thirty-six-year-old Colonel Gamal Abdel Nasser had become a major figure in international affairs. A champion of pan-Arabism, he aimed to build up Egypt and liberate the Middle East from the last vestiges of European colonialism. He had won Britain's agreement to withdraw its eighty thousand troops from the Suez Canal Zone, played a starring role at the Bandung conference, and defied the West with a spectacular arms deal with communist Czechoslovakia in 1955 and the establishment of diplomatic relations with the People's Republic of China in 1956.

By 1956 Nasser's feats had also raised alarm. Israeli leaders, worried over their neighbor's acquisition of sophisticated Eastern-bloc weapons, the escalating border violence, and the hostile propaganda emanating from Cairo radio, contemplated a preemptive strike. They found a kindred spirit in France, where the Guy Mollet government was obsessed with Nasser's support of the Algerian revolution. And Britain's prime minister, Anthony Eden, furious over Nasser's attempts to undermine British interests in Iraq and Jordan, viewed the Egyptian leader as an "Arab Mussolini" intent on using Soviet aid to dominate the Middle East and to threaten Western Europe's oil supplies.

The Superpowers were ineluctably drawn in. One year earlier, the United States, hoping to gain influence in the largest Arab state, had agreed to a generous $54 million loan to support the building of the Aswan High Dam. However, by the spring of 1956 Eisenhower had grown wary of Nasser's flirtation with Moscow, his anti-Western statements, and his hostility toward Israel. Khrushchev on the other hand—despite his nod to noncapitalist development—was absorbed in the tumult in Eastern Europe and skeptical of the dam project and therefore declined Nasser's request to enter a bidding contest with Washington. Suddenly, on July 19, an exasperated and suspicious Eisenhower withdrew the US loan, and Eden readily vacated Britain's $14 million offer as well.

Shocked and humiliated, Nasser took action, announcing the nationalization of the Suez Canal to pay for the dam, stirring his compatriots, electrifying the Arab world, and triggering a prolonged international crisis. In a stroke, Nasser had attained a commanding position over the lifeline of Britain's commonwealth and empire and over one of two principal routes of Middle Eastern oil deliveries to the West. With the closure of the Strait of Tiran, he had also gained a chokehold on Israel's maritime ties with East Africa and Asia.

The Superpowers' responses were a study in contrast. Khrushchev, caught off balance by what he termed Nasser's "ill-timed" move, neither spread a Soviet diplomatic mantle over Egypt nor offered additional arms, expecting the United States to rein in its allies. Thus during the next three months Eisenhower took the lead, striving to prevent an attack on Egypt, which, he was convinced, would destabilize the Middle East and encourage further Soviet moves into the region.

Pitted against the US president were his two agitated NATO partners: France, smarting over the loss of Indochina and the Algerian uprising and with a popular opinion solidly behind punishing Nasser, and Britain, with a divided cabinet and parliament and almost unanimous commonwealth opposition to the use of force, but led by an ailing and impulsive prime minister determined to assert his nation's power and protect its oil supply. Israel played a crucial role. Prime Minister Ben Gurion, who had vacillated out of fear of US or Soviet intervention, was won over by militant cabinet members with the prospect of joining a Western alliance. In early October Eden agreed to Mollet's audacious scheme for an Israeli invasion of Egypt as a cover for an Anglo-French seizure of the canal and the toppling of Nasser. Israel's agreement to strike first was sealed in a secret pact with France and Britain signed at Sèvres on October 24, 1956.

Operation Musketeer began smoothly. On October 29 Israeli paratroops landed in the central Sinai and quickly reached the Suez Canal. One day later Britain and France issued a twelve-hour ultimatum demanding that *both* sides withdraw from the Canal Zone; when Nasser refused, on October 31 they bombarded Egyptian airfields, and after a five-day delay, their troops began ground operations. In the meantime Nasser had responded on November 1 by blocking the canal with blown-up craft and equipment. During that explosive week a wave of outrage swept the world, almost obliterating the dire news from Hungary.

It was now up to the Superpowers. Khrushchev was again taken unaware, having been lulled through October by Nasser's overconfidence, faulty Soviet intelligence, and his underestimation of Eden's resolve. Once hostilities began, Khrushchev, absorbed by Hungary, ignored Nasser's pleas for military or diplomatic support, leaving the way open for US management of the crisis. Eisenhower, furious over his allies' deception, was determined to halt the aggression against Egypt and to do so before Moscow acted. The United States called on the United Nations, and after an Anglo-French veto blocked action by the Security Council, the General Assembly on November 1 voted 64–5 in favor of an immediate cease-fire. In an extraordinary Cold War moment, Soviet and American aims had become identical and the United Nations became a site of peacemaking.

Both Superpowers overplayed their hands. With the Hungarian uprising almost crushed, Khrushchev on November 5 warned Eden, Mollet, and Ben Gurion that the Soviet Union was prepared to use its nuclear weapons "to crush the aggression and to restore peace in the Middle East." Eisenhower, who had applied heavy political and economic pressure on the three belligerents, won both a second term and a cease-fire on November 6 and then took the lead in transporting a UN Emergency Force to Egypt and pressuring the invaders to withdraw their armies.

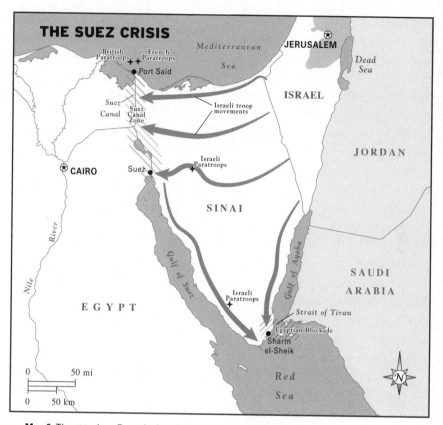

Map 9. The attack on Egypt by Israel, France, and Great Britain, October–November 1956.

Khrushchev's saber rattling was alarming, but America's desertion of its allies drew even heavier criticism at home and abroad. A humiliated Eden resigned, forcing Washington to reassure Britain and other NATO members of US protection and goodwill. France was even more disaffected over Eden's yielding to Washington and Eisenhower's nonchalance over Khrushchev's threats. Musketeer's author, Guy Mollet, resigned in May 1957, and the Suez fiasco undoubtedly prepared the way for the reemergence one year later of Charles de Gaulle, a leader imbued with a profound distrust of the Anglo-Saxons and determined to ensure France's national security outside a US-dominated NATO and to build its own nuclear force.

The Suez crisis also produced the West's first oil crisis. Almost immediately after Nasser blocked the canal, other Arab governments moved to choke the West's oil supply. Syria severed diplomatic relations with Britain and France, and the pipeline carrying oil through its territory from Iraq to the Mediterranean was immediately disabled when three of its pumping stations were blown up, reportedly by units of the Syrian army. On November 6 Saudi Arabia also broke its ties with the aggressors and banned tankers from carrying its oil to Britain or France. Everything now depended on the United States, still a major oil producer and exporter as well as home to five of the seven multinational oil companies. An incensed Eisenhower refused to relieve his allies' mounting oil shortages or rescue the plummeting British and French currencies until they withdrew their armies from Egypt.

To be sure, the oil scare had little impact at the time. Once Britain and France had caved in, the United States helped ease the delivery problem, and Anglo-American oil companies resumed their cooperation. Moreover, higher energy prices reduced consumption, and the unusually warm winter in Europe in 1956–1957 softened the impact of diminished supplies. By March 1957, the canal had been cleared, the pipelines repaired, and rationing ended in Western Europe. Worldwide oil production increased, and prices fell dramatically. Nonetheless, the specter of future shortages that could threaten the West's security, halt its industries, and bring hardship to its population had presented itself in 1956, along with the lessons of US dominance over supplies and the Arabs' willingness to use this weapon.

Israel, which had demonstrated its military prowess, emerged stronger from the Suez crisis. It now had a French ally willing to supply arms and even nuclear material. With strong French support it had secured an international guarantee of naval passage through the Strait of Tiran as well as a UN force to protect it against guerrilla raids from Egypt, although both gains were dependent on Nasser's compliance. On the other hand, the exiled Palestinian leadership based in Gaza, which had witnessed the Egyptians' rout firsthand, had become more determined than ever to pursue their goal of national liberation and sought more substantial Arab support. Israel's relations with Washington had also soured: the United States had forced Israel to relinquish the prizes of its stunning victory—the capture of Gaza and the Sinai from Egypt—and to recognize its minor role in Eisenhower's political calculations.

The Cold War had now spread into the Middle East. In the beginning of 1957 Eisenhower—echoing Truman ten years earlier—announced a new US doctrine, pledging military and financial aid to Arab countries threatened by the "spread of communism." But Washington overestimated the Arabs' fear of communism and underestimated their nationalism and political divisions along with their hatred of colonialism and of Israel. Meanwhile, Moscow, fixated on securing a foothold in a strategically important region, overestimated its resources and its influence over the Arabs and underestimated the US resolve to replace Great Britain as the major power in the region. The Suez crisis had demonstrated the readiness of Middle East actors to use the Superpowers but also the latter's insufficient knowledge and understanding of the region's populations and politics.

THE NUCLEAR QUESTION

The best-selling 1957 novel *On the Beach* by the Anglo-Australian writer Nevil Shute was set in a world devastated by nuclear war. In that year the Superpowers had accumulated enough weapons not only to annihilate each other but also to make the globe uninhabitable.

Khrushchev's nuclear bluff in November 1956 had been the threat of an underdog. The United States still held a clear superiority in strategic weapons: with nuclear bombs and long-range bombers outnumbering the USSR by a ratio of approximately 11:1. Moreover, the United States had encircled the Soviet Union with a chain of bases housing its Strategic Air Command bombers, which included 1,000 B47s, 150 B52s, and 250 B36s and were complemented by a worldwide fleet of aircraft carriers capable of launching long-range bombers from practically everywhere. Thus in 1956 the Soviet Union, with fewer bombs and aircraft, was vulnerable to a US first strike or a retaliatory attack, while the United States was still sheltered by numbers, distance, and a superior surveillance system.

Khrushchev was determined to overcome the Soviets' inferiority. Alongside his calls for peaceful coexistence, he ordered a buildup in Soviet bombs and bombers and launched the development of intercontinental ballistic missiles (ICBMs). With the appearance of the *Sputnik* satellite in 1957, thrust into space by a long-range Soviet rocket, the United States mainland suddenly became vulnerable to attack. Civil defense programs, which had already begun earlier in the decade, made Americans aware that Soviet rockets could now target any place on the globe. The Eisenhower administration hastened to regain US superiority by launching an ambitious space and missile program and providing government subsidies for higher education, especially in scientific and technical fields.

Europe stood precariously between the two Superpowers, and the Iron Curtain was its pervasive reality. Khrushchev's threats in November 1956 and Eisenhower's bland response had exposed Western Europe's weakness. Despite the latter's growing economic strength and the turmoil within the Soviet satellite nations, the Warsaw Pact's ground forces outnumbered NATO's by a ratio of about 6:1. Once mobilized and committed to war they could not be stopped before they reached the Rhine, even with the use of tactical nuclear weapons. Moreover, few West European leaders believed that the United States would expose its territory to retaliation by launching a nuclear strike against the Soviet Union.

West Europeans began to question two Cold War axioms: Was America's nuclear umbrella reliable, or should their governments act more independently in their own defense? Did US bases endanger their crowded population centers and necessitate a reconsideration of NATO membership?

East Europeans raised questions as well. In a speech to the UN General Assembly on October 2, 1957, Polish foreign minister Adam Rapacki called for the de-nuclearization of Central Europe, which would have blocked the stationing of Soviet bases in Poland and Czechoslovakia as well as US bases in West Germany. Washington, although recognizing the significance of this independent initiative, promptly denounced the plan as a threat to NATO's nuclear shield, a nonsolution to the German question, and a solidification of the Iron Curtain.

A global nuclear disarmament movement began to swell in the 1950s, drawing on memories of Hiroshima and Nagasaki, challenging the accelerating US-Soviet arms race, and bringing together people of different ages, races, and ideologies to demand a world free from the fear of a nuclear catastrophe.

BUILDING EUROPE

Among the most anxious witnesses to the Hungarian and Suez crises was West German chancellor Konrad Adenauer. The Federal Republic, NATO's newest member, had declared its neutrality in the war against Egypt, but it had been jarred by the Soviets' brutal repression in Hungary and by Moscow's threats to London and Paris as well as by America's cavalier treatment of its principal European allies. Seizing the moment of his arrival in Paris on November 6, just as the cease-fire was announced, Adenauer urged his hosts to work together to "build Europe."

The project of European unity had a long history and had gained force after World War II with the Marshall Plan and the European Coal and Steel Community, the 1951 agreement that had brought France, West Germany, Italy, and the Benelux countries (Belgium, Luxembourg, and the Netherlands) together under a common high authority. For more than a year the Benelux project of a Common Market—involving both economic and nuclear cooperation—had languished because of Franco-German hesitations, France over the future role of its empire and Germany caught in an internal debate over chaining itself institutionally and politically to its weaker neighbors.

The Suez crisis brought Bonn and Paris together in 1956 in a historic gesture of real and symbolic reconciliation. Adenauer believed that Western Europe needed to form a counterweight to the Soviet threat and American unilateralism, and Mollet wished to avenge the humiliation of Suez. The Treaty of Rome of March 25, 1957, which brought the European Economic Community (EEC) to life, grew out of a bargain involving substantial concessions to France's overseas territories and a major financial commitment by Bonn, but it was also a clear sign of West Germany's increased role in European affairs.

Britain's future role in Europe was also affected. Eden's successor, Harold Macmillan, accepted Britain's economic and strategic dependency on Washington. He also reduced ties with Paris, repaired the frayed bonds with the British Commonwealth, and acknowledged that the "wind of change" was blowing through Africa. However, EEC membership held little appeal for London. Britain, already a nuclear power, was disinclined to share secrets and techniques with the continent. Moreover, it still sent 74 percent of its exports outside Europe, thus diminishing the attraction of submitting to the tariff and political controls of continental bureaucrats.

The six-member EEC developed into a significant US Cold War ally, although more robust in economic and cultural influence than in its military capabilities. Britain stood out until 1973, until its empire had disappeared and its economic isolation from the continent had weakened it further. In another unanticipated development, the Treaty of Rome not only created a supranational bureaucracy and expanded its members' prosperity but also revived the dream of a whole, united, and democratic Europe that would exert a strong influence across the Iron Curtain.[*]

PEACEFUL COEXISTENCE?

Khrushchev's appeal for peaceful coexistence, echoing Lenin's bid in the early 1920s, had evoked a cautious response from Washington. Indeed, the "spirit of

---

[*] On the other side of Europe was the eight-member Comecon (the Council for Mutual Economic Assistance), founded by Stalin in 1949 in response to the Marshall Plan, charged with regulating economic relations among the socialist states, and dominated by the Soviet Union.

Geneva" in 1955 had rapidly dissipated over Khrushchev's bullying behavior in 1956, the ensuing Soviet arms buildup, and the general secretary's boasts of the future global triumph of socialism. After Khrushchev had rejected Eisenhower's Open Skies proposal* at the Geneva summit, the United States launched an ambitious aerial intelligence-gathering program involving high-altitude photoreconnaissance aircraft (U-2s) as well as the development of reconnaissance satellites to breach the barriers of the Soviets' nuclear program and see beyond Khrushchev's bluster.

The German question remained a fundamental source of contention among the World War II victors. After refusing the West's 1955 proposals for national elections and a united Germany that would maintain links with NATO (with adequate security guarantees for its neighbors), Khrushchev had impulsively committed the USSR to preserving the independence and survival of East Germany (which Stalin had considered merely a Cold War bargaining card), thereby saddling Moscow for more than three decades with the burden of propping up and defending a weak, unpopular regime. Moreover the Berlin problem (the status of the divided former German capital lying one hundred miles inside the GDR) exacerbated East-West tensions. By the mid-1950s West Berlin had become a glittering showcase of capitalist prosperity that provided an easy escape route for almost two million disaffected East Germans. It was also militarily indefensible by its small US, British, and French garrisons—except at the cost of a nuclear war.

On November 10, 1958, Khrushchev provoked another Berlin crisis, emboldened by the successful coup in Iraq (which had overthrown the monarchy and removed that country from the British-organized Baghdad Pact) and by the peaceful outcome of the US-Chinese standoff over the Quemoy and Matsu islands (in which, he believed, his own quiet saber rattling had averted America's nuclear threat to China). Almost ten years after Stalin's failed probe, the Soviet leader threatened to repudiate the four-power occupation regime in Berlin and allow East Germany to control access to West Berlin. In his ultimatum he gave the West six months to negotiate their treaty rights with the German Democratic Republic. Khrushchev's ostensible goal was to stabilize conditions in Central Europe: to crush Bonn's hopes for unification, prop up the faltering GDR, and transform Berlin's western sector—a "bone in the communists' throat"—into an

---

* Aiming at overcoming the Soviets' opposition to on-site inspection, the president had proposed a mutual exchange of blueprints and aerial photoreconnaissance.

Photo 4.3. During Khrushchev's two-week visit to the United States, he and Eisenhower spent three days, September 25–27, 1959, at the presidential retreat of Camp David, where they engaged in frank discussions of Cold War topics. *Courtesy of National Archives.*

unarmed and vulnerable free city that, stripped of Western protection, would inevitably be swallowed by East Germany.

Once more a Soviet leader underestimated US determination to maintain its presence in Berlin. Ignoring British reservations over risking annihilation for the sake of two million former enemies, Eisenhower took a tough stand, exceeding de Gaulle's strong response to Moscow's threat, reassuring an anxious Adenauer, and maintaining West Berlin as a powerful symbol of American credibility. The Berlin crisis temporarily evaporated. In May 1959 Khrushchev let the deadline pass in return for a foreign ministers' conference in August and an invitation to become the first Soviet leader to visit the United States in September.* At their meeting at Camp David, Khrushchev and Eisenhower agreed to put the Berlin problem "on ice" until the summit conference a year later. This represented a clear setback for the Kremlin, which had failed to halt the flight of East Germans westward—some 144,000 in 1959 and 200,000 would flee in 1960. It also raised concern in Beijing over Khrushchev's growing coziness with the capitalists.

The spirit of Camp David was also short-lived. Both Eisenhower and Khrushchev were committed to reducing their nuclear stockpiles, but both were under pressure by their respective militaries to maintain sufficient bombs and missiles—the United States to stay far ahead, the Soviets to catch up—to prevent the other side from exerting nuclear blackmail. Eisenhower, urged by the intelligence community to inspect Khrushchev's new ICBMs, in March 1960 reluctantly approved the resumption of U-2 reconnaissance flights—well aware that violating Soviet air space could compromise his efforts to achieve disarmament. On a particularly poorly chosen date, May 1, the annual celebration of International Workers' Day and a major Soviet holiday, a U-2 was launched from Peshawar, Pakistan, on a 3,800-mile flight over the USSR to have ended in Bodø, Norway. Instead the craft, tracked by Soviet radar, was apparently forced by engine trouble to descend from its impregnable 70,000-feet altitude, and as it approached three of the Soviets' five ICBM launch pads, it was shot down over Sverdlovsk in the Ural Mountains. The pilot, Francis Gary Powers, who had parachuted from the stricken plane, was captured immediately, and the wrecked U-2 plane went on display in Gorky Park near the center of Moscow.†

Only two weeks before the long-awaited four-power Paris summit to discuss Berlin and disarmament, the downing of the U-2 created a sensation. Eisenhower, dismissing his advisers' counsel, on May 11 took full responsibility for the espionage flights, which he deemed a "distasteful but vital necessity" to guard the United States against "massive surprise attacks." Khrushchev, infuriated by the president's admission and determined to defend Soviet skies from foreign surveillance, demanded an apology, which Eisenhower refused. Thereupon the

---

* That summer Khrushchev had held his famous "kitchen debate" with Vice President Richard Nixon at the American National Exhibition in Moscow, the first high-level meeting between the Superpowers since 1955.
† The details of the May 1 crash—how exactly Powers's plane was hit and also his failure to destroy the plane and himself—remain controversial to this day.

general secretary departed Paris on May 18, torpedoing the conference. In a vengeful gesture Khrushchev, en route to Moscow, stopped in East Berlin to reaffirm his commitment to "solving the German problem."

Some observers have suggested that a major opportunity to end the Cold War was lost in May 1960; others strongly disagree. To be sure, neither the United States nor the Soviets were in agreement over the future of Germany; nor could they harmonize their views over disarmament, particularly in light of the pressures each had encountered from within and without. Eisenhower, nearing the end of his second term, had become increasingly alarmed over the power of America's "military-industrial complex," the vast public and private resources allocated to national security. On leaving office he admitted "a definite sense of disappointment" that no "lasting peace [was] in sight."

Khrushchev's efforts toward complete and general disarmament were also opposed, not only by members of the politburo and the Soviet military and intelligence elite but also by Beijing. After the failed Paris summit he marked time until Eisenhower's departure and became more adventurous and truculent, courting Third World leaders, sending aid to the communist guerrilla movement in Laos and to the leftist regime of Patrice Lumumba in the Congo, and treating the world to a shoe-banging performance at the UN General Assembly in September 1960 in protest against the criticisms by the Philippines' delegate of Soviet behavior in Eastern Europe. The stage was thereby set for a new and even more dangerous round of US-Soviet confrontation.

CUBA AND BERLIN

John F. Kennedy's inaugural address on a wintry Friday, January 20, 1961, ushered in a new Cold War decade. The forty-three-year-old president, the first US leader born in the twentieth century, who had won the election by an extremely narrow margin, sent a mixed message. To Americans and the world he announced that "we shall pay any price, bear any burden, meet any hardship, support any friend, oppose any foe, in order to assure the survival and the success of liberty," but he also held out the prospect of renewed disarmament negotiations with the Soviet Union as well as a global alliance to assure "a more fruitful life for all mankind."

Khrushchev initially welcomed the new and pragmatic US leader, with whom he sought to settle the Berlin question once and for all and to continue the search for nuclear disarmament. Over Beijing's strong objections, Washington and

Moscow quietly cooperated in March to obtain a cease-fire in Laos and create a neutral government. In early April Khrushchev and Kennedy agreed to meet in Vienna in June. And on April 12 the Kremlin received another boost when the astronaut Yuri Gagarin became the first man to fly in outer space.

But a new barrier had been raised between the Superpowers. In January 1959 a revolution in Cuba led by the charismatic Fidel Castro had toppled the corrupt, US-backed dictator Fulgencio Batista. After Eisenhower, in retaliation for the nationalization of US landholdings, banks, and industries, imposed a crippling embargo, Castro turned to the Kremlin. Khrushchev in February 1960 grasped the opportunity to challenge the Monroe doctrine and enter the Western Hemisphere, offering to purchase Cuban sugar, grant low-interest loans, and provide substantial arms. Eisenhower, furious at Castro's defiance—made explicit in his four-and-a-half-hour denunciation of "Yankee imperialism" before the September 1960 meeting of the General Assembly—and the appearance of thousands of Soviet technicians and military and diplomatic personnel, broke off relations with Cuba in January 1961 and handed his successor a plan to invade the island and overthrow its leader.

Kennedy, although skeptical, approved the operation. It involved a landing on three beaches of the Bay of Pigs by exiled Cubans, trained by the CIA and US Special Forces, who would ostensibly stir a revolt against Castro's rule. However, at the last minute the new US president called off the air strikes that would have provided cover for the invasion force. Castro's Soviet-supplied tanks and planes easily overwhelmed the invaders, who also had no local guerrilla forces to support their operation. A rueful Kennedy took full responsibility for the Bay of Pigs disaster, in which 1,100 survivors were taken prisoner in Cuba.

America's second humiliation in two years formed the backdrop of the rough Vienna meeting in June 1961. Khrushchev, facing grim economic news at home, the collapse of his client Lumumba's regime in the Congo, and growing Chinese defiance, issued another Berlin ultimatum that sent Kennedy reeling back to Washington searching for an appropriate response. Both sides decided on prudence. Kennedy, disregarding his senior advisers, urged an increase in the US defense budget and called up reserve troops and the National Guard, but he did not declare a national emergency. Khrushchev on his part had decided to avoid a nuclear showdown and to solve the Berlin problem in August 1961 by encasing West Berlin inside a concrete wall. By allowing the East Germans to erect this heavily fortified structure, Khrushchev closed off the last escape route from the Iron Curtain and saved the GDR.

Photo 4.4. East German workers near the Brandenburg Gate reinforce the Berlin Wall dividing the city, October 1961. *Courtesy of National Archives.*

The Western powers' reaction was muted. Although protesting the limitations on inter-Berlin travel and communication, the United States, Britain, and France ultimately accepted the fait accompli that brought stability to the continent by removing the last dispute between Washington and Moscow. As Kennedy famously remarked to his aides, "A wall is a hell of a lot better than a war."

For almost three decades the Berlin Wall became the Cold War's most powerful symbol. In a surrounded West Berlin the West had gained an island outpost: a major intelligence site as well as a precious propaganda tool against communist repression. But for Chancellor Adenauer and West Berlin mayor Willy Brandt, the wall was also proof of America's acquiescence in the division of their homeland and an important spur to pursue a more independent and dynamic German foreign policy.

Once the storm over Berlin had subsided, Khrushchev embarked on an even riskier initiative. By October 1962, with Castro's approval, the USSR had begun construction of thirty-six medium-range missile and twenty-four ICBM sites in Cuba. Alerted by evidence from a U-2 overflight, Kennedy grimly informed the American public, announcing an air and naval "quarantine"* to block the arrival

---

* Kennedy avoided the term "blockade," which, according to international law, signified a state of war.

of additional nuclear armaments to Cuba, and demanding the removal of the existing missile sites while his administration secretly prepared for air strikes and an invasion of Cuba. With thirty Soviet ships headed for Cuba, the moment of a Superpower confrontation and a nuclear war seemed about to occur. Then both sides backed down, with Khrushchev agreeing to withdraw the missiles in return for an American pledge not to invade Cuba and to remove its missiles in Turkey.

For almost a half century US historians characterized Khrushchev's action as an unprovoked threat to the United States and praised Kennedy's courage and restraint in forcing a showdown and a unilateral Soviet withdrawal. However, recent research has modified this narrative. Khrushchev was, in fact, reacting to American aggressiveness toward his ally in Cuba[*] as well as the marked expansion of America's military power after 1961, including the installation of intermediate-range Jupiter nuclear-armed missiles in Turkey that had sparked fears of a first strike against the Soviet Union.[†] By placing the missiles in Cuba Khrushchev had boldly gambled on giving the Americans "a little of their own medicine."

Moreover, Kennedy, despite his public warning over the menace posed by the Soviet missiles, recognized that America's vast nuclear preponderance was unaltered (even if its first-strike capability had now been curtailed). Sensitive to the political fallout over the missiles' presence in Cuba, he responded with a display of brinkmanship that terrified the world, but he also refrained from the military showdown advocated by some of his advisers. And rather than inflicting a humiliating defeat, the president agreed to Khrushchev's terms over the Jupiter missiles.

Instead of stabilizing the Cold War, the near collision between the Superpowers in October 1962 had a problematic outcome. Khrushchev, who had refrained during the crisis from threatening West Berlin, emerged all the more determined to achieve nuclear parity with the United States, whose growing fleet of reconnaissance satellites continued to patrol Soviet skies. And America's NATO allies were less impressed with Kennedy's resolution than stunned over the dangers they had faced because of Washington's unilateral overreaction to a strategically insignificant event.[‡] Indeed, bolstered by their growing economic prosperity—and with the status quo now cemented by the Berlin Wall—West European governments had become less frightened of a Soviet invasion and sought ways of improving relations with the Eastern bloc.

---

[*] Which included assassination plots, sabotage, and large-scale military exercises in the Caribbean aimed at toppling Castro.

[†] Which had been under consideration during the Berlin crisis in 1961.

[‡] In the pithy words of French president de Gaulle: "annihilation without representation."

Photo 4.5. President John F. Kennedy meets in the White House Cabinet Room with members of the Executive Committee of the National Security Council (EXCOMM) regarding the crisis in Cuba. Left to right: Kennedy, Secretary of State Dean Rusk, Secretary of Defense Robert S. McNamara (seated), and White House Press Secretary Pierre Salinger, October 29, 1962. *Courtesy of National Archives.*

The nuclear alarm in October 1962 had the positive effect of prompting renewed efforts for strategic arms control. On June 20, 1963, the hotline agreement established direct communications between the White House and the Kremlin. In August the United States, Great Britain, and the Soviet Union signed a major treaty prohibiting nuclear testing in the atmosphere, in outer space, or at sea. But with the arrival of two new members in the nuclear club—France in 1960 and China in 1964 (which refused to adhere to the test ban)—the specter of proliferation shook Washington and Moscow.

EXIT KENNEDY AND KHRUSHCHEV

With the construction of the Berlin Wall and the removal of the Soviet missiles from Cuba, each Superpower had halted the other's incursions into their proper realms. Moscow's Iron Curtain was reinforced in East Central Europe in 1961, and a year later the United States curtailed the Soviets' military presence in the Western Hemisphere. After testing each other's nerve and mettle—and taking the world to the brink of a nuclear war—John F. Kennedy and Nikita Khrushchev suddenly disappeared from the international scene within a year of each other.

John Kennedy, who was assassinated in November 1963, left an ambiguous Cold War legacy. In his June 1963 American University commencement address he had expressed optimism over achieving peaceful coexistence with the Soviet Union. But within two weeks he set out to Europe to reassure his NATO allies of America's commitment to their defense (while also appealing for a greater contribution on their part), and in West Berlin he denounced the brutal system on the other side of the wall and chided those who believed "we can work with the communists." Moreover, the otherwise prudent Kennedy had markedly increased US military aid and advisers to the embattled government of South Vietnam and shortly before his death had also authorized the generals' successful coup against Diệm, thus expanding America's responsibility for another, even more distant, and indefensible ally.

Khrushchev was toppled in October 1964 by a politburo disgruntled by his brinkmanship over Suez, Berlin, and Cuba and also opposed to his erratic search for coexistence with the United States. During his nine-year rule, Khrushchev had attempted to square the impossible: while striving to dismantle the repressive elements of Stalinism, he had used Stalinist measures to crush popular revolutions in Eastern Europe; while seeking to unify global communism, he had created a powerful rival in Mao's China; while seeking to revive Marxist-Leninist revolutionary impulses in the Third World, he had not only raised Washington's hackles but also embraced nationalist leaders who crushed their left-wing opposition; and while seeking détente with the United States and the end of NATO, his inflammatory language and nuclear threats had underscored the need for a united West.

Despite their differences in age and temperament, Kennedy and Khrushchev were both hardened Cold Warriors who only dimly recognized the radical changes in the world landscape that were beginning to reduce the Superpowers' control. Their successors, less experienced in diplomacy and more intent on domestic reforms, would create a dangerous pause in the Superpowers' post-Berlin, post-Cuba search for détente.

SUGGESTIONS FOR FURTHER STUDY

Primary Sources

"The 1956 Hungarian Revolution: A History in Documents: Electronic Briefing Book." National Security Archive. 2002. http://www.gwu.edu/~nsarchiv/NSAEBB /NSAEBB76/.

"Bay of Pigs Release." Central Intelligence Agency. Last updated August 2, 2011. http://www.foia.ucia.gov/collection/bay-pigs-release.

"Berlin Wall." Newsreel Archive. British Pathé. Accessed February 26, 2013. http://www.britishpathe.com/workspaces/rgallagher/Berlin-Wall-4.

Castro, Fidel. "Castro Speech Data Base." Latin American Network Information Center. Accessed February 26, 2013. http://lanic.utexas.edu/la/cb/cuba/castro.html

"CIA and Assassinations: The Guatemala 1954 Documents." National Security Archive. Accessed February 26, 2013. http://www.gwu.edu/~nsarchiv/guatemala/.

"Cuba Documentation Project." National Security Archive. Accessed February 26, 2013. http://www.gwu.edu/~nsarchiv/latin_america/cuba.htm.

"Digital 1956 Archive." Open Society Archives. Accessed February 26, 2013. http://osaarchivum.org/digitalarchive/index.html.

"Final Communiqué of the Asian-African Conference of Bandung (24 April 1955)." Centre Virtuel de la Connaissance sur l'Europe. http://www.cvce.eu/obj/final_communique_of_the_asian_african_conference_of_bandung_24_april_1955-en-676237bd-72f7-471f-949a-88b6ae513585.html.

"Foreign Relations of the United States, 1961–1963, Volume XI, Cuban Missile Crisis and Aftermath." Office of the Historian, US State Department. http://history.state.gov/historicaldocuments/frus1961-63v11.

Kennedy, John F. "Inaugural Address, 20 January 1961." John F. Kennedy Presidential Library and Museum. Video, 16:00. http://www.jfklibrary.org/Asset-Viewer/BqXIEM9F4024ntFl7SVAjA.aspx?gclid=CPngl6eZyLUCFQ7NnAodaWcAhA.

———. "JFK's 'Cuban Missile Crisis' Speech (10/22/62) (Complete and Uncut)." YouTube video, 18:41. Posted by "DavidVonPein1," December 15, 2010. http://www.youtube.com/watch?v=bOnY6b-qy_8.

———. *The Kennedy Tapes: Inside the White House During the Cuban Missile Crisis.* Edited by Ernest R. May and Philip Zelikow. Cambridge, MA: Belknap Press of Harvard University Press, 1997.

Khrushchev, Nikita S. "Nikita S. Khrushchev: The Secret Speech—On the Cult of Personality, 1956." *Modern History Sourcebook.* http://www.fordham.edu/halsall/mod/1956khrushchev-secret1.html.

Nixon, Richard M., and Nikita S. Khrushchev. "Nixon-Khrushchev Kitchen Debate." C-SPAN Video Library, 15:00. July 1, 1959. http://www.c-spanvideo.org/program/110721-1.

"The Secret CIA History of the Iran Coup, 1953." National Security Archive. 2000. http://www.gwu.edu/~nsarchiv/NSAEBB/NSAEBB28/.

"Treaty Banning Nuclear Weapon Tests in the Atmosphere, Outer Space and Under Water." Entered into force October 10, 1963. NuclearFiles.org. http://www.nuclearfiles.org/menu/library/treaties/partial-test-ban/trty_partial-test-ban_1963-10-10.htm.

"The U-2 Spy Plane Incident." Dwight D. Eisenhower Presidential Library and Museum. Accessed February 26, 2013. http://eisenhower.archives.gov/research/online_documents/u2_incident.html.

Contemporary Writing

Djilas, Milovan. *The New Class: An Analysis of the Communist System*. New York: Praeger, 1957.

Kissinger, Henry. *Nuclear Weapons and Foreign Policy*. New York: Published for the Council on Foreign Relations by Harper, 1957.

Rostow, W. W. *The Stages of Economic Growth: A Non-Communist Manifesto*. Cambridge: Cambridge University Press, 1960.

Wright, Richard. *The Color Curtain: A Report on the Bandung Conference*. Foreword by Gunnar Myrdal. Cleveland: World, 1956.

Memoirs

Dayan, Moshe. *Diary of the Sinai Campaign*. New York: Harper and Row, 1966.

Kennedy, Robert F. *Thirteen Days: A Memoir of the Cuban Missile Crisis*. New York: Norton, 1969.

Khrushchev, Nikita Sergeevich. *Khrushchev Remembers*. Translated and edited by Strobe Talbott. Boston: Little, Brown, 1970.

———. *Khrushchev Remembers: The Last Testament*. Translated and edited by Strobe Talbott. Boston: Little, Brown, 1974.

———. *Khrushchev Remembers: The Glasnost Tapes*. Translated and edited by Jerrold L. Schecter and Vyacheslav V. Luchkov. Boston: Little, Brown, 1990.

Music

Cliburn, Van. "Van Cliburn." YouTube video, 1:59, from a performance of "Moscow Nights," 1958. Posted by "Posterfromus," October 3, 2009. http://www.youtube .com/watch?v=s1vZWJT-XGw.

Hvorostovsky, Dmitri. "Dmitri Hvorostovsky Moscow Nights." YouTube video, 3:25, from a concert recorded in Moscow, 2004. Posted by "Apomethe," January 29, 2007. http://www.youtube.com/watch?v=mIHPhFHjn7Q.

Films

The Atomic Café. Directed by Jayne Loader, Kevin Rafferty, and Pierce Rafferty. Los Angeles: The Archives Project, 1982.

Ballad of a Soldier. Directed by Grigoriy Chukhray. Moscow: Mosfilm, 1959.

Battle of Algiers. Directed by Gillo Pontecorvo. Rome: Rizzoli Film, 1966.

Come Back, Africa. Directed by Lionel Rogosin. New York: Milestone Films, 1959.

Funeral in Berlin. Directed by Guy Hamilton. Los Angeles: Paramount Pictures, 1966.

Gigant Berlin. Directed by Leo de Laforgue. Berlin: Leo Laforgue Filmproduktion, 1964.

Invasion of the Body Snatchers. Directed by Don Siegel. Los Angeles: Allied Artists Pictures, 1956.

Kanal. Directed by Andrzej Wajda. Warsaw: Studio Filmowe Kadr, 1957.

On the Beach. Directed by Stanley Kramer. Los Angeles: Stanley Kramer Productions, 1959.

One, Two, Three. Directed by Billy Wilder. Grünwald: Bavaria Filmstudios, 1961.

Fiction

Arévalo, Juan José. *The Shark and the Sardines.* Translated by June Cobb and Raul Osegueda. New York: L. Stuart, 1961.

Beauvoir, Simone de. *The Mandarins: A Novel.* Translated by Leonard M. Friedman. Cleveland: World, 1956.

Beti, Mongo. *Remember Ruben.* Translated by Gerald Moore. London: Heinemann, 1980.

Carpentier, Alejo. *Explosion in a Cathedral.* Translated by John Sturrock. London: Gollancz, 1963.

Deighton, Len. *The Ipcress File.* New York: Simon and Schuster, 1963.

Fleming, Ian. *From Russia with Love.* New York: Macmillan, 1957.

Greene, Graham. *Our Man in Havana: An Entertainment.* New York: Viking, 1958.

Lederer, William J., and Eugene Burdick. *The Ugly American.* New York: Norton, 1958.

Ngũgĩ wa Thiong'o. *A Grain of Wheat.* London: Heinemann, 1967.

Solzhenitsyn, Aleksandr Isaevich. *One Day in the Life of Ivan Denisovich.* Translated by Max Hayward and Ronald Hingley. New York: Praeger, 1963.

Wright, Richard. *The Outsider.* New York: Harper, 1953.

Secondary Sources

Allison, Roy. *The Soviet Union and the Strategy of Non-Alignment in the Third World.* Cambridge: Cambridge University Press, 1988.

Barghoorn, Frederick Charles. *The Soviet Cultural Offensive: The Role of Cultural Diplomacy in Soviet Foreign Policy.* Princeton, NJ: Princeton University Press, 1960.

Beschloss, Michael R. *The Crisis Years: Kennedy and Khrushchev, 1960–1963.* New York: Edward Burlingame Books, 1991.

Branch, Daniel. *Defeating Mau Mau, Creating Kenya: Counterinsurgency, Civil War, and Decolonization.* Cambridge: Cambridge University Press, 2009.

Castillo, Greg. *Cold War on the Home Front: The Soft Power of Midcentury Design.* Minneapolis: University of Minnesota Press, 2010.

Citino, Nathan J. *From Arab Nationalism to OPEC: Eisenhower, King Sa'ud, and the Making of U.S.-Saudi Relations.* Bloomington: Indiana University Press, 2002.

Connelly, Matthew James. *A Diplomatic Revolution: Algeria's Fight for Independence and the Origins of the Post–Cold War Era.* Oxford: Oxford University Press, 2002.

Dudziak, Mary L. *Cold War Civil Rights: Race and the Image of American Democracy.* Princeton, NJ: Princeton University Press, 2000.

Engerman, David C. *Staging Growth: Modernization, Development, and the Global Cold War.* Amherst: University of Massachusetts Press, 2003.

Freedman, Lawrence. *Kennedy's Wars: Berlin, Cuba, Laos, and Vietnam.* New York: Oxford University Press, 2000.

Fursenko, A. A., and Timothy J. Naftali. *Khrushchev's Cold War: The Inside Story of an American Adversary.* New York: Norton, 2006.

Gati, Charles. *Failed Illusions: Moscow, Washington, Budapest, and the 1956 Hungarian Revolt.* Washington, DC: Woodrow Wilson Center Press, 2006.

Giauque, Jeffrey Glen. *Grand Designs and Visions of Unity: The Atlantic Powers and the Reorganization of Western Europe, 1955–1963.* Chapel Hill: University of North Carolina Press, 2002.

Gilman, Nils. *Mandarins of the Future: Modernization Theory in Cold War America.* Baltimore: Johns Hopkins University Press, 2003.

Gleijeses, Piero. *Shattered Hope: The Guatemalan Revolution and the United States, 1944–1954.* Princeton, NJ: Princeton University Press, 1991.

Groys, Boris. *The Total Art of Stalinism: Avant-Garde, Aesthetic Dictatorship, and Beyond.* Princeton, NJ: Princeton University Press, 1992.

Harrison, Hope Millard. *Driving the Soviets Up the Wall: Soviet–East German Relations, 1953–1961.* Princeton, NJ: Princeton University Press, 2003.

Hixson, Walter L. *Parting the Curtain: Propaganda, Culture and the Cold War, 1945–61.* London: Macmillan, 1997.

Karnow, Stanley. *Vietnam: A History.* New York: Viking, 1983.

Kinzer, Stephen. *All the Shah's Men: An American Coup and the Roots of Middle East Terror.* New York: Wiley, 2004.

Krenn, Michael L. *Fall-Out Shelters for the Human Spirit: American Art and the Cold War.* Chapel Hill: University of North Carolina Press, 2005.

Kunz, Diane B. *The Economic Diplomacy of the Suez Crisis.* Chapel Hill: University of North Carolina Press, 1991.

Kyle, Keith. *Suez.* New York: St. Martin's, 1991.

Logevall, Fredrik. *Embers of War: The Fall of an Empire and the Making of America's Vietnam.* New York: Random House, 2012.

Marsh, Steve. *Anglo-American Relations and Cold War Oil: Crisis in Iran.* New York: Palgrave Macmillan, 2003.

Osgood, Kenneth Alan. *Total Cold War: Eisenhower's Secret Propaganda Battle at Home and Abroad.* Lawrence: University of Kansas, 2006.

Poiger, Uta G. *Jazz, Rock, and Rebels: Cold War Politics and American Culture in a Divided Germany.* Berkeley: University of California Press, 2000.

Puddington, Arch. *Broadcasting Freedom: The Cold War Triumph of Radio Free Europe and Radio Liberty.* Lexington: University Press of Kentucky, 2000.

Rabe, Stephen G. *Eisenhower and Latin America: The Foreign Policy of Anticommunism.* Chapel Hill: University of North Carolina Press, 1988.

Richmond, Yale. *Cultural Exchange and the Cold War: Raising the Iron Curtain.* University Park: Pennsylvania State University Press, 2003.

Rotter, Andrew Jon. *Comrades at Odds: The United States and India, 1947–1964.* Ithaca, NY: Cornell University Press, 2000.

Schlesinger, Stephen C., and Stephen Kinzer. *Bitter Fruit: The Story of the American Coup in Guatemala.* Cambridge, MA: Harvard University, David Rockefeller Center for Latin American Studies, 2005.

Scott-Smith, Giles. *The Politics of Apolitical Culture: The Congress for Cultural Freedom, the CIA and Post-War American Hegemony.* London: Routledge, 2002.

Stern, Sheldon M. *The Week the World Stood Still: Inside the Secret Cuban Missile Crisis.* Stanford, CA: Stanford University Press, 2005.

Tignor, Robert L. *Capitalism and Nationalism at the End of Empire: State and Business in Decolonizing Egypt, Nigeria, and Kenya, 1945–1963.* Princeton, NJ: Princeton University Press, 1998.

Von Eschen, Penny M. *Satchmo Blows Up the World: Jazz Ambassadors Play the Cold War.* Cambridge, MA: Harvard University Press, 2004.

Wang, Zuoyue. *In Sputnik's Shadow: The President's Science Advisory Committee and Cold War America.* New Brunswick, NJ: Rutgers University Press, 2008.

Wharton, Annabel Jane. *Building the Cold War: Hilton International Hotels and Modern Architecture.* Chicago: University of Chicago, 2001.

Wittner, Lawrence S. *Resisting the Bomb: A History of the World Nuclear Disarmament Movement, 1954–1970.* Stanford, CA: Stanford University Press, 1997.

Yaqub, Salim. *Containing Arab Nationalism: The Eisenhower Doctrine and the Middle East.* Chapel Hill: University of North Carolina Press, 2004.

Zhai, Qiang. *China and the Vietnam Wars, 1950–1975.* Chapel Hill: University of North Carolina Press, 2000.

Zubok, V. M., and Konstantin Pleshakov. *Inside the Kremlin's Cold War: From Stalin to Khrushchev.* Cambridge, MA: Harvard University Press, 1996.

Chapter 5

THE SIXTIES

A people who have courageously opposed French domina-
tion for more than eighty years [and] fought side by side
with the Allies . . . must be free and independent.

—Declaration of Independence, Democratic Republic
of Vietnam, September 2, 1945

The Great Power game . . . had distorted the social-
political development of the Middle East.

—Isaac Deutscher, *New Left Review,* June 23, 1967

Two overfed world powers have converted stupidity into
armored divisions and atomic warheads. And we sit in
between. . . . At last we have understood the lesson of
Prague.

—Günter Grass, *Die Zeit,* October 4, 1968

The storied half decade between 1963 and 1968 witnessed a fundamental change
in the Cold War. The two main contestants were faced with new actors and
new issues unanticipated in 1945, including a revived and restive Europe and a
nuclear-armed France and China as well as even more independent Third World
leaders. There was also the global impact of the postwar baby boom in which a

generation raised in an ideologically divided world began to challenge Cold War ideas and structures.

The mid-1960s witnessed the climax of the postwar global economic expansion. Whether measured by mounting raw-material, agricultural, and manufacturing production, or by high employment and consumption levels, the growth between 1945 and 1965 had been nearly universal. Primary-producer countries had also shared in this prosperity, increasing their annual gross domestic product by at least 4 percent in the 1950s. In the 1960s—which the United Nations designated the First Development Decade—this figure rose to 5 percent and was even higher in the oil-producing countries. The Green Revolution in agriculture (the application of technology, including irrigation, fertilizers, pesticides, and disease-resistant, high-yield crop varieties) increased the world's food supply.

But the new global landscape also had darker sides. Increased food yields and improved transportation networks led to steep population growth but also an alarming drop in local production. There were the first warnings of a "Silent Spring"—the threat of industrial chemicals to the natural environment.* Scientists feared the reduction in biodiversity as a result of applying technology to agriculture. There were also significant economic and social consequences, including a rise in class disparities in the countryside (wealthier farmers were better able to acquire loans and information, and men had easier access to credit than women), the delay or cancellation of land-distribution programs, and the mass rural migrations to Third World cities that lacked houses, jobs, schools, medical facilities, and social services for the new arrivals.

By the mid-1960s the Superpowers were experiencing the limits of their economic strength. The vast US and Soviet expenditures on their conventional and nuclear forces, ambitious space programs, and growing weaponry deliveries to their allies and overseas clients increasingly diverted capital from civilian investment—particularly from education, social services, public health, and infrastructure projects such as mass transportation—and promoted inflation (which the Soviets were better able to hide), leading to the erosion of the quality of public life in both the West and the East.

The Soviet Union, although faced with an acute contraction of its growth rate and productivity, in 1964 turned away from earlier efforts to modify its Stalinist economic structure. After Khrushchev fell, his decentralized system of regional management was immediately dismantled. The much-heralded Kosygin

---

* Made vivid in Rachel Carson's 1962 book by that name.

Reforms of October 1965 restored the centralization of Soviet industries but also failed to alleviate the chronic problems of waste and inefficiency, consumer shortages, and a dearth of quality goods for export abroad. Government ministries continued to collect rents, allocate supplies, set production targets, wages, bonuses, and prices, and restrain innovation and technological advances. Moreover, the Soviet Union, which was far advanced in cybernetic research (and in 1961 had alarmed Washington with its scientists' proposals to create a unified national computer system to plan and manage the communist national economy*) was unable to follow through after its leaders in the mid-1960s drew back from the political and social ramifications of a universal access to information.

The United States too was experiencing economic problems, having lost its postwar dominance of world trade to new rivals. The reduction of tariffs within Europe's Common Market and the rising productivity of its members contributed to America's mounting dollar gap with Western Europe. The entry into the US market of the homely and highly popular Volkswagen Beetle signaled a challenge to the powerful automobile industry. Ex-enemy Japan, with its highly organized links between business and government and its freedom from a major defense burden, was becoming Asia's foremost economic power, which, by the mid-1960s, had also begun to reverse its trade balance with the United States.

The world of the 1960s witnessed fighting on almost every continent. The brutal civil wars in the Congo, Indonesia, and Nigeria and the border wars between India and its neighbors drew in outside powers but were containable. However, the decade's three major crises—the US war in Vietnam, the June 1967 Middle East war, and the Soviet repression of the Prague Spring—emphasized the dangers of the new multipolar world. All three involved bold local actors and indirect forms of combat that Washington and Moscow strove to keep in bounds.

THE COLD WAR AND VIETNAM

The US intervention in Vietnam was not inevitable. It had evolved from the vacuum left by the collapse of Japan's Asian empire, followed by the communists' victory in China, the Korean stalemate, and France's defeat in 1954. But it also grew out of the Cold War decisions of three US presidents: Truman's to move

---

* Based on classified CIA reports, a Kennedy aide wrote that "by 1970 the USSR may have a radically new production technology, involving total enterprises or complexes of industries, managed by closed-loop, feedback control employing self-teaching computers."

away from Roosevelt's anticolonialism and back the French, Eisenhower's to block the Vietnamese national elections in 1956 and prop up the Diệm regime, and Kennedy's to increase the number of US military advisers, Special Forces, and CIA agents in South Vietnam. All three intended to transform Vietnam into a "proving ground for democracy in Asia."

By the 1960s American power in the world was no longer unchallenged. To be sure, despite Castro's survival, Latin America remained a secure US preserve.* But a cash-strapped United States was facing restive NATO allies in Europe, whose confidence in the US nuclear shield was diminishing and who were expressing more independent views on their defense against a Soviet attack.

Political conditions on the other side had also changed significantly as a result of the Sino-Soviet rupture. In the late 1950s Mao, resentful of Moscow's refusal to support China's atomic weapons program, condemned Khrushchev's abandonment of the doctrine of revolutionary warfare and his pursuit of peaceful coexistence. Khrushchev, a critic of Mao's disastrous Great Leap Forward and belligerence toward his neighbors, in 1960 suddenly withdrew Soviet experts and reduced Soviet assistance to China. After the split became public at the Twenty-Second Soviet Party Congress in October 1961, Mao openly mocked Khrushchev's retreat over the Cuban missile crisis, complained of Moscow's pro–New Delhi stance during the 1962 Sino-Indian border conflict, and denounced the test-ban treaty as a means of preventing China from developing its own nuclear weapons. By the end of 1963 the two communist giants were openly competing for leadership of the revolutionary movements in Asia, Africa, and Latin America.

North Vietnam, caught between its two rival patrons whose differences it had failed to resolve, chose initially in the summer of 1963 to side with nearby China over the more distant Soviet Union; Beijing responded with promises of full support against US aggression. North Vietnam's decision coincided with the growing political crisis in the south that climaxed in the November coup and murder of Diệm. Hanoi now had to decide between continuing its cautious infiltration policy aimed at creating a neutral South Vietnam that would eventually unite with the north (which Moscow and Beijing had supported) and an interventionist policy that risked a war with the United States. In early 1964, after deciding to

---

* Following its confrontation with the Soviet Union in 1962, the United States led a regional quarantine of Cuba. Moreover, the Johnson administration quickly abandoned the reformist impulses of the Alliance for Progress, and in 1965 intervened militarily in the Dominican Republic to overthrow an allegedly leftist government and prevent "another Cuba."

conduct large-scale operations, Hanoi developed plans to send whole regiments of troops and supplies over the Ho Chi Minh trail through Laos and Cambodia to South Vietnam.

That spring, with the Viet Cong controlling 40 percent of its territory, South Vietnam appeared doomed. But Kennedy's successor, Lyndon B. Johnson, was determined to reassure America's allies—particularly those he had encountered during his 1961 Asian journey—of Washington's resolve to protect them against communism. A novice in international diplomacy who was determined to produce major US domestic reforms, which he labeled the Great Society, Johnson deferred to his hawkish advisers and ignored the naysayers.* The president resolved to make South Vietnam the principal focus of America's renewed Cold War struggle in order, like his predecessors, to prevent falling dominoes in Southeast Asia and a victory for China. However, while continuing Kennedy's covert war against North Vietnam and preparing for military action nine thousand miles from the US mainland, Johnson had first to stand for election in November 1964, and he did so, ironically, as the peace candidate.†

Three months before the presidential election Johnson had already obtained his justification for going to war. From the beginning of 1964 the US military had taken over direction of the CIA/South Vietnamese covert commando attacks against North Vietnam as well as naval intelligence gathering in the coastal areas (known as the DeSoto Program). On August 1, 1964, shortly after a South Vietnamese commando attack on two islands, the US destroyer *Maddox* entered the Gulf of Tonkin for the purpose of collecting electronic intelligence. The next day, as it approached the island of Hon Me, it encountered three North Vietnamese torpedo boats whose signals had been intercepted. The *Maddox* fired, damaging only one of them. Two days later, the *Maddox*, now joined by a second intelligence vessel, *C. Turner Joy*, again fired on what appeared to be approaching enemy ships, although no evidence has ever been found of a second North Vietnamese interception.

Although neither US ship had been hit and there were no casualties, Johnson immediately ordered a retaliatory bombing raid against North Vietnamese naval

---

* The most prominent was French president Charles de Gaulle, who had negotiated Algeria's independence in 1962.

† Drawing on the American public's fears during the Cuban missile crisis, Johnson suggested that his Republican opponent, Barry Goldwater, would recklessly use nuclear weapons in Vietnam. In the notorious daisy ad featuring a young child counting flower petals immediately followed by a countdown before a nuclear explosion, Johnson appealed for voters' support "because the stakes are too high."

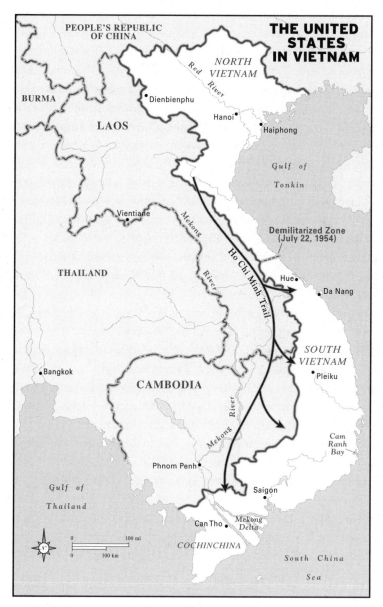

Map 10. Major sites of the US war in Vietnam, 1964–1973.

bases. Evoking America's dread of surprise assaults, Johnson appealed for public support against an "unprovoked attack" in international waters. After Defense Secretary Robert McNamara assured Congress that the US Navy had "played absolutely no part in, was not associated with, was not aware of any South Vietnamese actions, if there were any," Johnson on August 7, 1964, won near-unanimous Senate approval for a resolution authorizing him to use US armed force to defend the freedom of South Vietnam, a measure his administration had prepared earlier in the spring. The Tonkin Gulf Resolution enabled Johnson to spurn proposals that fall for another Geneva conference to achieve a negotiated settlement over Vietnam.

Shortly after his overwhelming electoral victory, Johnson moved quickly to rescue South Vietnam from an imminent collapse. In 1965 he launched Operation Rolling Thunder, a massive bombing campaign against North Vietnam, and by the end of the year he had dispatched 180,000 combat troops as well. Although this dramatic escalation contained several cautious elements,* Johnson had transformed South Vietnam into a Cold War struggle and one of the longest and most divisive wars in US history.

Johnson's decision was based on several problematic assumptions. The first was that the American people—stirred by Kennedy's ringing rhetoric but also increasingly sensitive to social and economic injustices in America and around the globe—would sustain a prolonged, distant, and costly war on behalf of an unpopular client regime and against a nationalist movement seeking to unify the country. The second was that Washington's allies would endorse a struggle that diverted America's attention and shrinking resources from the defense of Europe. And the third was that the Soviet Union—now in open competition with China, which strongly supported North Vietnam—would remain on the sidelines.

Even more crucial was his fourth assumption: that the North Vietnamese leadership would succumb to US power and abandon their resolve to unify the entire country. Instead North Vietnam, stung by the initial successes of US troops (which by the end of 1967 had reached a half million soldiers) and the installation of the strongman General Nguyễn Văn Thiệu as South Vietnam's president, disregarded Beijing's and Moscow's advice to conduct guerrilla

---

* In selecting bombing targets, Johnson avoided destroying North Vietnamese dams and ports and provoking a Chinese intervention; although the Ho Chi Minh trail was bombed, Johnson made no moves to invade Laos or attack the Viet Cong sanctuaries in Cambodia; and US forces confined themselves to search and destroy operations against enemy units and largely refrained from involvement in local politics.

warfare and aimed at a conventional military victory. On January 30, 1968, the first day of Tet (the lunar New Year festival), the North Vietnamese offensive began, spreading by April to the entire country (including attacks on the US embassy and the presidential palace), and continuing until August. Despite its ultimate military setback, heavy losses—some fifty thousand deaths—and failure to foment an uprising against the Thiệu regime, North Vietnam had achieved a major propaganda and political triumph. The searing images of Saigon and Hue and of dozens of seized provincial capitals—widely disseminated in the US press and on television—stunned the American public, belying the Johnson administration's predictions of a winnable war.*

Facing mounting criticism from America's Cold War architects and from Congress, the press, and the public—as well as damage to his Great Society program—Johnson now recognized that he could neither send more troops nor bomb North Vietnam into submission and became the first US president to leave office over an unwinnable Third World conflict. On March 31, 1968, Johnson issued the startling announcement of his withdrawal as a candidate for reelection and the discontinuation of the bombing. He also offered unconditional peace negotiations, which an exhausted North Vietnam readily accepted. The Republican candidate Richard Nixon was victorious in November largely because of his offer of a peace plan that would end America's costly and disruptive war, although under his leadership the United States would remain there for four even more costly and divisive years.

The US military intervention in Vietnam had a major effect on global politics. Antiwar movements developed rapidly in America, with young people burning their draft cards, fleeing the country, or serving jail sentences rather than go to Vietnam. By October 1965 protest demonstrations in forty American cities had spread to Europe and Asia. Critics of the war condemned America's atrocities against the civilian population—North and South—and its use of chemical weapons, and they called for an immediate US withdrawal. Antiwar activists derided Washington's claim of battling Chinese communism to save Asians from tyranny, and deplored America's opposition to the Third World's struggle for independence. To the generation raised after World War II and the Holocaust, America's professions of defending freedom through its unbridled

---

* US public support of the war was badly damaged by Eddie Adams's close-up photograph of the South Vietnamese police chief, Nguyễn Ngọc Loan, executing a suspected Viet Cong officer during the Tet offensive, which won the Pulitzer Prize in 1969. In the spring of 1968 the *Wall Street Journal* opined "no battle and no war are worth any price."

use of arms, air power, napalm, and Agent Orange against a tiny, tenacious people and its support of a corrupt and repressive puppet government rang increasingly hollow.

The escalation of the Vietnam War created a major challenge for the Soviet Union. Prime Minister Aleksei Kosygin, who witnessed the US bombing of Hanoi and Haiphong in February 1965, drastically increased deliveries of monetary aid, supplies, technical manpower, and missiles. Although by 1968 Soviet and Warsaw Pact members' aid to North Vietnam exceeded China's, the USSR had little control over its ally and was locked into a competition with Beijing. Moreover, Moscow's involvement in the Vietnam War had stifled its overtures for détente and disarmament with the United States.

The Soviet Union's increasing support of Hanoi (including the pledge that its nuclear arsenal would deter a US invasion and a nuclear attack on North Vietnam) also had several advantages. One was as an investment in a future Soviet presence in Southeast Asia. Second was the bolstering of the USSR's global image as a champion of national liberation movements. And third were the strategic and diplomatic benefits: a struggle that tied the United States down in Southeast Asia gave the Kremlin more freedom to act in other parts of the world and also to extract diplomatic concessions from Washington. Nonetheless, the Kremlin, concerned that the war might escalate into a larger East-West conflict, began working behind the scenes in 1968 to bring the parties to the negotiating table. But the Soviet Union's two-pronged policy—continuing to lavishly supply Hanoi while working for a peace settlement—exasperated the Chinese and the United States.

China's role in the Vietnam War was also a difficult one. Despite the economic ravages of the Great Leap Forward and the Cultural Revolution that began in 1966, China provided substantial manpower and materiel aid, assisted in major infrastructure and defense projects, and pledged to repulse a US/South Vietnamese invasion, only to share the Kremlin's inability to control North Vietnam's decision making. Moreover, beneath their comradeship in arms was the long-standing Chinese-Vietnamese rivalry over the future control of Indochina as well as memories of centuries of Chinese occupation made manifest in the strict limits placed on Chinese personnel by the North Vietnamese government. By 1966 Beijing was bristling over the rapprochement between Hanoi and Moscow, which was now providing advanced weaponry and, with its Security Council seat and diplomatic relations with Washington, representing North Vietnam to large parts of the world.

Predictably Mao expressed displeasure with Hanoi's agreement to commence negotiations with Washington in 1968 and withdrew the bulk of Chinese forces from North Vietnam. Nonetheless Johnson's startling announcement—coupled with China's deteriorating situation at home and its worsening relations with Hanoi and Moscow—would pave the way for Mao's decision a year later to normalize relations with Washington.

JUNE 1967: THE ARAB-ISRAELI WAR

The Arab-Israeli War in June 1967 was another local struggle that drew in the Superpowers but eluded their control. Israel's unexpectedly swift and overwhelming victory over Egypt, Jordan, and Syria, followed by the UN's failure to repeat its 1956 peacemaking role, changed the Middle East *and* the Cold War. To be sure, the principal actors who lit the fuse were also unprepared for the momentous consequences.

The antecedents of the 1967 war were several. The Palestinian problem fed the regional hostility to Israel, which had developed into a strong, prosperous, and Western-oriented state that physically divided the Arab world. Eighteen years after Israel's military triumph in 1948–1949, more than 1.3 million Palestinian refugees remained dispersed throughout the Middle East, 39 percent housed in UN-administered refugee camps. Under Egyptian sponsorship the Palestinian cause was taken up in 1964 during the first summit conference of the Arab League, which called for the creation of the Palestinian Liberation Organization (PLO). Although the Palestinians remained politically divided, they supported the PLO charter that called for the destruction of Israel.

In 1966 the Ba'ath regime in Syria—the Soviet Union's newest Middle East client—replaced Egypt as the Palestinians' principal sponsor and Israel's foremost antagonist. The Damascus regime armed Palestinian militants for border attacks on Israel, which generally originated across the more porous Jordanian border.[*] Middle East tensions escalated dramatically in April 1967, when Israeli pilots downed seven Syrian MiGs in an air battle over Damascus. Five weeks later, Syrian defense minister Hafez al-Assad warned Egypt that Israel's troops were massing on Syria's border in preparation for an invasion.

Nasser (who was beset with internal difficulties as well as a long, ruinous war in South Yemen and quarrels with Saudi Arabia and Iran) was roused by the alarm, which was reinforced by a similar message from Moscow. The Egyptian leader decided to seize the moment to refute domestic and foreign charges of his

---

[*] One of these operations in November 1966 provoked an Israeli military retaliation against three Jordanian villages that drew censure from Israel's friends and foes.

apathy toward Israeli aggression and to assert his leadership over the Arab cause. To reassure Syria and deter Israel, Nasser ordered Egyptian troops into the Sinai. When UN secretary general U Thant refused a partial removal of the UN Emergency Force (UNEF) that for ten years had separated Egypt from Israel, Nasser ordered UNEF's complete withdrawal and on May 22, 1967, announced the closure of the Strait of Tiran to Israeli shipping. With these bold actions, accompanied by belligerent speeches to rally the Egyptian population, Nasser crossed the boundary between peace and war.

Israeli prime minister Levi Eshkol, an elderly moderate, was now engulfed by his country's fear and war fever as well as by a serious economic recession. Although Israel was legally entitled to use force to keep the strait open, he recognized the danger of acting alone. He too ordered mobilization on May 16, but he also appealed for Washington's support against Nasser, who was threatening "to drive Israel into the sea" and return the Palestinians to their homeland.

The Arabs looked to the Soviet Union for support. Kosygin and General Secretary Leonid Brezhnev, in search of political influence and naval bases in the eastern Mediterranean, had been generously supplying Syria and Egypt with arms and aid and echoing their criticisms of Israel. But although at least one US intelligence source suspected that the Kremlin's warning to Egypt had been aimed at creating still another trouble spot for Washington, it is doubtful that Moscow's cautious rulers intended to unleash a Middle East war and risk another confrontation with the United States.

President Johnson, overwhelmed by Vietnam and constrained by congressional opposition to undertaking any further military action, acted promptly to restrain Israel from attacking Egypt or Syria and thereby drawing the United States into the conflict. To sweeten the pill, Johnson sent the Sixth Fleet to the eastern Mediterranean, approved a substantial military assistance package for Israel on May 23, and also tried to assemble an international flotilla to open the Strait of Tiran. But by the end of May, after King Hussein of Jordan had placed his army under Egyptian control and Nasser refused to back down, Johnson changed the red light to yellow. Although discounting Israeli reports of an imminent Egyptian attack, Johnson recognized that the delay he had imposed on the frightened, fully mobilized country could no longer be prolonged. In a fatalist mood reminiscent of statesmen on the eve of World War I, the US president took no steps to halt the Israeli attack, which he learned of twenty-four hours in advance.

The war was unexpectedly short. Early in the morning on June 5, Israel's air force attacked Egyptian, Syrian, and Jordanian airfields, destroying the bulk of

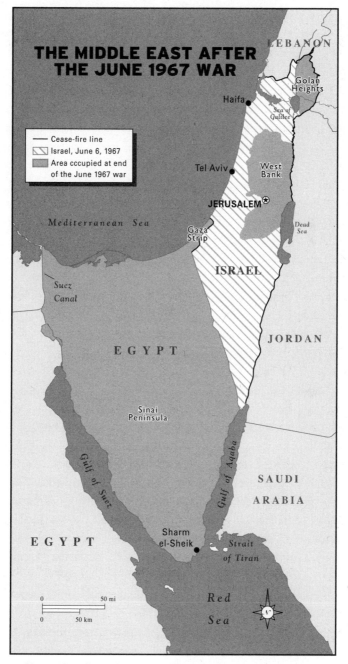

Map 11. Israeli conquests in the Sinai, East Jerusalem, the West Bank, and the Golan Heights.

their craft, which were still mostly on the ground. The Israeli army then went on to conquer Gaza and the Sinai from Egypt before capturing East Jerusalem and the West Bank from Jordan and the Golan Heights from Syria. In just six days Israel had tripled its size, and the Arabs faced the greatest military disaster in their modern history. The Superpowers also faced a setback, having exposed their inability to control their clients. During the brief but bloody conflict Johnson and Kosygin had made energetic use of the hotline between Washington and Moscow in an attempt to achieve a cease-fire, which was delayed until Israel had taken the Golan on June 10.

Once more the scene shifted to the United Nations, but the result was far different than in 1956. This time the United States prevented the Arabs from branding Israel as the aggressor and placed no pressure on Israel to withdraw. The Soviet Union acquiesced. On November 24, 1967, after two weeks of difficult deliberations, the Security Council unanimously passed Resolution 242, a British-drafted compromise that reflected Israel's lopsided victory, linking any withdrawal from the occupied territories with its neighbors' willingness to make peace and recognize its 1949 borders (which became known as "land for peace"), affirming the necessity of "freedom of navigation through international waterways," and, ignoring the Palestinians, simply calling for a "just settlement of the refugee problem."

Stifled by the Superpowers, the Arabs took matters into their own hands. Egypt and Syria broke off diplomatic relations with Washington, which they accused of colluding in the Israeli attack. In the summer of 1967 Middle Eastern oil producers imposed a second boycott, this time against the United States, Great Britain, and West Germany, which had allegedly provided arms to Israel. And the Arab League summit meeting in Khartoum adopted a resolution on September 1 refusing direct negotiations with a triumphant Israel and insisting on "the rights of the Palestinians in their own country." Behind the scenes, however, a chastened Nasser, defying the Arab militants, had held out the prospect of indirect peace talks through a UN mediator and an informal acceptance of Israel's existence. Nonetheless, Israeli leaders, flush with victory, took Khartoum's "three noes" (no peace treaty, no direct negotiations, no de jure recognition) at face value.

While the Israeli public exulted in its deliverance from Nasser's threats and the liberation of the holy places in Jerusalem and the West Bank that Jordan had seized during the 1948 war, the Eshkol government was hesitant over the next steps. Israel faced not only the problem of controlling a territory three times its former size and the responsibility for one million more Palestinian Arabs but also the prospect of an unremitting confrontation with its neighbors. A tiny minority advocating withdrawal (among them former prime minister David Ben Gurion) was quickly overpowered by the politicians and generals, who argued the value of strategic depth and of holding on to the territories in exchange for full peace and recognition. In the heady days of 1967 there was also an explosion of national sentiment—secular as well as religious—in favor of a Greater Israel that included East Jerusalem and all the land to the Jordan River. Scarcely noticed at the time was the emergence of the Palestinians as an independent political movement prepared to use violence to assert their disregarded national claims.

Outside the Middle East, Israel's supporters generally celebrated its survival and its lightning victory. To be sure, some leftist critics in Western Europe deplored Israel's resort to war in June 1967, its territorial conquests, and the creation of a new wave of Palestinian refugees who had fled the West Bank. Moreover, the June war had rent NATO's unity. Facing a dangerous eruption on its vulnerable southern flank, the alliance had been badly split, with France condemning Israel, the Netherlands defending it, and West Germany, frightened of a new threat to Berlin, announcing its neutrality.*

The year 1967, the fiftieth anniversary of the Bolshevik Revolution, was a grim one for Moscow. In Asia the Indonesian communists and their sympathizers had been decimated, and the United States was still asserting its military strength in Vietnam; in Europe Romania had essentially severed its ties with the Warsaw Pact; and in the Middle East the Soviet Union had sustained an unexpected blow to its arms and diplomacy, hyperbolically termed by one of its envoys "one of the greatest defeats in our history."† Mao lost no time in taunting Khrushchev's successors for betraying their Arab allies and caving in to US pressure at the United Nations.

The Kremlin wavered between restraint and assertiveness. At great cost, the Soviet Union dispatched replacement military supplies to Egypt and Syria, but it also decided to impose some fetters on its risk-taking clients, limiting the flow of offensive weapons, placing Soviet advisers in control of Arab troops and advanced armaments, and discouraging Arab leaders from provoking another war

---

* Although leading German politicians, sensitive to the Nazi past, announced that in the face of the Arabs' threat to Israel's existence they could not be neutral in spirit.

† Moreover, the October 1967 death of Che Guevara at the hands of CIA-trained Bolivian rangers gave President Johnson a rare moment of optimism over the prospects of halting communist insurgencies in the Third World.

to regain their lost territories. But Soviet cautiousness had its political limits: the politburo's ideologues insisted on compensating for the USSR's military inaction during the June 1967 war by severing diplomatic relations with Israel, thereby freezing Soviet diplomacy in the Middle East and making it hostage to Arab radicalism.*

At home, the USSR launched an anti-Zionist campaign aimed at intimidating Soviet and East European Jews who had rejoiced in Israel's victory. The KGB operation also led to a wave of Jewish emigration from Poland. But the campaign badly backfired. It not only failed to quench the newfound pride of millions of Jews living under communism but also raised strong disapproval in the West and charges of antisemitism and sparked a global movement on behalf of Soviet Jewry. Despite Moscow's vituperation against the Jews, Soviet and East European dissidents were also buoyed by plucky Israel's challenge to Soviet might.

Ostensibly the United States was a victor in the June 1967 war.† The huge caches of captured Soviet arms provided NATO with a treasure trove of information. Thanks to America's actions, the conflict had been brief and localized. The propaganda benefits were also considerable: a small, courageous nation had stood up to a communist-inspired threat, and the Soviet Union, although still in the Middle East and now with access to naval bases in Syria and Egypt, had suffered a major blow to its resources and prestige.

Cooler observers in Washington also recognized that Israel's overwhelming victory had failed to solve the region's problems and had only bought time. In the meantime, an important ally was about to retire from the scene. In 1966, the cash-strapped Labour government—without consulting Washington—announced the withdrawal of British forces east of Suez, from Aden and from Persian Gulf bases in 1971, placing the sole burden for protecting the Middle East against Soviet or Chinese-supported movements on the United States. But the Cold Warriors who dominated the Johnson administration, mistaking a military verdict for a long-term solution, were unable to grasp the brief opportunity in the summer and fall of 1967 to exert pressure on both the Arabs and the

---

* In 1970 the KGB recruited Wadi Haddad, the leader of the Marxist Popular Front for the Liberation of Palestine (PFLP) who had organized the 1968 hijack of an Israeli El Al flight, and for the next eight years the USSR supported PFLP terrorist operations against Israel, its Western allies, and targeted Arab governments.

† Which the Israelis, evoking Genesis, have named Milhemet Sheshet Hayamim (The Six-Day War), the Arabs, more prosaically, an-Naksah (The Setback), and outsiders have labeled the June 1967 Arab-Israeli War.

Israelis to come to the peace table. And while Johnson quickly turned his attention back to Vietnam, the rivals' positions hardened and festered.

PRAGUE: AUGUST 1968

Even after the building of the Berlin Wall, the West did not cease its efforts to overcome the Iron Curtain. Among the most avid advocates was French president Charles de Gaulle. Although he had stood staunchly behind the United States over Berlin, de Gaulle was fundamentally opposed to Europe's division into two hostile blocs dominated by the Superpowers. Thus, in March 1966 he suddenly announced France's withdrawal of its land and air forces from the NATO military command and ordered the removal of the alliance's headquarters and US and Canadian military bases from French territory. Three months later de Gaulle paid a celebrated state visit to Moscow seeking to resurrect Franco-Russian ties and reduce Cold War tensions in Europe. Soviet leaders, who warmly welcomed their renegade visitor, nonetheless recognized that the French president's long-term goals—German unification, greater autonomy for their satellites in Eastern Europe, and a "Europe from the Atlantic to the Urals"—were incompatible with Moscow's fundamental interest in maintaining the status quo.

West Germany, with seventeen million countrymen behind the Iron Curtain and an isolated outpost in West Berlin, had an even greater stake than France in reducing tensions in Europe. But until Adenauer left the chancellorship in October 1963, Bonn had adhered to an inflexible Cold War line that had alienated Moscow and its allies: refusing to recognize the GDR and ostracizing every country (except the USSR) that had relations with the East German government, which it scathingly termed the "so-called GDR"; refusing to recognize the post–World War II boundaries with Poland and Czechoslovakia; and insisting on German unification as the precondition for any form of European détente. However, once Adenauer departed, his Conservative successors changed the tone, hastening to conclude economic agreements with four of the FRG's eastern neighbors. Even more pointedly, Willy Brandt, the Social Democrat opposition leader and West Berlin mayor, now openly advocated an *Ostpolitik*: a new policy that radically changed Bonn's relationship with the East, replacing confrontation with accommodation and acceptance, and placing European reconciliation *before* German unification.

Soviet leaders were unreceptive to West Germany's overtures. Moscow recognized that any steps toward accommodation with Bonn would dismay its East

German, Polish, and Czech comrades, who had dutifully imitated the Kremlin's diatribes against the FRG's obsession with its lost territories and inclusion of former Nazis in key positions along with its nuclear ambitions, aid to Israel, and subservience to Washington. After Brandt failed to win the chancellorship in 1966, the USSR kept West Germany's Grand Coalition government (headed by the ex-Nazi Kurt-Georg Kiesinger and with Brandt as foreign minister) at arm's length.

On entering office US president Lyndon B. Johnson had also endorsed a policy of "building bridges" with Eastern Europe, and in 1966 he called for peaceful engagement to bring about greater freedom for the countries behind the Iron Curtain. Although Brezhnev had lashed out at Washington and Bonn's ambitions to undermine socialism, the Warsaw Pact took note of these overtures and in July 1966 declared its desire for détente. And that year, NATO in celebration of its twentieth anniversary commissioned a study that would integrate the defense of Western Europe with the prospect of expanding cooperation with the East.*

Behind the Berlin Wall there were societies in ferment, chafing at the economic slowdown and the Communist Party's heavy hand over the courts, the press, culture, and society. The population of Eastern Europe, which for more than a decade had been mobilized to declare its solidarity with the downtrodden people in the Americas, Asia, and Africa, was still heavily controlled in its freedom of thought, expression, association, and travel, and lived under governments that obediently followed Moscow's orders. By the mid-1960s the thaw, which had begun but was then halted by Khrushchev, flowed again in Eastern Europe in a remarkable outpouring of film, literature, art, and music.† In addition, a slight loosening of travel restrictions allowed selected citizens to go abroad for study and tourism that, along with the introduction of television, gradually opened a window to the West. But while Eastern Europe's writers railed against their governments' censorship, ordinary people simply longed for Western blue jeans, rock music, and soft drinks and for a beach holiday in a place other than the Black Sea.

---

* A seminal document in NATO's history, the 1967 Report of the Council on the Future Tasks of the Alliance (better known as the Harmel Report), acknowledging changes in the international environment since 1949, committed the alliance to a dual-track policy of maintaining military preparedness and seeking political détente.

† Among the leading East European cultural figures, the novelists Stefan Heym (GDR), Milan Kundera and Ludvík Vaculík (Czechoslovakia), and György Konrád (Hungary); the playwright Václav Havel (Czechoslovakia); and the filmmakers Miloš Forman (Czechoslovakia) and Andrzej Wajda (Poland) all ran afoul of communist authorities in the 1960s.

Czechoslovakia, with its strong communist tradition, had been the most loyal of satellites. Two years after Stalin's death it had erected the world's largest monument to the Soviet dictator only to dismantle it seven years later—the last to do so. Testifying to Czechoslovakia's reliability, no Soviet troops were stationed on its soil, despite the fact that it bordered on two noncommunist countries, produced the bloc's most advanced armaments, possessed considerable quantities of uranium, and was a prospective site for Soviet nuclear weapons. Earlier, Czechoslovakia's Communist Party chief, Antonín Novotny, an old-style Stalinist, had opposed Khrushchev's reforms and refused to rehabilitate Stalin's victims. Until the end of 1967 Novotny had also ignored Czechoslovakia's economic woes and his Slovak comrades' resentment of Prague's domination.

Brezhnev, gambling that a party shake-up would strengthen Czechoslovakia, in early 1968 approved the appointment of Alexander Dubček, a forty-six-year-old Slovak who believed deeply in socialism and in friendship with the Soviet Union. But as in Hungary twelve years earlier, events spun out of control. Dubček's selection of political and economic reformers to head the government, followed immediately by the lifting of censorship, caused an eruption of anticommunist sentiments throughout the country and calls for a free market and democracy.*

Even more menacing to Soviet interests was the Czechoslovak Communist Party's April Action Program, which envisaged "socialism with a human face": without relinquishing its leading role, it endorsed freedom of speech, the press, and association; working in partnership with other parties; promoting reforms in the justice system; and handing greater control over the economy to the parliament. In June, during the selection of delegates for the Extraordinary Party Congress that was expected to ratify this radical program in September, the dissident writer Ludvik Vaculík, in his fiery "Two Thousand Words" manifesto, urged the entire nation to rally around Dubček.

An anxious Brezhnev was deeply reluctant to crush the Prague Spring,[†] fearing bloodshed as well as a possible NATO intervention and counting on Dubček to restrain his countrymen. But like Khrushchev before him, Brezhnev faced a hard-line Soviet politburo and KGB as well as satellite governments

---

* The Czechs and Slovaks were also exultant over their hockey team's upset victory over the Soviets during the February 1968 Winter Olympics.

† In Czech *pražské jaro*, in Slovak *pražská jar*, Prague Spring was originally the name of an annual international music festival, but in 1968 it became linked to Czechoslovakia's seven months of political liberalization.

that were appalled by their Czechoslovak comrades' behavior and frightened of the spillover effect in their countries. When neither the Warsaw Pact's menacing maneuvers nor Brezhnev's direct threats halted the swift liberalization of Czechoslovakia, Moscow decided to rescue communism with force. On the night of August 20–21, 480,000 Soviet and Warsaw Pact troops invaded Czechoslovakia and crushed the Prague Spring. On November 13, 1968, Brezhnev, stating the doctrine that afterward bore his name, stressed the indivisibility of the communist bloc and the Soviet Union's right to prevent any deviation by its members. More a defensive than an aggressive posture, the general secretary had implicitly acknowledged Moscow's vulnerability to any weak link in its Cold War barrier against "Western imperialism."

The suppression of Czechoslovakia was in many ways a hollow triumph for the Kremlin. Ninety percent of the "liberated" population condemned the invasion, and a half year elapsed before the Soviet Union could replace Dubček with leaders willing to ratify the "temporary presence" of its troops on Czechoslovak soil.* Facing a hostile population, the occupation army soon had to be withdrawn from populated centers, and the formerly impressive Czechoslovak army, which had been confined to its barracks during the invasion, lost its soldierly spirit.

The occupation of Czechoslovakia was almost universally castigated.† Opposition was even expressed in the factories of East Berlin and Budapest, on the streets of Warsaw and Kiev, and in Red Square itself. The invasion worsened Moscow's already difficult relations with Beijing. Although Mao found Dubček's reforms repugnant, he also condemned the Kremlin's "fascist" behavior in August 1968. Beijing's fears that the Brezhnev doctrine provided a license for Moscow to interfere in China's affairs were heighted by alleged Soviet intrusions into Chinese air space one month later.

The Soviet invasion of Czechoslovakia provided a temporary propaganda boost to the United States, which was beleaguered by Vietnam and the race riots in America's cities. It created a swarm of protests in Western Europe and around the world. All at once NATO sprang into life: de Gaulle's overtures toward the

---

* Once more hockey created a provocation: after the Czechs twice defeated the Soviet team in the March 1969 World Ice Hockey Championships in Stockholm, some five hundred thousand joyous fans poured into the streets of Prague. In response to alleged acts of violence—which many suspected were stirred by Soviet provocateurs—the police suppressed the protests, and Moscow used the disorder as a pretext to place Gustáv Husák at the head of the Communist Party.

† While the governments of Yugoslavia and Romania stood on the sidelines, only North Korea, North Vietnam, and Cuba applauded the destruction of Czechoslovakia's "counterrevolutionary forces."

Soviet bloc were discredited, and a frightened West Germany increased its military budget.

But the West was unable to capitalize on the Soviets' predicament. The Johnson administration offered only mild protests, with some administration officials reminding the president of Czech arms deliveries to Hanoi. Despite the talk of bridge building, Washington had never intended to come to the assistance of Czechoslovakia and once more bore the opprobrium of deserting a people seeking freedom. National interests undoubtedly trumped moral sentiments. Waging a war nine thousand miles away in Asia, the United States could ill afford to condemn the USSR's defense of its borders, especially when Brezhnev had not threatened West Berlin. The personal and political costs fell heavily on Johnson, who had to cancel his trip to Moscow for a summit meeting, thereby abandoning the hope of ending his presidency on a high note and securing peace in Vietnam.

Soviet hard-liners exulted over the West's restraint in August 1968. Having expanded their supply of bombs and missiles, they were now brimming with confidence that any form of European détente would be on Soviet terms. On October 8, in his first meeting with Brandt during the UN General Assembly in New York, Soviet foreign minister Andrei Gromyko made it clear that Moscow's stiff conditions for improved bilateral relations had not changed: recognition of Europe's existing borders, recognition of the GDR, renunciation of the 1938 Munich agreement that had carved up Czechoslovakia, and adherence to the Nuclear Non-Proliferation Treaty.

Nonetheless, the destruction of the Prague Spring created a lasting moral and intellectual dilemma for Khrushchev's heirs, dispelling the illusion that the communist system could be reformed and become more popular and efficient by introducing elements of democracy.* For the next two decades Moscow tried to suppress the extraordinary seven-month occurrence in Czechoslovakia, and the West, fearing to provoke another round of repression, also refrained from stirring the hopes of the vanquished in August 1968.

1968: INTERNATIONAL HUMAN RIGHTS YEAR

The political claims of the East European dissidents echoed a global movement in the 1960s on behalf of human rights. From the American South to South

---

* A lesson imprinted not only on the anticommunist opposition but also on the thirty-seven-year-old communist official in Stavropol (and future party general secretary) Mikhail Gorbachev.

Africa and from Northern Ireland to Australia, minority and indigenous populations were demanding citizenship rights, equality under the law, and freedom of speech, the press, and association. People still living under colonial rule were demanding freedom, and those suffering under repressive governments were seeking outside defenders. Among their champions were a growing number of nongovernmental organizations that protested racial and religious discrimination and advocated rights for women, workers, aliens, refugees, and the incarcerated. In 1967, six years after its founding, Amnesty International was operating in eighteen countries, adopting prisoners of conscience and lobbying the United Nations to abolish the death penalty and later to abolish torture.[*]

Neither of the Superpowers gave significant support to the internationalist goals of the United Nations nor welcomed any form of outside intrusion in their internal affairs. US leaders, although professing support for international humanitarian standards, had insisted on their nonbinding, aspirational character. America's political culture contained a paradoxical mixture of concern for individual liberties, respect for law, and generous impulses toward the underprivileged abroad with a strong commitment to laissez-faire capitalism, its federal system of states' rights, and its assertion of an exceptionalism that made the United States immune from outside intrusion. The Soviet Union championed self-determination and antiracism abroad, if not at home. Guided by Marx's dicta, it dismissed the "bourgeois" principle of personal rights as a license for exploitation, defined freedom in economic and social terms (among them, the right to work and to free education and social services), and insisted on the *duties* of its citizens and the primacy of the state in building socialism.

Unsurprisingly, neither side had wished to enlarge the UN competence in the area of human rights, but both had used its machinery to trade barbs in the Commission on Human Rights and in the General Assembly: the West condemning the Soviets' ban on emigration and its forced labor system, and the East denouncing America's discriminatory laws and practices against its black population. Under the Eisenhower administration Congress, the American Bar Association, and US business groups had reinforced the president's refusal to draft or ratify UN human rights conventions, and things changed only slightly under Kennedy and Johnson. The Soviet leadership, while taunting America's reticence and endorsing Third World demands for decolonization, was equally leery of any instrument that exposed their regime to outside scrutiny.

---

[*] In 1977 Amnesty International was awarded the Nobel Peace Prize for "having contributed to securing the ground for freedom, for justice, and thereby also for peace in the world."

By 1960, the human rights cause had assumed a new direction, because an overwhelming majority of UN members now represented Asia, Africa, and Latin America. Inevitably, these governments were far less concerned with the barbarous acts committed in World War II than in redeeming the unfulfilled promises in the Atlantic Charter: removing the last remnants of Western imperialism, ending racial injustice in southern Africa, and taking up the cause of the Palestinians. They therefore identified human rights neither with individual freedom nor with the realization of socialism but with the imperatives of national self-determination, economic development, and control over natural resources.

The General Assembly sprang to life. The anti-imperialist bloc, joined by all the communist members, passed declarations calling for Independence for Colonial Peoples (1960) and the Elimination of All Forms of Racial Discrimination (1965). In 1966 they also broke the long deadlock over implementing the Universal Declaration of Human Rights. Recognizing the impossibility of bridging the East-West ideological division over human rights, the assembly finally passed *two* International Human Rights Covenants, one on Civil and Political Rights, the other on Economic, Social, and Cultural Rights.* The Third World attempted to transform the Cold War into a North-South debate between the white and colored peoples, and the developed and nondeveloped worlds. In 1967 an expanded UN Commission on Human Rights ended its two-decade-long period of inactivity and for the first time conducted investigations of conditions in South Africa and in the Arab lands occupied by Israel. The next year it sought to implant its political goals on the international discourse of human rights.

To commemorate the twentieth anniversary of the Universal Declaration, the United Nations had named 1968 "International Human Rights Year" and convened a global conference to review its progress and set an agenda for the future. The setting, ironically, was Tehran, site of the first Big Three summit in 1943 and also the capital of an absolutist regime installed by a 1953 Western-sponsored coup, which was maintained by a powerful army and secret police and whose victims were mobilizing worldwide protests against the shah.

The first International Conference on Human Rights met between April 22 and May 13, 1968, at a moment of considerable Superpower anxiety: it was the height of the Prague Spring and the Tet offensive and less than three weeks after assassination of the American civil rights leader Dr. Martin Luther King Jr. The Third World had amassed considerable power and experience since the Bandung conference. Echoing their host's provocative opening speech, the majority

---

* Both of which were ratified by the Soviet Union in 1973 but not by the United States.

of delegates paid lip service to the Universal Declaration of 1948 but also empha-sized its "empty promises." Several speakers denounced the UDHR's "cosmopol-itan" values, insisting on "the special circumstances of developing countries," the priority of "economic" over "political democracy," and the precedence of col-lective entities—nation, people, and state—over the individual.

The Superpowers shrank from confronting the majority over an issue they had long regarded as secondary. In a curious twist, US and Soviet diplomats at the scene quietly linked forces and refrained from attacking the other's weak points. Only the aged French jurist René Cassin, a veteran of the 1948 delib-erations over the Universal Declaration, dissented, insisting that human rights "could not be different for Europeans, Africans, Americans, and Asians" and warning against confusing the achievement of national independence with the necessity of protecting humans from arbitrary power. The only delegate who supported Cassin was the emissary of Dubček's reformist government. His ap-peal for "the rights of the individual" did draw warm applause from all except the Soviets.

The year 1968 ended on a high note when on Christmas Eve the US space craft *Apollo 8* orbited the moon and transmitted breathtaking photographs of the earth's satellite and of the earth itself. The United States had won another Cold War contest—the space race—and seven months later three American as-tronauts walked on the surface of the moon. But below, on a planet filled that year with turmoil and violence, some questioned the huge expense of the US space program. A striking cartoon depicted an urban slum dweller's impassive reaction to an astronaut's observation of the earth's beauty as seen from space.

By the late 1960s a youth revolt had erupted on every continent against so-cial, economic, and political injustice and against war, imperialism, and nuclear arms. Drawing no inspiration from the official ideologies of either the United States or the USSR or even from Dubček's socialism with a human face or from traditional trade union principles, the demonstrators—dressed in Mao jackets and carrying banners of Che Guevara and Ho Chi Minh—demanded a world that transcended the Cold War. Paul McCartney's 1967 lyrics suggested that it was time for Sergeant Pepper's (twenty-year-old) Lonely Hearts Club Band to leave the scene.

But the Cold War did not end. In response to the popular clamor, the Third World's assertiveness, and their near-clashes in Asia, the Middle East, and Eu-rope—and especially to the economic slowdown that was sapping their power—the United States and the Soviet Union sought new ways to manage their rivalry and reinforce their global hegemony.

SUGGESTIONS FOR FURTHER STUDY

Documents

China's Cultural Revolution, 1966–1969: Not a Dinner Party. Edited by Michael Schoenhals. Armonk, NY: M. E. Sharpe, 1996.

Cronkite, Walter. "Report from Vietnam (1968)." YouTube video 0:53, from a CBS News Television broadcast, February 27, 1968. Posted by "tpleines," May 22, 2010. http://www.youtube.com/watch?v=Nn4w-ud-TyE.

"Final Act of the International Conference on Human Rights, Tehran 22 April to 13 May 1968." United Nations. http://untreaty.un.org/cod/avl/pdf/ha/fatchr/Final _Act_of_TehranConf.pdf.

Johnson, Lyndon Baines. "Remarks Made Following the First Meeting with Soviet Premier Kosygin." Glassboro, NJ, June 1967. Lyndon Baines Johnson Presidential Library and Museum. http://glifos.lbjf.org/gsm/index.php/WHCA_594-4.

———. *Taking Charge: The Johnson White House Tapes*. Edited by Michael R. Beschloss. New York: Simon and Schuster, 1997.

Navrátil, Jaromír. *The Prague Spring 1968: A National Security Archive Documents Reader*. New York: Central European University Press, 1998.

"Palestine National Charter of 1964." United Nations. http://www.un.int/wcm /content/site/palestine/pid/12363.

The Pentagon Papers: The Defense Department History of United States Decisionmaking on Vietnam. 5 vols. Boston: Beacon, 1971–1972.

United Nations Security Council. "Resolution 242 (1967) of 22 November 1967." United Nations. http://daccess-dds-ny.un.org/doc/RESOLUTION/GEN/NR0 /240/94/IMG/NR024094.pdf?OpenElement.

Memoirs

Ellsberg, Daniel. *Secrets: A Memoir of Vietnam and the Pentagon Papers*. New York: Viking, 2002.

Johnson, Lyndon B. *The Vantage Point: Perspectives of the Presidency, 1963–1969*. New York: Holt, Rinehart and Winston, 1971.

Mailer, Norman. *The Armies of the Night*. New York: New American Library, 1968.

McNamara, Robert S., and Brian VanDeMark. *In Retrospect: The Tragedy and Lessons of Vietnam*. New York: Times Books, 1995.

Mlynář, Zdeněk. *Night Frost in Prague: The End of Humane Socialism*. Translated by Paul Wilson. London: C. Hurst, 1980.

Trương, Nhu Tang, David Chanoff, and Van Toai Doan. *A Vietcong Memoir*. San Diego: Harcourt Brace Jovanovich, 1985.

Photographs

Hobsbawm, E. J., and Marc Weitzmann. *1968 Magnum Throughout the World*. Paris: Magnum Photos, 1998.

Films

Apocalypse Now. Directed by Francis Ford Coppola. San Francisco: Zoetrope Studios, 1979.

The Bedford Incident. Directed by James B. Harris. Los Angeles: Columbia Pictures, 1965.

Commissar. Directed by Aleksandr Askoldov. Moscow: Gorky Film Studio, 1967.

The Deer Hunter. Directed by Michael Cimino. Los Angeles: Universal Pictures, 1978.

The Ditch. Directed by Bing Wang. Hong Kong: Wil Productions, 2010.

Dr. Strangelove, or How I Learned to Stop Worrying and Love the Bomb. Directed by Stanley Kubrick. Los Angeles: Columbia Pictures, 1964.

Fail-Safe. Directed by Sidney Lumet. Los Angeles: Columbia Pictures, 1964.

From Russia with Love. Directed by Terence Young. London: Eon Productions, 1963.

I Am Cuba. Directed by Mikhail Kalatozov. Moscow: Mosfilm, 1964.

Ice Station Zebra. Directed by John Sturges. Los Angeles: Metro-Goldwyn-Mayer Studios, 1968.

The Ipcress File. Directed by Sidney J. Furie. London: Lowndes Productions, 1965.

Kolya. Directed by Jan Sverák. Prague: Portobello Pictures, 1996.

The Mouse on the Moon. Directed by Richard Lester. London: Walter Shenson Films, 1963.

The Odessa File. Directed by Ronald Neame. Los Angeles: Columbia Pictures, 1974.

Panic in Year Zero. Directed by Ray Milland. Los Angeles: American International Pictures, 1962.

The Quiet American. Directed by Phillip Noyce. Los Angeles: Miramax Films, 2002.

The Red Detachment of Women. Directed by Jie Fu and Wenzhan Pan. Beijing: Beijing Film Studio, 1970.

The Russians Are Coming, the Russians Are Coming. Directed by Norman Jewison. Los Angeles: Mirisch Corporation, 1966.

Seven Days in May. Directed by John Frankenheimer. Los Angeles: Seven Arts Productions, 1964.

The Spy Who Came In from the Cold. Directed by Martin Ritt. London: Salem Films, 1965.

Torn Curtain. Directed by Alfred Hitchcock. Los Angeles: Universal Pictures, 1966.

The Unbearable Lightness of Being. Directed by Philip Kaufman. Los Angeles: Saul Zaentz Company, 1988.

When the Tenth Month Comes [*Bao gio cho den thang muoi*]. Directed by Nhat Minh Dang. Hanoi: Vietnam Feature Film Studio, 1985.

Fiction

Achebe, Chinua. *A Man of the People: A Novel*. New York: John Day, 1966.

Gordimer, Nadine. *The Late Bourgeois World*. New York: Viking, 1966.

Greene, Graham. *The Comedians*. New York: Viking, 1966.

Solzenitsyn, Aleksander. *The Cancer Ward*. New York: Dell, 1973.

Vargas Llosa, Mario, and Edith Grossman. *The Feast of the Goat.* New York: Farrar, Straus and Giroux, 2001.

Secondary Sources

Barnouin, Barbara, and Changgen Yu. *Chinese Foreign Policy During the Cultural Revolution.* London: Kegan Paul International, 1998.

Brands, H. W. *The Wages of Globalism: Lyndon Johnson and the Limits of American Power.* New York: Oxford University Press, 1995.

Brigham, Robert K. *Guerrilla Diplomacy: The NLF's Foreign Relations and the Viet Nam War.* Ithaca, NY: Cornell University Press, 1998.

Brocheux, Pierre. *Ho Chi Minh: A Biography.* New York: Cambridge University Press, 2007.

Burke, Roland. *Decolonization and the Evolution of International Human Rights.* Philadelphia: University of Pennsylvania Press, 2010.

Chang, Gordon H. *Friends and Enemies: The United States, China, and the Soviet Union, 1948–1972.* Stanford, CA: Stanford University Press, 1990.

Chen, Jian. *Mao's China and the Cold War.* Chapel Hill: University of North Carolina Press, 2001.

Dockrill, Saki. *Britain's Retreat from East of Suez: The Choice Between Europe and the World?* Houndmills, Basingstoke, UK: Palgrave Macmillan, 2002.

Gaiduk, I. V. *The Soviet Union and the Vietnam War.* Chicago: I. R. Dee, 1996.

Ginor, Isabella, and Gideon Remez. *Foxbats over Dimona: The Soviets' Nuclear Gamble in the Six-Day War.* New Haven, CT: Yale University Press, 2007.

Kaiser, David E. *American Tragedy: Kennedy, Johnson, and the Origins of the Vietnam War.* Cambridge, MA: Belknap Press of Harvard University Press, 2000.

Karnow, Stanley. *Vietnam, a History.* New York: Viking, 1983.

Kovrig, Bennett. *Of Walls and Bridges: The United States and Eastern Europe.* New York: New York University Press, 1991.

LaFeber, Walter. *The Deadly Bet: LBJ, Vietnam, and the 1968 Election.* Lanham, MD: Rowman and Littlefield, 2005.

Logevall, Fredrik. *Choosing War: The Lost Chance for Peace and the Escalation of War in Vietnam.* Berkeley: University of California Press, 1999.

Luthi, Lorenz M. *The Sino-Soviet Split: Cold War in the Communist World.* Princeton, NJ: Princeton University Press, 2008.

McDougall, Walter A. *The Heavens and the Earth: A Political History of the Space Age.* New York: Basic Books, 1985.

Moyn, Samuel. "Imperialism, Self-Determination, and the Rise of Human Rights." In *The Human Rights Revolution: An International History,* edited by Akira Iriye, Petra Goedde, and William I. Hitchcock, 159–178. Oxford: Oxford University Press, 2012.

Oren, Michael B. *Six Days of War: June 1967 and the Making of the Modern Middle East.* Oxford: Oxford University Press, 2002.

Radchenko, Sergey. *Two Suns in the Heavens: The Sino-Soviet Struggle for Supremacy, 1962–1967.* Washington, DC: Woodrow Wilson Center, 2009.

Schwartz, Thomas Alan. *Lyndon Johnson and Europe: In the Shadow of Vietnam.* Cambridge, MA: Harvard University Press, 2003.

Segev, Tom. *1967: Israel, the War, and the Year That Transformed the Middle East.* New York: Metropolitan Books, 2007.

Spector, Ronald H. *After Tet: The Bloodiest Year in Vietnam.* New York: Free Press, 1993.

Suri, Jeremi. *Power and Protest: Global Revolution and the Rise of Détente.* Cambridge, MA: Harvard University Press, 2003.

Tischler, Barbara L. *Sights on the Sixties.* New Brunswick, NJ: Rutgers University Press, 1992.

Williams, Kieran. *The Prague Spring and Its Aftermath: Czechoslovak Politics, 1968–1970.* Cambridge: Cambridge University Press, 1997.

Zhai, Qiang. *China and the Vietnam Wars, 1950–1975.* Chapel Hill: University of North Carolina Press, 2000.

Chapter 6

DÉTENTE, 1969–1975

It often takes more courage to change one's opinion than to keep it.

—Willy Brandt

I don't know why you use a fancy French word like détente when there's a good English phrase for it—Cold War.

—Golda Meir

In 1969 the Cold War entered a new stage. The United States and the Soviet Union, responding to the proliferation of nuclear arms, economic and political rivals, and volatile conditions in the Third World, attempted to revamp their global rivalry by establishing new ground rules, new practices, and a new relationship between themselves. Mindful of their limits after the shocks of Tet and Prague, Washington and Moscow embraced détente as a means of fortifying a status quo in which they would continue to lead the world.

Détente—the relaxation of Cold War tensions between the United States and the USSR—began in 1969. Its architects were the new US president, Richard Nixon, and the Soviet Union's general secretary, Leonid Brezhnev, two cautious, conservative political actors seeking to fortify their positions in power. Nixon took the lead, bolstered by his long anticommunist record and the deft support of his national security adviser Henry Kissinger. Seeking to reassert US power against the backdrop of the Soviets' spectacular achievement of nuclear parity and America's descent into the Vietnam morass, Nixon proposed a new format of US-Soviet relations. There would be concrete and reciprocal agreements and an overt linkage between the Superpowers' three major interests: arms control, expanding economic ties, and containing conflicts in Europe and the Third World. Brezhnev responded positively, seeking a means of increasing the Soviets' prestige, obtaining Western technology, and aiding a faltering economy as well as alleviating the growing threat from China.

Détente was affected by several factors. In announcing an "era of negotiations" in 1969 both leaders raised inflated hopes and fears at home and abroad. A Cold War–weary public welcomed a step back from nuclear saber rattling, but hard-liners on both sides were mistrustful and vocal in their criticism. The US and Soviet leaders also confronted a multipolar world in which other actors, particularly West German chancellor Willy Brandt and China's supreme leader, Mao Zedong, played significant roles in reshaping US-Soviet relations, as did the leaders of India and Pakistan, Israel and its Arab neighbors, and North and South Vietnam. Moreover, underlying US-Soviet efforts to create a more orderly and predictable international order was the old Cold War logic of falling dominoes and their core ideological quarrel: Would capitalism or socialism prevail? Consequently the launching of détente, which was predicated on establishing mutual agreements, a joint code of conduct, and military and political restraint—and in which the means and goals of the two rivals were intermingled or ambiguous—would inevitably stir suspicions of the other's bad faith.

REDUCING THE NUCLEAR THREAT

Ever since the dawn of the nuclear age both the United States and the Soviet Union had preached the virtues of arms control without achieving any agreement. The Soviets had initially rebuffed US calls for a ban on atomic weapons until they were able to produce their own arsenal, and in the 1950s Khrushchev's proposals for general disarmament had foundered on Eisenhower's insistence on verification.

The Soviet Union's spectacular military gains in the 1960s formed an important backdrop for détente. Now that Moscow had bridged the missile gap and achieved strategic parity with the United States, it was prepared to discuss mutual reductions in nuclear forces, but the initial discussions had been thwarted by the Vietnam War, the June 1967 war in the Middle East, and the Soviet invasion of Czechoslovakia. On the eve of the Prague invasion, on July 1, 1968, East-West cooperation reached a pinnacle with the signing of the Non-Proliferation

Treaty, an agreement that restricted the transfer of nuclear weapons or technology to nonnuclear states, called on the latter to renounce the acquisition or production of nuclear weapons, and established the UN International Atomic Energy Administration in Vienna to enforce compliance.*

By 1969 the Superpowers claimed the capacity for "mutual assured destruction" (MAD): regardless of who fired the first missile, both were equally vulnerable to annihilation, and no defensive weapon could shield them. Although neither side was confident in the other's restraint, the leaders of both countries recognized the political and economic advantages of curbing their extravagant military budgets and reducing a struggle that neither could win.

Nixon's accession to the presidency in January 1969—coupled with Brezhnev's determination to play a dominant role in the Kremlin—made the revival of talks on major arms limitations possible. In a daring political gambit, Brezhnev immediately probed a war-weakened America's willingness to negotiate as an equal. And in accepting the Soviet proposal for reciprocal nuclear limitations, Nixon became the first president to abandon the insistence on US superiority and sought to wrap the USSR in a web of agreements and understandings to detoxify the Cold War.

The start of serious US-Soviet arms-limitation talks was delayed by old layers of suspicion. The Nixon administration, obsessed with ending the Vietnam War, continued to demand Moscow's assistance with North Vietnam and in the meantime balked at a summit meeting. The president also discomfited Brezhnev by making friendly gestures toward communist China. The Soviet Union, on its side, maintained its insistence on a European security conference that would recognize the postwar borders, and the Soviet press continued to lambaste NATO and Nixon's "Cold War tactics": America's stepped-up war in Southeast Asia, the decision to expand its antiballistic missile (ABM) system, and its obsession with subverting the socialist world.

After months of mutual stalling (caused in part by the reluctance of their military leaders), the United States and the Soviet Union finally launched the Strategic Arms Limitation Treaty (SALT) talks in Helsinki on November 17, 1969. Under a bright spotlight of public attention, the negotiators during their first five weeks made a serious effort to understand the other side's views. Nevertheless,

---

* Opened for signature in 1968, the treaty came into force in 1970 but with India, Pakistan, and Israel declining to sign along with France and China (both of which acceded in 1992). North Korea, which signed in 1985, withdrew in 2003.

the subsequent SALT meetings, which alternated between Helsinki and Vienna, dragged on for two and a half years. Although both sides agreed on the necessity of curbing ABMs, the Soviets, until May 1971, resisted Washington's demand to include offensive weapons in their discussions, and when they did, the SALT talks became bogged down over the different categories of missiles and innovations in nuclear warheads.

The drawn-out SALT talks were also colored by developments in Europe, Asia, and the Middle East, where the two rivals remained at odds. The talks were closely managed behind the scenes by Kissinger through his Washington back channel with Soviet ambassador Anatoly Dobrynin. Another important element in the arms negotiations was their linkage to the prospect of increased US-Soviet trade. Brezhnev, who had stood up to the politburo hard-liners in advocating closer economic ties with the West, counted on Washington to deliver palpable benefits. But Nixon and Kissinger viewed any trade concession as a quid pro quo for Soviet good conduct over Vietnam and the SALT talks. Indeed, a major SALT breakthrough in May 1971 was directly tied to US grain sales to the Soviet Union. Meanwhile, the complicated negotiations between the Nixon administration and anticommunist US labor unions over fulfilling this deal underscored the domestic perils of linkage.

The SALT talks were ultimately successful, although contested by hawks on both sides. The result gave a decided edge to the United States. By controlling the pace of the negotiations, the United States had been able to maintain its strategic advantage despite obtaining only an interim agreement on offensive weapons and establishing missile numbers that gave an apparent benefit to the USSR. Nixon, by wielding the carrot and stick of the West's superior economic power as well as the shock of his breakthrough visit to China in February 1972, was able to elicit significant concessions from Brezhnev, particularly on excluding US nuclear weapons in Europe. Moreover, despite the resumption of America's bombing campaign against North Vietnam (during which Soviet merchant ships were accidentally hit and several sailors killed), Brezhnev did not cancel the Moscow summit. In May 1972 Nixon became the first US president to visit the Soviet Union, where he signed the Cold War's first Strategic Arms Limitation Treaty.

A second agreement signed in Moscow, the ABM treaty, was an attempt to curb the arms race by limiting the number of defense sites against a nuclear attack. In this treaty the United States and the USSR abandoned the establishment of a nationwide system of defenses, agreeing to establish only two fixed, ground-based systems, each with one hundred missile interceptors.* The goal was to reduce the arms race: if both Superpowers remained vulnerable, they would be deterred not only from a first strike but also from developing even more powerful offensive weapons.

Nixon and Brezhnev also concluded a Basic Agreement in Moscow laying out the new principles of US-Soviet relations. These included a pledge to avoid military confrontations and to prevent the outbreak of nuclear war, a promise of "restraint" in their mutual relations, and a foreswearing of "efforts to obtain unilateral advantage at the expense of the other, directly or indirectly." Although vaguely worded and largely unenforceable, these guidelines constituted the unofficial charter for détente and reverberated around the world as a formal renunciation by the Superpowers of exploiting regional conflicts for their own interests.

OSTPOLITIK

Unlike Nixon,[†] Brezhnev had warmly welcomed Willy Brandt's victory in the momentous West German elections in September 1969. As a potential partner, Brandt, the first Social Democrat chancellor of the Federal Republic, had impeccable credentials, with his anti-Nazi record, adherence to the Nuclear Non-Proliferation Treaty, outspoken support for rapprochement with the East, and, above all, promises of generous economic and technological assistance to the ailing Soviet economy. Other Kremlin leaders endorsed a Soviet *Westpolitik* as a means of weaning the Bonn government away from NATO and reducing US power in Europe. However, a few were less enthusiastic. In his response to Brandt's overtures, Brezhnev had to overcome strong Soviet memories of World War II, Moscow's two-decade-long propaganda tirades against the FRG, and the even longer hostility (dating back to 1917) between communists and Social Democrats—not to mention the awkward problem of the GDR.

Brandt and his close adviser and confidant Egon Bahr were prepared to move quickly and decisively to free the German question from its Cold War straitjacket. The FRG, now led by an awkward coalition of Social Democrats (SDP) and Center-Right Free Democrats (FDP), had become the world's third-largest exporter but was wracked by its first serious economic downturn since 1949 and

---

* The treaty explicitly banned sea-, air-, space-, and land-based mobile ABM systems, and the number of fixed sites was reduced to one in 1974.

† Who had preferred and prematurely congratulated Brandt's conservative opponent, the CDU leader Kurt-Georg Kiesinger.

by social and political unrest from increasingly militant left- and right-wing movements. Brandt, a charismatic politician and a realist, capitalized on Nixon's proposal for an era of negotiations. He intended to overcome the East's suspicions and bad memories by conducting an active campaign to conciliate the Soviet Union and its Warsaw Pact allies, including the GDR. He would reassure his US protector and his West European neighbors of Bonn's fidelity, quelling their fears of another Rapallo—the 1922 rapprochement between Germany and the Soviet Union that had ruptured the West's unity and laid the basis for close military and economic cooperation until Hitler came to power. Brandt's most difficult accomplishment was to convince most, if not all, of his fellow citizens that by abandoning Adenauer's hard-line stance toward Germany's lost territories and the priority of German unification, the FRG could stabilize relations in Central Europe and secure the future of West Berlin.

Ostpolitik consisted of a series of interlinked agreements brilliantly masterminded by Brandt and Bahr, who trod a careful line between accommodation and German national interests. The major breakthrough occurred in the Moscow Treaty (August 12, 1970), in which both sides renounced the use of force and any territorial claims against each other and also recognized the inviolability of Europe's borders. By accepting the Soviet demand to acknowledge the status quo and offering considerable economic inducements, Brandt was able to convince Brezhnev to accept his refusal to formally recognize the German Democratic Republic and to sanction West Germany's inroads into the Soviet bloc.

Four months later Brandt journeyed to Warsaw to sign a treaty with the even more wary Polish government. Again, the chancellor combined renunciatory gestures on borders and offers of increased trade with a forceful refusal to pay reparations to Poland and a demand to expedite the emigration of the remaining ethnic Germans wishing to leave. On December 7, 1970, in a stunning political gesture, the chancellor fell to his knees before the memorial to the slain Jews of the 1943 Warsaw ghetto uprising, thereby acknowledging West Germany's responsibility for its past and its determination to reconcile with its former victims.

Still to be won was security for West Berlin, whose morale and economy had languished since the Berlin Wall was built in 1961. During that decade the GDR had done its utmost to isolate the city by impeding traffic across its territory and blocking ties between West and East Berliners. In response Bonn had persisted in maintaining its links with the beleaguered outpost by establishing a few government offices and heavily subsidizing the West Berlin economy.

Although the fate of the former German capital rested with the four occupying powers, Bonn, through back channels, played an important role in the negotiations. The prospects began to improve in May 1971, when Brezhnev replaced the obdurate East German Communist Party leader Walter Ulbricht with the more obliging Erich Honecker. With the August 23, 1971, Quadripartite Pact, Brandt won another major victory, achieving security for his West Berliners. The agreement not only assured unimpeded access to the city, allowing them to visit East Berlin and other parts of the GDR, but also opened the way for Bonn to represent West Berlin abroad and to expand its political and economic ties with the isolated city.

Brandt's successes, culminating in his informal Crimean meeting with Brezhnev in September 1971 and the award of a Nobel Peace Prize at the end of the year, received grudging approval in Washington. But it also infuriated Brandt's domestic rivals, who accused him of betraying the nation's interests. In April 1972 the Christian Democrats sought to unseat him with a vote of no confidence and a month later to block passage of the core Soviet and Polish treaties. Brezhnev, on the eve of his summit with Nixon, anxiously observed these votes, on which the fate of his *Westpolitik* rested.

Soon Brandt achieved another triumph. On May 17 the Bundestag, by a razor-thin majority, passed the two treaties. Buoyed by his victory, the chancellor called for national elections as a referendum on *Ostpolitik*, and his government won handily in November 1972. Brandt was then able to conclude the most difficult agreement of all, the Basic Treaty with the GDR, containing recognition of the current borders and a renunciation of force but also setting more generous rules for human contact between the two Germanys. By accepting the existence of two states—while still withholding formal recognition—Brandt had abandoned West Germany's two-decade-long Cold War crusade against its communist neighbor and normalized its role in the international community, paving the way for the FRG and the GDR to enter the United Nations in 1973. That year *Ostpolitik* was completed with the establishment of diplomatic ties with Czechoslovakia, Hungary, and Bulgaria.

Ostpolitik was made possible not only by Brandt's determination and persuasiveness but also by a new stage of the Cold War that gave Bonn room to maneuver. With both Superpowers struggling to control their respective clients, finance their outsized military expenditures, and quell domestic dissatisfaction, Brandt between 1969 and 1974 was able to transform West Germany into a politically respectable, diplomatically vigorous, middle-sized actor. He laid the foundations for Bonn's extensive economic inroads into the Soviet Union and Eastern Europe, which profited both sides. He promoted the first expansion of the European Community in 1973, which not only brought in a supportive Great Britain but also raised the prospect of a stronger European voice in world affairs. And, finally, although Brandt anchored Bonn's diplomacy in its ties to Washington, the methods and goals of *Ostpolitik* were both more geographically limited and politically daring than Nixon's view of détente.

PING-PONG DIPLOMACY

Mao Zedong, who had reached his seventy-eighth year in 1969 and appointed Marshal Lin Biao as his successor, was still determined to combat China's dire economic and security situation. The country, ravaged by the Great Leap Forward in the 1950s and the Cultural Revolution, which began in 1966, had become increasingly poor and isolated, with enemies on almost all its borders. In addition to the American-led war in Vietnam, its hostile neighbors included Taiwan, Japan, South Korea, India, and especially the Soviet Union, whose invasion

Photo 6.1. Warm handshake between Chinese leader Mao Zedong and Richard Nixon during the president's visit to China, February 29, 1972. *Courtesy of National Archives.*

of Czechoslovakia and Brezhnev doctrine directly threatened China. Countering the Kremlin's efforts to gain the support of the world communist movement, China drew closer to Romania and Albania and on March 2, 1969, instigated the first Sino-Soviet armed clash along the Ussuri River.

The advent of détente and *Ostpolitik*—threatening to strengthen China's foremost antagonist—may well have persuaded Mao to rethink his two-decade-long hostility toward the United States. Drawing on Leninist vocabulary to accuse Moscow of "tsarism" and "social imperialism" and on traditional Chinese political culture calling for "borrowing the strength of the barbarians to check the barbarians," Mao could justify a momentous shift in world diplomacy.

Nixon was well prepared to woo a second communist power in order to free America from Vietnam, exert pressure on Moscow, and revive US global power. However, to do so, he had to abandon America's pro-Taiwan China lobby (which he had once championed) and deal with a regime the United States had not yet recognized, had long vilified, and had annually barred from taking a seat in the United Nations, and a government still supporting North Vietnam. Soon after assuming the presidency in 1969, Nixon set out boldly, initiating secret diplomatic soundings through the leaders of France, Pakistan, and Romania, which led to the resumption of the suspended Sino-American ambassadorial talks in Warsaw in early 1970.*

Washington, however, had many unfriendly habits to overcome. Not only had Nixon irritated Mao by publicly justifying his costly ABM program as a defense against "the Chinese threat," but he had also refused to end America's military presence in Taiwan and in May 1970 expanded the Vietnam War by invading Cambodia. Only when Kissinger recognized the serious split in the Chinese politburo between Prime Minister Zhou Enlai, who advocated rapprochement with Washington, and Lin Biao, who forcefully opposed it, did Washington begin to hone its signals and issue more conciliatory statements.

By 1971 Mao was ready to respond. In April he caused a sensation by inviting an American table tennis team to visit China. While the US press recorded the excitement of "ping-pong diplomacy," Nixon quietly lifted the twenty-one-year trade embargo and in May offered to dispatch Kissinger to China for a secret meeting with its leaders. Kissinger's two-day visit in July was a resounding political and propaganda success. The announcement of Nixon's forthcoming trip

---

* Between 1955 and 1970 (with a hiatus between 1968 and the beginning of 1970 due to the chaos caused by the Cultural Revolution), US and Chinese ambassadors had met 170 times, first in Geneva and afterward 1958 in Warsaw, to discuss outstanding issues relating to Korea and Taiwan.

to China—which would *precede* the long-delayed Moscow summit—alerted the world to a new US-Chinese relationship. In August the United States announced its support for the seating of the People's Republic of China in the United Nations, which occurred two months later. Of even greater significance was Lin Biao's mysterious death in a September 12 plane crash, which removed a major obstacle to the course set by Mao and Nixon.

Despite Nixon's hyperbolic toast at the end of his weeklong visit to China in February 1972, the president's trip did not "change the world." Replacing two decades of hostility, the carefully crafted Shanghai Communiqué on February 27 pledged both countries to work for normalization of relations and expand people-to-people contacts and trade opportunities.* But US-Chinese relations remained prickly over the future of Taiwan and ending the Vietnam War. Nonetheless, Washington's triangular diplomacy had measurably improved the US position in the Cold War. Although Nixon repeatedly denied that he was playing the "China card," the United States in fact had decided to tilt toward the weaker communist power against the Soviet Union. As proof, Kissinger repeatedly provided sensitive intelligence information to Beijing but none to the Soviet leaders.

There were additional benefits for the United States. Immediately after the Nixon visit, Beijing counseled North Vietnam against a military offensive, and when the United States ferociously bombed Hanoi, Beijing remained relatively silent. Moreover, China gradually began to diminish its aid to insurrectionary movements in Africa, and over the next three years, while Washington and Beijing began working in tandem to reduce tensions in Southeast Asia, the United States was able to reduce its armed forces.

For the aged and ill Mao, rapprochement with the long-reviled United States had risked domestic opposition and Hanoi's contempt. But Nixon's visit had also brought benefits. Although weak and vulnerable, the People's Republic of China could now become a major diplomatic player in the region and the world. By reaching out to the United States Mao had checked the danger of Soviet "imperialism," and with the winding down of the Cultural Revolution in 1971, China would be able to profit from expanded ties with the West to revive its shattered economy.

The Soviets were, of course, the major losers. Stunned by Kissinger's initial visit, Moscow continued to hammer away at "the Chinese menace," but it failed to halt Nixon's triangular diplomacy. Some have suggested that the USSR's

---

* In a bow to China's anti-Soviet stance, the communiqué also asserted that neither nation "should seek hegemony in the Asia-Pacific region" and that each was "opposed to efforts by any other country or group of countries to establish such hegemony."

willingness to conclude the Quadripartite Agreement on Berlin was hastened by Kissinger's July 1971 trip to Beijing. Even more persuasive are the suggestions that Brezhnev's concessions during the SALT negotiations and his refusal to cancel the Moscow summit grew directly out of the Soviet Union's ever-worsening relations with China.

Ping-pong diplomacy had also set the United States and China on a course that transcended the Cold War. The end of China's isolation not only changed the balance of power in Asia but also added China's voice on the UN Security Council as a champion of the old Bandung principles of noninterference and nondomination by the two Great Powers.

TESTING DÉTENTE, 1970–1974

Despite US-Soviet attempts to manage their affairs peacefully, the Cold War continued in the Third World. The three-year delay of the Moscow summit played a role, but even more important were the Superpowers' opposing views of the methods and goals of détente as it applied outside Europe. Khrushchev had earlier explained to a suspicious Mao that coexistence with the United States did not necessarily preclude seeking political advantage through aid to potential clients in Asia, Africa, and Latin America or protecting Moscow's interests against Western incursions. Consequently, Brezhnev, after the hiatus following the Soviets' setbacks in Cuba, the Congo, Ghana, Algeria, and Indonesia, cautiously reentered the fray in the late 1960s, encouraged by Nixon's announcement that the United States would no longer commit its troops to halt the spread of communism.* On the other hand, Nixon still insisted on keeping a scorecard on the Kremlin's gains and losses and refused to allow Moscow to exploit America's plight in Vietnam to gain advantage. Thus détente did not stop the Superpowers from deploying their intelligence, military, and economic resources to compete for influence and prestige in the Third World.

The Middle East

The Israeli-Egyptian conflict provided the first test of détente. Having heavily rearmed their respective clients after the June 1967 war, the Superpowers were

---

* In his press conference in Guam on July 25, 1969, the president proclaimed the Nixon doctrine. Returning to the more cautious formulations of Truman and Eisenhower doctrines, he announced the end of Vietnam-type military interventions, stating that although the United States would maintain its treaty commitments and continue to furnish requested military and economic assistance, he expected America's allies to play a major role in their own defense.

nonetheless unprepared for the outbreak of hostilities. In March 1969, just as the Kremlin was exchanging friendly signals with Washington, Nasser, irritated by the UN's failure to obtain an Israeli evacuation of Egyptian territory, unilaterally abrogated the 1967 cease-fire and launched the War of Attrition, with commando raids and the shelling and bombing of Israeli positions. Israel responded with aerial attacks. By January 1970, Israel's depth bombings of Egyptian military installations and urban centers precipitated Nasser's urgent plea to Moscow for support.

Brezhnev, bowing to his military and intelligence advisers against the more cautious counsel in the politburo, responded almost immediately with Operation Kavkaz (Caucasus), expanding Egypt's air defense system and dispatching 12,000 Soviet soldiers and 150 pilots to control the surface-to-air missiles (SAMs), fly surveillance missions, and conduct air-to-air combat with Israelis. Although his armed forces were stretched from Czechoslovakia to the Chinese frontier, Brezhnev shocked the United States by ordering the Soviet Union's most significant deployment outside the borders of the Warsaw Pact.*

Washington, although absorbed by the domestic outcry over the invasion of Cambodia,† was determined to stand firm against the Soviets' provocation and moved in as mediator. On August 7, Secretary of State William Rogers convinced Israel and Egypt to sign another cease-fire, restoring the status quo. Nasser, saved by US intervention, signed without consulting Moscow. The less enthusiastic Israeli prime minister, Golda Meir, was assuaged by the offer of new deliveries of US F-4 Phantom aircraft and by Nixon's assurances that the United States would not insist on a withdrawal until a "binding peace agreement satisfactory to you has been achieved." Under Kissinger's leadership, the United States had checked Soviet "adventurism" in the Middle East.

This resolve was immediately tested in September, when a radical Palestinian group—furious over Nasser's desertion—attempted to foment a civil war in Jordan.‡ Nixon, applauding King Hussein's formation of a military government,

---

* Smaller numbers of Soviet troops had been sent earlier to Korea, Cuba, South Yemen, and Vietnam.

† In April 1970, after US troops were sent into Cambodia to prevent North Vietnamese troops from using that country as a sanctuary to attack South Vietnam, there was a wave of domestic and foreign protests, culminating in the May 4 demonstration at Kent State University in Ohio, during which four students were killed by the National Guard.

‡ Underlining its rivalry with the far larger Egyptian-backed PLO, a splinter group, the Marxist Popular Front for the Liberation of Palestine (PFLP), had hijacked four Western planes on September 6 and 7 and, after freeing the passengers in exchange for the release of their comrades in Western prisons, blew up all four.

denounced the Palestinian militants, sent naval forces to the eastern Mediterranean, and warned against outside intervention. But on September 18 the crisis suddenly escalated when Syrian forces invaded Jordan in support of the Palestinians.

Washington immediately suspected a Soviet plot behind Syria's move. Nixon and Kissinger perceived a pattern of testing America's mettle, which included the Egyptians' violations of the cease-fire and Moscow's stalling over the SALT and the Berlin negotiations. Moreover, on the very day of the Syrian invasion of Jordan, U-2 photos had recorded evidence of the construction of a potential nuclear submarine base in Cienfuegos, Cuba, in violation of the 1962 Kennedy-Khrushchev agreement that prohibited offensive weapons on the island.*

A Superpower confrontation—which was underscored by the arrival of armed Soviet ships in the eastern Mediterranean to shadow the US fleet—appeared imminent. The United States and Israel began consultations over a possible intervention in Jordan to stave off Hussein's collapse and the establishment of a Palestinian Marxist state. However, in reality Washington was moving cautiously out of fear of unleashing an uncontrollable war.

In the end it was the local actors who ended the crisis. King Hussein, the thirty-five-year-old monarch who had been a major loser in June 1967, averted an Israeli intervention by unleashing his air force against the Syrians, who (under the threat of Israel's mobilization on their borders) beat a hurried retreat. The Jordanian crisis then ended bloodily with the massacre of thousands of Palestinians and the expulsion of their leaders to Lebanon. In still another startling development on September 28, Nasser, after calling an emergency Arab League meeting to solve the Jordanian crisis, died of a heart attack at age fifty-two.

Although Washington trumpeted its victory (and many scholars have repeated this claim), the Jordanian incident actually served as a crisis-management lesson for both sides. Whether or not Washington's pressure had been decisive, Brezhnev, with only limited influence over Syria, had his own good reasons to prevent a wider war that would sink the prospect of détente. Nixon, too, shrank from a Superpower confrontation. Despite the nuclear threat lurking behind the Cienfuegos dispute, he decided against escalating that crisis and instead negotiated a private agreement with Brezhnev in October. Under the new parameters

---

* Washington's hackles had been further raised on September 4, 1970, when, despite its efforts, the socialist Salvador Allende had won the presidency of Chile, adding a second left-wing government in the Western Hemisphere.

of détente, the need for alert, realistic policy making on distant and peripheral disputes had become evident.

South Asia

The struggle between India and Pakistan was another postcolonial rivalry that tested détente. The core source of antagonism was the region of Kashmir, whose division in 1948 was (and still is) contested by Pakistan. Initially, India had sought a neutral Cold War stance, but after the Sino-Indian War in 1962 it had gravitated toward the Soviet Union. Pakistan, a formerly staunch member of the Western bloc, after its 1965 war with India moved closer to China. In both instances, the United States, immersed in Vietnam, had stayed aloof, but the Soviet Union in 1966 had gained the gratitude of both parties for its positive role as a mediator.

In the beginning of 1971—just as the United States began its overtures to China—the Indo-Pakistani quarrel resumed. After a stunning electoral setback, the Pakistani government, led by the military dictator General Yahya Kahn, sought to suppress an autonomous movement in East Pakistan by declaring martial law and arresting leaders of the resistance.* The violence of the repression, claiming thousands of victims, led to the flight of almost ten million Bengali (and mostly Hindu) refugees into India. Prime Minister Indira Gandhi, having failed to obtain international support to halt the atrocities, prepared for war.

The United States, while acknowledging its ally's brutal behavior, had become dependent on Pakistan as its conduit to China. Thus in July Nixon decided both to tilt toward Pakistan and to warn India (whose leader he personally disliked) against any form of aggression against its neighbor. Unsurprisingly, the Soviet Union, following the bombshell of Kissinger's trip to Beijing, responded on August 9 with a Treaty of Peace, Friendship, and Cooperation with India.

After war broke out in December between India and Pakistan, Washington and Moscow employed the hotline to prevent an escalation. The Soviets, backing India, insisted on independence for East Pakistan, which the United States did not oppose. But the crisis escalated when Nixon and Kissinger, suspecting Kremlin support for an Indian attempt to dismember *West* Pakistan, dispatched a carrier battle group to the Bay of Bengal. Moscow's response was to send its own naval forces into the area.

---

* See Map 4 (p. 65). The state of Pakistan consisted of two regions separated by a thousand miles with India in between.

The brutal two-week war, which ended on December 17, was catastrophic for Pakistan, stripping it of over half its population (which formed the new state of Bangladesh) and establishing India's dominance of the subcontinent. Nonetheless, Kissinger took credit for halting aggression by a Kremlin proxy, although the reality was less convincing. Gandhi had no intention of becoming a Soviet satellite and being dragged into Moscow's quarrels with China. Moreover, not only had Washington misread Indian and Soviet intentions and failed to rein in Pakistan, but its show of naval force had not impressed Beijing, and its refusal to intervene militarily had infuriated the government in Islamabad.

The war's outcome also contributed to regional instability and to nuclear proliferation. Immediately afterward Pakistan decided to follow India's example and began to develop an atomic weapons program.

Vietnam

The Vietnam War remained the most critical issue in US-Soviet relations. Early in the Nixon administration, the president had signaled that these could not improve without Soviet aid in ending the war and had threatened to escalate hostilities if this was not forthcoming. The Soviets, while acknowledging their limited control over Hanoi, resented US pressure and the use of its opening to China to force them to stand aside.*

Nixon did fulfill his 1968 campaign promise to end the draft and reduce the number of US troops in Vietnam, but he also escalated the amount of violence and casualties. Far exceeding Johnson's approach, Nixon's moves included expanding the war into Cambodia in 1970 and into Laos in 1971 (destabilizing both countries) and responding to every North Vietnamese offensive with massive bombing attacks. Nonetheless, the United States failed to budge Hanoi at the meeting table. In the secret Paris talks that he directed after 1969, Kissinger failed to win North Vietnamese agreement on a mutual withdrawal of their forces from South Vietnam.

Facing reelection in 1972, Nixon stepped up the pressure on Moscow. In April Kissinger punished the Soviets' complicity in Hanoi's recent offensive by refusing to facilitate the passage of the two Eastern Treaties in the West German Bundestag. Nixon's badgering had some effect. At the May 1972 Moscow summit Brezhnev finally agreed to send an emissary to Hanoi, and during the fall and

---

* The United States had slightly more success with China, which urged the North Vietnamese to accept a compromise and in 1971 rebuffed Hanoi's pleas to cancel the Nixon visit.

winter of 1972 both of Nixon's summit partners urged restraint on their client. Hanoi responded by accusing China and the Soviet Union of becoming bogged down on "the dark, muddy road of compromise." North Vietnam denounced its two patrons—"lured by the chimera of peaceful coexistence and economic benefits"—for betraying "the great, all-conquering revolutionary idea of the age."

The United States also continued to wield its military power. Kissinger's announcement that "peace is at hand" undoubtedly contributed to Nixon's reelection in November 1972, but immediately afterward, the president ordered the fierce Christmas Day bombing of Hanoi and Haiphong to convince North Vietnam to return to the conference table and also to give proof to South Vietnam of America's lasting commitment to protect it. With the agreement on January 27, 1973, America's long, costly, and divisive war ended on a sour note with a cease-fire in place instead of a total North Vietnamese withdrawal.[*] Within two years, the Saigon government—weakened by the complete removal of US troops and a sharp decrease in US military aid—was overcome by North Vietnamese forces, and the governments of Cambodia and Laos also fell to the communists.

The conclusion of the Vietnam War had underscored the paradox of US-Soviet détente that had been complicated by the emerging US-Sino-Soviet triangle. Although the Superpowers had committed substantial resources to the struggle in Southeast Asia, neither had fully controlled its clients. Both had expected the other to be more accommodating than either was willing to be, or even capable of being. To be sure, Hanoi's victory in 1975 created more diplomatic and economic problems for Moscow as well as for Beijing, while America's defeat—although a severe political and psychological blow—had left its triangular diplomacy unimpaired. Nonetheless, America's war in Vietnam had reinforced the nation's growing conviction that the struggle against global communism must no longer be fought solely by US soldiers.

The October War in the Middle East[†]

After the Vietnam obstacle had been cleared away, US-Soviet relations appeared to improve. Despite a slowdown in the SALT II negotiations, Brezhnev's visit to the United States in June 1973 (the first by a Soviet leader in fourteen years and

---

[*] The 1973 Nobel Peace Prize was awarded jointly to Kissinger and the North Vietnamese negotiator Lê Đức Thọ (who declined to accept).

[†] Because the outbreak of the war on October 6 coincided with holy days in both the Jewish and the Muslim calendars, the Israelis (and much of the West) have called it the Yom Kippur War, while the Arabs have called it the Ramadan War.

Photo 6.2. Leonid Brezhnev and Richard Nixon meeting during the general secretary's visit to the United States, June 19, 1973. *Courtesy of National Archives.*

including a visit to Nixon's California home) was amicable. In the course of their private discussions, Brezhnev had added an ominous note with his repeated warnings of an imminent explosion in the Middle East, which Nixon, intent on excluding the Kremlin from the region, chose to ignore.

By September 1973 relations were cooling. With Nixon engrossed in Watergate,* Kissinger, who had replaced Rogers as secretary of state, took a harder line toward the Soviets. That month the spirit of détente was frayed by the US-supported coup in Chile. A right-wing military junta overthrew the government of Salvador Allende, who died during the attack, and then conducted a brutal wave of repression against his left-wing supporters. In addition, Congress was balking over granting most-favored-nation trade status to the Soviet Union, and Moscow was annoyed over another planned Kissinger trip to China.

Kissinger intended to maintain US predominance in the Middle East but had decided to delay a peace initiative until after the October Israeli general elections,

---

* The scandal that originated in the June 1972 arrest of five burglars who had broken into the Democratic National Committee Headquarters in the Watergate building in Washington, DC. With the discovery of the burglars' ties to Nixon's reelection committee and the subsequent cover-up attempts, Watergate had grown into a major political and constitutional crisis played live after July 1973 in the nationally televised hearings of a special congressional investigative committee.

which the seventy-five-year-old Golda Meir was expected to win. Washington was also in direct contact with Nasser's successor, Anwar Sadat, who, after expelling seventeen thousand Soviet military advisers and technicians, had sought US diplomatic support in regaining the Sinai. At the United Nations on September 25, Kissinger gave a weak assurance to Arab diplomats that the United States would soon "assist in finding a settlement" to end the Israeli occupation but also warned his audience about "expecting miracles."

Sadat, who had lost patience with the Superpowers, was determined to use Egypt's military power to force concessions on Israel. In April 1973 he had concluded an offensive agreement with Syrian president Hafez al-Assad and subsequently ignored repeated Soviet cautions against another disastrous military action. On October 6, in a well-coordinated surprise attack, Egypt sent its troops across the Suez Canal and overran Israeli defenses in the Sinai while Syria simultaneously attacked in the Golan Heights.

The United States and the Soviet Union moved immediately to control a war they had failed to prevent. Over the next two weeks, while conducting a tense diplomatic duet, they both ran nonstop airlifts to supply arms to their clients and jockeyed for a favorable cease-fire. After Israel launched a counteroffensive and recaptured practically all the occupied territory, the situation changed dramatically. Kissinger, in almost complete charge of US diplomacy, won Soviet consent for a cease-fire resolution by the UN Security Council on October 22.

The Superpowers' cooperation was immediately tested when Israeli forces, ignoring the cease-fire, threatened to encircle the Egyptian Third Army corps. On October 24 Brezhnev, in response to Sadat's urgent appeal, proposed the dispatch of joint US-Soviet military units to enforce the cease-fire. Kissinger, determined to keep control over the peace process, chose to interpret the general secretary's proposal as an ultimatum, one that (as in 1956) ostensibly threatened a unilateral Soviet intervention. That night US conventional and nuclear forces throughout the world went on high alert for the first time since the Cuban missile crisis. In response to Washington's vociferous reaction, Brezhnev withdrew his proposal. Kissinger then moved briskly to defuse the crisis, forcing Israel to accept the cease-fire and allow supplies to the beleaguered Third Army and convincing Sadat to accept an international peacekeeping force. Bypassing the UN peace conference in December, chaired jointly by the United States and the Soviet Union, Kissinger conducted a breathtaking round of negotiations leading to disengagement agreements between the Israeli and Egyptian and Syrian governments that excluded Moscow from the process.

The fourth Arab-Israeli war had global repercussions. On October 16, in retaliation against the West's support of Israel, the Arab oil producers cut production, quadrupled prices, declared a total embargo against shipments to the United States and the Netherlands, and drastically reduced supplies to Western Europe. The oil shock of 1973–1974 dealt a crippling blow to the noncommunist world, sending their economies into stagflation, a period of low economic growth and rising prices and unemployment.

The Soviet Union, a major oil and natural gas producer, initially profited from higher world prices. But this boon had a negative effect as well, reinforcing the command economy and blocking internal reforms. Brezhnev, who had staked his leadership on using oil and gas revenues to obtain Western technology, rejected the urgent proposals of Soviet economists to modernize, decentralize, and diversify the USSR's economy to face the challenges of the postindustrial age.

The October War also exposed the fragility of the 1972 Basic Agreement between the United States and the Soviet Union. Once more, both sides had poured arms into their clients but had difficulty controlling them, and neither had been willing to sustain a defeat by proxy. Moreover, there were serious domestic impediments to their managing the world's problems together. Brezhnev had become vulnerable to mounting criticism from military, intelligence, and politburo hard-liners for sacrificing Soviet interests on the altar of peaceful coexistence, and Nixon and Kissinger faced growing congressional opposition to appeasing Moscow in light of its persecution of Jews and political dissidents. Indeed, outrage over Brezhnev's "provocative" behavior during the October war fueled support for the Jackson-Vanik Amendment, which had been added to the 1974 Trade Act. Stirred by the Kremlin's restrictions on the emigration of Soviet Jewry, the amendment withheld most-favored-nation treatment from countries that violated human rights and was passed overwhelmingly, effectively foreclosing the Kremlin's economic payback for détente.* Kissinger, who had strongly opposed Jackson-Vanik, now recognized that negative linkage could cripple US-Soviet ties.

The October 1973 war also left a scar on US relations with its NATO allies, who were not consulted during the crisis, were terrified by the nuclear alert, and bore the major brunt of the Arab oil boycott. In 1974 the European Community, now consisting of nine members (including Great Britain), sought to exert its diplomatic

---

* Indeed Brezhnev, recognizing the high political cost of the KGB's anti-Jewish campaign, complained to a politburo meeting in March 1973, "Zionism is making us stupid."

muscle by initiating direct ties with the Arab world, only to be scolded by Kissinger for obstructing the peace process and breaking ranks with US leadership.

HELSINKI

Détente still had one more act to play. The Soviet Union had long sought a treaty recognizing its control of Eastern Europe, but the United States had refused to go beyond an acknowledgment of the status quo. However, once Bonn had launched its *Ostpolitik* and recognized Europe's post-1945 borders, Washington could no longer resist.

In December 1971, four months after the Quadripartite Agreement on Berlin, NATO formally accepted the Soviet proposal but insisted on US and Canadian participation in the Conference on Security and Cooperation in Europe. Following more than a year of preparation, the conference opened in 1973 in Helsinki. Over the next two years delegates engaged in tough negotiations and finally drafted a series of conventions, agreements, and confidence-building measures to improve East-West relations in Europe. On August 1, 1975, Brezhnev; Nixon's successor, Gerald Ford; and the leaders of thirty-three other governments signed the Helsinki Accords.

On the surface, the Soviet Union was the victor. The first two parts of the Helsinki Final Act (termed Baskets One and Two) pronounced the inviolability of Europe's borders and prohibited changes either by force or by economic coercion. The West thereby acknowledged the division of Germany and the borders of Poland and the Soviet Union (including the absorption of the Baltic states). In pledging to "respect each other's sovereign equality and individuality" and "refrain from any intervention . . . in the internal or external affairs . . . of another participating state," the West foreswore any political designs to alter the status quo. And in pledging to increase East-West trade relations, the West granted expanded access to its loans and technology to the communists.

However, in addition to legitimating the Soviet Union's European empire, the Helsinki Accords offered the daring prospect of its reform. The third section, known as Basket Three, drawing on a decade of human rights activism, contained a pledge to uphold such fundamental rights as "freedom of thought, conscience, religion, or belief" as well as freedom of movement, and "to promote and encourage the effective exercise of civil, political, economic, social, cultural and other rights and freedom, all of which derive from the inherent dignity of the human person."

Basket Three had raised a momentary alarm in Moscow. But Foreign Minister Gromyko, citing Stalin's signature on the Yalta Declaration of Liberated Europe in return for Western political and territorial concessions, calmed the Kremlin by repeating Kissinger's assurances that neither side would interfere in the other's domestic affairs and insisting, "We remain masters in our own house." Yet despite the tacit US-Soviet accord over nonintervention, the Helsinki Accords brought forth a wave of human rights activism that Moscow could only temporarily repress.

On balance, the Helsinki Accords revealed the ambivalent nature of détente and drew criticism for their ambiguity. For Europeans—East and West—Helsinki marked a relaxation of tensions while the Iron Curtain still stood; for the United States it represented a formal concession with the prospect of a future wedge issue; and for the Soviet Union it was a triumph that would soon place it on the moral and political defensive. Partisans of Helsinki evoked the spirit of the 1922 Genoa Conference, which had tried to rebind Europe after World War I and efface the ideological divide between the Soviet Union and the West. Thus Helsinki was both an end and a beginning of two distinct stages in the Cold War.

The six-year period of détente remains a highly controversial historical episode in the West. Its proponents were praised for lowering the decibels of the Cold War, but they were also castigated for replacing principled resistance to communism with Realpolitik, for extending the life of an enfeebled Soviet Union and betraying the dissidents, and, especially, for failing to prevent conflicts in the Third World. Similarly Brezhnev and his supporters were lauded for gaining political and economic concessions from the West but also scolded by domestic and foreign critics for abandoning the Marxist creed of international class warfare. In a broader perspective, the authors of détente had sought stability over change without anticipating the domestic backlash or fully understanding the new challenges of global politics.

To be sure, the Superpowers' embrace of détente was more superficial than real. Because of internal pressures and their old Cold War habits, they did not stop building bombs and missiles or attempting to seek political advantage wherever possible. Détente succeeded in establishing some permanent ground rules of US-Soviet behavior that lasted until the end of—and even beyond—the Cold War. But because its principal authors were not bold enough to abandon their domino theories, resist their clients' pressure, play by mutual rules, and, above all, give up the prospect of winning the Cold War, the principles of equality and compromise inherent in the Helsinki Accords were only short-lived.

CHAPTER 6: DÉTENTE, 1969–1975

SUGGESTIONS FOR FURTHER STUDY

Documents

"Conference on Security and Co-operation in Europe Final Act, Helsinki, 1975." Organization for Security and Co-operation in Europe. http://www.osce.org/mc /39501?download=true.

"Joint Statement Following Discussions with Leaders of the People's Republic of China." Shanghai, February 27, 1972. US State Department. Office of the Historian. http://history.state.gov/historicaldocuments/frus1969-76v17/d203.

Kissinger, Henry. *The Kissinger Transcripts: The Top Secret Talks with Beijing and Moscow*. Edited by William Burr. New York: New Press, 1999.

"Paris Peace Accords, 1973." *Wikisource*. http://en.wikisource.org/wiki/Paris_Peace _Accords.

"Strategic Arms Limitation Talks (SALT I)." Signed May 26, 1972. NTI: Nuclear Threat Initiative. http://www.nti.org/treaties-and-regimes/strategic-arms-limitation -talks-salt-i-salt-ii/.

"The Tilt: The US and the South Asian Crisis of 1971." National Security Archive. 2002. http://www.gwu.edu/~nsarchiv/NSAEBB/NSAEBB79/.

"Treaty Between the Federal Republic of Germany and the Soviet Union, Signed at Moscow, August 12, 1970." Centre Virtuel de la Connaissance sur l'Europe. http://www.cvce.eu/obj/the_moscow_treaty_12_august_1970-en-d5341cb5 -1a49-4603-aec9-0d2304c25080.html.

"Treaty on the Limitation of Anti-Ballistic Missile Systems (ABM Treaty)." Signed May 26, 1972. NTI: Nuclear Threat Initiative. http://www.nti.org/treaties-and -regimes/treaty-limitation-anti-ballistic-missile-systems-abm-treaty.

Memoirs

Arbatov, G. A. *The System: An Insider's Life in Soviet Politics*. New York: Times Books, 1992.

Brandt, Willy. *People and Politics: The Years 1960–1975*. Translated by J. Maxwell Brownjohn. Boston: Little, Brown, 1978.

Bruce, David K. E. *Window on the Forbidden City: The Beijing Diaries of David Bruce, 1973–1974*. Edited by Priscilla Mary Roberts. Hong Kong: Centre of Asian Studies, University of Hong Kong, 2001.

Bush, George. *The China Diary of George H.W. Bush: The Making of a Global President*. Edited by Jeffrey A. Engel. Princeton, NJ: Princeton University Press, 2008.

Dobrynin, Anatoly. *In Confidence: Moscow's Ambassador to America's Six Cold War Presidents (1962–1986)*. New York: Times Books, Random House, 1995.

Gandhi, Indira. *My Truth*. New Delhi: Vision Books, 1981.

Gromyko, Andrei Andreevich. *Memoirs*. New York: Doubleday, 1989.

Israeliyan, Viktor Levonovich. *Inside the Kremlin During the Yom Kippur War*. University Park: Pennsylvania State University Press, 1995.

Kissinger, Henry. *White House Years*. Boston: Little, Brown, 1979.
———. *Years of Upheaval*. Boston: Little, Brown, 1982.
Meir, Golda. *My Life*. New York: Putnam, 1975.
Nixon, Richard M. *RN: The Memoirs of Richard Nixon*. New York: Grosset and Dunlap, 1978.

Films

Born on the Fourth of July. Directed by Oliver Stone. Los Angeles: Ixtlan, 1989.
Go Tell the Spartans. Directed by Ted Post. Los Angeles: Mar Vista Productions, 1978.
Hamburger Hill. Directed by John Irvin. Los Angeles: RKO Pictures, 1987.
The Killing Fields. Directed by Roland Joffé. London: Enigma Productions, 1984.
Kippur. Directed by Amos Gitai. Jerusalem: Agav Hafakot, 2000.
Missing. Directed by Costa-Gavras. Los Angeles: Universal Pictures, 1982.
1971. Directed by Amrit Sagar. Mumbai: Sagar Art International, 2007.
Noch nad Chili (*Night over Chile*). Directed by Sebastián Alarcón and Aleksandr Kosarev. Moscow: Mosfilm, 1977.
Platoon. Directed by Oliver Stone. Los Angeles: Hemdale Film/Cinema 86, 1986.
Salvador Allende. Directed by Patricio Guzmán. Santiago: JBA Production, 2004.
Uncommon Valor. Directed by Ted Kotcheff. Los Angeles: Paramount Pictures, 1983.
Xiu, Xiu: The Sent Down Girl. Directed by Joan Chen. Beijing: Good Machine/Whispering Steppes, 1998.

Drama

Blessing, Lee. *A Walk in the Woods: A Play in Two Acts*. New York: New American Library, 1988.
Dorfman, Ariel. *Death and the Maiden*. New York: Penguin Books, 1992.
Frayn, Michael. *Democracy*. London: Methuen Drama, 2003.

Opera

Adams, John, Alice Goodman, and John McGinn. *Nixon in China: An Opera in Three Acts*. 1987.

Fiction

Del Vecchio, John M. *The 13th Valley: A Novel*. New York: Bantam Books, 1982.
Gao, Xingjian. *One Man's Bible: A Novel*. Translated by Mabel Lee. New York: Harper Collins, 2002.
Just, Ward S. *Stringer*. Boston: Little, Brown, 1974.
Mallon, Florencia E. *Beyond the Ties of Blood: A Novel*. New York: Pegasus Books, 2012.
Roa Bastos, Augusto Antonio. *I, the Supreme*. New York: Knopf, 1986.

Roth, Robert. *Sand in the Wind*. Boston: Little, Brown, 1973.

Sloan, James Park. *War Games*. Boston: Houghton Mifflin, 1971.

Stone, Robert. *Dog Soldiers: A Novel*. Boston: Houghton Mifflin, 1974.

Yu, Hua. *To Live: A Novel*. Translated by Michael Berry. New York: Anchor Books, 2003.

Secondary Sources

Asselin, Pierre. *A Bitter Peace: Washington, Hanoi, and the Making of the Paris Agreement*. Chapel Hill: University of North Carolina Press, 2002.

Bange, Oliver, and Gottfried Niedhart. *Helsinki 1975 and the Transformation of Europe*. New York: Berghahn Books, 2008.

Berman, Larry. *No Peace, No Honor: Nixon, Kissinger, and Betrayal in Vietnam*. New York: Free Press, 2001.

Bluth, Christoph. *Soviet Strategic Arms Policy Before SALT*. Cambridge: Cambridge University Press, 1992.

Buwalda, Piet. *They Did Not Dwell Alone: Jewish Emigration from the Soviet Union, 1967–1990*. Washington, DC: Woodrow Wilson Center Press, 1997.

Daigle, Craig. *The Limits of Détente: The United States, the Soviet Union, and the Arab-Israeli Conflict, 1969–1973*. New Haven, CT: Yale University Press, 2012.

Gao, Wenqian. *Zhou Enlai: The Last Perfect Revolutionary: A Biography*. Translated by Peter Rand and Lawrence R. Sullivan. New York: PublicAffairs, 2007.

Garthoff, Raymond L. *Détente and Confrontation: American-Soviet Relations from Nixon to Reagan*. Washington, DC: Brookings Institution, 1985.

Gelman, Harry. *The Brezhnev Politburo and the Decline of Detente*. Ithaca, NY: Cornell University Press, 1984.

Gleijeses, Piero. *Conflicting Missions: Havana, Washington, and Africa, 1959–1976*. Chapel Hill: University of North Carolina Press, 2002.

Golan, Galia. *Yom Kippur and After: The Soviet Union and the Middle East Crisis*. Cambridge: Cambridge University Press, 1977.

Goldman, Marshall I. *Détente and Dollars: Doing Business with the Soviets*. New York: Basic Books, 1975.

Gustafson, Kristian. *Hostile Intent: US Covert Operations in Chile, 1964–1974*. Washington, DC: Potomac Books, 2007.

Hakkarainen, Petri. *A State of Peace in Europe: West Germany and the CSCE, 1966–1975*. New York: Berghahn Books, 2011.

Hanhimäki, Jussi M. *The Flawed Architect: Henry Kissinger and American Foreign Policy*. New York: Oxford University Press, 2004.

Haslam, Jonathan. *The Nixon Administration and the Death of Allende's Chile: A Case of Assisted Suicide*. London: Verso, 2005.

Hoff, Joan. *Nixon Reconsidered*. New York: Basic Books, 1994.

Isaacson, Walter. *Kissinger: A Biography*. New York: Simon and Schuster, 1992.

MacMillan, Margaret. *Nixon and Mao: The Week That Changed the World*. New York: Random House, 2007.

Mansingh, Surjit. *India's Search for Power: Indira Gandhi's Foreign Policy, 1966–1982.* Beverly Hills: Sage, 1984.

Maresca, John J. *To Helsinki—the Conference on Security and Cooperation in Europe, 1973–1975.* Durham, NC: Duke University Press, 1987.

Möckli, Daniel. *European Foreign Policy During the Cold War: Heath, Brandt, Pompidou and the Dream of Political Unity.* London: I. B. Tauris, 2009.

Nelson, Keith L. *The Making of Détente: Soviet-American Relations in the Shadow of Vietnam.* Baltimore: Johns Hopkins University Press, 1995.

Newhouse, John. *Cold Dawn: The Story of SALT.* New York: Holt, Rinehart and Winston, 1973.

Pittman, Avril. *From Ostpolitik to Reunification: West German–Soviet Political Relations Since 1974.* Cambridge: Cambridge University Press, 2002.

Sarotte, Mary Elise. *Dealing with the Devil: East Germany, Détente, and Ostpolitik, 1969–1973.* Chapel Hill: University of North Carolina Press, 2001.

Shawcross, William. *Sideshow: Kissinger, Nixon and the Destruction of Cambodia.* New York: Simon and Schuster, 1979.

Sisson, Richard, and Leo E. Rose. *War and Secession: Pakistan, India, and the Creation of Bangladesh.* Berkeley: University of California Press, 1990.

Smith, Gerard C. *Doubletalk: The Story of the First Strategic Arms Limitation Talks.* Garden City, NY: Doubleday, 1980.

Stent, Angela E. *From Embargo to Ostpolitik: The Political Economy of West German–Soviet Relations, 1955–1980.* Cambridge: Cambridge University Press, 2002.

Terriff, Terry. *The Nixon Administration and the Making of US Nuclear Strategy.* Ithaca, NY: Cornell University Press, 1995.

Thomas, Daniel C. *The Helsinki Effect: International Norms, Human Rights, and the Demise of Communism.* Princeton, NJ: Princeton University Press, 2001.

Xia, Yafeng. *Negotiating with the Enemy: U.S.-China Talks During the Cold War, 1949–1972.* Bloomington: Indiana University Press, 2006.

Chapter 7
DÉTENTE COLLAPSES, 1975–1980

Peace is more precious than a piece of land.

—Anwar Sadat

In the Islamic government all people have complete free-dom to have any kind of opinion.

—Ayatollah Ruhollah Khomeini

As a nation we have the right to decide our own affairs.

—Lech Wałęsa

Détente and *Ostpolitik* had been heavily dependent on four individuals—Nixon, Brandt, de Gaulle's successor Georges Pompidou, and Brezhnev—and three of them suddenly departed the scene in 1974, leaving the Soviet leader with less than wholehearted partners.* Although Kissinger, who stayed on as President Gerald Ford's secretary of state, tried to stay the course, Congress's moves to curtail the president's powers plus the shock of South Vietnam's collapse placed

---

* Pompidou died on April 2, Brandt resigned on May 7 after the discovery of an East German spy in his immediate entourage, and Nixon on August 9 became the first US president to resign because of the Watergate scandal. Moreover, Golda Meir, one of détente's major opponents, also left office on June 3, 1974, after a National Inquiry Commission issued a critical preliminary report on the Israeli military's lack of preparedness for the October 1973 war.

a brake on further US-Soviet rapprochement.* In addition, the new German chancellor Helmut Schmidt and French president Valéry Giscard d'Estaing were less devoted to *Ostpolitik* than their predecessors.

The Helsinki Accords, signed on August 1, 1975, marked the climax of a string of Soviet gains. The steep oil price hikes in 1973–1974 had not only crippled the West economically but also raised the value of the Soviets' expanding oil and gas exports and lowered the cost of its grain imports. By the mid-1970s Soviet factories appeared to be churning out nuclear weapons, missiles, and conventional arms as well as steel, iron, and industrial goods, and Soviet trade with Western Europe and the Third World was bringing in increased foreign currency. Moreover, America's setback in Vietnam encouraged Moscow to shed its reticence over challenging the United States in Western Europe and in other parts of the Third World. Although the Soviet Union, in stark contrast with its Chinese rival, had tacitly abandoned the mission of fomenting world revolution and remained dedicated to the "peaceful coexistence of states with different social systems," the new 1977 Soviet constitution still endorsed the "struggle of peoples for national liberation and social progress."

Not only did détente expire, but between 1975 and 1980 the Cold War was reignited over ideological divisions and regional conflicts, which Washington and Moscow had lost both the will and the capacity to handle in tandem.

HUMAN RIGHTS

Détente and human rights stood at opposite poles. As the price of negotiating agreements on arms reduction and the relaxation of tensions over Berlin, the Soviet Union had insisted on the principle of nonintervention in its sovereign internal affairs. Brezhnev's partners in Washington and Western Europe had agreed to recognize Europe's post-1945 borders and also to refrain from encouraging dissident movements inside the Soviet realm. During the high era of détente this forced the West to passively observe the Kremlin's anti-Semitic campaign after the June 1967 Middle East War and the crackdown on Soviet and East European dissidents after the August 1968 invasion of Czechoslovakia.

Kissinger defended US policy by insisting that any effort to induce internal changes in the Soviet Union would "defeat what must remain our overriding

---

* Antidétente sentiments in the United States were stirred by the images of Soviet tanks aiding the capture of Saigon in 1975.

objective, the prevention of nuclear war." He argued that although the United States was not "neutral . . . in the age-old antagonism between freedom and tyranny, . . . consciousness of our limits is recognition of the necessity of peace—not moral callousness," and he vehemently opposed the temptation to apply pressure on the Soviet Union.[*] Moreover, under Nixon's leadership the United States also ignored human rights abuses by its Cold War allies Pakistan, Greece, South Korea, Indonesia, Brazil, Iran, and South Africa as well as in Chile after 1973.[†]

The emergence of human rights as an element of international affairs came from several sources. The US civil rights movement after World War II was an important model, and the 1960s saw the birth of a small, disparate, but also resolute grassroots movement in the Soviet Union. On December 5, 1965, a group of dissidents, alarmed over the demise of Khrushchev's reforms and the growing repressiveness of the Soviet legal system, had rallied in Pushkin Square in Moscow under the banner "Respect the Soviet Constitution." Even more challenging to the USSR were the protests by Soviet Jews against official discrimination, the persecution of their religion and culture, and the restriction on their right to emigrate to Israel. In 1969 a group of Soviet intellectuals formed the USSR's first human rights association, encompassing three perspectives. There were the dissenting Marxists, such as the historian Roy Medvedev and his twin brother, the biochemist Zhores, who advocated reforms within the Soviet system; the democrats, represented by the nuclear physicist Andrei Sakharov, who called for more elements of Western liberalism; and the nationalists, represented by the novelist Aleksander Solzhenitsyn, who viewed Marxism as an unredeemable foreign intrusion on Russian soil. After his expulsion from the Soviet Union in February 1974, Solzhenitsyn denounced the nonintervention principle and urged the United States to "interfere as much as you can."

The second factor was the expansion of the international human rights community in the 1970s and its increased activism. At the forefront was Amnesty International, whose research department documented human rights abuses on every continent. A global campaign on behalf of Soviet Jewry, strongly supported by the government of Israel after 1969, became closely connected with

---

[*] Underlined by his advice to Nixon's successor, Gerald Ford (on the eve of the signing of the Helsinki Accords), to refuse a White House visit to the exiled Soviet writer, Aleksander Solzhenitsyn.

[†] In a July 1975 speech titled "The Moral Foundations of Foreign Policy," Kissinger acknowledged, "Today we cooperate with many nations for the purpose of regional stability and global security even though we disapprove of some of their internal practices."

the struggle for human rights, and in 1971 the New York–based International League for Human Rights established ties behind the Iron Curtain and disseminated the texts of Soviet dissidents.

Third, the US Congress grasped the issue of human rights in reaction to Nixon's "imperial" presidency and the growing backlash against the questionable benefits and amoral characteristics of détente. A coalition of anticommunist liberals and conservatives conducted hearings in 1973 and, over Kissinger's objections, would force the State Department to submit annual reports on the state of human rights in more than one hundred countries.

After Nixon's resignation the US administration's stance toward human rights changed dramatically. Nixon's successor Gerald Ford, the unelected thirty-eighth president who had served for nearly thirty-five years in the US Congress, responded to America's yearning for a less devious and more upright foreign as well as domestic policy.* Ending two and a half decades of official US indifference, Ford marked the twenty-sixth anniversary of the Universal Declaration by inviting his fellow citizens to join the international commemoration and declaring December 10, 1974, Human Rights Day in the United States. Following a unanimous congressional vote, Ford reversed Nixon's opposition to punishing Moscow for its restrictions on Jewish emigration and enthusiastically signed the trade bill with the Jackson-Vanik Amendment on January 4, 1975. On August 1, at the signing ceremony in Helsinki, Ford placated détente's critics by looking directly at Brezhnev and proclaiming America's "deep devotion to human rights and individual freedoms."

Brezhnev gave the standard Soviet response: "No one should try to dictate to other peoples how they should manage their internal affairs." Yet, inexplicably, the Soviet leader authorized publication of the entire text of the Helsinki Accords, including the human rights provisions, which, unlike the UN covenants, contained a review process as well as follow-up meetings that placed sustained pressure on Moscow and its allies. Almost immediately after Helsinki, Soviet and East European dissidents formed organizations to test their governments' compliance, beginning with the Moscow Helsinki Watch Group in May 1976 and Charter 77 in Czechoslovakia.

The celebration of America's bicentenary in 1976 stirred popular hopes of replacing the devious pragmatism of the Nixon-Kissinger era with a renewed Wilsonian idealism. Ford's Republican rival, Ronald Reagan, and his Democratic

---

* To be sure, the latter initiative was undermined by Ford's controversial pardon of Nixon.

opponent, Jimmy Carter, bolstered by Congress and the military, the churches and the unions, the captive Baltic nations and the Jewish lobbies, transformed the 1976 presidential campaign into a referendum on détente. With Carter's victory in November, followed by his ringing inaugural address* and the assurance that dissidents could "depend on the United States," human rights moved to the forefront of global attention in 1977.

The one-term presidency of Jimmy Carter represented the high point of America's public espousal of human rights. The deeply religious but politically inexperienced former governor of Georgia sought to alter the terms of détente, posing a more robust challenge to the Soviet Union by elevating America's moral stature and demanding better behavior from Moscow. Guided by his national security adviser, Zbigniew Brzezinski—but against the warnings of the US State Department—the president announced that human rights would be a "central concern of my administration." Carter voiced support for the dissidents in Czechoslovakia who urged their government to conform to the Helsinki Basket Three principles. He responded personally to the appeal by Sakharov to speak out against Soviet repression.† And, breaking with his predecessors' practice, Carter received the prominent exiled dissident Vladimir Bukovsky‡ in the White House.

Because the Helsinki Accords had specified a series of follow-up conferences, Carter seized the opportunity to keep human rights at the center of the international agenda. At the Belgrade meeting of the CSCE (Conference on Security and Cooperation in Europe) in 1977–1978 the US delegate objected vigorously to the communists' human rights violations. Afterward Carter, increasingly irritated over Moscow's machinations in Africa, backed up his rhetoric. After a new wave of imprisonments of leading Soviet dissidents, the president tightened restrictions on exports to the Soviet Union. In 1978 the United States drew closer to the Soviet opposition through the founding of the US Helsinki Watch Committee. Funded by the Ford Foundation and led by major public figures with

---

* Which included the words "because we are free, we can never be indifferent to the fate of freedom elsewhere."

† "Every person serving a term in the hell of present-day Gulag for his beliefs or open profession of them—every victim of psychological repression for political reasons, every person refused permission to emigrate, to travel abroad—represents a direct violation of the Helsinki accord. . . . Is the West prepared to defend these noble and vitally important principles?"

‡ One of the original founders of the Soviet Union's human rights movement who had served a twelve-year incarceration in Soviet prisons, labor camps, and psychiatric institutions and exposed the misuse of psychiatry against political prisoners.

close ties to the administration and Congress, the committee monitored Moscow's compliance with the Helsinki Accords.

Brezhnev's response was indignant and defensive. Citing America's record of civil rights violations against its own population and its support of "terroristic" regimes in Chile and South Korea, he insisted that under the Soviet constitution "the exercise of individual freedoms must not injure the interests of society, and the State, and the rights of other citizens." Moscow, calling Carter's bluff, also expanded the crackdown on nationalists seeking autonomy in several Soviet republics and on religious groups, including Baptists, Pentecostals, Seventh Day Adventists, and Jehovah's Witnesses. After 1978 there was a sudden increase in Jewish emigration, but the Soviet Union imposed harsh prison sentences on leaders of the Moscow Helsinki Watch Group, and Brezhnev dismissed Carter's appeal on their behalf. In 1980 the Soviet government banished Sakharov* (one of the group's leaders) to Gorki, an industrial city 250 miles from Moscow that was closed to foreigners.

Carter's human rights crusade was aimed not only at the Soviet Union but also at some of America's more repressive Cold War allies (a task made easier in the mid-1970s by the restoration of democracy in Greece, Portugal, and Spain). The United States faced an acute challenge in South Africa, a strategically—and economically—important partner policy whose Apartheid† policies and repression of its black majority had drawn condemnation by the United Nations for more than a decade. In 1976 a brutal police attack on student protesters in Soweto resulted in at least 575 deaths, and a year later the death of the activist Stephen Biko in police custody brought worldwide protests.

Carter initially set out to reverse the Nixon-Kissinger hands-off policy toward South Africa. However, the president ended up zigzagging, in his first two years making futile attempts to convince the Pretoria government to undertake democratic reforms and in the last two easing off, reverting to a Cold War stance of placing the communist threat to southern Africa at the top of his priorities.

US relations with Iran, another key US ally, also exposed Carter's ambivalence toward human rights. In the 1960s Shah Mohammad Reza Pahlavi had used his enormous oil revenues to finance an ambitious program of industrialization and modernization, but he was also a despotic ruler who used his omnipresent

---

* In retaliation for his protest over the Soviet invasion of Afghanistan.
† Instituted in 1948, the regime of Apartheid mandated the strict separation of races, which led to discriminatory treatment of the non-European population in almost every aspect of their lives.

Photo 7.1. Jubilant Sandinista soldiers in the main square of Managua as they take control of the government of Nicaragua, June 20, 1979. *Courtesy of Corbis.*

intelligence agency (SAVAK) to suppress liberal and religious, as well as communist, opposition and drew worldwide criticism for his brutal methods. Nonetheless the Nixon administration, viewing Iran as an important anticommunist bastion, had sent sophisticated weaponry to the shah. Carter, following suit, in 1977 notoriously deemed Iran an "island of stability" in the Cold War world.

Finally, in Central and South America, where the Cuban threat still haunted Washington, Carter tried to reverse his predecessors' policy of supporting right-wing dictatorships in the name of Cold War imperatives. Bowing to global anti-imperialism and braving domestic opposition, Carter in 1977 renegotiated the Panama Canal treaty, relinquishing US control over the waterway and the five-mile-wide zone surrounding it. Carter also supported the return to democratic rule in Honduras and encouraged reforms in the Dominican Republic. However, the president failed to curtail government abuses in Guatemala, and his administration's abortive efforts to replace the long-standing right-wing Anastasio Somoza dictatorship with moderates left the region polarized between the triumphant left-wing Sandinistas in Nicaragua and a brutal US-backed junta in El Salvador. In South America Carter also used the human rights stick sparingly, urging reforms in Peru but having little effect on the authoritarian regimes in Argentina, Brazil, Chile, Paraguay, and Uruguay.

Carter's espousal of human rights not only contributed to US-Soviet estrangement but also left the United States at odds with its allies—with dictators who resented Washington's meddling and with European and Canadian partners who rued the damage to East-West détente. Moreover, Carter's crusade was selective, notably excluding Saudi Arabia and South Korea. And throughout the delicate process of establishing full diplomatic relations with China in January 1979, the president carefully refrained from raising human rights issues with Beijing.

Nonetheless, the humanitarian principle enshrined in the Helsinki Accords enabled the United States in the late 1970s to escape the doldrums of Watergate and Vietnam and to assert its moral superiority over the USSR. Some scholars believe that the revitalization of the international human rights movement planted a "time bomb" in the heart of the Soviet Empire, where the various dissident groups had found both a global audience and avid supporters. But at the same time America's new focus on human rights highlighted the North-South divide: the growing gap between the Cold War–dominated, developed world and the planet's poorer regions, whose populations had become increasingly vulnerable to Great Power rivalries over their resources and strategic locations.

THE COLD WAR IN AFRICA

Détente was also shattered in Africa, where the United States and the Soviet Union both intervened in the political struggle in Angola (1975–1976) and in the war between Ethiopia and Somalia (1977–1978). Drawn in by their clients, and insistent on the high stakes of these two bloody contests, Washington and Moscow resumed their old duel on a distant continent while still professing hopes of nuclear disarmament and peaceful negotiations elsewhere.

A left-wing military coup in Portugal in April 1974 had ended forty years of authoritarian rule and also accelerated the dissolution of Europe's oldest overseas empire in Africa.* The new Lisbon government immediately abandoned the almost two-decade-long struggle against left-wing guerrillas in Portugal's white-dominated colonies and announced its intention to grant independence to the Cape Verde Islands, Guinea, Mozambique, and Angola.

---

* The dissolution of the Portugal's Asian empire began in 1961 with India's seizure of Goa. In 1975 East Timor declared independence but was immediately invaded by Indonesia and achieved full independence only in 2002. In 1999 Macau, according to a 1987 agreement with Beijing, reverted to China.

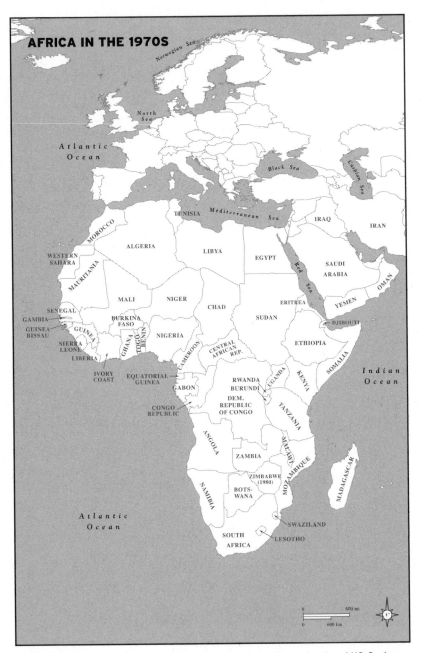

Map 12. Africa's resources and strategic location made it a major site of US-Soviet confrontation in the 1970s.

Shortly afterward, in 1975, civil war erupted in Angola, which contained vast reserves of oil, natural gas, and diamonds as well as iron, bauxite, and uranium. Three competing indigenous rebel factions—the Popular Movement for the Liberation of Angola (MPLA), the Front for the National Liberation of Angola (FNLA), and the National Union for the Total Independence of Angola (UNITA)—all had outside support, MPLA from Cuba and the Soviet Union, FNLA from the United States, and UNITA from South Africa (which feared a spillover into South West Africa [Namibia], which was still under its control).

On the eve of Helsinki, Washington and Moscow were drawn into a proxy conflict. Kissinger, terming the Angola war a test of America's "will and resolve" to halt the spread of communism, used some $32 million in CIA funds (which included payments to mercenary troops) to prop up FNLA, and the United States also backed South Africa's military intervention in October 1975. Brezhnev, intent on exerting Moscow's leadership over Africa's "anti-imperialist struggle," sent arms, intelligence officials, and military advisers to MPLA and in November and December 1975 began airlifting Cuban combat units to the front. After reports of the covert US funds were leaked to the press in December, an irritated, post-Vietnam Congress, by an overwhelming vote, banned any further aid for Angola—which might actually have dragged out the war.

In February 1976 the Soviets achieved a stunning victory when the MPLA proclaimed the People's Republic of Angola almost simultaneously with the triumph of the pro-Marxist Liberation Front (FRELIMO) forces in Mozambique. That month Brezhnev announced that Moscow's goals of world peace and nuclear disarmament did not prelude its support for "national liberation and social progress." A shocked and irate Kissinger aroused the hawks who had opposed détente with his denunciations of Soviet perfidy, blamed Congress for America's "first failure to check Moscow's incursion outside its immediate orbit," and spent his final year in office warning against "another Angola" and bolstering the communists' next ostensible targets, South Africa and Rhodesia.

Carter immediately reduced the heated rhetoric and took another tack to stem the left-wing tide in southern Africa. Seeking to regain the moral initiative, the United States terminated its nuclear collaboration with Pretoria, called for multilateral diplomacy to resolve the Namibia issue, and, working closely with Britain, achieved a Rhodesian settlement and the creation of an independent Zimbabwe in April 1980.

Yet Carter too became caught up in the US-Soviet rivalry, this time in the Horn of Africa, which, according to Washington's Cold War perspective, was a region of high strategic importance. Ethiopia until 1974 had been a major US ally and the recipient of substantial aid, but after the military coup that removed the aged emperor Haile Selassie, it had gravitated toward Moscow. In the spring of 1977, Carter, citing Ethiopia's human rights abuses and, more importantly, its major arms deal with the Soviet Union, suddenly cut off all aid to Addis Ababa.

Ethiopia's sworn opponent, Somalia, had been the recipient of generous Soviet aid in return for access to the port of Berbera.* Its leaders had long set their eyes on liberating Ogaden, a desert area comprising one-third of Ethiopia's territory and inhabited by ethnic Somalis. Carter, although hesitant to send arms and back an aggressor, was tempted at the prospect of obtaining a new US client and checking the Marxist threat to the Gulf region. In June 1977, in a carefully worded message, he assured the Somali government that it could "depend on the United States" for "defensive" weapons.

Based on this vague promise, Somalia, on July 23, 1977, committed the grave blunder of sending its troops into Ogaden, but after two months of heavy fighting, it failed to capture the entire province. Moving quickly and decisively to rescue its newest ally, the Soviet Union dispatched military advisers to the front and between November 1977 and March 1978 also airlifted some seventeen thousand Cuban combat troops, enabling Ethiopia to reconquer Ogaden. Carter, fending off charges of having sanctioned the debacle, turned down Somalia's pleas for arms but also warned Ethiopia to halt at the Somali border. The US government, although outraged at another successful Soviet-Cuban intervention, could neither remove the communists' military presence in Ethiopia nor alleviate this new blow to its prestige. But it had at least replaced the Soviets in Berbera.

The United States and the Soviet Union did not instigate the two conflicts in Africa, but both once more responded in a reflexive Cold War manner. Contrary to the Basic Principles established at the height of détente in 1972, neither side was now willing to hold direct discussions or to exercise a joint role of restraint over their clients. To be sure, there were also no clear-cut winners or losers. For the ostensibly victorious Brezhnev, his African involvement had gained two new, impoverished, and unstable allies and increased the cost of keeping Castro's Cuba afloat. And although Carter lost face in the spring of 1978, he paid back by accelerating the normalization talks with China, greatly unnerving Moscow.

---

* Where the Soviets had constructed an airfield, a communications center, a missile maintenance facility, and a naval base with access to the Indian Ocean.

SS-20 MISSILES AND SALT II

The Superpowers' efforts for arms control waned after 1975. While the Soviets continued to expand their nuclear and conventional weaponry, a growing segment of the American public fretted over alleged US weakness and viewed détente as a mechanism for managing their country's decline. Moreover, NATO members began pressing Washington to counter the Soviet preponderance in Europe. The Carter administration was deeply divided, with Secretary of State Cyrus Vance urging a continuation of the disarmament negotiations with Moscow, and National Security Adviser Zbigniew Brzezinski calling for a policy of "strength." Indeed, the new president got off to a bad start with the fiasco over the neutron bomb.* Washington's proposal of this new weapon in 1977 gave Moscow the opportunity to condemn Carter's nuclear saber rattling and mobilize the antinuclear movement in Western Europe. One year later, the president's withdrawal of his neutron bomb proposal infuriated the West German chancellor, Helmut Schmidt. A reluctant supporter of this initiative, Schmidt complained of America's "unreliability."

Next it was Brezhnev's turn to raise apprehensions. In 1977 the Soviet Union—in a move to counter the US, British, and French nuclear forces in Europe omitted from the SALT I agreement—began replacing its older missile systems on the continent with new, mobile, solid-fueled SS-20 intermediate-range missiles containing multiple warheads that could potentially destroy NATO's nuclear arsenal and its command system. Dismissing Moscow's claims that this simply represented a modernization of its weaponry (and that older missiles would be removed), Washington accused the Soviets of attempting to gain regional superiority. Schmidt, already apprehensive over the Superpowers' SALT II negotiations, voiced Bonn's alarm over decoupling Western Europe from the United States and leaving it vulnerable to Soviet political blackmail.

The NATO negotiations over a response to the SS-20 dragged on for two years, weighed down as much by political as by military considerations. In October 1979 Brezhnev issued a last-minute warning against stationing new

---

* The neutron bomb, also known as an enhanced radiation weapon (ERW), had been under development since the 1950s and was first tested in the 1960s. Its proponents believed it would be an effective deterrent to a Warsaw Pact attack because of its short-range destructiveness without endangering nearby population centers. Its opponents derided a thermonuclear weapon that killed people and left buildings intact.

intermediate-range nuclear weapons in Western Europe and offered to negotiate arms reductions with NATO. Two months later, on December 12, NATO issued its Double-Track (also called Dual-Track) decision: to station almost six hundred highly accurate US Pershing II and Tomahawk cruise missiles in five countries of Western Europe* but also offering to begin talks with Moscow over limiting theater (ground-based) tactical nuclear weapons.

The deployment announcements by the Soviet Union and NATO between 1977 and 1979 reflected the mounting coldness between both sides after Helsinki. Despite lingering references to détente, it had become clear that in evaluating strategic conditions each side viewed the military balance differently, neither took the other's perspective into account, and the habits of negotiation had broken down.

The backdrop to these European tensions was the prolonged, politically charged SALT II negotiations. With the interim SALT I agreement scheduled to expire in 1977, several issues stood in the way of a new US-Soviet arrangement. Innovations in missile technology (particularly the introduction of multiple, independently targetable reentry vehicles, or MIRVS) had not only undermined the goal of mutual deterrence and restored the advantage to a first strike but had also made the comparison and verification of US and Soviet forces far more difficult. Moreover, the United States continued to insist on excluding from any agreement its nuclear forces in Europe along with those of Britain, France, and China, although these were all capable of destroying targets in the Soviet Union, which had no nuclear allies that could similarly threaten the United States. America's strategy of extended deterrence was aimed not only at blocking an attack on US territory but also at balancing the Soviets' conventional superiority in Europe and thwarting what it termed Soviet "adventurism" in the Third World.

The outlines of a SALT II agreement had been drawn up in November 1974 by Ford and Brezhnev at their meeting in Vladivostok. Brezhnev had taken a considerable political risk by agreeing to a limit of 2,400 missile launchers and strategic bombers, of which 1,320 could be equipped with MIRV technology, and again accepting the exclusion of NATO's European arsenal. However, several issues were left unresolved. Although both parties had expected to sign a new treaty, Brezhnev's ill health, followed by the heated US debate over détente, delayed the conclusion of a new treaty while Ford was still in office.

---

* Britain, West Germany, Belgium, Italy, and the Netherlands.

Carter, responding to the critics of arms control, decided to abandon the Vladivostok framework. In March 1977 the new administration shocked Moscow by proposing disproportionately deeper cuts on the Soviet Union, which an outraged Brezhnev refused. Over the next two years the SALT II negotiations were stalled. While Washington condemned the Kremlin's human rights abuses, countered Soviet moves in the Horn of Africa, tacitly condoned the Chinese attack on Vietnam, and reunited its NATO allies against the SS-20s, Moscow dragged out the talks to fend off demands.[*]

In June 1979, almost five years after Vladivostok, Carter and Brezhnev finally met in Vienna and, under the glare of the world press, resumed the old Cold War sparring. Brezhnev answered Carter's complaint over the Cubans' presence in Africa by endorsing legitimate national struggles for freedom and independence and denying US charges of Moscow's "plots and intrigues." Privately the two leaders were more amicable, with Carter praising the recent rise in Soviet-Jewish emigration and assuring Brezhnev that the improvement in US-Chinese relations would not impair America's stance toward Moscow.

On June 18 Carter and Brezhnev signed the SALT II treaty, a historic agreement that limited both sides' strategic forces and committed them to work for even more significant cuts. SALT II, whose details represented an advance over the simple Vladivostok framework, created significant advantages for the United States. NATO quickly endorsed the document, only to watch it immediately unravel. The long delay had fueled US public opposition to appeasing Moscow, and the vote in the Senate Armed Services Committee was overwhelmingly negative. By December 1979, after new Superpower quarrels had erupted over the discovery of a Soviet brigade in Cuba, the deployment of new NATO missiles, and, especially, the Soviet invasion of Afghanistan, Carter withdrew the treaty from the Senate.

The SALT II debacle was not simply the result of a new direction by a new president in the White House but a reminder of fundamental Cold War realities. During the Carter administration an increasingly vocal part of the American public, convinced of the Soviet threat to its territory and the heinousness of the communist regime, was unwilling to concede any form of nuclear parity to Moscow, however skillfully camouflaged in the arcane figures of a disarmament treaty. For Soviet leaders it was a lesson that the United States still took linkage seriously and that their propaganda campaign to save the world from nuclear war had failed by ignoring the West's political and moral concerns.

---

[*] Brezhnev's illness may also have slowed down the negotiations.

THE MIDDLE EAST: 1979

Three striking events—the Egyptian-Israeli peace treaty, the Iranian revolution, and the Soviet invasion of Afghanistan—drew the Superpowers back into the Middle East, a region that détente had touched only briefly in late 1973. By the late 1970s the United States, increasingly dependent on imported oil, was more than ever determined to play a leading role from the eastern Mediterranean to the Persian Gulf, and the Soviet Union was equally intent on building a buffer against the expanding Western presence. In an updated version of the nineteenth-century Great Game between Britain and Russia, the United States and the USSR plunged into this strategically important environment laden with political rivalries, and there the last shreds of détente were unraveled.

After the October 1973 war the United Nations' efforts to create a Middle East settlement had been stillborn. The principal reason was the Nixon and Ford administrations' refusal to partner with the Soviet Union, but other causes included the serious divisions in the Arab world and Israel's refusal to negotiate with the Palestinians and its leaders' fear of a dictated peace.* By the end of 1976 leading US analysts, worried about a renewal of hostilities and facing sharply rising oil prices, urged Washington to change course.

Jimmy Carter came to office determined to negotiate a comprehensive peace treaty, even at the cost of an active Soviet role. However, this initiative suddenly halted in the fall of 1977 because of Carter's irritation over the Soviet-Cuban buildup in Ethiopia and the strong protests of Israel's new right-wing prime minister, Menachem Begin, but also because the US-Chinese rapprochement (which would lead to the establishment of full diplomatic relations in January 1979) had strengthened his position vis-à-vis Moscow.

Carter's abrupt reversal not only infuriated the Kremlin but also caused considerable disappointment in Cairo, where Sadat had counted on US pressure to force his rival, the hard-line Syrian leader Hafez al-Assad, to join him at the negotiating table. Suddenly Sadat, in an extraordinarily bold move to rescue Egypt's failing economy and regain the Sinai, on November 20, 1977, paid a dramatic visit to Jerusalem. Before the Israeli Knesset and the world's television cameras, Sadat issued an eloquent appeal for a "comprehensive" peace among all the former enemies and for a "just solution" to the Palestinian problem.

---

* Israeli leaders were determined to avoid another Munich—a Great Power dictate that would shape its post-1967 borders.

But lofty words aside, by his presence in Jerusalem the Egyptian leader had signaled his willingness to defy Moscow, break ranks with his Arab partners, and conclude a separate peace with Israel. When Begin proved obstreperous, it was Carter who would provide the crucial intervention by summoning the parties to Camp David, the US presidential retreat, in September 1978 and devising an astute solution that separated Middle Eastern issues into three distinct parts.

After thirteen days of seclusion at Camp David with Carter as their dogged intermediary, Sadat and Began finally agreed on a Framework for Peace in the Middle East. The middle section of the three-part agreement was straightforward: a plan for a bilateral treaty between Egypt and Israel involving a phased Israeli withdrawal from the Sinai in return for the establishment of full diplomatic, economic, and cultural relations between the two countries. The two other parts were murkier: the first outlining the prospect of future negotiations over the Israeli-occupied West Bank and Gaza among Egypt, Israel, Jordan, and "representatives of the Palestinian people," and the third proposing parallel treaties between Israel and Jordan, Syria, and Lebanon. On December 10, 1978, the thirtieth anniversary of the Universal Declaration of Human Rights, Sadat and Begin jointly received the Nobel Peace Prize for the Camp David Accords.

But Carter's work was not finished. After Camp David came six difficult months of negotiations between Egypt and Israel to work out details small and large. At the last minute, Carter, emulating Kissinger, conducted eight days of shuttle diplomacy. Finally, on March 26, 1979, Begin and Sadat came together in Washington to end thirty-one years of warfare between their two countries and to sign the Middle East's first peace treaty. Almost lost in the excitement were the exclusion of Palestinian self-rule* and the dim prospects of additional agreements between Israel and its other neighbors.

The Egyptian-Israeli treaty was a pragmatic alternative to a comprehensive peace, combining the UN's 1967 land-for-peace formula,† Israel's insistence on direct negotiations, and Sadat's national goals. It was a triumph for Washington, satisfying US Cold Warriors by once more eliminating the Soviets from the eastern Mediterranean. Moreover, the treaty utterly transformed the

---

* Indeed Begin referred twice in his speech to Israeli control over Jerusalem, and Sadat omitted the portion of his prepared text referring to the "grave injustice" that had been inflicted on the Palestinians.

† UN Resolution 242 had linked Israel's withdrawal from the territories it had occupied in 1967 with the right to every state in the region "to live in peace within secure and recognized boundaries free from force or threats of force."

Photo 7.2. President Jimmy Carter (center) shaking hands with Egyptian president Anwar Sadat, with Israeli prime minister Menachem Begin to his right, at the signing of the Egyptian-Israeli peace treaty on the grounds of the White House. *Courtesy of National Archives.*

three-decade-long Middle East conflict, removing the strongest member of the Arab bloc and bringing it into the Western orbit—although at the cost of substantial increases of US aid to both parties. It was also a victory for Israel, which by surrendering the Sinai and giving up its settlements had gained peace on its longest and most vulnerable border without making any concessions to the Palestinians or curbing its occupation and settlements in the West Bank and Gaza.

To be sure, these victories came with a high price for the parties and the region. Sadat's defection isolated Egypt from its Muslim neighbors and also made him a target for assassination two years later. Begin's withdrawal from the Sinai infuriated Israeli hard-liners, who would oppose any further retreats. The Arab and Muslim world became even more unstable, fragmented by the 1979 treaty and plunged into a leadership struggle, and the abandoned Palestinians stepped up their guerrilla operations against Israel from their bases in Lebanon.

Moreover, America's Middle East success was offset by a severe setback in Iran. During the 1970s under the shah, Mohammad Reza Pahlavi, Iran had become America's closest Middle Eastern ally and a major purchaser of US weapons and equipment. But Carter, on assuming the presidency, had decided to press this loyal anti-Soviet partner to curb its human rights abuses and received a striking rebuff. By 1978 the United States, which desperately needed to contain oil prices and enlist the shah's backing for the Israeli-Egyptian negotiations, wavered in its policies, failing to recognize the growing Iranian opposition and the futility of the regime's repressive measures that were resulting in the death of thousands of its citizens. Carter on December 12, 1978, declared, "The shah has our support and he also has our confidence."

Both Moscow and Washington were taken aback by the Iranian uprising in late 1978 and by the shah's sudden departure. On January 16, 1979, the shaken Iranian chief of state, ill with cancer and uncertain of his army's loyalty, fled the country. The political vacuum was quickly filled by Ayatollah Ruhollah Khomeini, the charismatic religious opposition leader who returned triumphantly from exile on February 1, 1979. Although the Kremlin may have welcomed the fall of a close US partner, it played no role in the Iranian revolution, which at once took on an anti-Soviet direction. Not only did Khomeini harshly suppress the local communists, but the establishment of an Islamic republic in Tehran created a new force in regional politics threatening to stir up restive Muslims in the Soviet Union's Central Asian borderlands.

The United States, which also exerted no control over the events in Iran, was even more vulnerable to the crowds' outrage and to Khomeini's political ambitions. Carter's efforts to bolster Prime Minister Shahpour Bakhtiar, the shah's last-minute appointee, incited suspicions in Tehran that Washington was plotting to return Pahlavi to power and bring back his hated secret police. Khomeini played an extremely clever game. In February he disavowed the Iranian leftists' seizure of the US embassy and allowed Bakhtiar to free the captives, but nine months later, once the Marxists had been disposed of, Khomeini was ready to mobilize Iranian sentiment against the United States (now called the "Great Satan") to remove the last moderates from power. After Carter provided the pretext by admitting the dying shah into the United States for medical treatment, on November 4, in a well-planned action, hundreds of Iranian demonstrators scaled the walls of the American embassy compound, overwhelming the guards and seizing more than seventy hostages. Khomeini seized the moment to consolidate power. Within a few weeks he became the supreme leader of the world's first Islamic republic, replacing Nasser's defunct pan-Arab nationalism with pan-Islamism and championing the rights of all Muslims oppressed by Soviet and US imperialism. The revolutionary government in Tehran denounced the Egyptian-Israeli treaty, embraced the Palestinians' cause, threatened the US client Saudi Arabia, and spread alarm in its secular neighbor Iraq.

Photo 7.3. Iranian women in a February 1, 1979, demonstration, carrying a poster of Ayatollah Khomeini. *Courtesy of Corbis.*

For the United States the 444-day Iranian hostage crisis represented a profound domestic and international blow.* Only four years after the collapse of the Saigon government, this new sign of America's vulnerability was reinforced by

---

* Other calamities in 1979 included the kidnapping and assassination of the US ambassador in
   Afghanistan in February and the burning of the American embassy in Islamabad in November,
   shortly after Islamic militants had seized the Grand Mosque in Mecca in protest against the
   Saudi monarchy's subservience to the United States.

Carter's failed attempt in April 1980 to rescue the hostages.* Indeed, the sudden collapse of America's position in Iran may well have emboldened the Kremlin in December 1979 to take far stronger measures in Afghanistan.

Until 1973 Afghanistan had not been a contested space between the Superpowers. The Soviet Union, although maintaining Russia's historic concern over the power balance in this mountainous, multitribal land that bordered its southern underbelly,† had accepted Afghanistan's nonaligned status, and the United States had declined to bid for the Afghans' loyalty.

Everything changed in 1973, after Muhammad Daoud Khan overthrew the Afghan monarchy and established a republic. Daoud not only suppressed the leftist, pro-Moscow political groups in Afghanistan but also began gravitating toward the West. After various factions rose against the Daoud regime's corruption and repressiveness, on April 27, 1978, he and his entire family were murdered in a bloody coup—which may or may not have been countenanced by the Kremlin. Daoud was succeeded by a communist-dominated government bound by a treaty of friendship to the Soviet Union and now with the red flag of a Soviet satellite and the official title of the Democratic Republic of Afghanistan. The Carter administration masked its surprise by reacting blandly to the events, signaling that the United States still considered Afghanistan within the Soviet orbit.

Despite Moscow's cautions, the new regime in Afghanistan, headed by the longtime communist activist Nur Muhammad Turaki, immediately imposed a radical blueprint of social, economic, and political transformation that provoked widespread opposition: Islamists decried its atheism, the landlords opposed collectivization, local and tribal leaders resisted centralization, and parts of the army also turned against the government. A major turning point occurred on March 24, 1979, when defecting soldiers and mujahideen‡ temporarily seized Herat, Afghanistan's second-largest city, killing thousands of people including Soviet advisers and their families. Moscow was alarmed by its satellite's inability to quell the rebellion and the cost (estimated at $9 million per day) of propping up its client. Even more shocking was the September 13–16 coup, during which Turaki was replaced (and murdered) by his far more independent rival,

---

* After the commander aborted the mission because of the mechanical failure of one of the rescue craft, a helicopter collided with a C-130 tanker aircraft, killing eight servicemen and injuring several more.

† After the Bolshevik Revolution there had been three brief episodes of Soviet intervention when its troops crossed the frontiers of Afghanistan in 1925, 1929, and 1930.

‡ The Islamic rebels who called themselves "holy warriors."

Hafizullah Amin. By the beginning of December 1979 the Kremlin was shaken by reports of Amin's purges of left-wing forces, his overtures to the Muslim and tribal opposition, and his approaches to the Western powers. In addition there were rumors of Chinese and Pakistani support for Amin. Moscow thus faced the prospect of a hostile regime in Kabul on top of its two other setbacks that year.*

The Soviet leadership was divided in its response. Brezhnev was furious at Amin's perfidy, and several influential politburo members strongly favored intervention, but the military chiefs were almost unanimously opposed to sending troops into Afghanistan. After the KGB failed to assassinate Amin, the politburo on December 12, 1979, by a unanimous vote,† decided to intervene in Afghanistan to establish a more broad-based government and quell the rebellion. On Christmas Eve some thirty thousand Soviet troops began the occupation of Kabul and all the other major cities as well as Afghanistan's strategic points, main lines of communications, and border entries. Three days later, after Soviet special forces had murdered Amin, his family, and his colleagues, his Soviet-installed replacement, Babrak Karmal, issued a belated "request" for assistance under the terms of their two countries' friendship treaty.

According to the now-available records of the politburo deliberations, Moscow's momentous decision in December 1979 emerged less from an expansionist impulse than from fear, miscalculation, and the inertia of an out-of-touch and inflexible regime. In a disastrous underestimation of the Afghan resistance, Defense Minister Dimitriy Ustinov and KGB chairman Yuri Andropov had argued, incredibly, that a military intervention in this historically unconquerable land would be quick, decisive, and unopposed. Moreover, there was almost no expectation of US disapproval or a threat to détente. In an extraordinary blunder, the Kremlin interpreted Washington's bland response to the April 1978 coup, the absence of warning signals throughout 1979, and Carter's preoccupation with Iran as signs of America's acquiescence.‡

But Carter did react strongly. Seeking reelection in the face of the ongoing hostage crisis and a new spike in oil prices caused by the unrest in Iran that

---

* The Egyptian-Israeli peace treaty and the Islamic revolution in Iran.
† The principal opponent of intervention, Prime Minister Alexei Kosygin, was absent from this crucial meeting.
‡ To be sure, some politburo members may have been rattled by NATO's December 12 decision to station new US medium-range Cruise and Pershing-2 missiles in Western Europe, which may have reinforced Soviet fears that Amin might "pull a Sadat," move his country into the American camp, and conceivably acquiesce in US bases and the deployment of US missiles in Afghanistan.

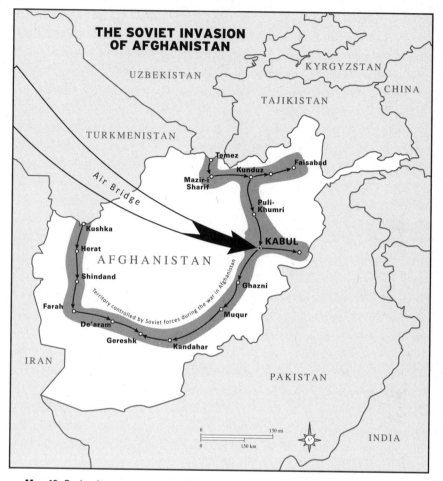

Map 13. During its ten-year war in Afghanistan, the Soviet army, facing a determined, outside-armed resistance, suffered high casualties, while the Afghan population's losses numbered two million deaths and five million refugees.

had intensified America's economic woes and stagflation, the president in January 1980 hyperbolically termed Moscow's entry into Afghanistan "the greatest threat to peace since the Second World War." Interpreting the invasion as a menace to America's vital oil and strategic interests, he issued a Trumanesque doctrine that bore his name: "An attempt by any outside force to gain control of the Persian Gulf region will be regarded as an assault on the vital interests of the United States and . . . will be repelled by any means necessary, including military force."

Carter bolstered his tough words with action, including a major increase in the US military budget, reviving the registration of draft-aged males, and accelerating the creation of a rapid deployment force to respond to threats in the Middle East. The president also unleashed a global propaganda campaign against the Soviet Union* and ordered a boycott of the 1980 Summer Olympic Games in Moscow. Moreover, Carter withdrew SALT II from Congress, discontinued technology exports to the USSR, and ordered a punishing grain embargo, forcing the Soviets to pay an additional $1 billion for their imports on the international market and making them more dependent on Western Europe. Even more potently, Carter authorized a substantial CIA-directed campaign of military assistance to the Afghan Islamist rebels. Reversing his negative stance toward the military dictatorship in Pakistan (hitherto shunned by Washington because of its human rights abuses), Carter designated the Islamabad government as a front-line state, a conduit of assistance to the Afghan rebels, and a tacit US ally. To put further pressure on Moscow, Washington strengthened its strategic bonds with Beijing by increasing its deliveries of advanced military equipment and also by countenancing a secret supply route for weapons, support systems, and technology between Israel and China.

America's NATO allies, who viewed Afghanistan as fully within the Soviet orbit, were reluctant to follow Carter's militant path. By 1980 France, Italy, and West Germany had all established important trade links with Moscow, were increasingly dependent on Soviet oil and natural gas deliveries, and were therefore opposed to disrupting détente. British prime minister Margaret Thatcher, who fully endorsed the US position, faced criticism in the House of Commons over Washington's failure to consult its partners.

By the end of 1980, Moscow's war in Afghanistan had been transformed from a well-executed operation into a quagmire. The invasion was highly unpopular among the Afghan population, the Afghan army performed poorly, and Soviet forces, undermanned and unprepared for counterinsurgency warfare in the rugged mountainous terrain, maintained control over the urban areas but not over the countryside. In the meantime international pressure mounted because of the flood of millions of refugees into Pakistan, the drumbeat of criticism led by the United States and China, the almost universal condemnation from the Muslim

---

* After the Soviets blocked a debate in the UN Security Council, the General Assembly on January 14, 1980, by a vote of 104–18 adopted a US-sponsored resolution condemning the Soviet invasion of Afghanistan.

Photo 7.4. Anti-Soviet mujahideen soldiers, January 1, 1980. *Courtesy of Corbis.*

world, the weak support of Moscow's East European satellites (as well as Cuba), and, especially, the mounting arms deliveries to the various groups of Afghan rebels, who grew daily in strength and confidence.

SOLIDARNOŚĆ

Poland, Moscow's largest European ally with one-quarter of the Eastern bloc's population, had always been a restive satellite. Its population—scarred by more than a century of tsarist rule, the Soviet occupation between 1939 and 1941 (during which some twenty-two thousand prisoners of war had been murdered), and Moscow's imposition of a communist regime after World War II—was fiercely resistant to Marxist ideology and practice. For the Soviet Union, four decades of control over Poland had brought mixed results; while ensuring its land route to front-line East Germany, it had been burdened by Warsaw's weak economic performance and frequently independent communist leadership.

With the onset of détente and West German *Ostpolitik* in the early 1970s, Moscow had loosened its reins, allowing increased cultural and trade relations between Poland and the West, but exposing its satellite to mounting foreign debt, rising prices, and domestic unrest. The Kremlin's decision to discontinue subsidizing oil and gas exports to its East European allies undoubtedly contributed to Poland's economic misery. In 1976, spurred by the Helsinki Accords' human rights provisions and incensed over the government's brutal suppression of workers' protests in several Polish cities, the opposition group KOR was born, the communist world's first grassroots civic organization, which included intellectuals, students, and workers.[*]

On October 16, 1978, another charismatic religious figure entered the world stage. That year, as Poland was suffering widespread shortages and a looming political crisis, the Polish cardinal Karol Józef Wojtyła was unexpectedly elected Pope John Paul II. On his first visit to his homeland as head of the Catholic Church in June 1979, the eloquent, physically commanding, and fervently anticommunist patriot urged a crowd of 250,000 ecstatic listeners in Warsaw's Victory Square, "Be not afraid."

One year later the Polish tinderbox exploded. In the summer of 1980, just as the Soviet war in Afghanistan had bogged down, Poland erupted with strikes against announced wage reductions and food-price hikes. The center of resistance was the Lenin shipyards in Gdańsk (the former Danzig), where workers, supported by KOR and the church and led by the sacked electrician Lech Wałęsa, set off a tidal wave of strikes throughout the country. In late August and early September, in a series of unprecedented agreements, the Polish government surrendered to almost all the workers' demands, which included the relaxation of censorship and of restrictions on the Catholic Church as well as the right to strike and to form an independent trade union. On September 17, 1980, Solidarność (Solidarity),[†] the communist world's first independent, nationwide trade union was established, and over the next year it enrolled some ten million

---

[*] Komitet Obrony Robotników, or the Workers' Defense Committee.

[†] Niezależny Samorządny Związek Zawodowy (NSZZ) or Solidarność (Independent and Self-Governing Trade Union, or Solidarity), a name suggested by the Polish historian and political dissident Karol Modzelewski.

workers, farmers, students, and intellectuals and transformed itself into a powerful social and political movement that challenged communist rule.

The West reacted warily, welcoming the August accords but also fearing political chaos and Soviet intervention. Carter, pressed by Congress, labor unions, churches, and the Polish American community to support Solidarność, praised the workers' "courage" and "resilience" but in September also released a substantial loan to stabilize the Warsaw government and encouraged America's NATO's allies to adopt a strict noninterference policy to deny the Kremlin any pretext to intervene. Britain, France, and West Germany—still hoping to preserve détente—were happy to follow the president's cautious lead.

Quickly recognizing Solidarność's threat not only to communist rule in Poland but also to its western borderlands, Moscow moved quickly to quarantine the infection through heavy domestic censorship and "anti-antisocialist" propaganda. But stung by the punishing Western response to its invasion of Afghanistan and its inability to impose its will there by force, the Kremlin hesitated to suppress the Polish union. Moreover, Moscow's socialist partners were divided between East German and Czechoslovak hard-liners who strongly favored intervention and the Hungarian and Romanian leaders who were vehemently opposed.

Chastened by Afghanistan, this time Brezhnev chose caution. Although authorizing the military exercises that raised alarm in the West, he had abandoned his doctrine and decided that the Poles must bring order in their own house. At the crucial Warsaw Pact summit in Moscow on December 5, 1980, Brezhnev used the threat of "international assistance" (a Soviet-led intervention) to pressure his Polish comrades to stand firm against Solidarność. Hence Carter, who in his last days in office had carefully monitored the Polish situation, was spared the challenge of responding to another Soviet military strike.

One month earlier, the landslide election of archconservative Ronald Reagan marked the rebirth of US-Soviet confrontation. Reagan not only disliked the principles and practice of détente but was ideologically committed to destroying Soviet communism and winning the Cold War. He began his presidency on a high note with Iran's release of the US hostages on the day of his inauguration.

On the Soviet side the West faced an aged, ailing general secretary anxious over the growing power of China, which after Mao's death in 1976 had embarked on major economic reforms and strengthened its ties with the West. Brezhnev was also alarmed over the high price of maintaining his overseas clients and the cost of the disastrous intervention in Afghanistan. Détente had enabled the Soviet leader to avoid economic and political modernization while still pursuing the USSR's interests overseas. But détente had crumbled, and by the end of 1980 the Kremlin had acquired new and resolute adversaries within its empire and outside its borders and had been made aware of its vulnerability to the political, economic, and diplomatic challenges of a more unstable global environment.

SUGGESTIONS FOR FURTHER STUDY

Documents

"Afghanistan: Lessons from the Last War." National Security Archive. 2001. http:// www.gwu.edu/~nsarchiv/NSAEBB/NSAEBB57.

Carter, Jimmy, "Inaugural Address, Jan. 20, 1977." Yale Law School Avalon Project: Documents in Law, History and Diplomacy. http://avalon.law.yale.edu/20th _century/carter.asp.

Comrade Kryuchkov's Instructions: Top Secret Files on KGB Foreign Operations, 1975–1985. Edited by Christopher M. Andrew and Oleg Gordievsky. Stanford, CA: Stanford University Press, 1993.

"Documents on the Soviet Invasion of Afghanistan." Woodrow Wilson Center Cold War International History Project. 2001. http://www.wilsoncenter.org/sites /default/files/e-dossier_4.pdf.

"Foreign Relations of the United States, 1969–1976, Volume XXVIII, Southern Africa: Angola Document List." US State Department Office of the Historian. 2011. http://history.state.gov/historicaldocuments/frus1969-76v28/ch3.

"Hostage Report (1981)." Video produced by the National Archives and Records Administration, 22:28. Internet Archive. http://archive.org/details/gov.archives .arc.4524406

"Jimmy Carter Oral Histories." University of Virginia Miller Center of Public Affairs. Accessed February 28, 2013. http://millercenter.org/president/carter/oralhistory.

"Soviet Deliberations During the Polish Crisis of 1980–1981." Special Paper No. 1. Edited by Mark Kramer. Woodrow Wilson Center Cold War International History Project. 1999. http://www.wilsoncenter.org/sites/default/files/ACF56F.PDF.

"Strategic Arms Limitation Talks (SALT II)." Signed June 18, 1979. NTI: Nuclear Threat Initiative. http://cns.miis.edu/inventory/pdfs/aptsaltII.pdf.

Supplemental Websites

"The Carter-Brezhnev Project." National Security Archive. Accessed February 28, 2013. http://www.gwu.edu/~nsarchiv/carterbrezhnev/.

Contemporary Writing

Medvedev, Zhores A., and Roy Aleksandrovich Medvedev. *A Question of Madness.* New York: Knopf, 1971.

Roth, Stephen J. *The Helsinki "Final Act" and Soviet Jewry.* London: Institute of Jewish Affairs in association with the World Jewish Congress, 1976.

Memoirs

Brzezinski, Zbigniew K. *Power and Principle: Memoirs of the National Security Advisor, 1977–1981.* New York: Farrar, Straus and Giroux, 1985.

Carter, Jimmy. *Keeping Faith: Memoirs of a President.* Toronto: Bantam Books, 1982.

Jordan, Hamilton. *Crisis: The Last Year of the Carter Presidency.* New York: Putnam, 1982.

Pahlavi, Mohammad Reza. *Answer to History.* Translated by Michael Joseph Ltd. New York: Stein and Day, 1980.

Sadat, Anwar. *In Search of Identity: An Autobiography.* New York: Harper and Row, 1978.

Sakharov, Andrei. *Memoirs.* New York: Alfred A. Knopf, 1990.

Schmidt, Helmut. *Men and Power: A Political Memoir.* Translated by Ruth Hein. New York: Random House, 1989.

Snepp, Frank. *Decent Interval: An Insider's Account of Saigon's Indecent End.* New York: Random House, 1977.

Vance, Cyrus R. *Hard Choices: Critical Years in America's Foreign Policy.* New York: Simon and Schuster, 1983.

Wałęsa, Lech. *A Way of Hope.* New York: H. Holt, 1987.

Films

Charlie Wilson's War. Directed by Mike Nichols. Los Angeles: Universal Pictures, 2007.

Do Not Be Afraid: The Life and Teachings of Pope John Paul II. Directed by Krzysztof Zanussi. World Film Services and Eurovideo. New York: HBO Home Video, 1996.

Man of Marble. Directed by Andrzej Wajda. Warsaw: Vision Film Distribution, 1976.

Persepolis. Directed by Vincent Paronnaud and Marjane Satrapi. Paris: France 3 Cinéma, 2007.

Under Fire. Directed by Roger Spottiswoode. Los Angeles: Lion's Gate Films, 1983.

Fiction

Coetzee, J. M. *Waiting for the Barbarians.* Harmondsworth, UK: Penguin Books, 1982.

García Márquez, Gabriel. *The Autumn of the Patriarch.* New York: Harper and Row, 1976.

Greene, Graham. *The Human Factor.* New York: Simon and Schuster, 1978.

Hirsh, M. E. *Kabul.* New York: Atheneum, 1986.

Hosseini, Khaled. *A Thousand Splendid Suns.* New York: Riverhead Books, 2007.

Maḥfūẓ, Najīb. *The Day the Leader Was Killed.* Translated by Malak Hashem. New York: Anchor Books, 2000.

Ondjaki. *Good Morning Comrades: A Novel.* Translated by Stephen Henighan. Emeryville, ON: Biblioasis, 2008.

Secondary Sources

Ansari, Ali M. *Confronting Iran: The Failure of American Foreign Policy and the Next Great Crisis in the Middle East.* New York: Basic Books, 2006.

Barber, James P., and John Barratt. *South Africa's Foreign Policy: The Search for Status and Security, 1945–1988.* Cambridge: Cambridge University Press, 1990.

Bill, James A. *The Eagle and the Lion: The Tragedy of American-Iranian Relations.* New Haven, CT: Yale University Press, 1988.

Caldwell, Dan. *The Dynamics of Domestic Politics and Arms Control: The SALT II Treaty Ratification Debate.* Columbia: University of South Carolina Press, 1991.

Frost, Howard. *The Bear and the Eagles: Soviet Influence in the 1970 and 1980 Polish Succession Crises.* Pittsburgh: University of Pittsburgh Center for Russian and East European Studies, 1988.

George, Edward. *The Cuban Intervention in Angola, 1965–1991: From Che Guevara to Cuito Cuanavale.* London: Frank Cass, 2005.

Hammond, Thomas Taylor. *Red Flag over Afghanistan: The Communist Coup, the Soviet Invasion, and the Consequences.* Boulder, CO: Westview, 1984.

Henze, Paul B. *The Horn of Africa: From War to Peace.* New York: St. Martin's, 1991.

Jackson, Donna R. *Jimmy Carter and the Horn of Africa: Cold War Policy in Ethiopia and Somalia.* Jefferson, NC: McFarland, 2007.

Keddie, Nikki R., and Richard Yann. *Modern Iran: Roots and Results of Revolution.* New Haven, CT: Yale University Press, 2003.

Khalidi, Rashid. *Soviet Middle East Policy in the Wake of Camp David.* Beirut, Lebanon: Institute for Palestine Studies, 1979.

Kramer, Mark. *The Kuklinski Files and the Polish Crisis of 1980–1981: An Analysis of the Newly Released CIA Documents on Ryszard Kuklinski.* Cold War International History Project. Working Paper No. 59. Washington, DC: Woodrow Wilson International Center of Scholars, 2009. http://www.wilsoncenter.org/sites/default/files/WP59_Kramer_webfinal1.pdf.

Laïdi, Zaki. *The Superpowers and Africa: The Constraints of a Rivalry, 1960–1990.* Chicago: University of Chicago Press, 1990.

Lampton, David M. *The Making of Chinese Foreign and Security Policy in the Era of Reform, 1978–2000.* Stanford, CA: Stanford University Press, 2001.

LeoGrande, William M. *Our Own Backyard: The United States in Central America, 1977–1992.* Chapel Hill: University of North Carolina Press, 1998.

Liakhovskiĭ, Aleksandr Antonovich. *Inside the Soviet Invasion of Afghanistan and the Seizure of Kabul, December 1979.* Translated by Gary Goldberg, and Artemy Kalinovsky. Cold War International History Project. Working Paper No. 51. Washington, DC: Woodrow Wilson International Center for Scholars, 2007. http://wilsoncenter.org/sites/default/files/WP51_Web_Final.pdf.

MacEachin, Douglas J. *Predicting the Soviet Invasion of Afghanistan: The Intelligence Community's Record.* Washington, DC: Center for the Study of Intelligence, Central Intelligence Agency, 2002.

Mishra, Ajay Kumar. *Soviet Policy Towards Anti-Colonial Movements in Southern Africa*. Delhi, India: Vista International, 2006.

Muravchik, Joshua. *The Uncertain Crusade: Jimmy Carter and the Dilemmas of Human Rights Policy*. Lanham, MD: Hamilton, 1986.

Njølstad, Olav. *Peacekeeper and Troublemaker: The Containment Policy of Jimmy Carter, 1977–1978*. Oslo: Institutt for Forsvarsstudier (IFS, Norwegian Institute for Defense Studies), 1995.

Pastor, Robert A. *Condemned to Repetition: The United States and Nicaragua*. Princeton, NJ: Princeton University Press, 1987.

Quandt, William B. *Camp David: Peacemaking and Politics*. Washington, DC: Brookings Institution, 1986.

Ross, Robert S. *Negotiating Cooperation: The United States and China, 1969–1989*. Stanford, CA: Stanford University Press, 1995.

Rubenstein, Joshua. *Soviet Dissidents: Their Struggle for Human Rights*. Boston, MA: Beacon, 1980.

Saikal, Amin. *The Rise and Fall of the Shah: Iran from Autocracy to Religious Rule*. Princeton, NJ: Princeton University Press, 2009.

Sarantakes, Nicholas Evan. *Dropping the Torch: Jimmy Carter, the Olympic Boycott, and the Cold War*. Cambridge: Cambridge University Press, 2011.

Savel'yev, Aleksandr' G., and Nikolay N. Detinov. *The Big Five: Arms Control Decision-Making in the Soviet Union*. Translated by Dmitriy Trenin. Edited by Gregory Varhall. Westport, CT: Praeger, 1995.

———. *The Hot "Cold War": The USSR in Southern Africa*. London: Pluto, 2008.

Sick, Gary. *October Surprise: America's Hostages in Iran and the Election of Ronald Reagan*. New York: Times Books, 1991.

Sikkink, Kathryn. *Mixed Signals: U.S. Human Rights Policy and Latin America*. Ithaca, NY: Cornell University Press, 2004.

Strong, Robert A. *Working in the World: Jimmy Carter and the Making of American Foreign Policy*. Baton Rouge: Louisiana State University Press, 2000.

Talbott, Strobe. *Endgame: The Inside Story of SALT II*. New York: Harper and Row, 1979.

Thomas, Daniel C. *The Helsinki Effect: International Norms, Human Rights, and the Demise of Communism*. Princeton, NJ: Princeton University Press, 2001.

Thomson, Alex. *US Foreign Policy Towards Apartheid South Africa, 1948–1994: Conflict of Interests*. New York: Palgrave Macmillan, 2008.

Wasserman, Sherri L. *The Neutron Bomb Controversy: A Study in Alliance Politics*. New York: Praeger, 1983.

Chapter 8

THE SECOND COLD WAR, 1981–1985

Right now in a nuclear war we'd lose 150 mil. people. The Soviets could hold their loss down to less than were killed in W.W. II.

—Ronald Reagan, diary entry, December 3, 1981

In the end, the people's will is what achieves victory.

—Hezbollah leader Hassan Nasrallah

The second Cold War arose in the early 1980s, when the new US administration took the offensive—ideologically and strategically—against the Soviet Union. Unlike his immediate predecessors, who had viewed the USSR as a permanent presence in international affairs and an unavoidable if difficult partner, Reagan viewed the Soviet Union as an incorrigible adversary that he was determined to vanquish. In a 1982 UN speech Reagan condemned the USSR for violating human rights and spreading "political terrorism" throughout the world. That year he stunned the Soviets and his NATO allies by announcing the replacement of détente and peaceful competition with a "global campaign for democracy." And in an address to the National Association of Evangelicals on March 8, 1983, Reagan described the Soviet Union as an "evil empire."

Reagan matched his tough words with action. Taking aim at the 1968 Brezhnev doctrine (that the establishment of a communist regime was irreversible), the Reagan doctrine led to a substantial increase of US aid to anti-Soviet forces in Afghanistan and also to the opponents of Marxist regimes in Africa, Asia, and Central America. The US president even contested Soviet rule in Eastern Europe. In addition, Reagan directed the largest expansion and diversification of America's military and nuclear forces since the late 1940s in order to establish US predominance and force concessions on the USSR.[*]

Reagan's anti-Soviet crusade was supported by a substantial segment of the US public. Stung by Solzhenitsyn's 1978 lament over the West's loss of courage, many Americans yearned to reassert US strength and global leadership against the perceived Soviet advances of the 1970s. Reagan was also bolstered by the emerging neoconservative ideology in the United States that extolled capitalism and individualism and denounced the leftists' creed of revolution and national liberation that had led to Stalin's gulags, Mao's Red Guards, and Castro's tyranny, and had also shaped the welfare-state mentality that had caused Western economies to stagnate.

Moscow was duly alarmed over this major shift in US policy. Still a global power, the USSR was devoting an outsized portion of its resources to military spending and overseas aid and now faced an accelerated weapons competition with Washington. To be sure, foreign tensions also invigorated the Kremlin's hard-liners. But Brezhnev (who died in November 1982) and his two short-lived successors, Yuri Andropov (who died in February 1984) and Konstantin Chernenko (who died in March 1985), tried futilely to interest Reagan in a summit meeting and a resumption of the arms-limitation negotiations.

America's NATO allies were also distressed by Washington's unilateralism and the unraveling of détente. In Western Europe the antinuclear peace movement had revived and was strengthened in the early 1980s by a new generation of feminist, religious, and environmental activists.[†] Even China, although sharing Reagan's antipathy toward Moscow, openly distanced itself from Washington's anti-Soviet and Third World policies.

Moreover, Reagan's drive to flay the Soviet Union with America's overwhelming moral and military power arose in a far more complicated world than the 1940s and 1950s. By identifying the Afghan mujahideen and the Nicaraguan contras as "freedom fighters"[‡] and lumping together the governments of Nicaragua, Libya, Ethiopia, Angola, Vietnam, and Cambodia, and the guerrillas in

---

[*] US annual military spending rose from approximately $155 billion in 1980 to almost $300 billion in 1986.

[†] Two spectacular manifestations were the 1980 Krefeld Appeal in West Germany against US missiles, signed by 2.7 million people, and the 1981–1983 women-led siege of the Royal Air Force base at Greenham Common in Britain to block their installation.

[‡] A label originally applied to the Hungarian rebels in 1956.

El Salvador, the PLO, and the rebels in Namibia as "Soviet proxies," Washington blurred complex local and regional issues, which led to consequences beyond the Cold War itself.

THE DETERIORATION OF US-SOVIET RELATIONS

As the calendar approached George Orwell's ominous year 1984, US-Soviet relations hit rock bottom. Not since the Cuban missile crisis had a Superpower conflict appeared this imminent. A series of mounting crises, which threatened to escalate beyond verbal denunciations, created some of the most dangerous moments of the Cold War.

Martial Law in Poland

General Wojciech Jaruzelski, who led Poland between 1981 and 1989, helped solve the Kremlin's dilemma over the political crisis that had erupted in his country.* In the year following Brezhnev's decision against intervention, Solidarność had become increasingly popular, organizing mass strikes and demonstrations, calling for democratic reforms and economic concessions, and threatening the collapse of communism in Poland as well as beyond its borders.† In Jaruzelski, a World War II veteran and minister of defense since 1968, Moscow found a loyal and tough comrade willing to save the Soviet Union the expense and international opprobrium of another invasion. On December 13, 1981, martial law was declared throughout Poland. Catching the opposition off balance, Jaruzelski proceeded to arrest the leaders of Solidarność as well as scores of other dissidents.

A startled Washington reacted swiftly and severely. In addition to declarations of outrage, the Reagan administration imposed stiff economic sanctions on the Warsaw government, banning the export of US agricultural products, suspending Poland's most-favored-nation status, and blocking it from receiving assistance from the International Monetary Fund. To punish Moscow for the crackdown, the United States also halted grain exports to the USSR, suspended negotiations on scientific and technological cooperation, and prohibited the sale of American technology for the construction of the Soviet gas pipeline to Western Europe.

---

* The only professional soldier to lead a European communist country, Jaruzelski first served as premier and first secretary of the Communist Party and, after 1985, as the country's president.

† According to 1981 KGB reports, there were also mass strikes in the Baltic republics, Belarus, and western Ukraine, causing Soviet authorities to close the borders with Poland.

Although deploring Jaruzelski's coup, West European leaders were riled by Washington's unilateralism. German chancellor Helmut Schmidt and newly elected French president François Mitterrand protested the Reagan administration's blow to the pipeline project—a major investment aimed at cushioning their economies against future oil shocks. Even British prime minister Margaret Thatcher, shocked by the repression but unconvinced that harsh methods would either bring the Soviet Union to its knees or alleviate Poland's political and economic crisis, imposed far milder sanctions than Washington's. America's NATO allies were also irritated by US accusations of their dependency on communist regimes and quietly maintained their ties with the East.

China too was unreceptive to America's campaign. However much Beijing welcomed any challenge to Moscow, Deng Xiaoping was uninterested in supporting Poland's grassroots labor movement. Thus China threw its support behind Jaruzelski and actually increased its trade with Warsaw.

For the Soviet Union, the Jaruzelski solution was nonetheless a costly one. Western sanctions forced Moscow to spend billions of rubles to prop up Poland and also to purchase expensive grain on the world market, depleting its hard-currency reserves and exacerbating the consumer crisis in the USSR caused by the growing expense of the war in Afghanistan. Although Poland's communist regime had been saved, the local military solution could only be temporary. Moreover, the vivid media reports of imprisoned Solidarność leaders and the onerous restrictions on personal freedom in Poland, bolstered by the press campaigns of the Vatican and US labor unions, had reinforced the Reaganites' claim that the future belonged to the free world and that Marxism was headed for the "ash heap of history."

Reagan's Strategic Defense Initiative (SDI)

On March 23, 1983, in a televised address from the Oval Office, Reagan shocked the world (and his own administration) with his proposal to develop a new antiballistic system. Known as the Strategic Defense Initiative (SDI), its purpose was to shield the United States from the threat of a Soviet nuclear attack by "intercepting and destroying missiles before they reached our own soil or that of our allies." Although the president's proposal outlined a range of conventional defensive options (including land-based and submarine launchers), it was the space-based component that stirred the public: the computer-guided, ground-based, X-ray lasers and space-based antinuclear craft. Media critics immediately gave SDI the nickname "Star Wars," permanently linking the president's

Photo 8.1. Thousands of World Peace activists march on Forty-Second Street in New York en route to Central Park, where some five hundred thousand demonstrators gathered to protest the expansion of America's nuclear arsenal, June 12, 1982. *Courtesy of Corbis.*

program with the popular 1977 science fiction film in which the forces of good employing advanced technology fought an evil empire.

Reagan's extraordinary proposal to make nuclear weapons "impotent and obsolete" had several purposes. It was a strong and effective response to the peace offensive that had been launched by Brezhnev's successor Andropov to resume arms negotiations. It was aimed at altering the president's warmonger image without offering the Soviets any major concessions. SDI presented the prospect of an ingenious technological solution to assuage the public's mounting terror of atomic warfare. It was also an attempt to neutralize the burgeoning nuclear-freeze movement that had taken hold in the United States.* And it was timed to convince Congress to pass another giant military budget.

But above all, SDI was inherently a move to extricate the United States from three decades of mutual deterrence, the principle that underlay the 1972 ABM treaty. Because neither the United States nor the USSR could defend more than a fraction of its territory, both had been dependent on the deterrent effect of the other's strategic forces, reinforcing the concept of MAD (mutually assured destruction), in which the prospect of annihilation would prevent either side from going nuclear. Notwithstanding the improbability of its technical realization, SDI—by providing a one-sided defense from attack while leaving the other side vulnerable—altered the political as well as the strategic balance. For Reagan, SDI represented an escape from the "shackles of interdependence": the abandonment of the principle of arms control and a one-sided US version of national survival. As such, it also posed a new and powerful threat to the economically and technologically weaker USSR.

The responses were predictable. Moscow was shocked and indignant. Already smarting over Reagan's "evil empire" charge, Andropov accused the United States of seeking first-strike capability, extending the arms race into space, and using the threat of SDI to extract concessions from the Kremlin, and he warned of an "unprecedented sharpening" of the East-West confrontation. West European leaders not only questioned the technical feasibility of SDI and its breach of long-standing NATO defense policy but also quietly fretted over possible Soviet countermeasures. Even the usually loyal British warned against provoking "new instabilities and new arms races."

The Downing of KAL 007

Hostility between the Superpowers continued to escalate. On the morning of September 1, 1983, US secretary of state George Shultz grimly informed the press that a missile fired by a Soviet aircraft had destroyed a South Korean airliner, whose 269 passengers and crew, among them 69 Americans (including a member of the House of Representatives), had been lost. One hour before the

---

* On May 4, 1983, the US House of Representatives had voted 278–149 in support of a freeze.

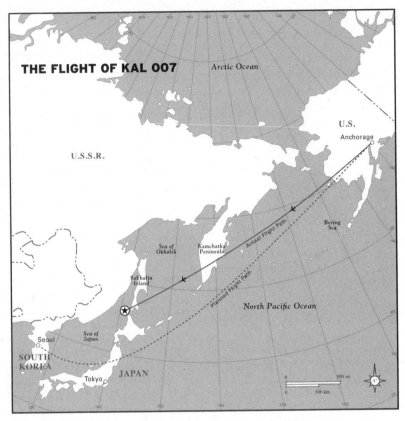

Map 14. The route of the South Korean airliner in September 1983.

attack, KAL flight 007, which had inexplicably veered some two hundred miles off course, had strayed into Soviet airspace and flown over highly restricted missile and submarine bases on the Kamchatka Peninsula. The Korean airliner was immediately tracked by Soviet air defense units, which were on high alert because of repeated incursions by US fighter-bombers probing gaps and vulnerabilities in the Soviets' early warning intelligence system as well as by periodic US surveillance flights, including one that same night by an American RC-135 reconnaissance plane. After crossing Sakhalin Island, another sensitive Soviet territory, KAL 007 was shot down over the Sea of Japan.*

---

* In 1996, Gennadiy Osipovich, the Soviet pilot who downed the Korean aircraft, admitted to the *New York Times* that he had recognized the civilian airliner but, following his chief's orders and believing it was on a spying mission, had nonetheless fired.

Although Reagan was absent from Washington, his administration rushed to condemn the Soviet Union. Based on hastily assembled US and Japanese intercepts of Soviet communications that clearly indicated the misidentification of the Korean craft, Shultz called it a deliberate "mass murder." In his address to the nation on September 5, the president labeled the attack "an act of barbarism, born of a society which wantonly disregards individual rights and the value of human life and seeks constantly to expand and dominate other nations."

The Kremlin, its leadership in disarray, responded poorly. Stunned by the Soviet military's blunder and Washington's overreaction, the politburo withheld an apology, constructed a feeble cover-up—insisting that the Korean aircraft was conducting a Washington-inspired espionage mission—and accused the United States of recklessly provoking "a global anti-Soviet campaign." From his sickbed Andropov called Washington's response "hysterical," lambasted America's "outrageous military psychosis," and declared that war might come.

"White Hot, Thoroughly White Hot"*

The downing of KAL 007 was a striking manifestation of the revived Cold War. While Washington sought to embarrass Moscow and imposed diplomatic and legal punishments on the Kremlin, the Soviets retaliated by obstructing the search for survivors and denying their discovery in October of the plane's blackbox recording of its flight plan and communications.† This appalling accident stirred both sides not only to distort the facts and frighten their publics but also to restate their mutual grievances: the Americans against the heinous and irredeemable Soviet system, the Soviets against the unrelenting violation of their sovereign space and Washington's obsession with using its military supremacy to blackmail Moscow.

For the first time since the Cuban missile crisis, the Superpowers appeared to be heading toward a confrontation. Each side, now possessing over twenty thousand nuclear warheads, had grown more and more nervous over the other's increasingly menacing land and naval maneuvers. Fear and mistrust reached a peak in November 1983, when NATO's military exercises created a panic in

---

* Phrase used on November 7, 1983, by politburo member Gregory Romanov to characterize the international climate.

† Among the remaining mysteries is KAL 007's twelve-minute-long descent after the firing of the missiles and the fact that practically no human remains or luggage and little debris were found, feeding CIA theories of either a ditching at sea or a landing on Sakhalin and subsequent Soviet captivity, neither of which have ever been proven.

Moscow over a surprise nuclear attack.* That month, after the first US Cruise and Pershing missiles were deployed in Britain and Germany (some six to ten minutes' striking distance from the USSR), Moscow halted the Intermediate-Range Nuclear Forces (INF) negotiations in Geneva and suspended the resumption of Strategic Arms Reduction Talks (START) with Washington. For the first time in more than a decade the Superpowers had ceased speaking to each other.

On November 20, 1983, *The Day After*, a television docudrama depicting the effects of nuclear war on a small Midwestern city, struck terror in a hundred million Americans.† Faced with a panicked public, a looming reelection campaign, and a bulging arsenal, Reagan suddenly reversed course. In his January 16 speech to the nation, the president called for renewed negotiations with Moscow and deemed 1984 "a year of opportunities for peace." However, Andropov's death in February and his successor's infirmity (Konstantin Chernenko was suffering from severe emphysema) created a thirteen-month pause while US-Soviet relations neither improved nor deteriorated.

Human Rights

Although Reagan had been an outspoken opponent of the Helsinki Accords and a bitter critic of Jimmy Carter's inconsistent human rights policies, he trod carefully in this delicate diplomatic terrain. His first secretary of state, Alexander Haig, who famously announced that "international terrorism will take the place of human rights," adopted a conservative approach: promoting the evolution of friendly right-wing *authoritarian* regimes (such as Chile and South Africa) toward a more humane society and working to prevent the establishment of new *totalitarian* (i.e., communist) regimes that would inevitably repress their populations. Moreover, in dealing with Moscow's ill-treatment of dissidents and religious and national minorities, Reagan was far more pragmatic than Carter, acknowledging the limits of US influence, declining to publicly "embarrass" the Soviets, and confining himself to personal letters to Brezhnev, private meetings with dissidents, and critical diary entries.

Reagan's reticence stirred an immediate backlash from the human rights community, especially the US Helsinki Watch Group, which feared the loss of a

---

* The Able Archer exercises, which were conducted between November 2 and 11 at a moment of heightened Superpower tensions for the purpose of testing new codes, involving NATO heads of government and simulating a period of conflict escalation that would culminate in the release of a nuclear weapon, convinced some nervous Soviet officials of the imminence of a genuine attack and resulted in the placing of Soviet air units in Poland and East Germany on alert.

† It was later seen by hundreds of millions of people in forty countries.

powerful state ally. The US Congress, which since 1976 had compelled successive administrations to monitor global human rights, passed resolutions condemning Soviet misconduct and chastising Reagan for withholding public support for the oppressed. By the summer of 1982, after Shultz came to office, the State Department weighed in, rebuilding its human rights apparatus, formulating a program of public and private diplomacy, mobilizing America's NATO allies, and raising America's voice in the UN and at the CSCE conference in Madrid.*
Meanwhile, US diplomats in Moscow and Leningrad maintained quiet contact with Soviet citizens who were denied permission to emigrate.

But Reagan, still more intent on military and ideological mobilization, was reluctant to wave the human rights banner. To appease the activists, between 1981 and 1983 he responded with showy gestures, increasing funds for Voice of America and Radio Liberty; designating special days for Americans to honor Solidarność, the people of Afghanistan, and the Soviet dissident Andrei Sakharov; and reviving Baltic Freedom Day and Captive Nations Week. But Reagan refused to use tougher methods—wielding the trade weapon or terminating cultural exchanges—to modify the Soviets' behavior.

There was an ostensible shift in US policy in 1984. In his otherwise conciliatory January 16 speech, the president for the first time identified human rights as a "major problem" in US-Soviet relations, expressed America's "deep concern over prisoners of conscience in the Soviet Union and over the virtual halt in the emigration of Jews,† Armenians, and others who wish to join their families abroad," and called on the Soviet Union to live up to its Helsinki obligations. Yet despite the president's reputation among Soviet dissidents as a liberator, it is probable that he was responding to election-year domestic pressures and continued to believe that the most effective way to alleviate the plight of Moscow's victims was to demolish the entire Soviet system.

CENTRAL AND SOUTH AMERICA

Cold War tensions were also reignited in the Western Hemisphere. The Kremlin, although reluctant to increase its already heavy military and economic burdens,

---

* Toward the end of this gathering, which took place over three years, between 1980 and 1983, there was a heated US-Soviet debate over the implementation of the Helsinki human rights provisions.
† Following the chill in US-Soviet relations after the Soviet invasion of Afghanistan, the numbers of Jewish emigrants dropped from a high of 51,320 in 1979 to 21,471 in 1980; 9,447 in 1981; 2,688 in 1982; 1,315 in 1983; and only 896 in 1984.

was still committed to supporting left-wing (in its own parlance "progressive") Third World movements, including those in Washington's own backyard. The Reagan administration, convinced that communism was on the rise in Central America, abandoned Carter's efforts to curb human rights abuses by pro-US rulers and devoted an unprecedented amount of time, effort, and resources to asserting American power in the region.

Beginning in 1981 Washington provided substantial assistance to the military governments of El Salvador and Guatemala to fend off leftist insurgencies. But the president's principal target was Nicaragua, which he labeled a communist and totalitarian regime and was determined to overthrow. To punish the Sandinista government for funneling Soviet and Cuban arms to the guerrillas in El Salvador, his administration cut off all aid to Managua. In addition, Reagan authorized covert CIA actions* and provided funding, training, equipment, and logistical support to the Honduras-based paramilitary opposition (*contrarevolucionarios*), known as the Contras. Faced with Washington's challenge, the Soviet Union greatly increased its military and economic assistance to Nicaragua, which also received aid from Western Europe and other Latin American countries.

The ensuing violence in Central America shocked the world public. In the US-supported counterinsurgency in Guatemala, the military destroyed hundreds of villages and hamlets, killed between fifty thousand and seventy-five thousand people, and created a million refugees; in tiny El Salvador the rulers' death squads left seventy thousand dead and hundreds of villages destroyed; and in Nicaragua the Contras, after failing to defeat the Sandinista army, resorted to widespread terrorist attacks against civilian targets in a war resulting in thirty thousand deaths, a hundred thousand refugees, and a ruined economy. By 1983, the Democrat-controlled US Congress, fearing another Vietnam, sought to curb Reagan's anticommunist crusade in Central America, reducing aid to Guatemala and El Salvador, refusing to fund the Contras, and ruling out the use of American troops.

Undeterred, the Reagan administration took bold action elsewhere. In the first US military intervention in the Western Hemisphere in eighteen years,† the president in October 1983 launched an air, land, and sea invasion of the tiny

---

* In 1984 Nicaragua brought a complaint against the United States to the International Court of Justice at The Hague for numerous violations of its sovereignty, including the mining of its harbors. The court, rejecting US insistence that its jurisdiction did not apply to matters relating to Central America, ruled against Washington, which then blocked enforcement by the Security Council. In 1992, after the Sandinista government was replaced through the electoral process, Nicaragua withdrew the complaint.

† In April 1965 Lyndon Johnson, fearing the creation of a "second Cuba," had ordered the invasion of the Dominican Republic, resulting in a pro-US government.

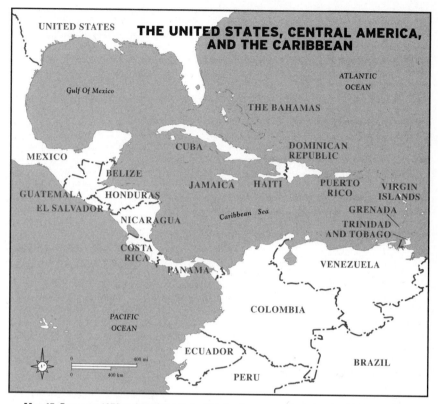

Map 15. Between 1978 and 1990 the United States became actively involved in its southern neighbors' political developments.

Caribbean island of Grenada for the purpose of toppling its Marxist government. Having secured marginal support from the Organization of Eastern Caribbean States, Washington announced its goals as protecting American medical students, thwarting the construction of a ten-thousand-foot airfield that could be used by Soviet or Cuban military aircraft, and restoring law and order and democratic institutions to Grenada. Seven thousand US troops easily overwhelmed the six-hundred-man Grenadian army and some seven hundred Cubans and installed a pro-US regime.

The American intervention in Grenada conveyed a clear Cold War message. In addressing the nation on October 27, Reagan underlined the Soviet Union's responsibility for the spread of subversion in the Caribbean (and also linked Moscow with the bombing of the marine barracks in Beirut four days earlier), and he reiterated his commitment to fight terrorism and roll back world communism. Although Andropov issued only a mild protest against the invasion, the Kremlin was stunned by Washington's use of military power. Cuba removed some one thousand personnel from Nicaragua, and the Managua government was put on notice of the consequences of provoking Washington.

International reaction was largely negative. Although the United States was able to veto a Security Council resolution, the UN General Assembly, by a lopsided vote of 108–9, condemned the invasion as "a flagrant violation of international law." The British government, fending off public criticism of the cruise missile deployment, took a dim view of Reagan's Big Stick diplomacy, which harked back to Theodore Roosevelt's assertion of the moral imperative of US dominance. Prime Minister Margaret Thatcher, whom Washington had not consulted beforehand, as leader of the British Commonwealth of Nations (of which Grenada was a member) publicly opposed the invasion.

The heightened risks of unilateralism and the erosion of multilateral peacekeeping had already been exposed a year earlier by the Falklands War, the world's first major naval engagement since World War II. This seventy-four-day conflict had pitted two US Cold War allies, Britain and Argentina—one a key NATO member, the other an active anticommunist partner in Central and South America—in a dispute over sovereignty of a remote group of South Atlantic islands.[*] Because of mounting tensions, the Superpowers were incapable of bringing the two countries to the negotiating table and avoid a war that cost a thousand lives.[†]

Indeed, the Falklands War was more than a remote sideshow, and neither Superpower exhibited adroit statesmanship. The United States sided with the British: the Reagan administration provided a satellite communications channel for their warships and stymied efforts by the UN and the Organization of American States[‡] to mediate the conflict. By doing so it provoked considerable resentment in Argentina and the rest of Latin America as well as in non-Western countries

---

[*] Called the Malvinas by Argentina (and most Latin American and European countries), the Falklands, lying 290 miles east of the Argentinean coast and 8,000 miles southwest of the British Isles, had been under British control since 1833, which had been contested by the Argentineans ever since.

[†] On April 2, 1982, the Argentinean military junta, angered over five years of futile negotiations with the British and attempting to divert public attention from the debt crisis, which had brought inflation and high unemployment, and from its human rights abuses ordered an invasion of the islands. A shocked Thatcher government, aiming to reverse its sagging popularity over Britain's economic troubles, demanded a complete withdrawal, refused US offers to mediate, and launched a naval force to retake the islands, which was completed on June 14. After the debacle, the junta was forced to resign, and Margaret Thatcher's popularity soared.

[‡] One of the world's oldest regional organizations (originally founded in 1889 and established in its new structure in 1948), the OAS is a thirty-five-member institution, headquartered in Washington, DC, whose purpose is to promote security and solidarity in the Americas.

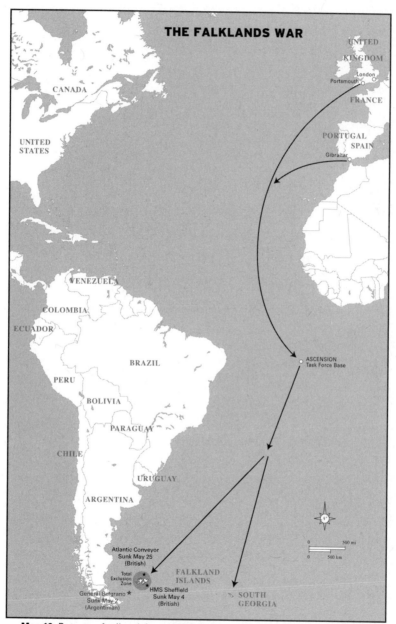

Map 16. Between April and June 1982 Britain and Argentina fought a costly war over the control of the contested Falkland Islands.

without incurring much gratitude from Thatcher. For the Soviets, the Falklands War provided a welcome distraction from their troubles in Poland and Afghanistan, an opportunity to lambaste Western colonialism, and a glimpse at the performance of British NATO forces. Nevertheless, Moscow failed to gain credit in the Third World because of its refusal to provide aid to Argentina (which had been an important grain supplier during the US embargo) and its failure to stand up to the West in the Security Council. The Falklands War not only revealed the Superpowers' continuing indifference toward multilateral peacekeeping but also the limits of US and Soviet control over conflicts precipitated by desperate and determined third parties.

ASIA

The renewed Cold War of the early 1980s also affected Asia. With the demise of détente, Moscow and Washington stepped up their competition to woo China and play a major role in Asia, but these efforts were complicated after the People's Republic under Deng Xiaoping launched a "second revolution" that established market-oriented economic reforms at home and an independent voice abroad. Resolved to back neither Superpower, China used its permanent Security Council seat to reaffirm the 1955 Bandung principles of anticolonialism and peaceful coexistence.

Both Superpowers approached Beijing with serious liabilities. The Reagan administration was initially cool toward the People's Republic, because of the president's long-standing anticommunist stance and his commitment to Taiwan, and China not only was adamantly against Washington's arms sales to its opponent but also critical of America's interventionist policies in Central America, Africa, and the Middle East. The Kremlin, now facing a potent rival promoting an alternative model of economic development in the Third World, nonetheless hoped to exploit the Sino-US rift and repair its broken ties with Beijing, but it was thwarted by China's three demands—the Soviets' withdrawal from Afghanistan, a Vietnamese withdrawal from Kampuchea (Cambodia), and a rollback of the Soviet military buildup on its northern borders, which included fifty divisions and SS-20 intermediate-range ballistic missiles.

Deng Xiaoping, facing a divided politburo and immense domestic challenges, trod warily in international affairs, evenhandedly resisting Washington's pleas for a more belligerent anti-Soviet stance* and Moscow's offers for a nonaggres-

---

* The one exception was Chinese-American collaboration in arming the mujahideen in

sion pact. In 1984 Beijing hosted two high-level visitors: in April Ronald Reagan (who later claimed to have fallen under a "China spell" and lauded its government for embracing "capitalist principles") and in December Soviet first deputy prime minister Ivan Arkipov (the highest-level contact since Kosygin's 1969 talks with Zhou Enlai). But neither guest succeeded in convincing the Chinese leadership to end their straddling and support his side.

US-Soviet rivalry took a more lethal form in Cambodia. On Christmas Day 1978 Vietnamese forces had invaded Cambodia and set up a puppet communist government, the PRK (People's Republic of Kampuchea). Although expressing relief over the end of the murderous Khmer Rouge regime, most of the world condemned Hanoi's violation of its neighbor's sovereignty and refused to recognize the PRK. Two months later, China launched a brief punitive attack on Vietnam. Moscow, responding to Hanoi's pleas, had agreed to provide military support in return for the lease of naval and air bases at the former US facilities in Da Nang and Cam Ranh Bay, thus bringing some seven thousand Soviet military personnel into the region.

After more than thirty years of conflict, Cambodia descended into a bloody civil war. Bolstered by some 180,000 Soviet-armed Vietnamese troops (whose presence Hanoi repeatedly denied), the PRK leader Heng Samrin faced three disparate insurgent movements, among them the Chinese-backed Khmer Rouge, which made deep cross-border forays from refugee camps and military bases in Thailand. In 1982, the United States and China put pressure on the communist and noncommunist rebels to form the Coalition Government of Democratic Kampuchea (CGDK) under the presidency of Prince Norodom Sihanouk. Over Soviet protests, the CGDK was seated by the United Nations.

Cambodia's neighbors played a major role in its civil war. China and Thailand (Vietnam's historic enemies) were determined to check Hanoi's efforts to dominate all of Indochina and demanded a full withdrawal of its troops. But the CGDK remained a tense alliance of opposites, with China supporting the Khmer Rouge, Thailand and other ASEAN* members providing economic and military aid to the noncommunist elements, and the United States (swallowing its misgivings over the Khmer Rouge's involvement) sending substantial aid to the coalition as well.

Afghanistan, in which the United States purchased Soviet-designed arms produced in China and transmitted them through Pakistan.

* The Association of Southeastern Asian Nations was an anticommunist organization founded in 1967 by Indonesia, Malaysia, the Philippines, Singapore, and Thailand and endorsed by the United States, Canada, Britain, and Australia.

As in Afghanistan, the struggle over Cambodia represented a high-stakes US-Soviet proxy war. Washington sought to topple a Soviet- and Vietnamese-backed regime, and Moscow, risking US and Chinese ire, paid huge sums to bolster its Vietnamese ally (estimated at some $3 million per day) as the price of acquiring two former US bases, which gave the USSR enhanced intelligence capability and increased its air force's range in East and Southeast Asia.

Despite the CGDK Coalition's vast resources and their own growing economic weakness and international isolation, the Vietnamese and their PRK allies held out. Fed by Chinese, US, and Soviet arms, the Cambodian civil war became a grinding stalemate.

AFRICA

The US-Soviet contest also intensified in Southern Africa. The key player here was South Africa, whose regional position had changed dramatically with the attainment of independence by Angola, Mozambique, and Zimbabwe. The Pretoria government saw itself facing a barrage of threats from its Soviet-armed neighbors and opponents: from the three black-ruled front-line states; from the exiled ANC (African National Congress), based in Angola and Mozambique; from SWAPO (Southwest Africa People's Organization), headquartered in Angola and demanding independence for its longtime trust-colony Namibia; and from the South African Communist Party (SAC). In addition, South Africa faced increased pressure by Western governments to ease white-minority rule, growing diplomatic isolation, and an expanding domestic opposition.

In response, the Nationalist prime minister P. W. Botha in 1979 launched his "total strategy."* It included strong presidential government at home and a campaign of subversion in Zimbabwe, clandestine air and ground operations in Mozambique and Angola, and continued support of opposition movements in both countries: RENAMO (Resistência Nacional Moçambicana) in Mozambique and UNITA (União Nacional para a Independência Total de Angola) in Angola. Botha also refused to relinquish control over Namibia to a Marxist SWAPO regime.

The Reagan administration, which regarded South Africa as a valuable strategic ally and raw-materials provider, was highly receptive to its fears of a Soviet master plan to control all of southern Africa. Reversing Carter's coolness toward

---

* In 1977, Botha, as defense minister, had begun South Africa's nuclear weapons program.

the Pretoria government, Washington revived the policy of constructive engagement, stressing quiet diplomacy to induce reforms by the white-minority government and withholding criticism of its security forces' use of violence against unarmed protesters. Moreover, Reagan not only countenanced South Africa's air and ground raids against its neighbors but also demanded the withdrawal of the twenty-five thousand to thirty thousand Cuban troops remaining in Angola. In addition, Washington provided clandestine direct and indirect aid to UNITA, even hailing its leader Jonas Savimbi as a "freedom fighter."

The Soviet Union, a longtime supporter of armed independence movements in southern Africa, had seemed triumphant in 1980. In response to South Africa's stepped-up aggression, the Kremlin dispatched some two thousand military advisers to Angola to train government- and ANC-armed forces and increased its shipments of arms to Angola and Mozambique. But in the face of mounting East-West tension, unrest in Eastern Europe, its protracted entanglement in Afghanistan, and a dangerous situation in the Middle East, the Kremlin found itself unable to maintain a leading position in southern Africa. Lacking the military forces and economic resources to bolster its clients, Moscow bleakly watched the leaders of Angola and Mozambique approach Pretoria and the United States in 1984 to secure their future.

THE MIDDLE EAST

The Superpower competition in the Middle East was shaped by violent clashes in this region, which included the 1980–1988 Iraq-Iran War and the ongoing Israeli-Palestinian conflict as well as the appearance of radical Islamic jihadists (religious warriors) in Afghanistan, Lebanon, and Egypt.[*] With the demise of détente, nothing remained of Nixon and Brezhnev's 1972 pledge to refrain from exploiting quarrels in the world's most volatile region for their own benefit.

On September 22, 1980, Saddam Hussein, who only a year before had seized control of Iraq,[†] launched an invasion of Iran, pitting a charismatic secular Arab leader against Khomeini's revolutionary Shi'ite forces. Hussein's grave

---

[*] Manifested dramatically in the 1981 assassination of Egyptian president Anwar Sadat by members of the Muslim Brotherhood.

[†] After being named president, army commander in chief, head of government, and secretary-general of its ruling Ba'ath Party in the summer of 1979, Hussein instigated a bloody purge of his political rivals, created a powerful security network, and suppressed Shi'ites, Kurds, and other potential dissident groups.

Map 17. Between 1979 and 1989 the Middle East and the Horn of Africa were major sites of Superpower confrontation.

miscalculation—that the Arab world would rally to Baghdad's side and that Iran would quickly collapse—led instead to an eight-year war between two heavily armed old rivals that cost over a million lives and calcified the two repressive political regimes.

According to official records so far available, this was a war neither Superpower had encouraged and both had tried to stay out of.* But shortly after taking office, the Reagan administration reversed Carter's neutral stance toward the combatants. Washington, seeking to punish Iran's sponsorship of international

---

* One year before the invasion, the United States learned of Saddam Hussein's intentions and passed on word to Iran, but neither the Carter administration nor the Kremlin gave Iraq a green light to invade.

terrorism and ignoring Iraq's human rights abuses, tilted toward Baghdad. In response to Iran's 1982 counteroffensive, the United States stepped up civilian, technological, and ultimately military aid to Iraq, shared crucial satellite intelligence, and reestablished full diplomatic relations in 1984. The United States also encouraged its allies to provide arms to Iraq and watered down UN resolutions condemning Hussein's use of chemical weapons.

Moscow's situation was far more delicate. Concerned over Tehran's threat to its Islamic border republics and over both sides' ferocious anticommunist campaigns, the Soviet Union decided to straddle. It tilted first toward Tehran, then declared its neutrality, and then in late 1983 resumed arms sales to Baghdad but also continued sending supplies to Iran and countenancing weapons deliveries to Tehran by its allies Libya, Syria, and North Korea.

More than an appalling sideshow, the Iran-Iraq War underlined the Superpowers' obsession with checking each other's influence in the Gulf region, even at the cost of expanding the violence.* Neither side endorsed Hussein's pan-Arab dream or the collapse of Iran, nor did they wish for an Iranian victory and the dismemberment of Iraq. Yet despite the convergence of Washington and Moscow's interests, the new chill between the two capitals checked any initiative to bring the warring parties to the peace table until 1987. America's principal interests, to protect its anticommunist Gulf allies (Saudi Arabia, Qatar, the United Arab Emirates, Kuwait, Oman, and Bahrain) and to secure the West's oil supplies, kept it solidly in the arms game, while the Soviet Union, capitalizing on the world's distraction from its imbroglio in Afghanistan, succeeded in expanding its influence in the Muslim world. In the meantime, more than thirty countries sent weapons to the belligerents, with China and several others arming both sides.

The next Superpower crisis was precipitated by Israel's June 6, 1982, invasion of Lebanon, a country that had been engulfed in civil war since 1975, was occupied by thirty thousand Syrian troops, and was also the headquarters of the PLO leadership. Just two months after Israel's complete evacuation of the Sinai Peninsula (as specified in the 1979 Egyptian-Israeli peace treaty), the Begin government, perceiving Washington's indecisive signals as a green light,† sent an army

---

* That included the world's first attacks on a nuclear facility: Iran's unsuccessful bombing of Iraq's Osirak reactor in September 1980, followed by the Israeli strike in June 1981, which destroyed it and brought unanimous condemnation by the UN Security Council.
† Despite State and Defense Department concerns over damaging US-Arab relations, Secretary of State Alexander Haig had voiced no opposition to the invasion.

into Lebanon to eliminate the Palestinian threat to its northern border. But rather than halting in southern Lebanon—as the United States and the world expected—Israel expanded the campaign. Following air attacks on the PLO headquarters in Beirut and on the Syrian Soviet missile sites in the Bekaa Valley, Israeli ground forces on June 13 reached Beirut, where they hoped to install a friendly government under the Christian Maronite leader Bashir Gemayel.

Israel achieved a major military triumph. It captured large numbers of Palestinian prisoners and their Soviet arms and forced the evacuation of Yasser Arafat, the entire PLO leadership, and some fourteen thousand Palestinian troops to Tunisia under the supervision of a US-led multinational force. But victory quickly turned sour. Large segments of the world public, including Israeli peace groups, condemned the Begin government for inflicting high casualties on Lebanon's civilian population. In September Israel lost a crucial partner when Gemayel was assassinated on the orders of Syrian intelligence. Even more damaging to Israel were the massacres in the Sabra and Shatila refugee camps. On September 16, under its soldiers' watch, Israel's Lebanese Christian allies, seeking revenge for Gemayel's murder, slaughtered some eight hundred Palestinians, creating an international scandal in which Israel was widely blamed for failing to stop the atrocities. Moreover, Israel ultimately failed to dislodge the Syrian forces, and a new organization, Hezbollah (Party of God), backed by Syria and Iran, emerged in Lebanon as a powerful Islamic, anti-Israeli force.

The Reagan administration, aroused by the violence in Lebanon and the public outcry, attempted to take charge. On September 20 Washington announced the formation of a second multinational peacekeeping force and the dispatch of 1,800 marines to Lebanon to bolster the central government. The Kremlin (unlike Khrushchev's bombastic response to Eisenhower's 1958 intervention in Lebanon*) issued only a mild protest. But the installation of a US-dominated force in Lebanon immediately raised opposition from the antigovernment Muslim militias, which accused Washington of supporting Israel and the Christians.

Although characterizing the US intervention in Lebanon as part of the East-West global conflict, neither Reagan nor Secretary of State Shultz was prepared to engage vigorously in the problems of the Middle East. Because of this US leadership gap, Israel and Syria's positions hardened, the Palestinian problem remained unresolved, and the sectarian violence escalated in Lebanon. The year

---

* When the president, answering the Beirut government's appeal, had sent fourteen thousand troops to Lebanon to thwart a Nasserite coup and form a new pro-Western government.

1983 also saw a wave of suicide attacks against American targets, beginning with the April assault on the US embassy in Beirut that claimed 63 lives, including 17 American citizens, and culminating in the October bombing of the Beirut marine barracks in which 241 US servicemen were killed. In response to this deadliest assault on US forces abroad since World War II, the White House ordered no military retaliation but faced congressional pressure to pull out. Reagan, now preparing his reelection campaign, in February 1984 ordered the departure of all US troops by April. It was a humiliating US withdrawal.

The Kremlin was also shaken by the Lebanon conflict. It had gambled on sitting on the sidelines in order to avoid a confrontation with the United States and inciting even stronger Israeli military action. Stung by radical Arab criticisms of its inferior weaponry, its failure to support the PLO and the Syrians, and its brutal war in Afghanistan, Moscow responded to Washington's intervention by greatly expanding its military commitment to Syria. This included the delivery of more than $2 billion in new sophisticated weaponry and aircraft, along with the first long-range SA-5 missile batteries outside the Warsaw Pact countries, which were operated by 1,500 Soviet military personnel.

More than any other site of Superpower controversy, the Middle East defied a bipolar structure. In this region of colonial-drawn borders and rival religions and ethnic groups as well as crucial oil supplies, neither Washington nor Moscow controlled its clients, but both were still trapped by their Cold War reflexes to seek advantage wherever possible. It was nonetheless an unequal competition. Although neither side understood the rising anti-Western sentiments in the region, America exerted a stronger attraction to all sides because of its greater economic and military power.

Cold War rhetoric continued to reverberate in Washington. Following his overwhelming reelection victory, Reagan in his January 21, 1985, inaugural address vowed to seek an agreement with Moscow over nuclear weapons but also reaffirmed his commitment to SDI, insisted that the United States must remain militarily strong, and declared that "human freedom is on the march and nowhere more so than our own hemisphere."

But in Moscow a shift was taking place. On March 11, the politburo unanimously selected as the successor to Chernenko its youngest member, Mikhail Gorbachev. Three months earlier, the new general secretary of the Soviet Union had already signaled a change in Moscow's direction by pronouncing the Cold War an "abnormal" condition of international relations and calling for "new political thinking" (*novoe politicheskoe myshlenie*) to combat the menace of nuclear war.

SUGGESTIONS FOR FURTHER STUDY

Documents

Morozov, Boris. *Documents on Soviet Jewish Emigration*. London: Frank Cass, 1999.

Reagan, Ronald. "Foreword Written for a Report on the Strategic Defense Initiative, December 28, 1984." The American Presidency Project. http://www.presidency.ucsb.edu/ws/index.php?pid=38499&st=strategic+defense+initiative&st1.

———. "Remarks at the Annual Convention of the National Association of Evangelicals in Orlando, Florida." Evil Empire Speech, March 8, 1983. Ronald Reagan Presidential Foundation and Library. http://www.reaganfoundation.org/bw_detail.aspx?p=LMB4YGHF2&h1=0&h2=0&sw=&lm=berlinwall&args_a=cms&args_b=74&argsb=N&tx=1770.

"Shaking Hands with Saddam Hussein: The US Tilts Toward Iraq, 1980–1984." National Security Archive. 2003. http://www.gwu.edu/~nsarchiv/NSAEBB/NSAEBB82/index.htm.

"Solidarity and Martial Law in Poland: 25 Years Later." National Security Archive. 2006. http://www.gwu.edu/~nsarchiv/NSAEBB/NSAEBB211/index.htm#docs.

Contemporary Writing

Friedman, Thomas L. *From Beirut to Jerusalem*. New York: Farrar, Straus and Giroux, 1989.

Havel, Václav. *The Power of the Powerless: Citizens Against the State in Central-Eastern Europe*. Edited by John Keane. Armonk, NY: M. E. Sharpe, 1985.

Hersh, Seymour M. *"The Target Is Destroyed": What Really Happened to Flight 007 and What America Knew About It*. New York: Random House, 1986.

Konrád, György. *Antipolitics: An Essay*. San Diego: Harcourt Brace Jovanovich, 1984.

Michnik, Adam. *Letters from Prison and Other Essays*. Translated by Maya Latynski. Berkeley: University of California Press, 1985.

Talbott, Strobe. *Deadly Gambits: The Reagan Administration and the Stalemate in Nuclear Arms Control*. New York: Knopf, 1984.

Memoirs and Diaries

Banī Ṣadr, Abū al-Ḥasan. *My Turn to Speak: Iran, the Revolution and Secret Deals with the U.S.* Washington, DC: Brassey's, 1991.

Gates, Robert Michael. *From the Shadows: The Ultimate Insider's Story of Five Presidents and How They Won the Cold War*. New York: Simon and Schuster, 1996.

Reagan, Ronald. *An American Life*. New York: Simon and Schuster, 1990.

———. *The Reagan Diaries*. Edited by Douglas Brinkley. New York: Harper Collins, 2007.

Shultz, George Pratt. *Turmoil and Triumph: My Years as Secretary of State*. New York: Scribner's, 1993.

Weinberger, Caspar W. *Fighting for Peace: Seven Critical Years in the Pentagon*. New York: Warner Books, 1990.

Films

Alsino and the Condor. Directed by Miguel Littin. Havana: Instituto Cubano del Arte e Industrias Cinematográficos, 1983.

The Day After. Directed by Nicholas Meyer. Los Angeles: ABC Circle Films, 1983.

Heartbreak Ridge. Directed by Clint Eastwood. Los Angeles: Jay Weston Productions, 1986.

The Hunt for Red October. Directed by John McTiernan. Los Angeles: Paramount Pictures, 1990.

The Iron Lady. Directed by Phyllida Lloyd. London: Pathé, 2011.

Lebanon. Directed by Samuel Maoz. Tel Aviv: Ariel Films, 2009.

Man of Iron. Directed by Andrzej Wajda. Łódź: Film Polski, 1981.

No End. Directed by Krzysztof Kieślowski. Łódź: Film Polski, 1985.

Pictures from a Revolution. Directed by Alfred Guzzetti, Susan Meiselas, and Richard P. Rogers. New York: GMR Films, 1991.

Red Dawn. Directed by John Milius. Los Angeles: United Artists, 1984.

Repentance. Directed by Tengiz Abuladze. Tbilisi, Georgia: Qartuli Pilmi, 1984.

Threads. Directed by Mick Jackson. London: BBC, 1984.

Waltz with Bashir. Directed by Ari Folman. Jaffa: Bridgit Folman Film Gang, 2008.

World War III. Directed by David Greene and Boris Sagal. Los Angeles: NBC, 1982.

Fiction

Brinkley, Joel. *The Circus Master's Mission.* New York: Random House, 1989.

Jabrā, Jabrā Ibrāhīm. *In Search of Walid Masoud: A Novel.* Translated by Roger Allen, and Adnan Haydar. Syracuse, NY: Syracuse University Press, 2000.

Khūrī, Ilyās, and Humphrey T. Davies. *Gate of the Sun.* Brooklyn: Archipelago Books, 2005.

Paton, Alan. *Ah, but Your Land Is Beautiful.* New York: Scribner, 1982.

Sammān, Ghaādah. *Beirut Nightmares.* London: Quartet Books, 1997.

Children's Literature

Dr. Seuss [Theodore Geisel]. *The Butter Battle Book.* New York: Random House, 1984.

Secondary Sources

Alekseeva, Ludmila. *Soviet Dissent: Contemporary Movements for National, Religious, and Human Rights.* Middletown, CT: Wesleyan University Press, 1985.

Barber, James P., and John Barratt. *South Africa's Foreign Policy: The Search for Status and Security, 1945–1988.* Cambridge: Cambridge University Press, 1990.

Ben-Zvi, Abraham. *The United States and Israel: The Limits of the Special Relationship.* New York: Columbia University Press, 1993.

Blight, James G. *Becoming Enemies: U.S.-Iran Relations and the Iran-Iraq War, 1979–1988.* Lanham, MD: Rowman and Littlefield, 2012.

Cannon, Lou. *President Reagan: The Role of a Lifetime.* New York: Simon and Schuster, 1991.

Dannreuther, Roland. *The Soviet Union and the PLO*. New York: St. Martin's, 1998.

Diggins, John P. *Ronald Reagan: Fate, Freedom, and the Making of History*. New York: Norton, 2007.

Evron, Yair. *War and Intervention in Lebanon: The Israeli-Syrian Deterrence Dialogue*. Baltimore: Johns Hopkins University Press, 1987.

Freedman, Robert Owen. *Moscow and the Middle East: Soviet Policy Since the Invasion of Afghanistan*. Cambridge: Cambridge University Press, 1991.

Halverson, Thomas E. *The Last Great Nuclear Debate: NATO and Short-Range Nuclear Weapons in the 1980s*. Basingstoke, UK: Macmillan, 1995.

Herf, Jeffrey. *War by Other Means: Soviet Power, West German Resistance, and the Battle of the Euromissiles*. New York: Free Press, 1991.

Jaster, Robert S. *South Africa in Namibia: The Botha Strategy*. Lanham, MD: University Press of America, 1985.

Laïdi, Zaki. *The Superpowers and Africa: The Constraints of a Rivalry, 1960–1990*. Chicago: University of Chicago Press, 1990.

Lawson, Fred Haley. *Why Syria Goes to War: Thirty Years of Confrontation*. Ithaca, NY: Cornell University Press, 1996.

Lynch, Edward A. *The Cold War's Last Battlefield: Reagan, the Soviets, and Central America*. Albany: State University of New York Press, 2011.

Medvedev, Zhores A. *Andropov*. New York: Norton, 1983.

Monaghan, David. *The Falklands War: Myth and Countermyth*. Basingstoke, UK: Macmillan, 1998.

Richardson, Sophie. *China, Cambodia, and the Five Principles of Peaceful Coexistence*. New York: Columbia University Press, 2010.

Schweizer, Peter. *Victory: The Reagan Administration's Secret Strategy that Hastened the Collapse of the Soviet Union*. New York: Atlantic Monthly Press, 1994.

Scott, James M. *Deciding to Intervene: The Reagan Doctrine and American Foreign Policy*. Durham, NC: Duke University Press, 1996.

Sjursen, Helene. *The United States, Western Europe and the Polish Crisis: International Relations in the Second Cold War*. Basingstoke, UK: Palgrave Macmillan, 2003.

Smith, Geoffrey. *Reagan and Thatcher*. New York: Norton, 1991.

Taylor, Alan R. *The Superpowers and the Middle East*. Syracuse, NY: Syracuse University Press, 1991.

Vogel, Ezra F. *Deng Xiaoping and the Transformation of China*. Cambridge, MA: Belknap Press of Harvard University Press, 2011.

Wittner, Lawrence S. *Toward Nuclear Abolition: A History of the World Nuclear Disarmament Movement, 1971 to the Present*. Stanford, CA: Stanford University Press, 2003.

Young, Marilyn J., and Michael K. Launer. *Flights of Fancy, Flight of Doom: KAL 007 and Soviet-American Rhetoric*. Lanham, MD: University Press of America, 1988.

Chapter 9
THE END OF THE COLD WAR, 1985–1991

I really do inhabit a system in which words are capable of
shaking the entire structure of government, where words
can prove mightier than ten military divisions.

—Václav Havel

Nothing will ever be the same as it was.

—Willy Brandt

In his 1987 book, *The Rise and Fall of the Great Powers*, the Yale historian Paul
Kennedy surveyed five centuries of imperial overstretch. Significantly, the concluding chapters focused primarily on the United States, which, Kennedy believed, was slipping from its place as the world's Number One. This was due not
only to economic competition from Europe, Japan, and China but primarily to
the escalating cost of America's Cold War defense establishment, which had
raised the national debt in 1985 to the stratospheric figure of $1.8 trillion.

However, by the winter of 1986, many observers drew an even bleaker picture
of the USSR. Drained by the war in Afghanistan and by subsidies to its satellites
and overseas clients; jarred by the precipitous drop in world oil and gas prices,
the fall in its foreign currency earnings from trade, and declining agricultural
and industrial production; crippled by its technological backwardness and rigid
bureaucracy (which that year were underscored by the Chernobyl disaster); and
fending off increasingly restive national minorities, the Soviet Union seemed to
be facing an existential crisis.

Yet no one in 1985 expected the peaceful end of US-Soviet rivalry, the fall of the communist regimes in Eastern Europe, the reunification of Germany, and the demise of the Soviet Union—all of which occurred in the next six years. These unforeseen developments have created a lively historical debate over how and why they occurred and when the Cold War actually ended.

THE GORBACHEV REVOLUTION IN INTERNATIONAL AFFAIRS

After his arrival in Moscow from Stavropol in 1978, Mikhail Gorbachev quickly became one of the politburo's most active members and caught the eye of Andropov as a fellow reformer and likely successor. In nominating him to succeed the Brezhnev-loyalist Chernenko, Gromyko praised the new leader's "unquenchable energy" and commitment to "put the interests of the Party, society, and people before his own." Young, well-educated, and articulate, and backed by the party and military chiefs, Gorbachev accepted a mandate in March 1985 to reform and strengthen the Soviet Union and to "realize our shining future."

Nevertheless, during his first two years Gorbachev's domestic policies were erratic and largely ineffective. Without challenging the centerpiece of the Soviet regime—the planned economy—or its outsized military budget, the new general secretary and his political allies launched the politically damaging anti-corruption and anti-alcoholism campaigns and also made futile attempts to boost industrial production and labor discipline. On February 25, 1986, thirty years after Khrushchev had exposed Stalin's misdeeds, Gorbachev promoted his perestroika (reconstruction) policy before the Twenty-Seventh Party Congress. Unlike the mix of reforms occurring concurrently in China that allowed decentralization and focused on agriculture and light industry as the motors of modernization, Gorbachev's was a top-down centralized program emphasizing heavy industry and maintaining many of the macroeconomic aspects of the Stalinist command system. It failed to alleviate the bottlenecks and shortages in the Soviet economy.

Gorbachev's political views were more audacious. Unlike Deng Xiaoping, who, after the chaos of the Cultural Revolution, was obsessed with stability and ruled out democratic reforms, Gorbachev linked perestroika with a policy of glasnost (openness). Taking aim at the USSR's encrusted party and bureaucracy, Gorbachev adopted a stillborn project of Andropov's to reduce their power by introducing new—even Western—ideas into the Soviet environment and engaging the Soviet population in modernizing the country. He went so far as to authorize the opening of the records of Soviet history, including its darkest moments, which ignited an explosion of criticism reaching back to Lenin's rule. To be sure, Gorbachev's purpose was to *preserve* the communist system by revitalizing it from above, but by combining perestroika with glasnost the Soviet leader risked unleashing forces he was ultimately unable to control.

Gorbachev was even more daring in his foreign policy, because he believed that the relaxation of international tensions was indispensable to his political reforms at home. Convinced that the Soviet Union's greatest threat was nuclear war but that its huge military budget was unsupportable, he intended to achieve security by scaling down the global rivalry between Moscow and Washington and reviving détente. After assembling a group of like-minded liberal internationalists, among them the new foreign minister, Eduard Shevardnadze, and his foreign policy adviser, Anatoly Chernyaev, Gorbachev boldly embarked on a step-by-step program of reducing the USSR's isolation and reaching out to the other side, which included Western Europe, Japan, and China as well as the United States. Yet there would be no precipitate surrender of strategic interests. In 1985 Moscow increased its military operations in Afghanistan and its flow of aid to Cuba, Nicaragua, Vietnam, Ethiopia, and Syria.

Gorbachev faced a wary Western audience, which he hoped to woo with vows to end the arms race. Before taking office, during his December 1984 visit to Britain, he had referred to Europe as "a common home . . . and not a theater of military operations" and had convinced Thatcher that he was a man with whom the West could "do business." But the Reagan administration, facing unexpectedly strong congressional opposition to its military budget, was unreceptive to the new leader's message and intensified its charges of the Soviets' untrustworthiness and deplorable human rights record. Nonetheless, in a private message Reagan expressed interest in a summit meeting and assured Gorbachev of his hope to resume the search for "mutual understanding and peaceful development."

The US and Soviet leaders met in Geneva in November 1985. At this first Superpower summit in six years, no treaty was signed, but the two-day meeting gave Reagan and Gorbachev an opportunity to evaluate each other and air their differences. Although they jointly declared that "a nuclear war can never be won and must never be fought" and agreed to accelerate work on arms control, Reagan defended SDI, and Gorbachev refused to expand the agenda to include Afghanistan and human rights.

The rift continued to widen in 1986. Seeking to draw the world's support for his peace offensive (signaled by a unilateral moratorium on Soviet nuclear tests

Photo 9.1. President Ronald Reagan and General Secretary Mikhail Gorbachev at their first summit meeting in Geneva, November 19, 1985. *Courtesy of National Archives.*

and his appeals to revive START, the stalled Strategic Arms Reduction Talks), Gorbachev boldly called for complete nuclear disarmament by the year 2000 and, reversing four decades of Soviet resistance, expressed his willingness to accept on-site inspections.

The Reagan administration continued to rebuff what it termed Moscow's "propaganda ploy," deriding Gorbachev's campaign against SDI and dismissing his proposal for extensive reductions in conventional military forces in Europe as a tactic to divide NATO. Washington underlined its forceful stance by announcing a new series of atomic tests, stepping up anti-Soviet actions in Afghanistan, launching several highly provocative intelligence-gathering activities, arming its B-52 bombers with air-launched cruise missiles,* and conducting air strikes against Moscow's ally Libya, which it accused of sponsoring global terrorism. US-Soviet relations were also frozen in 1986 because of two sensational spy scandals.†

But Gorbachev's persistence led to a second summit in Reykjavik on October 11–12, 1986, one of the most astonishing encounters of the entire Cold War. On

---

* Breaching the SALT II limitations that each side had agreed upon.
† The first involving the arrest and death sentences against US spies in the USSR based on information provided by the CIA double agent Aldrich Ames; the second over Soviet retaliation for the arrest of its KBG agent Gennady Zakharov with the arrest of the US correspondent Nicholas Daniloff.

day 1, Gorbachev startled the Americans by proposing a 50 percent reduction in all strategic weapons, eliminating all intermediate-range missiles in Europe, extending the ABM treaty for at least ten years, and reopening the stalled talks on a comprehensive nuclear test-ban treaty. After the Americans presented their response on the second day—the elimination of all strategic missiles everywhere in the next decade—Gorbachev countered by proposing the abolition of *all nuclear weapons*. Reagan, sensing a unique opportunity to stop the threat of nuclear wars, readily agreed. Much to the chagrin of their advisers and allies, the two leaders suddenly agreed to halve their atomic arsenals by 1991 and to eliminate them entirely by 1996.

But no deal was cut at Reykjavik because of their differences over SDI, which, regardless of its impracticability, had immense symbolic importance to both leaders. Gorbachev had linked his substantial concessions with a demand that the program be confined to the laboratory, and Reagan refused. After the summit's disappointing end, each used bitter words to blame the other, and a chill descended on US-Soviet relations. Their public setback, emphasized by the media, was all the more painful because both leaders also suffered major reversals at home: Reagan over the Democrats' capture of both houses of Congress and the eruption of the Iran-Contra scandal,* and Gorbachev over the swelling death toll from the explosion at the Soviet nuclear plant in Chernobyl, the mounting casualties in Afghanistan, the plummeting of oil and gas revenues, and the Soviet Union's economic meltdown and ballooning national deficit.

Refusing to abandon his peace offensive, Gorbachev produced more surprises. Intent on rehabilitating the Soviet Union's reputation before world public opinion, he initiated major breakthroughs in human rights, beginning with the February 1986 freeing of the famed Jewish political prisoner Natan Sharansky. On December 19, 1986, Gorbachev personally phoned the dissident Andrei Sakharov to inform him of his release from his Gorki exile. One month later the Soviets ceased jamming the BBC, the Voice of America, and Germany's Deutsche Welle broadcasts and lifted censorship of banned books, such as Boris Pasternak's *Dr. Zhivago*. The KGB reduced the number of arrests for political

---

* After seven US hostages were seized by a pro-Iranian group in Lebanon, Reagan in 1985 secretly authorized arms sales to Iran to secure their release, whereupon a member of the president's National Security Council, Lieutenant Colonel Oliver North, diverted some of the substantial profits to support the Contras. When news of these illegal transactions broke in November 1986, Reagan denied all knowledge, thereby tarnishing either the president's credibility or his ability to manage his underlings.

crimes, and the government released almost all political dissidents and allowed greater religious freedom and freedom of expression. In 1987 the number of Jews granted exit visas rose to almost eight thousand from fewer than one thousand the year before.

Still, Reagan was skeptical over the Soviet leader and hammered away at the evil empire. On his June 1987 visit to celebrate Berlin's 750th anniversary, the president, standing in front of the Brandenburg Gate, urged Gorbachev to "tear down this wall" that surrounded West Berlin.[*]

Both leaders continued to express support for arms control, but it was Gorbachev, by suspending his objections to SDI and removing strategic-weapon reductions from the negotiations, who made a breakthrough treaty on intermediate-range nuclear forces (INF) possible. In 1981 Reagan had overridden NATO's Dual-Track initiative[†] by proposing the "zero option" (removing *all* missiles from Europe), which Moscow, predictably, had refused. The talks, suspended by Andropov in 1983, now resumed.

Following months of difficult negotiations, the United States and the USSR concluded a path-breaking agreement to destroy all short- and intermediate-range ground-based nuclear missiles in Europe by 1991. Conceding what Andropov had rejected, Gorbachev also agreed to retire the SS-20 missiles from sites in Soviet Asia. This first strategic arms agreement between the Superpowers for almost a decade was unprecedented, calling for the removal of an entire class of nuclear weapons and establishing elaborate verification measures.

Gorbachev's reward was his celebrated trip to the United States in December 1987. Fourteen years after Brezhnev's visit, Gorbachev's American journey was a brilliant performance, during which he mingled with Washington crowds and signed the INF treaty on December 8 in a White House brimming with warmth. Yet the Cold War had not ended. The INF treaty eliminated only 4 percent of the Superpowers' nuclear warheads, and long months of acrimonious discussion lay ahead.

Gorbachev then took major steps to end the Soviet Union's military and economic activities abroad. In February 1988 he announced the phased withdrawal

---

* "There is one sign the Soviets can make that would be unmistakable, that would advance dramatically the cause of freedom and peace. General Secretary Gorbachev, if you seek peace, if you seek prosperity for the Soviet Union and Eastern Europe, if you seek liberalization come here to this gate. Mr. Gorbachev, open this gate. Mr. Gorbachev, Mr. Gorbachev, tear down this wall!" The Soviet press agency Tass called it an "openly provocative, war-mongering speech."

† NATO in 1979 had coupled the deployment of US Pershing and cruise missiles in Western Europe with a call for negotiations with the Soviet Union to limit total deployments.

of all Soviet troops from Afghanistan, to be completed in two years.* That year Moscow prodded Hanoi to remove its troops from Cambodia, thus ending another major conflict with Washington and Beijing. Also, the Soviet Union reduced its aid to the allied governments in Vietnam, Angola, and Ethiopia and prepared to evacuate Cam Ranh Bay.

Reagan now responded. With only six months remaining in his presidency (and still under the cloud of the Iran-Contra scandal), the US president made his first—and extraordinarily memorable—visit to Moscow. With no treaties to sign, it was nonetheless a gala event, with the Soviet capital lavishly adorned to greet its seventy-seven-year-old former adversary. Reagan met with human rights activists. Standing before a giant Lenin statute, he addressed students at Moscow State University, calling for "freedom [to] blossom forth at last in the rich fertile soil of your people and culture" and for "a new world of reconciliation, friendship, and peace." He also strolled with Gorbachev in Red Square and recanted his evil empire charge. Yet despite all the signs of geniality, Reagan underscored the power imbalance by refusing to issue a joint statement that echoed the Kremlin's old creed: "Equality of all states, noninterference in internal affairs, and freedom of sociopolitical choice [are] inalienable and mandatory standards of international relations."

Gorbachev's most impressive moment was still to come. On December 7, 1988, in his address to the UN General Assembly he declared the end of the Cold War, renouncing not only the 1945 Yalta settlement† but also the ideological struggle between the Soviet Union and the West since November 1917. According to the Soviet leader, the Bolshevik Revolution had entered the realm of history, and class conflict would no longer dominate global politics. "We are entering an era in which progress will be based on the common interests of the whole of mankind. . . . The common values of humanity must be the determining priority in international politics [requiring] the freeing of international relations from ideology."

Gorbachev also repudiated the Brezhnev doctrine: "Force or the threat of force neither can nor should be instruments of foreign policy. . . . To deny a

---

* Gorbachev's retreat was magnified when, in the April 1988 UN-brokered Geneva Accords on Afghanistan, the United States reversed its earlier pledge to cease providing arms to the insurgents after the Soviet troop withdrawal. Both sides continued to pour in weapons until 1992, and there is some evidence that a small number of Soviet troops remained as well.

† Which Chernyaev, in a reference to Churchill's 1946 Iron Curtain speech, called "Fulton in reverse."

nation of freedom of choice, regardless of the pretext or the verbal guise in which it is cloaked, is to upset the unstable balance that has been achieved. . . . Freedom of choice is a universal principle, which knows no exception."

Gorbachev's third point was to pronounce a new reality in the arms race: given the unlikelihood of a Superpower conflict, the principle of stockpiling arms was to be replaced with one of "reasonable sufficiency." To make this clear, he announced a unilateral cut of five hundred thousand men from the Soviet army and a withdrawal of fifty thousand soldiers and five thousand tanks from the Soviet forces in Eastern Europe, and he proposed negotiations on even greater reductions. One day later, during his private New York meeting with the outgoing Reagan and the new US president George H. W. Bush, Gorbachev pressed for rapid progress in arms control leading to the complete abolition of nuclear weapons.

Thus within three years the former Andropov protégé had totally transformed Soviet foreign policy, replacing its messianic Marxist creed with a radical internationalism. Among the strongest reactions was in the *New York Times*, whose December 8 editorial stated: "Perhaps not since Woodrow Wilson presented his Fourteen Points in 1918 or since Franklin Roosevelt and Winston Churchill promulgated the Atlantic Charter in 1941 has a world figure demonstrated the vision Mikhail Gorbachev displayed yesterday at the United Nations."

A number of scholars believe that the Cold War ended in December 1988 with neither a winner nor a loser.[*] According to this view, one of the Superpowers simply called off the ideological rivalry that began in 1917, withdrew from the post-1945 arms race, and relinquished control over regimes dependent on Soviet force and economic subsidies for their survival. Although not everyone agrees, it is certainly reasonable to assert that without Gorbachev's bold international agenda the world may well have remained divided into two armed camps, and the events that followed would have had entirely different outcomes.

1989: THE TRANSFORMATION OF EASTERN EUROPE

Although the year 1989 marked the two hundredth anniversary of the French Revolution, there was little radical spirit in either Europe or the rest of the world. The excesses of Lenin and Stalin, Mao Zedong and Pol Pot as well as of the Khomeini regime had discredited the mass uprising as a means of achieving political

---

[*] Nonetheless, the first triumphalist interpretation came from US senator Daniel Patrick Moynihan, who called Gorbachev's UN speech "the most astounding statement of surrender in the history of ideological struggle."

and social justice. The twentieth century's major revolutions, co-opted by ruthless revolutionary cliques, had led to terror, dictatorship, and the human nightmare recounted by Solzhenitsyn and many others.

Left-wing ideology had also been weakened in the 1980s by the revival of neoliberal political and economic regimes in the West, by the spectacular success of capitalist experiments in the developing world (particularly in Asia), and also by Gorbachev's attempt to reform communism. Filling the ideological gap left by orthodox Marxism were two old and powerful forces. One was religion, represented by the militant Islam of Iran but also by the forceful Christian doctrine of Pope John Paul II, the charismatic Polish leader who visited 129 countries during his pontificate championing anticommunism and human rights. The second was nationalism, long suppressed by communists, which the peoples of the Soviet Republics and of Eastern Europe now viewed as an agent of progressive historical development. In the 1980s even the orthodox East German leadership, in an effort to win popular support, honored Martin Luther, Frederick the Great, and the socialists' old nemesis Otto von Bismarck as national heroes.

Yet there was scant indication that 1989 would witness a stunning transformation in the very site where the Cold War began. On January 15 thousands gathered peacefully in Prague, Czechoslovakia, to mark the twentieth anniversary of the student Jan Palach's self-immolation in protest against the Soviet invasion, some shouting "Gorbachev" to rebuke the Czech leadership's refusal to institute reforms. Nervous party leaders ordered a brutal police crackdown using riot sticks, dogs, and water cannon, and almost nine hundred protesters were arrested.* Although outgoing Secretary of State George Shultz denounced this violation of the Helsinki Accords, the incoming Bush administration was unprepared to challenge Soviet control over Eastern Europe.

Nonetheless, the communist regimes in Eastern Europe had become exceedingly fragile. Their economies were in ruins, burdened by huge debts to the West, rising prices, and stagnant wages. Their leadership was dispirited and lacking ideological fervor, the opposition was becoming more defiant, and the media were becoming less restrained in its criticisms. Moscow weighed in by reaffirming its renunciation of the Brezhnev doctrine. In March, Kremlin spokesman Gennadii Gerasimov reaffirmed that each nation "had the right to decide its own fate."†

---

* Among them the playwright Václav Havel, who would become president of Czechoslovakia at the end of the year.

† Later that year, in an interview on a US television program, Gerasimov characterized the Kremlin's decision as the "Sinatra doctrine," after the US crooner's song "I Did It My Way."

Gorbachev's vow before the United Nations was backed by his actions toward two of the Kremlin's most rebellious satellites: Poland and Hungary. In Poland, where, despite Jaruzelski's attempts to imitate perestroika, the economy continued to deteriorate, Moscow approved the roundtable negotiations with Solidarność leaders that in April 1989 led to the legalization of the labor union and national elections and in August to a coalition government led by the Solidarność candidate Tadeusz Mazowiecki. In Hungary, where the 1956 Soviet-installed party chief János Kádár had been toppled in May 1988, the new communist leader Károly Grósz, with the Kremlin's blessing, instituted radical constitutional changes, scheduled free national elections (including a multiparty system), and on May 2, 1989, opened the barbed-wire fences separating his country from Austria.

The negotiated, top-down changes in Poland and Hungary had been encouraged by the Kremlin, but the grassroots protests that erupted that spring in China created a powerful challenge for both Beijing and Moscow. The Chinese government, enjoying heightened prosperity and international standing in 1989, had prepared to welcome Gorbachev's visit on May 15 to seal the Sino-Soviet rapprochement resulting from Moscow's dramatic withdrawals a year earlier. But during his stay in China Gorbachev and the world press also witnessed the gathering in Tiananmen Square of hundreds of thousands of peaceful demonstrators demanding greater democracy and sparking a movement that spread throughout the country. Two weeks after the Soviet leader's departure, on the night of June 3–4 the government ordered a military crackdown in Tiananmen Square that left some 1,300 dead, tens of thousands wounded, and uncounted numbers imprisoned.

Almost the entire Soviet bloc was aghast at the violence in China; only East Germany's hard-line leaders applauded Deng Xiaoping's "victory over counter-revolution." Gorbachev, although stunned by the bloodshed, was not ready to sever his new ties with Beijing, but he also cautioned his East European comrades to show more "flexibility" toward their populations. Before the Council of Europe on June 6 Gorbachev publicly distanced himself from the Chinese actions, ruling out the threat or the use of force and reasserting the USSR's ties with our "common European home."

A populist revolt was also brewing in the German Democratic Republic. Despite its relatively high standard of living, East Germany had spawned considerable discontent against the police state ruled by party chief Erich Honecker,

Photo 9.2. Crowds in Beijing's Tiananmen Square, June 3, 1989, calling for greater democracy. In the background are the Goddess of Democracy statue, the Gate of Heavenly Peace, and a portrait of Mao. *Courtesy of Corbis.*

controlled by the infamous Stasi,* and walled in from its richer and freer compatriots in the Federal Republic, which its citizens could view nightly on unjammable television broadcasts. After Hungary opened its borders, thousands of GDR citizens poured into that country intent on escaping to the West. When blocked from doing so, they went to Czechoslovakia and overwhelmed the West German embassy in Prague, insisting they would remain until allowed to leave for the FRG. But even while arrangements were being made between the two

---

* The acronym for the Ministerium für Staatssicherheit, the GDR's secret service, which employed anywhere between a half and two million informers.

Germanys for their emigration, other GDR citizens demanded a total renovation of East German society and took to the streets chanting, "We are the people," and "We are staying here." As demonstrations spread throughout the country, the GDR leadership contemplated a Tiananmen solution.

On his arrival in East Berlin on October 6 for the commemoration of East Germany's fortieth anniversary, Gorbachev found a regime stunned by the exodus of tens of thousands of its young, educated citizens and by huge crowds calling for democracy. Standing next to Honecker on the reviewing stand before a torchlit parade of party youth, Gorbachev heard the East Germans' appeal for his help in bringing them freedom. The next day he urged his hosts to heed the people's needs "before it was too late," insisting that "dangers await only those who do not react to life." Significantly, he also ordered the half million Soviet troops in East Germany to remain in their barracks and give no support to the GDR's attempts to suppress the opposition.

The GDR leadership, attempting to stanch the refugee flood and defuse the protests but shrinking from a military solution, engineered a change from above, replacing the ailing Honecker on October 18 with his protégé, Egon Krenz. The new leader, after journeying to Moscow on November 1 for instructions, announced major reforms of the party and government.* But it was too late. When the refugees and crowds kept growing, the GDR leadership plunged headlong into the abyss. On November 9, Krenz announced that East Germany was lifting most travel restrictions to the West. That night a confused party spokesman assured the press that this policy would be implemented "at once," forgetting to mention that passports and visas would be required. On hearing this news, masses of people thronged to the transit points of the Berlin Wall, forcing the guards to open the gates, and flooded into West Berlin, where they were received with champagne and flowers. Within hours, the world watched Berliners standing on and dismantling the Cold War's foremost symbol, the barrier that had divided Germany for twenty-eight years.

The fall of the Berlin Wall took Moscow by surprise. The throng's spontaneous move westward on November 9, 1989, abruptly ended Gorbachev's hope for a *gradual* reconciliation between Europe's East and West: the East was not only shedding its communist overlords but also disintegrating as a bloc, each nation "hurling itself through the Berlin Wall" toward the West. The carefully crafted compromises achieved in Poland and Hungary quickly collapsed,

---

* Gorbachev, reportedly shocked at the size of the GDR's $26.5 billion debt and its $12.1 billion budget deficit, had warned that the Soviets could not save East Germany.

Photo 9.3. East and West Germans converse at the newly created opening in the Berlin Wall after a crane removed a section of the structure beside the Brandenburg Gate, December 21, 1989. *Courtesy of National Archives.*

and the communists fled; even loyalist Bulgaria on November 9 dismissed its long-standing leader, Todor Zhivkov, and announced free elections.

In Czechoslovakia, there was the mostly peaceful "Velvet Revolution." The hard-line president Gustáv Husák had attempted to use force to put down the protests, but when the demonstrators refused to disperse and Moscow refused a military solution, the regime crumbled. On December 29, after Husák resigned, the playwright and dissident leader Václav Havel, who had spent five years in and out of communist prisons, became president of Czechoslovakia.

Only Romania experienced widespread violence. The communist leader Nicolae Ceauşescu, who had ruled with an iron hand since 1965 and resisted all of Gorbachev's pleas for reform, was determined to crush the opposition. On December 22, after his troops refused to fire on the crowd, the dictator and his wife fled the capital but were captured, tried, and sentenced to death by a firing squad three days later.

All in all some 110 million people in six countries were affected by the unexpected events of 1989.* During the next year the peoples of Eastern Europe

---

* This figure does not include Albania, whose long-standing communist regime collapsed in 1990, or Yugoslavia, which began its violent disintegration after 1990.

held their first free multiparty elections in four and a half decades and, with the exception of Romania, replaced communists with democrats, including recently imprisoned dissidents. They gradually instituted free markets and eventually withdrew from Comecon, the communists' trading bloc, and also from the Warsaw Pact. They opened their archives, honoring the victims of the Soviet interventions in 1953, 1956, and 1968; rehabilitating those who had suffered government persecution and violence; and naming (and in some cases punishing) communist informers and torturers. Gorbachev, in a gesture of giant symbolic importance, in 1990 acknowledged Soviet guilt for the massacre of thousands of Polish prisoners in 1940.

Without minimizing the courage and tenacity of the opposition forces, it is fair to say that the transformation of Eastern Europe was unthinkable without Mikhail Gorbachev, who was awarded the Nobel Peace Prize in 1990. The Soviet leader had not only inspired the reformers but also shaken up their rulers with his withdrawal from Afghanistan, his refusal to prop them up economically, and his announced troop withdrawals in Europe. By embracing new thinking, which stressed mutual security, interdependence, and a common European home, and making good his pledges before the United Nations, Gorbachev had relinquished Moscow's great gain in World War II: the ideologically conformist regimes that for forty-five years had formed the Soviet Union's Western security zone.

The United States, although regarded as the liberator of Eastern Europe, had played a remarkably restrained role in 1989. The incoming Bush administration had been rattled by the Gorby mania that had overtaken the world, fearing its challenge to the Western alliance. It also rejected Kissinger's proposal to establish joint Superpower control over the political changes in Eastern Europe—a détente-era maneuver that the American public and Washington no longer found palatable. On the other hand, although Bush was suspicious of Gorbachev's motives, he was also hesitant to encourage the Kremlin's hard-liners to topple the general secretary and use force to maintain Soviet dominance over Eastern Europe.

Facing divisions within his administration, Bush (much like Gorbachev) opted to support gradual transitions in Eastern Europe over radical change, hoping to avoid the political chaos and violence that had occurred in China. Indeed Washington was initially skeptical toward the diverse and disunited Polish opposition movements. Although publicly welcoming the process of reform and proclaiming its dedication to a "whole and free" Europe, Bush offered only modest financial assistance to Poland and Hungary (as did America's West European allies). During his July visits to Poland and Hungary, the president offered generous praise to the old-guard leaders who were managing the transitions peacefully, thereby helping them to maintain power. Only after November 9, when communist dominance had been shattered, did Washington drop its cautious stance toward the democratic forces in Eastern Europe.

Some scholars regard the Bush-Gorbachev meeting in Malta in December 1989 as the key date in the end of the Cold War.* The cascade of events in Central and Eastern Europe had ended both the Dulles rollback doctrine against the communist empire and the Brezhnev doctrine of forceful intervention to preserve it. Despite bumpy seas, the Malta shipboard summit was amicable. But in the larger realm of US-Soviet relations Gorbachev was a weakened figure. He failed to convince Bush of his objections to SDI, admitted that his economic reforms were foundering, and openly appealed for US help. He also told the president: "We do not consider you an enemy anymore."

By selecting this moment at the end of 1989, analysts have marked a substantial Soviet defeat: despite their almost parallel policies toward Eastern Europe, the United States and the USSR had achieved an unequal result. While Washington's efforts to avert violence on the other side of the Iron Curtain had earned it a propaganda victory, Moscow's loss of all its satellites, unplanned and irretrievable, was a major blow to its prestige *and* its security. To be sure, just as Britain and France had ultimately benefited from the surrender of their empires, the shedding of its costly and disgruntled dependencies might well have strengthened the USSR and facilitated its entry into a unified Europe. But by allowing Eastern Europe to secede and elect noncommunist governments, Gorbachev had also risked a major political backlash within the Soviet Union itself.†

1990: GERMAN REUNIFICATION‡

Nothing symbolized the Cold War more strongly than the division of Germany. The Soviets' control over East Germany had been a major gain for Stalin, and

---

* Significantly, that month the president ordered an invasion of Panama to topple a former ally, General Manuel Noriega, America's first military operation since 1945 not justified by a communist threat.

† In a test of Gorbachev's pledge of noninterference, the legislatures in Lithuania, Estonia, and Latvia in May and June 1989 had declared the preeminence of their laws over those of the Soviet Union.

‡ There are two terms, "reunification" and "unification," to describe the epochal event in 1990. The former, referencing Germany's initial unification under Bismarck in 1871, was widely used in 1989 after the wall fell down; the latter originated with those claiming that the events of 1990 had led to the creation of an entirely new German entity that had never existed before. To avoid this controversy, FRG politicians introduced the neutral term *"Deutsche Einheit"* (German unity) in 1990; many historians use the two terms interchangeably.

his successors had been committed to maintaining the Kremlin's strongest and most orthodox Warsaw Pact member. And although the Western powers officially favored reunification, they had not counted on its actually happening and were content to retain the Federal Republic as a major pillar of NATO and the European Community.

The conservative nationalist West German chancellor Helmut Kohl had a different goal: to unite and free his people from Superpower control. Sensing that the collapse of the GDR was imminent, Kohl seized the moment of the fall of the Berlin Wall to demand the right of *all* Germans to self-determination. Before the Bundestag on November 28, he announced his Ten-Point program calling for free elections in the GDR and the eventual reunification of Germany within a "pan-European framework."

Kohl's speech shocked the West as much as the East. Germany's NATO allies Britain and France, who had not been consulted beforehand, were as horrified as Poland and the Soviet Union at the sudden prospect of a united Germany, eighty-two million strong. Kohl, with no timetable in mind, was insistent: the continuing flood of refugees and the GDR's rapid disintegration compelled Bonn to respond forcefully and expeditiously.

Kohl's only supporter was Bush, who immediately backed the Ten-Point program. The president, recognizing the risks and opportunities created by the fall of the Berlin Wall, was determined to steer the German question in an American direction. Alert to the dangers of a neutral Germany, Bush pressed Kohl to accept full NATO membership for a reunified Germany as the price of US support and then took on the task of convincing the Soviets and the West Europeans to accept both. At Malta he assured Gorbachev that the United States would not seek advantage from the German question. At the NATO summit in December 1989 Bush quashed Thatcher's vociferous objections and won over French president François Mitterrand by agreeing to tie German reunification to deeper European integration and to the construction of a European monetary union.

As 1990 began, Bush sought to exploit this moment of Soviet weakness and GDR decline to exert leadership over the process of German reunification. The US State Department devised an ingenious solution—the "2 + 4"—in which the two Germanys would negotiate the substance of reunification while the four occupying powers (Britain, France, the United States, and the USSR) would confer over the international aspects. Bush convinced all the parties that their interests would be served.

Nonetheless, the key to German unity was still in Moscow. By February 1990, when Kohl traveled to the Soviet capital, Gorbachev had radically changed his stance—moving from anger over the Ten-Point plan to acceptance of German reunification. It was a daring step, not only reversing decades of Soviet policy but also negating the Soviet population's still-vivid memories of the bloodletting in World War II. Gorbachev had agreed with Bush that the Germans could now be trusted. But his abrupt abandonment of the GDR was also based on practical considerations, on the hope of substantial direct German aid in modernizing the Soviet economy—an initiative the United States had declined to join.

Trouble arose immediately over Germany's NATO membership. Exposing the huge extent of Washington's potential triumph, it posed a danger to Gorbachev's political survival and was firmly resisted by the Kremlin. Bush (without consulting his NATO partners) responded by proposing a radical overhaul of the alliance, and at his summit meeting with Gorbachev in Washington in May the president added the prospect of a grain and trade agreement and a commitment to speed up the current arms control negotiations to gain Gorbachev's agreement. He convinced the Soviet leader that, according to the principles of the Helsinki Final Act, "a sovereign state had the right to choose its own alliances."

When protests by outraged Soviet officials forced Gorbachev to backtrack, Bush (aided by Kohl) pressured their allies to enact reforms. At the London summit on July 5–6, 1990, NATO radically revised its four-decade military strategy and structure, offered to establish formal links with the Warsaw Pact, and proposed to expand and upgrade the role of the CSCE—Gorbachev's favored instrument for refashioning European security. In its eloquent "Declaration on a Transformed North Atlantic Alliance" NATO assured Moscow that "we are no longer enemies."

Bush's strategy prevailed. Ten days later, Gorbachev, his position bolstered by the NATO declaration and his reelection as CPSU general secretary, hosted Kohl in Moscow and the Caucasus. Relieving the German leader's anxiety, Gorbachev lifted all his objections to reunification, a withdrawal made easier by the Bonn government's substantial economic concessions, specified in treaties between the two countries.

Under Kohl's strong hand the inter-German negotiations began promisingly. The GDR's first free elections in March 1990 had brought victory to the chancellor's CDU party, which ran on a reunification platform, and the monetary union between West and East Germany (ordained by Kohl over the experts' overwhelming opposition) took effect on July 1. The East Berlin government, reeling from the exodus of more than two thousand of its citizens each day and pressured by a public demanding unification, formally agreed to accession. Alert to its neighbors' concerns, the Kohl government assured Moscow that it would assume the GDR's debts and trade commitments and promised the European Community that it would not request its partners' aid for the collapsed East Germany.* The Bonn government also agreed to limit the size of the Bundeswehr (the Federal Republic's army) to 370,000, uphold the Nuclear Non-Proliferation Treaty, and maintain its commitment to the existing border with Poland.

After only eight weeks of negotiations, the Treaty on German Unity was signed by representatives of the FRG and GDR on August 31, 1990, and approved by large majorities of both legislatures on September 20. The form of reunification was as important as its occurrence. Instead of a negotiated union between two sovereign governments (which would have necessitated the drafting of a new constitution), the Federal Republic simply incorporated the five new states (*Länder*) that comprised the former GDR and extended its treaties, political structure, and economic, social, and judicial system to the annexed territory.† The upshot was not only the disappearance of a political entity that in 1990 still maintained diplomatic missions in seventy-three countries but also the ensuing effort by the Federal Republic to erase the GDR's history and culture (including the names of towns, streets, and buildings) and to convince its former citizens that they were returning to Germany after a forty-one-year absence.

The German-German negotiations were overshadowed by the dramatic events in the Middle East, where, on August 2, 1990, a cash-strapped Iraq had invaded and annexed its wealthy neighbor Kuwait. In this first test of East-West cooperation, Gorbachev supported the UN condemnation of Moscow's longtime ally. After failing to convince Saddam Hussein to withdraw, the Soviet leader reluctantly endorsed an even tougher US-sponsored resolution threatening the use of force. For the first time since 1956 the United States and the Soviet Union were on the same side.

Not surprisingly, international ratification of the German treaty went smoothly. The four occupying powers agreed to terminate their "rights and responsibilities" in Berlin and in Germany, and the FRG (which had added forty-two thousand square miles and some 16.6 million people) achieved full sovereignty over its internal and external affairs. The final settlement, signed by the foreign ministers of the 2 + 4 governments on September 12 and ratified on October 1 by the foreign ministers of the CSCE meeting in Moscow, took effect

---

* Although by financing the rehabilitation of East Germany not only by taxes but also by raising interest rates, the FRG indirectly forced its European partners to share the burden of reunification.
† The 1949 Basic Law had to be amended in several significant ways to formalize the process of reunification.

two days later. On October 3, 1990, forty-five years after the end of World War II and forty-one years after Germany's division, the GDR ceased to exist, and the country was reunited.

German reunification, forged by Bush and Kohl, represented a third significant marker in the end of the Cold War and another setback for the Soviet Union. Gorbachev may have traded a difficult satellite for a grateful and potentially generous economic partner, but there was no masking the fact that his passivity and indecision had produced far fewer gains than losses and created a significant backlash at home.

By 1990, the Soviet Union was no longer in a position to block German reunification. Despite his wavering in other instances, Gorbachev remained committed to the principles of his UN declaration. Moreover, the Soviets' internal weakness prevented him from playing obstructionist politics—either by joining the naysayers Thatcher and Mitterrand or by reviving a Rapallo policy to lure Germany away from the West. Behind Gorbachev's step-by-step retreat in 1990 was an increasingly chaotic situation in the Soviet Union itself that included a sharp decline in the economy, ethnic violence, and separatist movements as well as growing opposition by the military and the KGB. According to his swelling number of critics, not only had Gorbachev sold out the GDR for a "bowl of porridge," but he had also ceded his expansive vision of a new Europe based on the CSCE to a revived, renovated, and eastward-moving NATO.

1991: THE COLLAPSE OF THE SOVIET UNION

The collapse of the Soviet Union was an epochal event in world history, brought on by both internal and external causes. Domestically, the sixty-nine-year-old entity disintegrated from above, the middle, and below: destabilized by Gorbachev's reformist projects that undermined the communist system and the central command economy, challenged by disgruntled and dispossessed Soviet elites, and undermined by grassroots nationalist movements demanding independence.

Outside influences had an almost equal importance. Gorbachev between 1985 and 1989 had substantially reduced the costs of the Soviet Union's European and overseas empires, drawn down the arms race with the United States, and retreated from Afghanistan. But his liberal foreign policy—his acceptance of the Helsinki human rights principles; his opening the USSR to Western people, media, culture, and ideas; and his allowing the peaceful transformation in

Central and Eastern Europe—had all helped to catalyze centrifugal pressures the Kremlin had neither predicted nor was able to control.[*]

Rebellion began first in the Baltic states, which were the Soviet republics most directly influenced by the events in Poland. On August 23, 1989, the fiftieth anniversary of the 1939 Molotov-Ribbentrop Pact, about one million people from Estonia, Latvia, and Lithuania joined hands along the 403-mile road that connected Tallinn, Riga, and Vilnius to protest the "illegal" Soviet occupation. One year later the three republics had virtually declared their independence, and their example was emulated by Georgia, Ukraine, Armenia, and Moldova. Russia, the Soviet Union's largest and most populous republic, followed. Boris Yeltsin, its populist leader, declared that Russia's laws had priority over Soviet laws and called for political democracy and a free market.

The international dimension remained significant. While seeking Western aid for perestroika, managing the complex negotiations over Germany, and conducting the difficult CFE[†] and START negotiations in 1990, Gorbachev applied conciliation rather than force toward the rebellious republics—and he was backed by the Bush administration. Washington, fearing that the disintegration of the Soviet Union would produce political and economic instability and also violence against minorities, took a restrained view toward the separatist movements. Despite America's long-standing support for the Baltics' independence, Washington urged their leaders to conduct peaceful negotiations with Moscow.

The struggle over the Soviet Union's future came to a head in 1991, signaled by departing foreign minister Shevardnadze's public warning that "dictatorship is coming." Gorbachev, alarmed over the breakdown of law and order, tacked to the right, appointing a new cabinet of hard-liners who were determined to maintain party control over the state. With the world distracted by the looming war to remove Iraqi troops from Kuwait, Gorbachev in January 1991 dispatched the Soviet military to Lithuania and Latvia to regain control over the breakaway republics, provoking strong criticism at home and abroad. In March he backtracked, proposing a new union treaty designed to preserve the central authority while giving the republics more freedom, but the March 17 referendum

---

[*] One of the first signs of trouble was the outbreak of ethnic violence in 1988 in Azerbaijan, which spread to Turkmenistan, Kazakhstan, and Georgia and which the Kremlin had difficulty controlling. There were also riots in Tajikistan and Kirghizia (Kyrgyzstan) requiring intervention by Soviet troops.

[†] A treaty on reducing conventional forces in Europe, begun in 1973 between NATO and the Warsaw Pact.

to transform the Soviet Union was boycotted by six of the fifteen republics (the Baltic states, Armenia, Georgia, and Moldova).

The Bush administration was divided between the Pentagon's long-standing desire to destroy the Soviet Union and the State Department's cautions over destabilizing a known and increasingly accommodating entity. Bush, while still resisting Gorbachev's pleas for substantial economic aid, continued to support him politically. The US president, although disturbed by the crackdown in the Baltics, repeated his muted reaction two years earlier to the Tiananmen massacre, favoring a familiar partner over a leap into the unknown. In July Bush gave a significant boost to Gorbachev by traveling to Moscow to sign the START treaty: a major accomplishment making significant reductions in the Superpowers' nuclear arsenals. With the removal of Soviet troops from Central and Eastern Europe, the end of Superpower competition in the Third World, and the close of the nuclear arms race in 1991, the international revolution forged by Gorbachev was completed—and largely on Western terms.

The last Cold War summit in Moscow saw an amicable exchange of views. Bush, who acknowledged Gorbachev's cooperation in the war against Iraq, envisaged future bilateral cooperation in Africa, Asia, the Middle East, and Central America—where, however, US power had measurably gained and Soviet influence had greatly diminished. On his stopover in Ukraine, the president praised Gorbachev's "astonishing achievements," endorsed the union treaty, and cautioned those seeking independence against promoting a "suicidal nationalism based on ethnic hatred."*

But three weeks later the Soviet Union began to unravel. Despite warnings of a coup, Gorbachev was taken by surprise. On August 18 Gorbachev was in the Crimea, planning to return to Moscow the next day for the August 20 signing of the union treaty transforming the USSR into a federation of independent republics with a common president, military, and foreign policy.† That day four members of Gorbachev's inner circle suddenly arrived at his dacha. Intent on blocking the treaty (which they feared would destroy the Soviet Union), they demanded he declare a national state of emergency. When Gorbachev refused,

---

* A right-wing *New York Times* columnist dubbed Bush's August 1 speech "Chicken Kiev," claiming its pro-Gorbachev sentiments had flattened the spirits of those seeking independence from the Soviet Union.

† The eight republics that were to form the Union of Sovereign States were: Russia, Belarus, Kazakhstan, Turkmenistan, Tajikistan, Azerbaijan, Uzbekistan, and Kyrgyzstan. Ukraine, which had participated in the March referendum, rejected the treaty.

they placed him under house arrest and cut off his communication with the outside world.

The next morning the world learned of the coup. Claiming that Gorbachev was suffering ill health, an eight-member Emergency Committee had taken the reins, sending tanks and troops into Moscow and other Soviet cities and blockading the Baltics. Bush immediately condemned the "unconstitutional resort to force" and called for the restoration of Gorbachev to power. The Soviet population was divided among liberals, such as the poet and parliamentary deputy Yevgeny Yevtushenko, who called on his fellow citizens to defend the Motherland; the communist faithful welcoming the return to centralized power; and a majority of the population that passively awaited the outcome.

The Emergency Committee made several blunders. Among them was the absence of a young, charismatic leader who could offer the public more than a return to the grim Soviet past. They had also failed to secure the support of key military and KGB officers, many of whom refused to carry out their orders. But above all, the conspirators' failure to arrest Yeltsin changed the course of history. The Russian leader headed to the White House (the seat of the Russian parliament), where he declared the takeover unconstitutional and called on the population to obey only his government. In an extraordinarily potent gesture, Yeltsin placed himself atop a tank and appealed for resistance, whereupon tens of thousands of Muscovites formed a protective cordon around the White House and erected barricades against an impending attack. Crowds also assembled in Leningrad and other major Russian cities. And because the phone lines had not been cut, Yeltsin was able to receive supportive calls from Bush, Kohl, Mitterrand, and British prime minister John Major.

The coup collapsed in three days. The conspirators, unsure of the troops' loyalty, called off the assault on the White House and allowed Gorbachev to return to Moscow. But the Gorbachev who returned to Moscow was a broken leader. His domestic revolution had been taken over by his rival Yeltsin and by the Russian people, who had defended a democracy yet to be built. After Gorbachev's efforts to reconstruct the USSR were rebuffed, a triumphant Yeltsin proposed the creation of a far looser Commonwealth of Independent States (CIS), which the Baltics and Georgia declined to join, that left no place for the Soviet leader.

The end came swiftly. Yeltsin, in full control of his Russian base, systematically stripped Gorbachev of his authority, and eight of the fifteen republics—including the Slavic heartlands of Belarus and Ukraine—followed the Baltic states and declared their full independence. On Christmas Day 1991 the Soviet

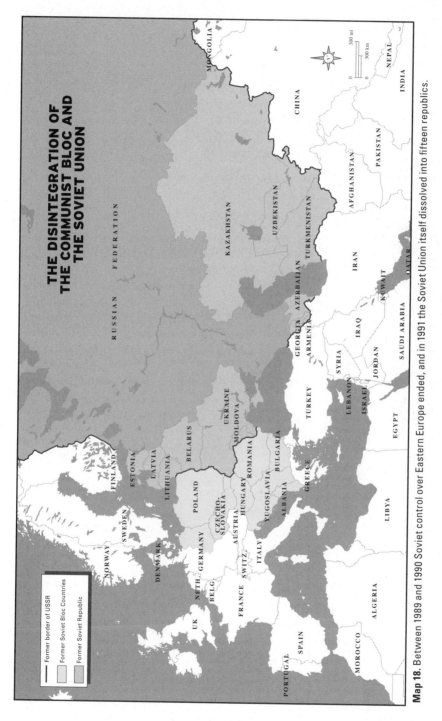

THE DISINTEGRATION OF THE COMMUNIST BLOC AND THE SOVIET UNION

Former border of USSR
Former Soviet Bloc Countries
Former Soviet Republic

Map 18. Between 1989 and 1990 Soviet control over Eastern Europe ended, and in 1991 the Soviet Union itself dissolved into fifteen republics.

Union's first elected president and its last party general secretary resigned, and that night the hammer and sickle came down from the Kremlin, replaced by the blue, white, and red flag of Russia.

The Bush administration had been in no hurry to dismiss Gorbachev until the remaining Cold War issues were settled. In September 1991, Washington had secured Soviet agreement to withdraw all its troops from Cuba. Subsequently, both sides agreed on a January 1 date to cease sending arms to Afghanistan,* to work together for a UN-mediated peace settlement in El Salvador, and to make major reductions of tactical nuclear weapons on land and sea. In October the United States and the USSR joined China in forging a peace settlement for Cambodia. Finally, in a major shift, the United States offered the Soviet Union a role in the Middle East settlement. At the end of the Gulf War Moscow reestablished diplomatic relations with Israel (which it had severed in 1967), and on October 30, 1991, Bush and Gorbachev jointly convened the Arab-Israeli peace conference in Madrid.

However, by December Washington recognized that Gorbachev's—and the Soviet Union's—days were numbered. Bush, under increasing pressure from Ukrainian Americans (and without consulting London, Paris, or Bonn), dropped his neutral stance toward the dissolution of the USSR. On the eve of Ukraine's December 1 vote on independence, the president outraged Gorbachev and even Yeltsin by signaling his willingness to recognize the new state unconditionally. On December 12 Secretary of State James Baker, in a Princeton address titled "America and the Collapse of the Soviet Empire," assured the successor republics that the United States was willing to work with them, especially on the issues of security, democracy, free-market economies, and nuclear nonproliferation. After Gorbachev's resignation, Bush praised the Soviet leader for his "sustained commitment to world peace" but also welcomed the new CIS led by "its courageous president Boris Yeltsin." Fifty-eight years of US-Soviet relations—begun by Roosevelt in 1933 and destroyed by the implosion of the USSR—were over, leaving even triumphant Americans uncertain of the global and regional consequences.

The Cold War's third major actor, China, also played a role in the events of 1991. Despite its longtime rivalry with the Kremlin, the Chinese leadership had hoped for the survival of Soviet communism both to bolster its own legitimacy and to restrain Western dominance. After a period of revived acrimony over

---

* Leading to the fall in April 1992 of the Soviet-backed Najibullah regime, followed by a brutal four-year-long civil war that ended with the Taliban's seizure of power in 1996.

Gorbachev's "counterrevolutionary" reforms and his betrayal of Eastern Europe, East Germany, and Iraq, Beijing found it expedient to resume its rapprochement with Moscow. In 1991 China approved high-level visits, increased trade, and, in March, a commodity credit of $750 million at a crucial time, when the United States was punishing Moscow politically and economically for its crackdown in the Baltics. Moreover, the long-postponed visit to Moscow in May by CCP General Secretary Jiang Zemin was an important signal of support for Gorbachev, now facing a more radical rival in Yeltsin.

Beijing, which had also maintained close ties with antireformist factions of the Soviet Communist Party, may well have had foreknowledge of the August coup. After the Emergency Committee seized power, China's official media responded approvingly and ignored Yeltsin's words and activities. There was no official response to Gorbachev's return to Moscow. In its postmortem on the failed coup, the Chinese leadership blamed the Emergency Committee. Infected by Gorbachev's new thinking, its members had shrunk from a June 4 (Tiananmen Square) response to Yeltsin's defiance and thereby failed to prevent the collapse of Soviet communism.

Over the next four months Beijing took a pragmatic stance, recognizing the independence of all the republics and offering to establish formal diplomatic relations. Now the world's largest surviving communist state, China faced the prospect of US global hegemony or a Moscow-Washington détente. At home, Deng Xiaoping's leftist critics warned of a Soviet-style demise, but the eighty-seven-year-old architect of China's reforms won the day by insisting that his "nondogmatic methods in the construction of socialism" were the surest way to prevent chaos and catastrophe.

The disappearance of one of the two Superpowers and the world's first Marxist state—which had played a major role in defeating Nazi Germany, put the first man in space, and for four decades vied with the West in the former colonial world—was a momentous event. Although the global Cold War ended between 1988 and 1990, the Soviet Union was unable to reap the political benefits of a more peaceful world before its dissolution.

In his farewell address Gorbachev proudly reviewed his achievements as a diplomat and world statesman but also acknowledged his failure at home: the old system had collapsed "before the new one had time to begin working."* Whether

---

* "We live in a new world. The Cold War has ended, the arms race has stopped, as has the insane militarization which mutilated our economy, public psyche and morals. The threat of a world

or not the Soviet Union was savable (and scholars still disagree over this point), Gorbachev failed to recognize the link between his extraordinary role in ending the Cold War—in particular, relinquishing Soviet control over Central and Eastern Europe—and the collapse of his country in 1991.

SUGGESTIONS FOR FURTHER STUDY

Documents

"Bush and Gorbachev at Malta: Previously Secret Documents from Soviet and US Files on the 1989 Meeting, 20 Years Later." National Security Archive. 2009. http://www.gwu.edu/~nsarchiv/NSAEBB/NSAEBB298/index.htm.

"A Different October Revolution: Dismantling the Iron Curtain in Eastern Europe." National Security Archive. 2009. http://www.gwu.edu/~nsarchiv/NSAEBB /NSAEBB290/index.htm.

"End of the Cold War." Wilson Center Digital Archive. Accessed February 28, 2013. http://digitalarchive.wilsoncenter.org/collection/37/end-of-the-cold-war.

"The Fall of the Berlin Wall." CBS News. Accessed February 28, 2013. http://www .cbsnews.com/2300-500283_162-5554834.html.

Gorbachev, Mikhail. "End of the Soviet Union; Text of Gorbachev's Farewell Address." New York Times. December 26, 1991. http://www.nytimes.com/1991/12/26 /world/end-of-the-soviet-union-text-of-gorbachev-s-farewell-address.html.

———. "Europe as a Common Home: Address Given by Mikhail Gorbachev to the Council of Europe (Strasbourg, 6 July, 1989). Making the History of 1989." http:// chnm.gmu.edu/1989/archive/files/gorbachev-speech-7-6-89_e3ccb87237.pdf.

Han, Minzhu, and Sheng Hua. Cries for Democracy: Writings and Speeches from the 1989 Chinese Democracy Movement. Princeton, NJ: Princeton University Press, 1990.

Havel, Václav. Open Letters: Selected Writings, 1965–1990. New York: Knopf, 1991.

"Iran-Contra Affair 20 Years On." National Security Archive. 2006. http://www .gwu.edu/~nsarchiv/NSAEBB/NSAEBB210/index.htm.

Jiang, Jin, and Qin Zhou. June Four: A Chronicle of the Chinese Democratic Uprising. Fayetteville: University of Arkansas Press, 1989.

Munteanu, Mircea. "The End of the Cold War." CWIHP Document Reader. Wilson Center Cold War International History Project. 2006. http://www.wilsoncenter .org/publication/the-end-of-the-cold-war.

Oksenberg, Michel, Lawrence R. Sullivan, Marc Lambert, and Qiao Li. Beijing Spring, 1989: Confrontation and Conflict: The Basic Documents. Armonk, NY: M. E. Sharpe, 1990.

---

war has been removed. . . . Everything was done . . . to preserve reliable control of the nuclear weapons. We opened ourselves to the world, gave up interference into other people's affairs, [and] the use of troops beyond the borders of the country, and trust, solidarity and respect came in response."

"One Germany in Europe (1989–2009)." German Historical Institute: German History in Documents and Images. Accessed February 28, 2013. http://germanhistory docs.ghi-dc.org/section.cfm?section_id=16.

Reagan, Ronald. "Remarks on East-West Relations at the Brandenburg Gate in West Berlin, June 12, 1987." Ronald Reagan Presidential Foundation and Library. http://www.reaganfoundation.org/tgcdetail.aspx?session_args=EEAA0989-1000-45E4 -852F-473AC8E79D37&p=TG0923RRS&h1=0&h2=0&sw=&lm=reagan&args_a =cms&args_b=1&argsb=N&tx=1748.

"The Revolutions of 1989." National Security Archive. 1999. http://www.gwu .edu/~nsarchiv/news/19991105.

"The Reykjavik File: Previously Secret Documents from the US and Soviet Archives on the 1986 Reagan-Gorbachev Summit." National Security Archive. 2006. http://www.gwu.edu/~nsarchiv/NSAEBB/NSAEBB203/index.htm.

"To the Geneva Summit: Perestroika and the Transformation of US-Soviet Relations." National Security Archive. 2005. http://www.gwu.edu/~nsarchiv /NSAEBB/NSAEBB172/index.htm.

Music

Bernstein, Leonard (conductor). *Ode to Freedom: Bernstein in Berlin*. Deutsche Grammophon, 1990, compact disc. Recorded in 1989. Includes Beethoven's Ninth Symphony.

Films

"The Gate of Heavenly Peace." *Frontline*, season 14, episode 12. Directed by Richard Gordon and Carma Hinton. New York: Independent Television Service, 1995.

Good Bye Lenin! Directed by Wolfgang Becker. Berlin: X-Filme Creative Pool, 2003.

The Lives of Others. Directed by Florian Henckel von Donnersmarck. Berlin: Bayerischer Rundfunk, 2006.

Summer Palace. Directed by Ye Lou. Beijing/Paris: Dream Factory/Centre National de la Cinématographie, 2006.

Wings of Desire. Directed by Wim Wenders. Berlin: Road Movies Filmproduktion, 1987.

Contemporary Works

Gorbachev, Mikhail Sergeevich. *Perestroika: New Thinking for Our Country and the World*. Cambridge: Harper and Row, 1987.

———. *A Time for Peace*. New York: Richardson and Steirman, 1985.

Memoirs

Baker, James Addison. *The Politics of Diplomacy: Revolution, War, and Peace, 1989–1992*. New York: Putnam, 1995.

Boldin, V. I. *Ten Years That Shook the World: The Gorbachev Era as Witnessed by His Chief of Staff*. Translated by Evelyn Rossiter. New York: Basic Books, 1994.

Brucan, Silviu. *The Wasted Generation: Memoirs of the Romanian Journey from Capitalism to Socialism and Back*. Boulder, CO: Westview, 1993.

Bush, George, and Brent Scowcroft. *A World Transformed*. New York: Knopf, 1998.

Chernyaev, Anatoly S. *My Six Years with Gorbachev*. Translated and edited by Robert English and Elizabeth Tucker. University Park: Pennsylvania State University Press, 2000.

Drakulić, Slavenka. *How We Survived Communism and Even Laughed*. London: Hutchinson, 1992.

Dubček, Alexander, with András Sugár. *Dubcek Speaks*. London: I. B. Tauris, 1990.

Genscher, Hans Dietrich. *Rebuilding a House Divided: A Memoir by the Architect of Germany's Reunification*. Translated by Thomas Thorton. New York: Broadway Books, 1998.

Gorbachev, Mikhail Sergeevich. *The August Coup: The Truth and the Lessons*. New York: Harper Collins, 1991.

———. *Memoirs*. New York: Doubleday, 1996.

Gorbachev, Mikhail Sergeevich, and Zdenek Mlynár. *Conversations with Gorbachev: On Perestroika, the Prague Spring, and the Crossroads of Socialism*. Translated by George Shriver. New York: Columbia University Press, 2002.

Grachev, Andrei S. *Final Days: The Inside Story of the Collapse of the Soviet Union*. Translated by Margo Milne. Boulder, CO: Westview, 1995.

Iliescu, Ion. *Romania at the Moment of Truth*. Paris: Editions Henri Berger, 1994.

Li, Lu. *Moving the Mountain: My Life in China from the Cultural Revolution to Tiananmen Square*. London: Macmillan, 1990.

Ligachev, E. K. *Inside Gorbachev's Kremlin*. Translated by Catherine A. Fitzpatrick, Michele A. Berdy, and Dobrochna Dyrcz-Freeman. New York: Pantheon Books, 1993.

Matlock, Jack F. *Autopsy on an Empire: The American Ambassador's Account of the Collapse of the Soviet Union*. New York: Random House, 1995.

Palazhchenko, P. *My Years with Gorbachev and Shevardnadze: The Memoir of a Soviet Interpreter*. University Park: Pennsylvania State University Press, 1997.

Sakharov, Andrei. *Moscow and Beyond, 1986–1989*. Translated by Antonina W. Bouis. New York: Knopf, 1991.

Shultz, George Pratt. *Turmoil and Triumph: My Years as Secretary of State*. New York: Scribner's, 1993.

Thatcher, Margaret. *The Downing Street Years*. New York: Harper Collins, 1993.

Wałesa, Lech. *The Struggle and the Triumph: An Autobiography*. Translated by Franklin Philip and Helen Mahut. New York: Arcade, 1992.

Fiction

Cheng, Terrence. *Sons of Heaven: A Novel*. New York: William Morrow, 2002.

Grass, Günter. *Too Far Afield*. Translated by Krishna Winston. New York: Harcourt, 2000.

Schneider, Peter. *The Wall Jumper: A Berlin Story.* Translated by Leigh Hafrey. New York: Pantheon Books, 1983.

Wang, Annie. *Lili: A Novel.* New York: Anchor Books, 2002.

Wolf, Christa. *What Remains and Other Stories.* New York: Farrar, Straus and Giroux, 1993.

Yevtushenko, Yevgeny Aleksandrovich. *Don't Die Before You're Dead.* Translated by Antonina W. Bouis. New York: Random House, 1995.

Secondary Sources

Adamishin, A. L., and Richard Schifter. *Human Rights, Perestroika, and the End of the Cold War.* Washington, DC: United States Institute of Peace Press, 2009.

Beissinger, Mark R. *Nationalist Mobilization and the Collapse of the Soviet State.* Cambridge: Cambridge University Press, 2002.

Beschloss, Michael, and Strobe Talbott. *At the Highest Levels: The Inside Story of the End of the Cold War.* Boston: Little, Brown, 1994.

Bozo, Frédéric. *Mitterrand, the End of the Cold War and German Unification.* New York: Berghahn Books, 2009.

Bradley, J. F. N. *Czechoslovakia's Velvet Revolution: A Political Analysis.* Boulder, CO: East European Monographs, 1992.

Brook, Timothy. *Quelling the People: The Military Suppression of the Beijing Democracy Movement.* New York: Oxford University Press, 1992.

Brown, Archie. *The Gorbachev Factor.* Oxford: Oxford University Press, 1996.

———. *Seven Years That Changed the World: Perestroika in Perspective.* Oxford: Oxford University Press, 2007.

Chafetz, Glenn R. *Gorbachev, Reform, and the Brezhnev Doctrine: Soviet Policy Toward Eastern Europe, 1985–1990.* Westport, CT: Praeger, 1993.

Checkel, Jeffrey T. *Ideas and International Political Change: Soviet/Russian Behavior and the End of the Cold War.* New Haven, CT: Yale University Press, 1997.

Collins, Alan. *The Security Dilemma and the End of the Cold War.* New York: St. Martin's, 1997.

Combs, Dick. *Inside the Soviet Alternate Universe: The Cold War's End and the Soviet Union's Fall Reappraised.* University Park: Pennsylvania State University Press, 2008.

D'Agostino, Anthony. *Gorbachev's Revolution.* New York: New York University Press, 1998.

Dannreuther, Roland. *Creating New States in Central Asia: The Strategic Implications of the Collapse of Soviet Power in Central Asia.* London: Brassey's for the International Institute for Strategic Studies, 1994.

Dockrill, Saki Ruth. *The End of the Cold War Era: The Transformation of the Global Security Order.* New York: Oxford, 2003.

Ekedahl, Carolyn McGiffert, and Melvyn A. Goodman. *The Wars of Eduard Shevardnadze.* University Park: Pennsylvania State University Press, 1997.

English, Robert. *Russia and the Idea of the West: Gorbachev, Intellectuals, and the End of the Cold War*. New York: Columbia University Press, 2000.

FitzGerald, Frances. *Way out There in the Blue: Reagan, Star Wars, and the End of the Cold War*. New York: Simon and Schuster, 2000.

Freedman, Lawrence, and Efraim Karsh. *The Gulf Conflict, 1990–1991: Diplomacy and War in the New World Order*. Princeton, NJ: Princeton University Press, 1993.

Gaddis, John Lewis. *The United States and the End of the Cold War: Implications, Reconsiderations, Provocations*. New York: Oxford University Press, 1992.

Garthoff, Raymond L. *The Great Transition: American-Soviet Relations and the End of the Cold War*. Washington, DC: Brookings Institution, 1994.

Garton Ash, Timothy. *In Europe's Name: Germany and the Divided Continent*. New York: Random House, 1993.

———. *The Polish Revolution: Solidarity*. New Haven, CT: Yale University Press, 2002.

Grachev, A. S. *Gorbachev's Gamble: Soviet Foreign Policy and the End of the Cold War*. Cambridge: Polity, 2008.

Hahn, Gordon M. *Russia's Revolution from Above, 1985–2000: Reform, Transition, and Revolution in the Fall of the Soviet Communist Regime*. New Brunswick, NJ: Transaction Publishers, 2002.

Hutchings, Robert L. *American Diplomacy and the End of the Cold War: An Insider's Account of U.S. Policy in Europe, 1989–1992*. Washington, DC: Woodrow Wilson Center Press, 1997.

Jarausch, Konrad Hugo. *The Rush to German Unity*. New York: Oxford University Press, 1994.

Kotkin, Stephen. *Armageddon Averted: The Soviet Collapse, 1970–2000*. Oxford: Oxford University Press, 2001.

Kuzio, Taras, and Andrew Wilson. *Ukraine: Perestroika to Independence*. New York: St. Martin's, 1994.

Lévesque, Jacques. *The Enigma of 1989: The USSR and the Liberation of Eastern Europe*. Berkeley: University of California Press, 1997.

Lieven, Anatol. *The Baltic Revolution: Estonia, Latvia, Lithuania, and the Path to Independence*. New Haven, CT: Yale University Press, 1993.

Maier, Charles S. *Dissolution: The Crisis of Communism and the End of East Germany*. Princeton, NJ: Princeton University Press, 1997.

Matlock, Jack F. *Reagan and Gorbachev: How the Cold War Ended*. New York: Random House, 2004.

Meyer, Michael. *The Year That Changed the World: The Untold Story Behind the Fall of the Berlin Wall*. New York: Scribner, 2009.

Oberdorfer, Don. *From the Cold War to a New Era: The United States and the Soviet Union, 1983–1991*. 2nd ed. Baltimore: Johns Hopkins University Press, 1998.

Ost, David. *Solidarity and the Politics of Anti-Politics: Opposition and Reform in Poland Since 1968*. Philadelphia: Temple University Press, 1990.

Pond, Elizabeth. *Beyond the Wall: Germany's Road to Unification*. Washington, DC: Brookings Institution, 1993.

Prados, John. *How the Cold War Ended: Debating and Doing History.* Washington, DC: Potomac Books, 2011.

Sarotte, Mary E. *1989: The Struggle to Create Post–Cold War Europe.* Princeton, NJ: Princeton University Press, 2009.

Schweizer, Peter. *Reagan's War: The Epic Story of His Forty-Year Struggle and the Final Triumph over Communism.* New York: Doubleday, 2002.

Sebestyen, Victor. *Revolution 1989: The Fall of the Soviet Empire.* New York: Pantheon Books, 2009.

Siani-Davies, Peter. *The Romanian Revolution of December 1989.* Ithaca, NY: Cornell University Press, 2005.

Snyder, Sarah B. *Human Rights Activism and the End of the Cold War: A Transnational History of the Helsinki Network.* New York: Cambridge University Press, 2011.

Stokes, Gale. *The Walls Came Tumbling Down: The Collapse of Communism in Eastern Europe.* New York: Oxford University Press, 1993.

Suny, Ronald Grigor. *The Revenge of the Past: Nationalism, Revolution, and the Collapse of the Soviet Union.* Stanford, CA: Stanford University Press, 1993.

———. *The Soviet Experiment: Russia, the USSR, and the Successor States.* New York: Oxford University Press, 1998.

Tőkés, Rudolf L. *Hungary's Negotiated Revolution: Economic Reform, Social Change, and Political Succession, 1957–1990.* Cambridge: Cambridge University Press, 1996.

Vogele, William B. *Stepping Back: Nuclear Arms Control and the End of the Cold War.* Westport, CT: Praeger, 1994.

Zelikow, Philip, and Condoleezza Rice. *Germany Unified and Europe Transformed: A Study in Statecraft.* Cambridge, MA: Harvard University, 1996.

Zheng, Zhuyuan. *Behind the Tiananmen Massacre: Social, Political, and Economic Ferment in China.* Boulder, CO: Westview, 1990.

Chapter 10
AFTERMATH, 1992–2001

Globalization is not something we can hold off or turn off.

—Bill Clinton

The rivalry of the superpowers is replaced by the clash of civilizations.

—Samuel Huntington

Unlike most prolonged conflicts, the Cold War ended without a formal surrender, treaty, or celebration. Nonetheless, the remarkably peaceful demise of the Soviet Union touched the entire world. Moscow's former clients such as Cuba, Vietnam, North Korea, and the Palestinians—already living on reduced subsidies—were set adrift, but the end of the Soviet threat also dealt a blow to right-wing governments in Africa and Latin America that had gained US support based on their anticommunism. In Eastern Europe the former satellite states, no longer in the Soviet shadow, gravitated toward the West; with the discrediting of Marxist ideology, India and other socialist-leaning Third World countries moved toward a market economy; and in the 1990s Vietnam adopted the Chinese model of economic liberalization (combined with the Communist Party's political control).

Broader developments, originating during the Cold War, also shaped the last decade of the twentieth century. On the one hand, these included the acceleration of technological, economic, and social changes that offered the promise of global cooperation and prosperity (although not without creating new problems); on the other, there was an intensification of radical national and religious movements that frustrated hopes for a more unified and peaceful world.

THE 1990S: A GLOBAL VIEW

The technological breakthroughs of the 1990s were built on achievements during the Cold War. Both the United States and the Soviet Union had invested heavily in developing computers for military purposes. But it was in the West—with its open and decentralized capitalist system—that major advances in information technology had occurred in the 1970s and 1980s, first with the introduction of high-speed copiers, fax machines, and cellular phones, but especially with the personal computer and the Internet, which enabled individuals and businesses to overcome barriers of time, distance, and access to information. Similarly, the internationalization of world production and trade began in the West in the 1970s, spurred by the oil crisis and by major technological advances in transportation and communications.

The end of the Cold War underscored the East's technological backwardness, which Brezhnev and Gorbachev had failed to overcome. The uprisings of 1989, fueled by transistor radios and television as well as by handmade banners and underground samizdat* publications, sprang from populations as fed up with poor service, shoddy goods, and chronic consumer shortages as with official spying and corruption. With the seeming triumph of Western-style capitalism in Europe and throughout the world, borders were opened, markets and currencies were deregulated, and international arrangements were expanded. "Globalization" became the catchword of the post–Cold War decade.

The interconnected world of the 1990s—of swift data transfer and capital movements that facilitated a global supply chain—had its darker side, threatening the livelihood of farmers and industrial workers and making debtor nations vulnerable to the vagaries of international speculators. The swelling migrations of the poor to richer countries—already begun in the 1970s and 1980s—created a backlash that aroused exclusionist sentiments in the receiving countries. Globalization also enabled the spread of diseases, including AIDS, SARS,† and swine flu.

---

* A means of overcoming censorship, samizdat (self-published) tracts—either handwritten or typed and reproduced on mimeograph or hidden copying machines—had been passed from hand to hand.

† SARS (severe acute respiratory syndrome).

The global environmental movement was born during the Cold War, creating a counternarrative to the Superpowers' support of unbridled economic development and their competing large-scale, high-tech projects in the Third World. Rachel Carson's 1962 book, *Silent Spring* (translated into sixteen languages), which detailed the human and environmental dangers of unlimited use of pesticides, had stirred activists to demand stronger regulation of chemicals. Mounting public concern over the release of toxic substances into the ground, air, and water was taken up by the United Nations, which proposed the first Earth Day in 1970 and convened the Stockholm Conference in 1972 to enunciate principles for protecting the global environment. In his influential 1973 book *Small Is Beautiful* the British economist E. F. Schumacher urged the world's people to reject the destructive impact of "gigantism."

Until the 1980s the communist regimes had resisted pressure from the environmentalists. Struggling to raise production figures at all costs, they had created vast areas of environmentally degraded territory and severe health problems even before the Chernobyl disaster. Once the Cold War ended, the United Nations again sought to lead the collective effort to stop or reverse the damage to the world's fragile ecosystems that now transcended national borders. In 1992 the Rio Conference addressed the problem of global warming—the rise in the world's temperatures that was the result, many scientists believed, of sharply rising gas emissions from industry, agriculture, and transportation. The ensuing struggle over the 1997 Kyoto Protocol—the first international attempt to reduce greenhouse emissions—pitted the proponents of national sovereignty, economic growth, and human betterment against the protectors of the environment.

On the political side, nationalism, one of the forces that had helped end the Cold War and bring down the Soviet Union, took on a more lethal form in the 1990s. In the former communist world, the Czechs and Slovaks, freed from Moscow's control, peacefully separated with their "velvet divorce" in 1992. But Yugoslavia, which had been held together for forty years by Tito's pragmatic Marxism and his bargains among its nations, descended into four wars of succession and the persecution, murder, and displacement of millions of Bosnians, Croats, Kosovars, and Serbs. In the former Soviet Union, the Baltic states took steps to disenfranchise their Russian inhabitants, and the new governments of Azerbaijan, Georgia, Moldova, and Tajikistan attempted to purge the religious and national minorities within their borders. Moreover, soon after Germany's reunification there was an eruption of xenophobic attacks on foreign workers who had been imported by the GDR and also on newly arrived asylum seekers from the Third World.

Assaults on religious minorities and foreigners were not confined to Europe. In Asia, the Middle East, and Africa long-suppressed antagonisms were unleashed against vulnerable populations. In 1991 the attacks by Myanmar's ruling military junta forced 250,000 Rohingya Muslims to flee to Bangladesh. That year Kuwait expelled some 450,000 Palestinian workers in retaliation for the PLO leader Yasser Arafat's support of Saddam Hussein's invasion. And in Rwanda in 1994 nearly 1 million Tutsis were slaughtered by the Hutu majority.

Militant Islamic movements, which had left their mark on the Cold War, posed an even more radical threat in the 1990s. The United States became the target of Al Qaeda (The Base), a fundamentalist Arab group that had joined the anti-Soviet struggle in Afghanistan and afterward announced a global fight against Western dominance of the Muslim world. Al Qaeda's leader, Osama bin Laden, who settled in Sudan in 1992, directed jihadist operations in the Balkans, Kashmir, and the Philippines and also against US military personnel in Yemen, Somalia, and Saudi Arabia.[*]

Postcommunist Russia was also engaged in a struggle with Islamists. In 1994 Yeltsin's government sent forty thousand troops into the largely Muslim province of Chechnya but failed to reestablish control over the breakaway region. In 1999, after Chechen forces had attempted to stir a Muslim rebellion in Dagestan and were accused of organizing terrorist bombings in Moscow, a full-scale Russian invasion followed.

China too faced a militant Islamic opposition in the form of Uighur separatist groups in western Xinjiang province, inspired by the independence of the neighboring Central Asian republics from the USSR. Beijing's major enemy was the ETIM (East Turkestan Islamic Movement), founded in 1993 and revived in 1997, which the Chinese government accused of some two hundred terror attacks, including arson, bus bombings, and assassinations, resulting in approximately 160 deaths and 440 injuries, as well as of links with Al Qaeda.

Europe, with a population of some thirty-two million Muslims in 1990, also experienced rising Islamic militancy. Among the descendants of the labor migrants from North and Central Africa and the Middle East were those disillusioned by their joblessness and their separation from mainstream society who gravitated toward radical Islamic networks preaching anti-Western and anti-Israel messages and calling for attacks on Jews. France suffered the spillover from Algeria's civil war when armed Islamists hijacked an Air France plane in

---

[*] There is some evidence of Al Qaeda involvement in the first attack on the New York World Trade Center in 1993.

1994, conducted a series of bombings in 1995 and 1996, and declared a jihad on French territory in 1999.

The United Nations, born in World War II and largely ignored during the Cold War, sought to fill the structural and security gap after 1991. Between 1945 and 1991 the UN Security Council's authority had been largely paralyzed by its permanent members, who applied their veto nearly three hundred times. The Great Powers generally did their own peacekeeping, except when the UN provided a convenient forum for deliberation and decision making, especially over the Middle East. UN forces had performed a series of important tasks in Lebanon, Cyprus, Egypt, and Angola, but one of the United Nations' major operations—to manage secession and civil war in Congo (1960–1964)—had exacted a heavy political, economic, and human price on the organization and on Africa.

When the Cold War ended, the United Nations' partisans, hoping for a second chance to fulfill its founders' aspirations, pointed to the organization's productive role in ending the Iran-Iraq War, facilitating the Soviet troop withdrawal from Afghanistan, establishing a coalition government in Cambodia, and ending El Salvador's civil war. But the failures of UN peacekeeping missions in Rwanda, Angola, Somalia, and Yugoslavia and the continuing tendency of the Great Powers to police their near abroad*—combined with the organization's financial limitations and its split personality (as both a forum of international diplomacy and one of its actors)—weakened its position as an aspiring global player in the post–Cold War world.

On the other hand, in 1994 the UN General Assembly—faced with the atrocities in former Yugoslavia and Rwanda—boldly revived the principles of the Nuremberg trials and the abortive Cold War attempts to establish a permanent judicial institution to punish violators of international law. After four years of contentious negotiations, 120 UN members signed the Rome Statute in 1998, establishing an International Criminal Court in The Hague to examine war crimes, crimes against humanity, and genocide.† Although the court's jurisdiction was severely limited,‡ it nonetheless represented a significant development in the post–Cold War world, eventually bringing government and military leaders to trial.

---

* Regions within their own spheres of influence: the Western Hemisphere for the United States, the former Soviet Republics for Russia.

† The seven members who voted against were China, Iraq, Israel, Libya, Qatar, the United States, and Yemen.

‡ Under US pressure the court's reach has been limited to citizens of states accepting its jurisdiction and to cases referred by the UN Security Council.

Another promising development, building on the remarkable advances between 1985 and 1991, was in the area of strategic arms control. In 1992 the United States obtained the agreement of the four successor states—Russia, Ukraine, Belarus, and Kazakhstan—that housed the former USSR's nuclear arsenal to adhere to START I and the Nuclear Non-Proliferation Treaty (NPT). That year Bush and Russian president Yeltsin also concluded START II, which promised, by 2007, to eliminate heavy intercontinental missiles and multiple-warhead ICBMs and reduce total nuclear warheads. Although START II never came into effect,* it led the way to international efforts in the 1990s to end nuclear testing, strengthen nonproliferation regulations, and abolish the production and sale of chemical weapons under international supervision, which had, however, only limited success. Despite the withdrawal of the massive US and Soviet nuclear arms from Europe, the world of the 1990s was only slightly safer than before.

ASIA

After Cambodia's civil war ended in 1991, Asia was at peace for the first time in over six decades, but the end of the US-Soviet rivalry raised the issue of regional order and security, in which China's role had become paramount.[†]

The PRC's extraordinary economic development—its impressive growth rate and burgeoning trade figures—was matched in the 1990s by its increasingly assertive foreign policy. Responding to the perceived threat of US hegemony, Beijing's leadership reached out to its noncommunist Asian neighbors Japan, South Korea, Indonesia, Singapore, Australia, and even India, and participated in regional forums such as APEC (Asia-Pacific Economic Cooperation) and ASEAN. Moreover, China reestablished ties with Vietnam in 1991 and in 1992 forged a "strategic partnership" with Yeltsin's Russia. But by contesting possession of several islands in the South China Sea (reportedly having major gas and oil reserves) with its neighbors, exerting military pressure on Taiwan in 1995, and

---

* The Russian Duma, irritated over NATO's expansion and its bombing campaign against Serbia in 1999 and especially over US insistence on the option of building a national missile defense system (in violation of the ABM treaty), delayed ratification of START II, which was then superseded by the SORT (Strategic Offensive Reductions Treaty), concluded in 2001 between presidents Bush and Putin.

† The Soviet Union's collapse had isolated its Vietnamese client, forcing Hanoi to accept a settlement dictated by the United States and China: a cease-fire supervised by UN peacekeeping forces and UN-monitored elections that led to the restoration of the monarchy under King Sihanouk—only to be toppled in 1997 by a coup that placed Hun Sen (a communist and former Khmer Rouge soldier) in power.

removing the British from Hong Kong in 1997, China also kept the region off balance, combining restraint and conciliation with a willingness to defend its interests forcefully.

At the same time, China sought to repair its ties with the United States, and under the administration of President Bill Clinton Sino-US relations measurably improved. The PRC pledged to adhere to international conventions on nonproliferation and nuclear testing as well as on environmental protection and human rights, and it negotiated new economic arrangements with Washington in order to facilitate its entry into the World Trade Organization. But sources of tension had not disappeared, particularly over America's lingering Cold War strategy of nuclear deterrence, alliance formation, and the use of military force to intervene in the internal affairs of foreign governments.* Nonetheless, Beijing, chastened by the 1997–1998 Asian financial crisis and faced with growing unrest at home, chose domestic economic development over a direct challenge to US power.

In northeast Asia the Cold War still remained vivid, because of the partition of Korea. In the 1980s the economic gap between North and South Korea had drastically widened, and in the early 1990s Russia and China abruptly terminated their subsidies to Pyongyang and avidly courted Seoul, whereupon a desperate North Korea played the nuclear card. A reluctant signatory of the nonproliferation treaty, the dictator Kim Il Sung sought to save his regime from collapse and absorption by building nuclear weapons and a missile program that would threaten South Korea (and possibly Japan), destabilize the region, and force the United States into negotiations.† But when North Korea refused to permit UN inspections of its nuclear waste sites, the Clinton administration reacted strongly, condemning Pyongyang and engineering tough UN sanctions that drove it to the conference table.

Clinton also defused the crisis. Ending more than four decades of ostracism of North Korea and defying congressional opposition to appeasing a rogue regime, he sent former President Carter to Pyongyang on a mediating mission and in October 1994 concluded an agreement (the Agreed Framework) with Kim Il Sung's successor, Kim Jong Il. In return for Pyongyang's closure of its nuclear

---

* On the US side, these included revelations in 1999 of Chinese espionage at US nuclear facilities and Beijing's repression of political and religious dissidents and its harsh rule in Tibet; on the Chinese side there was opposition to US proposals to construct an antimissile system in Japan and America's continued commitment to Taiwan as well as outrage over the accidental bombing of the PRC's Belgrade embassy during NATO's 1999 war against Serbia.

† As part of its disarmament arrangements with the Soviet Union, the United States had removed all its tactical nuclear weapons from South Korea in 1991.

facilities and allowing international inspections, the United States would provide assistance in building light-water reactors (not capable of plutonium production) and supplying heavy oil for heating and electricity until the new plants were built. After floods devastated North Korea's farmland in 1996 and 1997, the United States also provided food, medicine, and other forms of humanitarian aid at a total of more than $61 million.

However, the bribe did not work. Not only did North Korea continue to obstruct UN inspections and develop its nuclear capacity, but in 1998 it fired a ballistic missile over Japanese territory. In 2002 North Korea repudiated the framework and evicted the inspectors, and the next year it seceded from the NPT, precipitating a second international crisis. This time, however, the United States did not act alone. Beijing (which in 1994 had only quietly backed Washington out of fear of destabilizing its longtime ally and precipitating its demise) now called for multilateral negotiations, which included the two Koreas, China, Russia, and the United States. But North Korea was not to be halted. In 2006 it exploded its first nuclear weapon, and the unsolved Korean question lingered over Asia.

AFRICA

Africa fared badly during the last two decades of the Cold War when the Superpowers intervened with arms and military advisers to promote their respective interests, but the end of the US-Soviet rivalry was also ruinous for many parts of the continent, which were largely removed from the world's attention. The collapse of the Washington- and Moscow-backed dictatorships in Somalia and Ethiopia in 1991 led to the disintegration of both countries, and the civil wars in Sudan and Angola and the genocide against the Tutsi minority in Rwanda underscored the absence of solid regional or international arrangements.

Two new players moved into the breach. The United Nations provided humanitarian aid to war-ravaged populations, brokered a temporary power-sharing arrangement in Angola in 1994, and ministered to refugees from Rwanda and Somalia. By the 1990s, China was also playing a significant role in Africa, purchasing its raw materials and energy resources and providing investment funds for infrastructure politics, but also maintaining a strict policy of noninterference in local politics.

The most striking result of the end of the Cold War occurred in South Africa. Five months after assuming the presidency in September 1989, the Nationalist leader F. W. de Klerk startled the world by announcing the end of Apartheid, the legalization of the African National Congress, and the release of political prisoners, including Nelson Mandela after his twenty-seven-year incarceration. Subsequently, the Pretoria government quietly destroyed South Africa's entire secret nuclear arsenal and launched political negotiations between black and white leaders. South Africa's peaceful transition to democracy in 1989 had many causes, among them the spirit of the 1976 Soweto Uprising, which was not quenched by government repression, and the international boycott movement of the 1980s, which sought to change Pretoria's racist policies. Moreover, the collapse of European communism in 1989 and Gorbachev's decision to cease funding resistance movements in Africa greatly diminished the influence and resources of local Marxists and of the militant left-wing elements of the African National Congress over the border in Angola. The government of South Africa could no longer claim it was a Cold War battlefield.

De Klerk's initiative was also related to the settlement over Namibia, which his country had long obstructed in the United Nations. The mounting costs of holding onto its truculent colony had convinced Pretoria it was time to leave. It was also time to end South Africa's covert intervention in Angola, where casualties were mounting. Under patient and persistent US mediation, a grand bargain was struck whereby the Cuban troops were removed from Angola in return for South Africa's withdrawal and for the termination of its occupation of Namibia.

The Angola/Namibia Accords, signed in New York on December 22, 1998 (two weeks after Gorbachev's UN speech), marked a decisive moment in Cold War history. They not only ended more than two decades of Superpower-fueled fighting and a communist withdrawal* but also marked the end of colonialism in Africa with the surrender of a territory seized during World War I. In November 1989 Namibia held its first free elections and gained its independence in March 1990. Under South Africa's close scrutiny, Namibia established a multiparty democracy and free-market economy. In the meantime de Klerk was managing the changeover from white-minority rule to a democratic South Africa. In May 1994, one month after the country's first multiracial elections, Nelson Mandela was inaugurated as South Africa's president.†

---

* Cuba, although outwardly defiant over Moscow's endorsement of the accords, was also ready to liquidate a long, costly, and seemingly unwinnable military mission, especially having gained the prestige of contributing to the liberation of Namibia and removing South African troops from Angola.

† One of the most striking developments in the new South Africa was the 1995 creation of the Truth and Reconciliation Commission, whose purpose was to examine human rights abuses under the Apartheid regime between 1960 and 1994, formulate proposals for reparation and rehabilitation of the victims, and examine petitions for amnesty by the accused. After hearing

Like the USSR's, South Africa's transition to democracy arose from popular protests and top-down decisions, an outstanding leader and a favorable international climate. However, its first post-Apartheid decade was marred by high rates of capital flight and emigration, unemployment and violent crime,* along with the scourge of the AIDS epidemic. Still Africa's richest and most powerful state, South Africa after 1994 was no longer an anticommunist bastion and a regional and global pariah. It had become a middle-sized power that wavered between supporting liberal principles and endorsing a radical democratic foreign policy, more inclined to play the role of a good international citizen, projecting its influence through multinational institutions, than to act alone.

THE MIDDLE EAST

Throughout the Cold War the Superpowers had fluctuated between confrontation and cooperation in the Middle East leaving one of its core problems—Israel and the Palestinians—unresolved. The outbreak of the Palestinian Intifada (uprising) in 1987 had focused the world's attention on Israel's two-decade-long occupation of the West Bank and Gaza and the unresolved problem of self-determination for the Palestinian people. But the collapse of the Soviet Union and the victory of the US-led coalition in the 1991 Gulf War had not only widened the rifts in the Arab world† but also tipped the balance of power in the Middle East.

The Bush administration, seizing this extraordinary moment, convened a peace conference in Madrid in October 1991. Although technically cosponsored by the fading Gorbachev, Washington's intention was to complete the unfinished work of Carter's Camp David agreement by producing a comprehensive Middle East settlement. Yet despite Secretary of State James Baker's best efforts, the participants brought little enthusiasm to the negotiations. The follow-up talks in Washington were fruitless, and with Bush's electoral defeat in November 1992 the American initiative expired the following June.

---

testimonies from over twenty-one thousand victims in venues throughout South Africa (many of which were broadcast over national television), the commission concluded its work with a 3,500-page report in October 1998. Despite some criticisms of the TRC's effectiveness, this countermodel to the Nuremberg Trials has been emulated elsewhere.

* Among the more prominent victims was de Klerk's ex-wife, Marike, who on December 4, 2001, was found stabbed and strangled to death in her Cape Town flat, the victim of a twenty-one-year-old security guard.

† Syria, Egypt, Saudi Arabia, and the Gulf States had supported the coalition, while the PLO, Jordan, and Libya backed Iraq.

Once more in the Middle East, a breakthrough came from an unexpected source. From his Tunisian exile, the PLO leader Yasser Arafat had fretted over his new rival Hamas,* which had sparked the Intifada and was gaining influence in the West Bank and Gaza. Isolated internationally, the PLO was also strapped financially by the termination of Moscow's subsidies and the withdrawal of Saudi and Gulf State funding in retaliation for Arafat's support of Saddam Hussein. Excluded from the Madrid talks, Arafat feared a US-brokered Syrian-Israeli agreement, which would further weaken the Palestinian cause.

In June 1992 Arafat found a partner when the legendary military chief and Labor Party leader Yitzhak Rabin became Israel's prime minister on a platform of trading land for peace with Israel's neighbors, including the Palestinians. The Israeli public—stung by international criticism of its government's forceful repression of the Intifada and stunned by the attacks of the Iraqi Scud missiles on Tel Aviv during the 1991 Gulf War—had become open to an accommodation with the Palestinians. The once-reviled and now-weakened Arafat represented a far more acceptable negotiating partner than Hamas and the even more radical Islamic jihad.

In a bold move that sidestepped the faltering Washington negotiations, Israeli and PLO negotiators began secret talks in Oslo, guided by tough but patient Norwegian mediators, and by late summer 1993 produced a breakthrough agreement. The new Clinton administration, which had been apprised of the negotiations but not the details, hosted a gala signing ceremony on the south lawn of the White House on September 13, 1993. The historic Oslo Accords, which brought its authors† the 1994 Nobel Peace Prize, consisted of two parts: a mutual recognition between Israel and the PLO, and a Declaration of Principles (DOP) setting forth a five-year agenda for Palestinian self-government in the West Bank and Gaza under the auspices of a newly created Palestinian Authority.

Israel reaped considerable benefit from the Oslo Accords, gaining praise and increased contacts with the world community. Recognition by the Palestinians ended five and a half decades of collective Arab opposition to its existence. A peace treaty with Jordan was signed in October 1994, followed by the establishment of consular relations with four other Arab states and expanded economic relations with others. But Syria, which Arafat had not consulted, refused to deal with Israel.

---

* Hamas (the Islamic Resistance Movement) was an offshoot of the Egyptian organization the Muslim Brotherhood.
† Rabin and Arafat as well as Israel's foreign minister, Shimon Peres, who played a major role in the Oslo negotiations.

Moreover, the Oslo Accords, which had been concluded between two highly unequal parties—a sovereign state and an occupied people—left serious elements unsolved, above all the shape of a permanent settlement and of a future Palestinian entity. Moreover, the DOP was silent over such crucial issues as the future of Jerusalem (which both Israelis and Palestinians claimed as their capital), the right of return of the Palestinians refugees who had left Israel in 1948–1949, and the future of the Jewish settlements in the West Bank and Gaza.

Not surprisingly, the accords raised vociferous opposition on both sides. The Israeli Right (still traumatized by the return of the entire Sinai to Egypt between 1979 and 1982) accused Rabin of a sellout, and the religious parties were outraged over his abandonment of Judea and Samaria (the biblical terms for the West Bank). On the Palestinian side, the Islamic radicals were irate over Arafat's betrayal, and even moderate PLO members scorned his surrender to Israel. Terrorist groups on both sides attacked the other.* In November 1995 a fanatical right-wing Israeli shot Rabin at a Tel Aviv peace rally. Following Israel's assassination of a Hamas bomb maker in Gaza in January 1996 and a wave of Palestinian suicide bombings inside Israel, the anti-Oslo Likud Party leader Benjamin Netanyahu became prime minister in May, and the Israeli-Palestinian peace process was brought to a halt.

Two years passed. In 1998 the Clinton administration attempted to revive the Oslo Accords by bringing Netanyahu and Arafat together at the Wye River plantation in rural Maryland for marathon negotiations without a positive result. Netanyahu's successor, the renowned military leader and Labor Party head Ehud Barak, who took office in 1999 and was prepared to discuss a final settlement with Arafat, urged the US president to try again. But the return to Camp David in July 2000 failed to produce agreement on the four key issues separating the two parties: the borders of a Palestinian state, control over Jerusalem and the city's sacred sites, the Palestinians' right of return, and Israel's security requirements (entailing continuing military control over the proposed Palestinian state). Arafat refused to sign.

The failure of the Camp David negotiations marked the end of the Oslo era, which had stirred hopes and fears of a breakthrough Israeli-Palestinian agreement. Both sides blamed the other for the breakdown, and scholars still debate its causes. Not unexpectedly, a second Palestinian Intifada erupted in September

---

* On February 25, 1994, a Jewish settler, Baruch Goldstein, opened fire on Arab worshippers in the Ibrahim Mosque in Hebron, killing 29 and wounding 125, setting off riots throughout the West Bank. The Israeli government and Jewish religious leaders condemned the attack, but Goldstein's deed was celebrated by Oslo's opponents.

2000, bringing a wave of violence to Israel, the West Bank, and Gaza.* In March 2001, after Barak was replaced by the hard-line Likud leader Ariel Sharon, Israeli-Palestinian negotiations were again suspended.

Despite its enormous power the United States in the decade after the Madrid Conference had proved incapable of wringing enough concessions from the Israelis and Palestinians to bring them to a two-state settlement. Moreover, unlike at the first Camp David, Washington was unable to offer sufficient security guarantees to both sides to resuscitate the Oslo Accords.

LATIN AMERICA

Although the Cold War had ended in Europe, it persisted in the Caribbean, where US enmity against the Castro regime grew even stronger. With the termination of the Soviet-Cuban alliance, the new Russian Federation withdrew its troops and ended all subsidies to Castro. Cuba on its part repatriated all its soldiers from Angola, Ethiopia, and Nicaragua; suspended its assistance to foreign revolutionary movements; and invited investments from abroad. But the United States remained determined to overthrow the Western Hemisphere's sole communist regime. Accusing Havana of human rights violations and pressuring it to move toward democracy, the Clinton administration tightened the international economic boycott against Cuba but failed to topple Castro.

The legacy of the Cold War also weighed heavily on Central America, where the Superpowers had engaged in three brutal proxy wars. Although the fighting in Nicaragua, El Salvador, and Guatemala in the 1980s gave way to peace agreements in the 1990s, the region faced the tasks of reconstruction and recovery along with continuing problems of urban and rural poverty and violence. Some two hundred thousand people had been killed in Central America, most of them civilians, and two million were uprooted internally or forced to flee their countries. The perpetrators were not prosecuted.

Central America emerged from its civil wars heavily dependent on international political guidance and economic assistance, which included a major role

---

* There is considerable evidence that Arafat preplanned the Second Intifada to reassert the PLO's leadership over the disgruntled Palestinians and cover Camp David's failure, but a few PLO spokesmen have insisted that it was a spontaneous response to Likud candidate Ariel Sharon's provocative September 28 visit to the Temple Mount complex in Jerusalem (accompanied by one thousand security guards) for the purpose of asserting Jewish control over a sacred Muslim site (where the Dome of the Rock shrine and the Al-Aqsa mosque are located).

for the United Nations.* Private aid organizations provided important services, but they also failed to coordinate their agendas and may have contributed to the increase in poverty. The spread of globalization—with its emphasis on deregulation and minimal state intervention—also impaired local efforts to rebuild local and national governments, provide help to the needy, and repatriate the masses of refugees.

The United States remained the dominant figure in Central America. US aid in the 1990s centered largely on promoting large-scale, nontraditional agricultural exports (NTAEs) for the global market with heavy use of fertilizers and pesticides, which not only hurt small farmers but also damaged public health and the environment. And although the Cold War was winding down, the United States continued to intervene militarily. Bush in December 1989 used the "War on Drugs" and the goal of restoring democracy in Panama to topple a former US ally, General Manuel Noriega, and Clinton in September 1994 ordered a US occupation of Haiti to restore political order and stanch the flow of refugees to the United States.

In South America the transition from Cold War conditions had begun earlier but was equally striking. By 1990 the US-backed dictatorships in Argentina, Brazil, Paraguay, and Chile had all disappeared, and political reforms had reduced the power of the military. In the near absence of a leftist opposition, the new regimes embraced neoliberal economic policies along with a commitment to free elections and constitutional guarantees. The defeat of Marxist guerrilla movements (most notably in Peru†) spread a mantle of peace over the continent.

Dollar diplomacy also resumed. The Washington Consensus promoted by the US Treasury, the World Bank, and the IMF called for the adoption of Western economic standards, including balanced budgets and reduced taxes, decontrolling interest and exchange rates, lowering trade barriers and attracting foreign investment, and ending subsidies and privatizing industries. This represented a major departure from the region's historic reliance on governments to promote capital ownership and economic growth, control key industries and infrastructure, and erect tariff barriers to protect domestic industries, a program that had bogged down by the 1980s in comparison with the remarkable free-market advances in eastern and southern Asia.

---

* In El Salvador in particular, where it monitored the implementation of the peace accords and investigated the activity of the notorious death squads.
† Where the Maoist Shining Path, which had waged guerrilla warfare throughout the 1980s, was defeated in 1992.

Latin America's post–Cold War development model initially proved successful: investment capital flowed into the region, and rapid growth ensued, including a dramatic rise in intraregional trade spurred by Mercosur.* However, by the latter half of the 1990s a series of financial crises shook the Southern Hemisphere. The downside of free markets was manifested by the mounting gap between rich and poor and the rise of violent crime. By the end of the twentieth century, left-wing populist movements had reappeared in many parts of South America, demanding a curb to unfettered capitalism.

EUROPE

For Europe, the end of the Cold War had a physical as well as a political dimension. Beginning in 1990 the double barbed-wire fences, armed guard houses, and mined strips extending some 6,800 kilometers from Finland to Greece were quickly dismantled and the continent's physical and ideological division was no more. For eighty-two million Germans in particular, reunification ended forty years of separation between two hostile regimes and ushered in the laborious task of integrating the east into the Federal Republic's political, judicial, and economic system. And although the feared migration of millions of easterners westward did not materialize, the end of communism made possible the emigration of over a million Jews from the former Soviet Union in the decade after 1987.

The Wars in Yugoslavia

The peaceful demise of communism in Eastern Europe was shattered by the brutal civil wars in Yugoslavia. Like other East European countries, Yugoslavia in the mid-1980s had suffered an economic meltdown and enormous foreign debts along with rampant corruption. With communism now discredited, long-suppressed national rivalries resurfaced, exacerbated by Tito's dispersion of various ethnic groups, which had created minorities throughout the country.†

---

* Founded in 1990 by Brazil, Argentina, Paraguay, and Uruguay, which Chile joined in 1996.

† The Socialist Federal Republic of Yugoslavia consisted of six republics, three religions, and a mixture of South Slavs, Albanians, Hungarians, and several smaller minorities. Among them, Serbia and Montenegro contained largely Orthodox Christian Slavs; Slovenia and Croatia largely Catholic Slavs (but the latter with a substantial Serb minority); Bosnia-Herzegovina was a mixed region of Muslim, Orthodox, and Catholic Slavs; and Macedonia was a mixed region of Orthodox Christian Slavs and Muslim Albanians. There were also two autonomous regions within Serbia, where the division fell along ethnic lines: Kosovo (Orthodox Christian Slavs and Muslim Albanians) and the Vojvodina (Orthodox Christian Serbs and Protestant and Catholic Hungarians).

Map 19. As a result of the wars between 1991 and 1995 the former Yugoslavia was replaced by six successor states.

Unlike the USSR, Tito's federal, multinational Yugoslavia collapsed in violence. Fighting erupted in 1991, when Slovenia and Croatia (the two most Westernized, prosperous, and anticommunist republics) declared their independence. The Serbian president, Slobodan Milošević—who controlled Yugoslavia's federal army—sought to block them. After only ten days of fighting, Milošević agreed to free Slovenia, which had only a miniscule Serb minority. However, Croatia's secession led to a fratricidal war because almost a third of its territory was inhabited by Serbs. In these regions, local Serbian forces (aided by the Yugoslav army) engaged in ethnic cleansing: the murder and forced deportation of Croats in the Krajina and Slavonia in order to create compact Serb strongholds within the breakaway state.*

---

* The civil war in Croatia lasted until 1995, when government forces captured the Serb-held territories and drove out much of the Serbian population.

Bosnia-Herzegovina, the next to secede, was an even greater tinderbox, consisting of roughly 44 percent Muslim Slavs (Bosnians), 33 percent Serbs, and 17 percent Croats. The Serbs, fearing Muslim domination, immediately declared their independence from the new state and created the Republika Srpska. Armed by the Yugoslav government and joined by Yugoslav troops, they waged a ferocious war on the non-Serb population, looting, killing, and setting up concentration camps, and placing the capital, Sarajevo, under a three-year siege. By the end of 1992 the Serbs controlled 70 percent of Bosnia.

Europe's first major conflict since the end of the Cold War shook the international community. Although Bosnia's fate involved no Great Power interests, the Serbs' well-publicized violence stunned the public, who put pressure on their leaders to respond. In May 1992 the United Nations voted sanctions against Yugoslavia for aiding the Republika Srpska and dispatched a multinational force of seven thousand unarmed peacekeepers (UNPROFOR) to aid Bosnian civilians. In October the Security Council established a no-fly zone, banning all military flights over Bosnia. The European Community attempted to mediate: the Vance-Owen Plan in early 1993 proposed a partition of Bosnia into ten cantons (administrative subdivisions), which the ascendant Bosnian Serbs rejected.

The Clinton administration was disinclined to commit US ground forces to Bosnia after its debacle in Somalia.* US calls to enforce the no-fly zone and for air strikes against the Serbs were rebuffed by its NATO partners and Russia, the major contributors to the UNPROFOR troops, which were unwilling to expose their soldiers to Serb reprisals and opposed to encouraging the Bosnians to prolong a futile struggle. In another controversial move, the Security Council in May 1993 dispatched an additional 7,600 troops and designated six besieged Muslim enclaves as safe areas. Both sides exploited these areas for their military advantage, and the understaffed, underfunded, unarmed UN forces proved incapable of protecting civilians or avoiding being taken hostage by the Serbs.

The tide began to turn in 1994. The Bosnian government obtained arms and fought on, and Washington's attitude toughened. On February 5, 1994, CNN television broadcast a bomb explosion in the Sarajevo central market that killed 68 and wounded 144 civilians. To stave off a retaliatory NATO airstrike, Russia

---

* Under President Bush twenty-five thousand US troops had been sent to Somalia to support a UN relief mission. But in March 1993 the Clinton administration had changed the mission and involved US soldiers in the Somalian civil war. When US casualties mounted and the American public protested, the president reversed course in October, announcing a total withdrawal, which was completed by March 1994.

engineered a Serb pullback from the capital. But the United States pushed ahead. Without consulting the UN, NATO bombers, in their first military action since 1949, attacked Serb positions, and Moscow responded with restraint.

Adding diplomacy to the use of force, the Clinton administration forged an alliance between the Croatian and Bosnian governments and formed a Croat-Muslim federation inside Bosnia. Washington also began supplying arms to the Muslim forces. Sidelining UN and European mediation efforts, Clinton in April 1994 established the five-member Contact Group, consisting of Britain, France, Germany, Russia, and the United States, to bring the Bosnian Serbs to the peace table.

The war in Bosnia reached a climax in the summer of 1995. In July the Serb forces massacred some seven thousand people who had taken refuge in Srebrenica and attacked several other UN safe areas. But US-trained and armed Croatian troops, which had driven most of the Serbs out of their country, now entered Bosnia. By the end of August, NATO (over strong Russian objections) unleashed devastating air attacks against Serb military targets and communications, Croat and Muslim forces pushed the Serbs back to roughly 49 percent of the territory of Bosnia, and the chief US negotiator, Richard Holbrooke, began the negotiations with Milošević that ultimately ended the war.

The Bosnian peace talks took place in November 1995 at a US air base in Dayton, Ohio. With the UN excluded and the Contact Group acting as formal guarantors, the presidents of Serbia, Croatia, and Bosnia agreed to maintain Bosnia as a single, united republic but with a dual identity: a Bosnian-Croat Federation and a Bosnian Serb Republic, which would share power in all government institutions. Although Bosnia's sovereignty had been preserved, it had been de facto partitioned and become a NATO protectorate occupied by sixty thousand foreign troops. Moreover, two of the principal terms of the Dayton Peace Agreement proved impossible to enforce: the Muslim refugees were never able to return to their homes, and the two major Bosnian Serb war crimes suspects were not apprehended for more than a decade—Radovan Karadžić in 2008 and Ratko Mladić in 2011.

The Bosnian War touched outside parties as well. For the Europeans, the massacres in Bosnia represented a grim link with their past and a warning of their post–Cold War immobility and divisions,* as well as a sign of America's

---

* During the course of the Bosnian War, France and Britain had supported Russia in opposing military action against the Bosnian Serbs, and Germany had stood with the United States in opposing a partition of Bosnia.

still powerful role on the continent. For the United States, which despite the public outcry had remained inactive for almost two years, and which had opposed appeasement in any form only to belatedly arrange Bosnia's partition, the Dayton settlement represented less than a clear-cut triumph. And for Russia, the Bosnian war was an undoubted setback: heavily dependent on Western economic aid, Yeltsin had pursued a pragmatic foreign policy, serving as mediator between the Contact Group and the Serbs but also acquiescing in NATO's military intervention in the Balkans and in its new post–Cold War role as Europe's dominant security organization. Indeed, it was during the Bosnian War that Washington set the wheels in motion to expand the Atlantic alliance eastward to three former communist states, raising alarms and anger in Moscow.*

Four years later, NATO, now celebrating its fiftieth anniversary, took even stronger action. At issue was Kosovo, a province in southwestern Serbia where Albanians constituted some 82 percent of the population. Over the previous ten years Milošević had systematically eroded Kosovo's autonomy, and the Albanians had responded with a nonviolent resistance movement. However, in 1997 a radical group, the KLA (Kosovo Liberation Army), had taken up arms and demanded independence, whereupon Milošević dispatched troops to crush the rebellion.

Fueled by fears of massive Albanian civilian casualties, NATO used the threat of bombing to demand a Serbian withdrawal. In February 1999 it pressured Belgrade to hold a referendum at the end of three years on the political future of Kosovo. Milošević, unwilling to surrender this mineral-rich province with its powerful ties to Serbian history, refused to allow NATO peacekeepers into Kosovo.

NATO responded swiftly. There were no plans to send ground troops to rescue the Albanians, but on March 24 NATO bombers began seventy-eight days of attacks on Serbia's military installations and also on civilian infrastructure.† In the meantime the civil war escalated in Kosovo, resulting in some 5,000 civilian deaths and the dispersal of 860,000 Albanians, who either fled or were driven into refugee camps outside the province. Finally, with a nudge from Moscow, Milošević caved in on June 10, agreeing to withdraw his troops, permit a NATO-led force (KFOR) to disarm the local combatants and supervise the return of the refugees, and allow a UN mission to administer the province.

---

* In 1999, after considerable debate within NATO and over Russian objections, Poland, Hungary, and the Czech Republic joined the Western alliance, followed, in 2004, by Estonia, Latvia, Lithuania, Slovenia, Slovakia, Bulgaria, and Romania.

† Including bridges, factories, power stations, telecommunication facilities, the state television offices and broadcasting tower, and the headquarters of Yugoslavia's leftist party as well as oil refineries and chemical plants.

On the surface NATO's action was deemed highly successful. Kosovo had been freed and now resumed its quest for independence.* Only one year later the Serbs voted Milošević out of office, and in 2001 the new Serbian government handed him over to the International Criminal Court at The Hague to stand trial. The Kosovo war, won entirely through aerial bombardment, had produced no combat casualties for NATO. Not only had the alliance worked harmoniously, but for the first time in fifty years a German government had exerted diplomatic leadership and had committed its forces offensively outside of the area, in a region scarred by its Nazi past. US secretary of state Madeleine Albright exulted that Kosovo was "simply the most important thing we have done in the world."

But the war's cost was also considerable. Returning to their ruined homes and villages, many Albanians took revenge on the Serbs, driving 186,000 from the province and terrorizing those who remained. A devastated Kosovo became another NATO protectorate dependent on outside donors for its economic survival. The impact of the bombing on Serbia was also considerable, including approximately five hundred civilian casualties. On May 7 an American B-2 bomber accidentally struck the Chinese embassy in downtown Belgrade, killing three, wounding another twenty, and greatly damaging relations between Washington and Beijing.†

Relations between Russia and the West also deteriorated. Moscow, no longer a partner, could neither prevent NATO's war against Serbia nor secure an independent place in the postwar occupation of Kosovo. Russian Nationalists assailed the new Pax Americana that had extended to the Balkans. Even Gorbachev spoke out critically; he insisted that the Kosovo issue could have been solved by political means but for the "bossy US alliance" that had precipitated a military decision in order to demonstrate the "ineffectiveness of the UN and the OSCE."‡

Some Western critics condemned NATO for collusion with KLA atrocities against the Serbs, for exaggerating the number of Albanian victims and refugees, and for subjugating Eastern Europe's last socialist country. There were also legal objections to the Kosovo war: Clinton had ignored the US War Powers Act, and in the name of an international humanitarian emergency the NATO powers had violated the UN Charter by attacking a member state without the Security

---

* Which was declared in 2008 over Russian and Serbian objections.

† The official explanation was that US intelligence had misidentified the embassy as the Yugoslav Bureau of Federal Supply and Procurement and placed it on the list of approved targets, but critics suspected a deliberate hit, either to thwart communications or possibly to catch Milošević at this site.

‡ The Organization for Security and Cooperation in Europe, successor to the CSCE.

Council's authorization and inflicted suffering on innocent Serb civilians in violation of the 1949 Geneva Convention.* On a broader scale, the war's opponents chided NATO for making war to prevent mass murder instead of daring to secure the peace.

The European Union

Even before the Cold War's end—and after two decades of sluggish progress—the twelve-member European Community† took steps in the mid-1980s to create a stronger union. The relaunch of the European project was manifested in two significant acts: the Schengen Agreement (1985), eliminating border controls between members, and the Single European Act (1986), removing all trade barriers within six years. The next step, aired in 1988, was the establishment of a monetary union.

The fall of the Berlin Wall greatly affected the European Community. In return for French support of German unification, Chancellor Kohl had dropped all of Bonn's objections to a common European currency. The 1992 Maastricht Treaty incorporated the strict German criteria for membership in the common currency‡ and set a 1999 deadline for its adoption, but Kohl had failed to convince Mitterrand to accept what Germany considered (and turned out to be) an essential counterpart: a *political* framework that would ensure the new currency's stability. The renamed European Union (1993) admitted three new members in 1995§ and in 1999 launched the world's first common currency—the euro—in eleven of its member states.⁋ Nevertheless, as the crisis in Yugoslavia demonstrated, post–Cold War Europe still lacked a unified voice to implement a common foreign and security policy on its own.**

---

* Some Western military observers were also unimpressed with the alliance's performance, particularly its decision-by-consensus arrangements that hindered the bombing campaign, the Europeans' military unpreparedness, several weaknesses in the US arsenal, and NATO's vulnerability to the Serbs' low-tech defense strategies.

† In additional to the six founding members, the following had joined: Denmark, Ireland, and Britain in 1973; Greece in 1981; and Portugal and Spain in 1986.

‡ Including low inflation and long-term interest rates, stable exchange rates, budget deficits less than 3 percent of GDP, and government debt less than 3 percent of GDP, as well as the establishment of an independent European Central Bank to exert control over the monetary policies of member states.

§ The former Cold War neutrals Austria, Finland, and Sweden.

⁋ Austria, Belgium, Finland, France, Germany, Ireland, Italy, Luxembourg, the Netherlands, Portugal, and Spain. Greece, late in meeting the Maastricht criteria, joined in 2001. Britain, Denmark, and Sweden opted to stay out.

** For example, the two EU members, Britain and France, that hold permanent seats on the UN Security Council generally cast votes according to their national interests.

The collapse of communism in Eastern Europe also raised the issue of European Union expansion, which the newly independent governments desired. At its Copenhagen summit in 1993 the European Union established unprecedented and exacting political, economic, and legal criteria for admission, setting the bar deliberately high to promote political stability and economic and judicial reforms by the applicants.* In the course of their arduous negotiations with EU officials, the ten candidates were compelled to alter many of their institutions and practices to meet the Copenhagen standards.† On the other hand, Turkey, a loyal NATO member that had applied in 1987, continued to be excluded along with the successor states of the USSR.

Born of the historical longings for a united Europe and forged by Franco-German reconciliation during the Cold War, the European Union in 2000 had a €93.3 billion budget, the world's largest number of supranational institutions,‡ and a dense bureaucracy that affected the lives of some 378 million people. Nonetheless, national interests continued to dominate its decision making. Moreover, by the beginning of the twenty-first century, the European Union had failed to create Europeans in either spirit or behavior—as witnessed by popular opinion polls and the low turnouts in European parliamentary elections. With fading memories of World War II and of the Soviet menace that had brought Western elites together between 1957 and 1989, no external threats to promote further integration, and the prospect of a large and heterogeneous membership, the European Union's future after the Cold War had become uncertain.

THE UNITED STATES AND 9/11

After almost a half century of Cold War, the unexpected disintegration of the Soviet Union—much like imperial Germany's collapse in 1918—left the United States faced with an unruly world. But the Clinton administration in the 1990s took no steps to forge a new multilateral form of international order—either

---

* (1) "Stability of institutions guaranteeing democracy, the rule of law, human rights, and respect for and protection of minorities"; (2) a "functioning market economy with the capacity to cope with competitive pressure and market forces within the Union"; and (3) the ability to "fulfill all EU laws and treaties governing trade, farm subsidies, monetary union, the environment, health and safety, energy, transport, justice, etc."

† The ten that entered the European Union together in May 2004 were: (Greek) Cyprus, the Czech Republic, Estonia, Hungary, Latvia, Lithuania, Malta, Poland, Slovakia, and Slovenia.

‡ Including the Council of Ministers, the European Commission, the European Parliament, the European Court of Justice, the European Central Bank, and the European Court of Auditors.

through a revival of Roosevelt's regional policemen or through a resuscitated United Nations. Instead, in his second inaugural address on January 20, 1997, Clinton announced his vision of global governance: "America stands alone as the world's indispensable nation."

By the end of the 1990s the United States, with the world's largest military and economy, had become the target not of a superpower or group of enemy states but of a radical Islamic group, Al Qaeda, which possessed no territory and operated in cells throughout the world. In 1996 its leader, Osama bin Laden, returned to Afghanistan, now controlled by a fundamentalist Taliban regime, and two years later issued a fatwa. In this Islamic-style legal pronouncement, he declared it the duty of all Muslims to kill Americans anywhere in the world because of US threats to Islam, including Washington's support of its Arab allies and of Israel. In August bin Laden's forces used truck bombs to attack the US embassies in Kenya and Tanzania, killing 224 people and wounding thousands more, and in October 2000 an Al Qaeda team attacked the USS *Cole* in Yemen, almost sinking the vessel and killing 17 American sailors.

The Clinton administration, aware of the threat, took countermeasures. On August 20, 1998, the president ordered retaliatory missile attacks on bin Laden's camp near Khowst and also on a pharmaceutical plant in Sudan suspected of producing chemical weapons for Al Qaeda. The air strike missed bin Laden, and the total destruction of the al-Shifa factory producing medicines for Sudan was widely condemned as a human rights violation and an intelligence failure.

Washington then turned to diplomacy. It enlisted Saudi Arabia and Pakistan in the abortive effort to convince the Taliban to expel bin Laden but also won UN support for tough sanctions against the Afghan government for sheltering terrorists and forged an alliance with the anti-Taliban opposition for the purpose of capturing the Al Qaeda leader. Clinton, constrained by his predecessors' executive orders banning the assassination of foreign leaders,* concerned over the risk of collateral damage, and hindered by disagreements between the CIA and the US military over responsibility for operations—and also embroiled in a growing personal scandal—held back from further strikes against bin Laden. His administration did thwart at least two Al Qaeda attacks against the United States and Jordan in early 2000.

---

* Originating in the post-Watergate congressional investigations of secret CIA assassination attempts, they had been issued by Carter, Ford, and Reagan.

In 2001, the new US president, George W. Bush, a Republican with little foreign policy experience, received some thirty-six alerts relating to Al Qaeda and bin Laden, including an August 6 CIA report entitled "Bin Laden Determined to Strike in the US," but these warnings lacked specifics of time, place, method, or target. On September 11, 2001, four American passenger planes were hijacked. Two struck the towers of the World Trade Center in New York, the third crashed into the Pentagon, and the fourth fell into an open field in Pennsylvania after the crew and passengers fought the hijackers.

The world reaction to the events of September 11, in which more than three thousand people from more than ninety countries died, was generally one of shock and sympathy. Church bells rang throughout Europe, tens of thousands of Beijing residents left condolences at the US embassy, firefighters in South Africa flew American flags, and children in India taped up signs that read, "This is an attack on all of us."

The post–Cold War era had abruptly ended. On September 18 Bush signed legislation that had been approved overwhelmingly by both houses of Congress authorizing him to "use all necessary and appropriate force against those nations, organizations, or persons he determines planned, authorized, committed, or aided" the 9/11 attacks.* Two days later, in a speech to the nation, the president declared a sweeping, open-ended war on terror not only against Al Qaeda but also "until every terrorist group of global reach has been found, stopped and defeated."

The drumbeat to war commenced, and the US gathered allies. On September 28, three days after the Taliban government refused Washington's request to hand over bin Laden, the United States introduced a UN Security Council resolution calling on all states "to prevent and suppress terrorist acts and take action against perpetrators," which neither China nor Russia vetoed.† Indeed, Russian president Vladimir Putin, despite serious differences with Washington over NATO expansion and the US defense missile program, offered broad support in battling the "common enemy" of terrorism by Islamic militants, which he claimed to be facing in his attempt to suppress the uprising in Chechnya.

---

* The Bush administration had submitted this bill in accordance with the November 7, 1973, War Powers Resolution, passed by a two-thirds congressional vote, which overrode Nixon's veto and was designed to curb presidential power to commit US troops without congressional authorization and review. In ordering US military action in Central America and the Caribbean in the 1980s and in the Balkans in the 1990s, both Reagan and Clinton had ignored this resolution.

† However, this resolution was not an authorization to go to war under Article 51 of the UN Covenant.

On October 2 NATO announced that the United States had provided "clear and compelling proof" of Al Qaeda's responsibility for the 9/11 attack and declared its readiness to join the United States in its fight—a decision that would draw the Atlantic alliance into the first out-of-area action in its history.

On October 7, 2001, Operation Enduring Freedom began. US forces launched an air and military attack on Afghanistan, supported by troops from Australia, Britain, and France, with NATO logistic assistance, and using Russian airspace for transporting men and supplies. The operation was also coordinated with the anti-Taliban forces of the Afghan United Front (Northern Alliance) and with the cooperation of the governments of Pakistan, Uzbekistan, and Tajikistan. Although bin Laden and other Al Qaeda leaders escaped, within two months the US-led coalition had captured the major cities, toppled the Taliban regime, and installed an interim government under the United Front leader Hamid Karzai. On December 20, 2001, the UN Security Council set up the US-led ISAF (International Security Assistance Force) to assist the Afghan government in maintaining security and expanding its authority.[*]

Bush, in his State of the Union address on January 29, 2002, warned the nation and the world that the war in Afghanistan was only the beginning of the US war on terrorism. Echoing Reagan's 1983 charge against the Soviet Union, the president announced that United States now faced an "axis of evil" consisting of three countries—Iraq, Iran, and North Korea—that sponsored terror, sought weapons of mass destruction, and endangered America and its allies. On September 22 the president announced the Bush doctrine: that the United States was free to take preemptive action against states developing weapons of mass destruction. Over the objections of Russia, China, and two key US NATO allies, France and Germany, this doctrine led to the US-led invasion of Iraq on March 19, 2003.[†] But after the overthrow of Saddam Hussein US forces were to remain for eight years in Iraq to quell insurgencies, tamp down on civil war, and attempt to produce a stable Iraqi government. The war in Afghanistan also continued. After the Taliban forces regrouped in the countryside, US and NATO forces attempted to protect the Karzai government, leading to the longest conflict in US history.

Since 2001 the war on terror (and terrorism)—the open-ended struggle against Al Qaeda, other militant anti-Western groups, and their rogue-state supporters—has dominated US foreign policy. Although the enemy is a new one,

---

[*] Over which NATO assumed responsibility in October 2003.

[†] In which the United States was joined by Britain, Australia, and Poland.

some Cold War elements have survived, including America's global campaign to promote democracy but also its embrace of questionable strategic allies, its disputes with NATO over US unilateralism, and the unraveling of support from Russia and China. Washington has also abandoned several hard-won Cold War and post–Cold War agreements.*

There were domestic consequences as well. Like the US war in Vietnam, the long conflicts in Afghanistan and Iraq kindled opposition to the human and material costs. And because of its ubiquitous range and indefinite duration, the war on terror has once more raised legal and constitutional objections at home and abroad.

SUGGESTIONS FOR FURTHER STUDY

Documents

"The Central Intelligence Agency's 9/11 File." National Security Archive. 2012. http://www.gwu.edu/~nsarchiv/NSAEBB/NSAEBB381/.

"Declaration of Principles on Interim Self-Government Arrangements (Oslo Agreement). http://unispal.un.org/unispal.nsf/0/71DC8C9D96D2F0FF85256117007 CB6CA.

"Enlargement." European Union. Last updated February 8, 2013. http://europa.eu /pol/enlarg/index_en.htm.

Milošević, Slobodan, and Ramsey Clark. *The Defense Speaks: For History and the Future: Yugoslav President Slobodan Milosevic's Opening Defense Statement before the International Criminal Tribunal for the Former Yugoslavia (ICTY) at The Hague, August 31–September 1, 2004.* New York: International Action Center, 2006.

"NATO 2020: Assured Security; Dynamic Engagement." NATO. 2010. http://www .nato.int/cps/en/natolive/official_texts_63654.htm?selectedLocale=en.

"Study on NATO Enlargement." NATO. 1995. http://www.nato.int/cps/en/natolive /official_texts_24733.htm?selectedLocale=en.

War Powers Resolution: Joint Resolution Concerning War Powers and the President. http://avalon.law.yale.edu/20th_century/warpower.asp.

Contemporary Writing

Fukuyama, Francis. *The End of History and the Last Man.* New York: Free Press, 1992.

Galeano, Eduardo H. *Upside Down: A Primer for the Looking-Glass World.* Translated by Mark Fried. New York: Metropolitan Books, 2000.

---

* Among them the 1972 Anti-Ballistic Missile Treaty with the former USSR and also the Comprehensive Test-Ban Treaty, the Land Mines Convention, the Biological Weapons Convention, the International Criminal Court, and the Kyoto Protocol.

Huntington, Samuel P. *The Clash of Civilizations and the Remaking of World Order.* New York: Simon and Schuster, 1996.

Kagan, Robert. *Of Paradise and Power: America and Europe in the New World Order.* New York: Knopf, 2003.

Nye, Joseph S. *The Paradox of American Power: Why the World's Only Superpower Can't Go It Alone.* Oxford: Oxford University Press, 2002.

Primakov, E. M. *Russian Crossroads: Toward the New Millennium.* Translated by Felix Rosenthal. New Haven, CT: Yale University Press, 2004.

Memoirs

Albright, Madeleine, with Bill Woodward. *Madam Secretary.* New York: Miramax Books, 2003.

Christopher, Warren. *Chances of a Lifetime.* New York: Scribner, 2001.

Clinton, Bill. *My Life.* New York: Knopf, 2004.

Goldstone, Richard. *For Humanity: Reflections of a War Crimes Investigator.* New Haven, CT: Yale University Press, 2000.

Havel, Václav. *To the Castle and Back.* Translated by Paul R. Wilson. New York: Knopf, 2007.

Holbrooke, Richard C. *To End a War.* New York: Random House, 1998.

Malan, Magnus. *My Life with the SA Defence Force.* Pretoria: Protea Book House, 2006.

Mandela, Nelson. *Long Walk to Freedom: The Autobiography of Nelson Mandela.* Boston: Little, Brown, 1994.

Peres, Shimon. *Battling for Peace: A Memoir.* New York: Random House, 1995.

Rabin, Yitzhak. *The Rabin Memoirs.* Berkeley: University of California Press, 1996.

Yeltsin, Boris Nikolayevich. *Midnight Diaries.* Translated by Catherine A. Fitzpatrick. New York: PublicAffairs, 2000.

Films

Babel. Directed by Alejandro González Iñárritu. Los Angeles: Paramount Pictures, 2006.

Before the Rain. Directed by Milcho Manchevski. London: Aim/British Screen Productions, 1994.

Black Snow. Directed by Fei Xie. Beijing: Beijing Youth Film Studio, 1990.

Burnt by the Sun. Directed by Nikita Mikhalkov. Paris/Moscow: Caméra One/Studio Trite, 1994.

Cabaret Balkan. Directed by Goran Paskaljevic. Bitola, Macedonia: Gradski Kina, 1998.

Chronicle of a Disappearance. Directed by Elia Suleiman. Paris: Centre National de la Cinématographie, 1996.

Cry the Beloved Country. Directed by Darrell Roodt. Los Angeles: Miramax Films, 1995.

Fahrenheit 9/11. Directed by Michael Moore. Los Angeles: Miramax Films, 2004.

Farewell My Concubine. Directed by Kaige Chen. Beijing: Beijing Film Studio, 1993.
Invictus. Directed by Clint Eastwood. Los Angeles: Warner Brothers, 2009.
No. Directed by Pablo Larraín. Paris: Funny Balloons, 2012.
No Man's Land. Directed by Danis Tanović. Paris: Noé Productions, 2001.
Of Gods and Men. Directed by Xavier Beauvois. Paris: France 3 Cinéma, 2010.
The Official Story. Directed by Luis Puenzo. Buenos Aires: Historias Cinematograficas Cinemania, 1985.
Pretty Village, Pretty Flame. Directed by Srđjan Dragojević. Belgrade: Cobra Films, 1996.
Three Seasons. Directed by Tony Bui. Hanoi: Giai Phong Film Studio, 1999.
Vukovar, jedna priča (Vukovar). Directed by Boro Drašković. Zagreb: Iskra, 1994.
Wag the Dog. Directed by Barry Levinson. Los Angeles: New Line Cinema, 1997.

Music

Adams, John, Mark Grey, and Lorin Maazel. *On the Transmigration of Souls*. New York: Nonesuch Records, 2004.
Del Tredici, David, and Marc Peloquin. "Missing Towers." *Gotham Glory Complete Piano Works 1*. Hong Kong: Naxos, 2012.
Penderecki, Krzysztof. *Concerto per Pianoforte ed Orchestra, "Resurrection."* Mainz: Schott, 2007.
Reich, Steve, et al. *WTC 9/11 Mallet Quartet; Dance Patterns*. New York: Nonesuch Records, 2011, 2004.

Fiction

Ali, Monica. *Brick Lane: A Novel*. New York: Scribner, 2003.
DeLillo, Don. *Falling Man: A Novel*. New York: Scribner, 2007.
Hirvonen, Elina. *When I Forgot*. Translated by Douglas Robinson. Portland, OR: Tin House Books, 2009.
McEwan, Ian. *Saturday*. New York: Nan A. Talese/Doubleday, 2005.
Messud, Claire. *The Emperor's Children*. New York: Knopf, 2006.
O'Neill, Joseph. *Netherland*. New York: Pantheon Books, 2008.
Pamuk, Orhan. *Snow*. Translated by Maureen Freely. New York: Knopf, 2004.
Saramago, José. *Blindness*. Translated by Giovanni Pontiero. New York: Harcourt, 1998.
Yehoshua, Abraham B. *The Liberated Bride*. Translated by Hillel Halkin. Orlando: Harcourt, 2003.

Secondary Sources

Akonor, Kwame. *Africa and IMF Conditionality: The Unevenness of Compliance, 1983–2000*. New York: Routledge, 2006.
Anderson, Jeffrey J. *German Unification and the Union of Europe: The Domestic Politics of Integration Policy*. Cambridge: Cambridge University Press, 1999.

Baehr, Peter. R., and Leon Gordenker. *The United Nations in the 1990s*. New York: St. Martin's, 1992.

Bajpai, Kanti P., and Stephen P. Cohen. *South Asia After the Cold War: International Perspectives*. Boulder, CO: Westview, 1993.

Baldwin, Richard E., and Charles Wyplosz. *The Economics of European Integration*. London: McGraw-Hill Higher Education, 2009.

Beasley, Thomas W. *Poverty in Africa*. New York: Nova Science, 2009.

Brautigam, Deborah. *The Dragon's Gift: The Real Story of China in Africa*. Oxford: Oxford University Press, 2009.

Calleo, David P. *Follies of Power: America's Unipolar Fantasy*. Cambridge: Cambridge University Press, 2009.

Chow, Gregory C. *China's Economic Transformation*. Malden, MA: Blackwell, 2007.

Cohen, Stephen F. *Failed Crusade: America and the Tragedy of Post-Communist Russia*. New York: Norton, 2000.

Cohen, Warren I. *America's Failing Empire: US Foreign Relations Since the Cold War*. Malden, MA: Blackwell, 2005.

Coicaud, Jean-Marc. *Beyond the National Interest: The Future of UN Peacekeeping and Multilateralism in an Era of U.S. Primacy*. Washington, DC: United States Institute of Peace Press, 2007.

Crandall, Russell. *The United States and Latin America After the Cold War*. Cambridge: Cambridge University Press, 2008.

Davidson, Basil. *The Black Man's Burden: Africa and the Curse of the Nation-State*. New York: Times Books, 1992.

Dedring, Juergen. *The United Nations Security Council in the 1990s: Resurgence and Renewal*. Albany: State University of New York Press, 2008.

Enderlin, Charles. *Shattered Dreams: The Failure of the Peace Process in the Middle East, 1995–2002*. New York: Other Press, 2003.

Fewsmith, Joseph. *China Since Tiananmen: The Politics of Transition*. Cambridge: Cambridge University Press, 2001.

Fromkin, David. *Kosovo Crossing: American Ideals Meet Reality on the Balkan Battlefields*. New York: Free Press, 1999.

Ganguly, Sumit, and S. Paul Kapur. *India, Pakistan, and the Bomb: Debating Nuclear Stability in South Asia*. New York: Columbia University Press, 2010.

Gibbs, David N. *First Do No Harm: Humanitarian Intervention and the Destruction of Yugoslavia*. Nashville: Vanderbilt University Press, 2009.

Golan, Galia. *Israel and Palestine: Peace Plans and Proposals from Oslo to Disengagement*. Princeton, NJ: Markus Wiener, 2007.

Guelke, Adrian. *Rethinking the Rise and Fall of Apartheid: South Africa and World Politics*. Basingstoke, UK: Palgrave Macmillan, 2005.

Haacke, Jürgen. *ASEAN's Diplomatic and Security Culture: Origins, Development and Prospects*. London: Routledge Curzon, 2003.

Hallams, Ellen, *The United States and NATO Since 9/11: The Transatlantic Alliance Renewed*. New York: Routledge, 2010.

Jones, Seth. *In the Graveyard of Empires: America's War in Afghanistan*. New York: Norton, 2010.

Judah, Tim. *The Serbs: History, Myth, and the Destruction of Yugoslavia*. New Haven, CT: Yale University Press, 1997.

Kang, David C. *China Rising: Peace, Power, and Order in East Asia*. New York: Columbia University Press, 2007.

Khalidi, Rashid. *Resurrecting Empire: Western Footprints and America's Perilous Path in the Middle East*. Boston: Beacon, 2004.

Makovsky, David. *Making Peace with the PLO: The Rabin Government's Road to the Oslo Accord*. Boulder, CO: Westview, 1996.

Mamdani, Mahmood. *Good Muslim, Bad Muslim: America, the Cold War, and the Roots of Terror*. New York: Pantheon Books, 2004.

Marsh, David. *The Bundesbank: The Bank That Rules Europe*. London: Heinemann, 1992.

Moir, Lindsay. *Reappraising the Resort to Force: International Law, Jus ad Bellum and the War on Terror*. Oxford: Hart, 2010.

Pfister, Roger. *Apartheid South Africa and African States: From Pariah to Middle Power, 1961–1994*. London: Tauris Academic Studies, 2005.

Quandt, William B. *Peace Process: American Diplomacy and the Arab-Israeli Conflict Since 1967*. Washington, DC: Brookings Institution, 1993.

Ross, Dennis. *The Missing Peace: The Inside Story of the Fight for Middle East Peace*. New York: Farrar, Straus, Giroux, 2004.

Rutherford, Ken. *Humanitarianism Under Fire: The US and UN Intervention in Somalia*. Sterling, VA: Kumarian, 2008.

Schrecker, Ellen, ed. *Cold War Triumphalism: The Misuse of History After the Fall of Communism*. New York: New Press, 2004.

Sheehan, James J. *Where Have All the Soldiers Gone? The Transformation of Modern Europe*. Boston: Houghton Mifflin, 2008.

Shubin, Vladimir G. *ANC: A View from Moscow*. Bellville, South Africa: Mayibuye, 1999.

Snow, Donald M. *The Shape of the Future: World Politics in a New Century*. Armonk, NY: M. E. Sharpe, 1999.

Soler Torrijos, Giancarlo. *In the Shadow of the United States: Democracy and Regional Order in the Latin Caribbean*. Boca Raton: Brown Walker, 2008.

Stalker, Peter. *Workers Without Frontiers: The Impact of Globalization on International Migration*. Boulder, CO: Lynne Rienner, 2000.

Stevenson, Jonathan. *Thinking Beyond the Unthinkable: Harnessing Doom from the Cold War to the War on Terror*. New York: Viking, 2008.

Walker, William. *Weapons of Mass Destruction and International Order*. Oxford: Oxford University Press, 2004.

CONCLUSION

What's the point of being the greatest, most powerful nation in the world and not having an imperial role? It's unheard of in human history.

—Irving Kristol

Since the end of the Cold War, hegemonism has become increasingly unpopular.

—Li Peng

Each success only buys an admission ticket to a more difficult problem.

—Henry Kissinger

Peace is not the absence of war; it is a virtue; a state of mind; a disposition for benevolence, confidence, and justice.

—Baruch Spinoza (1632–1677)

There is, curiously, a certain amount of nostalgia for the Cold War. Among those who lived its history, the US-Soviet struggle ostensibly created a sense of order—imposed, to be sure, by the Superpowers' huge stockpile of nuclear weapons, which, however, neither side ever intended to use for a first strike. Moreover, although they were avowed enemies, the United States and the Soviet Union maintained normal diplomatic relations, traded with each other, concluded agreements, and maintained control over their alliances.

There were other seeming advantages to the bipolar world between 1945 and 1991. The flourishing US and Soviet military-industrial complexes provided jobs as well as technological spinoffs; the two nations' space programs were spiritually uplifting, and their intense cultural, scientific, and sports competitions provided a bracing stimulus for each side's institutions. Each Superpower aimed (with, to be sure, greater achievements in the capitalist than in the communist world) to bring the good life to its people, to strengthen its allies economically, and to aid the underdeveloped and undeveloped world.

That said, the negative aspects of the Cold War were more significant. These included the incessant espionage and propaganda against the enemy and the curtailment of domestic freedoms (which were far greater in the communist than in the capitalist realm), the mountain of domestic debt accumulated, as well as the high-handedness toward allies and the manipulation of Third World countries and the catering to dictators. The Superpowers weakened the United Nations, ignored their environmental depredations, failed to take human rights seriously, and ultimately contributed to global poverty. Their Cold War rivalry distorted the process of decolonization and stirred (or failed to stop) almost constant internal and external warfare—in Asia, Africa, and the Western Hemisphere—which produced some tens of millions of casualties and enduring material losses.

There was also the damaging political dimension. In creating a zero-sum game, Washington and Moscow precluded a resolution of the Cold War short of the other's total defeat: the collapse of either communism or liberal democracy. This totalizing goal gave the advantages to each side's hawks over its doves, and tempted leaders to exaggerate the other's threats, exploit the other's weakness, and take risks to gain advantage. Despite periods of coexistence, every agreement was deemed temporary because it inherently fell short of the ultimate goal.

Some Cold War habits survived the end of the Cold War, among them America's tendency to view the world in messianic and Manichean terms and to prefer unilateral solutions over multinational diplomacy. Moreover, the loss of its longtime Cold War enemy may have left some US leaders overconfident in victory and inclined to view America's alleged triumph in universal terms, as validating its singular (and unreproducible) model of national success. Thus, the attack on the US mainland on 9/11 developed into a war on terror not simply to apprehend the culprits but also to defend and expand the American way of life to Central Asia and the Middle East.

Other players have also retained their Cold War perspectives. Russia and China have been consistent opponents of US global dominance. Both have used their UN vetoes to oppose America's interference in the internal affairs of other states, and both are wary of US military alliances and armament buildups in Europe and Asia. On the other hand, neither has shrunk from using force within its borders to prevent separatism or withheld arms and aid to regimes condemned by the international community. Moreover, the Gorbachev legacy still hangs heavy in both countries, with some Russian politicians continuing to lament the loss of empire and their Chinese counterparts citing the policies of the last Soviet leader as a cautionary tale of political disintegration.

A definitive Cold War history has yet to be written. A comprehensive study may require further years of research and reflection and will undoubtedly reflect the ideas and developments of the unfolding twenty-first century. Future historians will need to ponder the Cold War's human and environmental costs, how non-Soviet and non-US actors influenced the Superpower conflict, and how the militarization of large parts of the world affected the daily lives of ordinary people. In retrospect, there may be a broadening list of winners (China and Germany) and losers (much of Africa and parts of Central and South America). And if a more dynamic capitalism overwhelmed a failed communism in 1991, future scholars will need to grapple with the long-term impact of the economic globalization, the imperial aspirations, and the blowback by opposing groups that have followed.

INDIVIDUALS

Note: The offices listed are only those relevant to the individual's role in the Cold War and international affairs.

Acheson, Dean (1893–1971). United States. Secretary of state, 1949–1953.

Adenauer, Konrad (1876–1967). West Germany. Chancellor, 1949–1963.

Albright, Madeleine (1937–). United States. Secretary of state, 1997–2001; US ambassador to the UN, 1993–1997.

Allende, Salvador (1908–1973). Chile. President, 1970–1973.

Amin, Hafizullah (1929–1979). Afghanistan. President, 1979.

Andropov, Yuri (1914–1984). USSR. General secretary of the Communist Party, 1982–1984; head of the KGB, 1967–1982; USSR ambassador to Hungary, 1954–1957.

Arafat, Yasser (1929–2004). Palestinian Authority. President, 1996–2004; chairman of the Palestine Liberation Organization, 1969–1996.

Árbenz Guzmán, Jacobo (1913–1971). Guatemala. President, 1951–1954.

al-Assad, Hafez (1930–2000). Syria. President, 1971–2000; prime minister, 1970–1971; defense minister, 1966–1970.

Attlee, Clement (1883–1967). United Kingdom. Prime minister, 1945–1951.

Bahr, Egon (1922–). West Germany. Minister for economic cooperation, 1974–1976; special ambassador and head of Foreign Ministry Planning, 1966–1972.

Baker, James (1930–). United States. Secretary of state, 1989–1992.

Barak, Ehud (1942–). Israel. Prime minister, 1999–2001; minister of defense, 2007–; chief of General Staff of the Defense Forces, 1991–1995.

Begin, Menachem (1913–1992). Israel. Prime minister, 1977–1983.

Ben Gurion, David (1886–1973). Israel. Prime minister, 1948–1953, 1955–1963.

Beneš, Eduard (1884–1948). Czechoslovakia. President, 1935–1938, 1945–1948; president in exile, 1940–1945; minister of foreign affairs, 1918–1935.

Bevin, Ernest (1881–1951). United Kingdom. Foreign secretary, 1945–1951.

bin Laden, Osama (1957–2011). Born in Saudi Arabia. Al Qaeda founder and leader, 1990s–2011.

Botha, Pieter Willem (1916–2006). South Africa. Prime minister, 1978–1984.

Bourguiba, Habib (1903–2000). Tunisia. President, 1957–1987.

Brandt, Willy (1913–1992). West Germany. Chancellor, 1969–1974; mayor of West Berlin, 1957–1966.

Brezhnev, Leonid (1906–1982). USSR. General secretary of the Communist Party, 1964–1982.

Brzezinski, Zbigniew (1928–). United States. National security adviser, 1977–1981.

Bush, George Herbert Walker (1924–). United States. President, 1989–1993; vice president, 1981–1989; director of Central Intelligence Agency, 1976–1977; chief US liaison officer, People's Republic of China, 1974–1976; US ambassador to the United Nations, 1971–1973.

Bush, George W. (1946–). United States. President, 2001–2009.

Byrnes, James (1882–1972). United States. Secretary of state, 1945–1947.

Carter, Jimmy (James Earl; 1924–). United States. President, 1977–1981.

Castro, Fidel (1926–). Cuba. Prime minister, 1959–1976; president, 1976–2008.

Ceauşescu, Nicolae (1918–1989). Romania. President, 1967–1989.

Chamberlain, Neville (1869–1940). United Kingdom. Prime minister, 1937–1940.

Chernenko, Konstantin (1911–1985). USSR. General secretary of the Communist Party, 1984–1985.

Chernyaev, Anatoly (1921–). USSR. Chief foreign policy adviser, 1986–1991

Chiang Kai-shek (1887–1975). China. President of the Republic of China, 1948–1949, 1950–1975; director-general of the Kuomintang, 1938–1975; chairman of the National government of China, 1928–1931, 1943–1948; chairman of the National Military Council, 1931–1946; premier of the Republic of China, 1930–1931, 1935–1938, 1939–1945, 1947.

Churchill, Winston (1874–1965). United Kingdom. Prime minister, 1940–1945, 1951–1955.

Clinton, Bill (William Jefferson; 1946–). United States. President, 1993–2001.

Daoud Kahn, Mohammad (1909–1978). Afghanistan. President, 1973–1978.

de Klerk, Frederik Willem (1936–). South Africa. President, 1989–1994.

Deng Xiaoping (1904–1997). China. Vice premier, 1975–1983; paramount leader (various titles), 1978–1992.

Diệm, Ngô Đình (1901–1963). South Vietnam. President, 1955–1963.

Dubček, Alexander (1921–1992). Czechoslovakia. General secretary of the Communist Party, 1968–1969.

Dulles, John Foster (1888–1959). United States. Secretary of state, 1953–1959.

Eden, Anthony (1897–1977). United Kingdom. Prime minister, 1955–1957; foreign minister, 1935–1938, 1940–1945, 1951–1955.

Eisenhower, Dwight David (1890–1969). United States. President, 1953–1961; supreme commander of NATO Forces, 1951–1952; supreme commander of the Allied Expeditionary Force, 1943–1945.

Eshkol, Levi (1895–1969). Israel. Prime minister, 1963–1969.

Ford, Gerald (1913–2006). United States. President, 1974–1977; vice president, 1973–1974.

Gandhi, Indira (1917–1984). India. Prime minister, 1966–1977; 1980–1984.

Gaulle, Charles de (1890–1970). France. President, 1959–1969; prime minister, 1958–1959; president of the provisional government, 1944–1946.

Gomułka, Władysław (1905–1982). Poland. Secretary of the Communist Party, 1956–1970.

Gorbachev, Mikhail (1931–). USSR. President, 1990–1991; general secretary of the Communist Party, 1985–1991.

Gromyko, Andrei (1909–1989). USSR. Foreign minister, 1957–1985.

Guevara, Che (1928–1967). Born in Argentina, assassinated in Bolivia. Marxist revolutionary, 1956–1965.

Haig, Alexander (1924–2010). United States. Secretary of state, 1981–1982.

Hammarskjöld, Dag (1905–1961). Sweden. UN secretary general, 1953–1961.

Havel, Václav (1936–2011). Czechoslovakia and Czech Republic. President, 1989–2003.

Hitler, Adolf (1889–1945). Germany. Chancellor, 1933–1945; führer, 1934–1945.

Ho Chi Minh (1890–1969). Vietnam. President of the Democratic Republic of Vietnam, 1945–1969; founder, Indochina Communist Party (later known as Viet-Minh), 1930.

Holbrooke, Richard (1941–2010). United States. Assistant secretary of state for European and Canadian Affairs, 1994–1995.

Honecker, Erich (1912–1994). East Germany. Secretary of the Socialist Unity Party of East Germany, 1971–1989; chairman of the Council of State, 1976–1989.

Hopkins, Harry (1890–1946). United States. Secretary of commerce, 1938–1940; presidential adviser and diplomat, 1940–1945.

Husák, Gustáv (1913–1991). Czechoslovakia. General secretary of the Czechoslovak Communist Party, 1969–1989; president, 1975–1989.

Hussein I of Jordan (1935–1999). Jordan. King, 1952–1999.

Hussein, Saddam (1937–2006). Iraq. President, 1979–2003.

Jaruzelski, Wojciech (1923–). Poland. President, 1989–1990; prime minister, 1981–1985; first secretary of the Polish United Workers' Party, 1981–1989.

Jiāng Zémín (1926–). China. General secretary of the Communist Party of China, 1989–2002; president, 1993–2003.

Johnson, Lyndon B. (1908–1973). United States. President, 1963–1969; vice president, 1961–1963.

Karadžić, Radovan (1945–). Yugoslavia and Bosnia. President of the Bosnian Serbian Democratic Party, 1990–1995; head of state of the Serbian Republic, 1992–1995; imprisoned by UN Tribunal on War Crimes, 2008–.

Karmal, Babrak (1929–1996). Afghanistan. President, 1979–1986.

Karzai, Hamid (1957–). Afghanistan. President of the Islamic Republic of Afghanistan, 2004–; president of the Afghan transitional administration, 2002–2004.

Kennan, George (1904–2005). United States. Ambassador to Yugoslavia, 1961–1963; ambassador to USSR, 1952–1953; State Department counselor, 1949–1951; director of policy planning, 1947–1949; author of "Mr. X" article detailing containment policy in *Foreign Affairs*, 1947; minister-counselor to the USSR, 1944–1946; second secretary, US embassy, Moscow, 1933–1935.

Kennedy, John Fitzgerald (1917–1963). United States. President, 1961–1963.

Keynes, John Maynard (1883–1946). United Kingdom. Economist; leader of the British delegation to the Bretton Woods Conference and chairman of the Commission on the World Bank, 1944; Treasury representative at the Paris Peace Conference, 1919.

Khomeini, Ruhollah (1902–1989). Iran. Supreme leader of Iran, 1979–1989; ayatollah, 1950s–1989.

Khrushchev, Nikita (1894–1971). USSR. Premier of the Soviet Union, 1958–1964; first secretary of the Communist Party, 1953–1964.

Kiesinger, Kurt-Georg (1904–1988). West Germany. Chancellor, 1966–1969.

Kim Il Sung (1912–1994). North Korea. Chief of state, 1948–1994.

Kim Jong Il (1941–2011). North Korea. Premier or "dear leader," 1994–2011.

Kissinger, Henry (1923–). United States. Secretary of state, 1973–1977; national security adviser, 1969–1975.

Kohl, Helmut (1930–). Germany. Chancellor of Germany, 1990–1998; chancellor of West Germany, 1982–1990.

Kosygin, Aleksei (1904–1980). USSR. Premier, 1964–1980.

Krenz, Egon (1937–). East Germany. Head of state, 1989.

Litvinov, Maxim (1876–1951). USSR. People's commissar of foreign affairs, 1930–1939; vice commissar of foreign affairs, 1920–1930.

Lloyd George, David (1863–1945). United Kingdom. Prime minister, 1916–1922.

Lumumba, Patrice (1925–1961). Congo. Prime minister of the Democratic Republic of the Congo, 1960; cofounder, Congolese National Movement, 1958.

MacArthur, Douglas (1880–1964). United States. Commander of UN Forces in Korea, 1950–1951; allied commander of the Japanese occupation, 1945–1951; commander of US Army Forces in the Pacific, 1945; commander of Allied Forces in the Southwest Pacific theater, 1942–1945.

Macmillan, Harold (1894–1986). United Kingdom. Prime minister, 1957–1963.

Mandela, Nelson (1918–). South Africa. President, 1994–1999; one of the founders of Umkhonto we Sizwe (Spear of the Nation), the military wing of the African National Congress, 1960; imprisoned for treason, 1964–1990.

Mao Zedong (1893–1976). China. Chairman of the Communist Party of China, 1943–1976; president of the People's Republic of China, 1954–1958.

Marshall, George (1880–1959). United States. Secretary of defense, 1950–1951; secretary of state, 1947–1949; chief of staff of the army, 1939–1945.

McNamara, Robert (1916–2009). United States. Secretary of defense, 1961–1968.

Meir, Golda (1898–1978). Israel. Prime minister, 1969–1974; foreign minister, 1956–1966.

Mikołajczyk, Stanisław (1901–1966). Poland. Prime minister in exile, 1943–1944.

Milošević, Slobodan (1941–2006). Yugoslavia and Serbia. President, 1989–1997; president of the Federal Republic of Yugoslavia, 1997–2000; arrested by the UN International Criminal Tribunal for the Former Yugoslavia, 2001.

Mitterrand, François (1916–1996). France. President, 1981–1995.

Mladić, Ratko (1943–). Yugoslavia and Bosnia. General of the Bosnian Serb army, 1992–1996; indicted by the UN International Criminal Tribunal for the Former Yugoslavia, 1995; arrested, 2011.

Mollet, Guy (1905–1975). France. Prime minister, 1956–1957.

Molotov, Vyacheslav (1890–1986). USSR. Foreign minister, 1939–1949, 1953–1956.

Mossadeq, Mohammad (1882–1967). Iran. Prime minister, 1951–1953.

Mussolini, Benito (1883–1945). Italy. Prime minister, 1922–1943; leader of Fascist Party, 1919–1943.

Nagy, Imre (1896–1958). Hungary. Prime minister, 1953–1955, 1956.

Nasser, Gamal Abdel (1918–1970). Egypt. President, 1956–1970; prime minister, 1954–1956.

Nehru, Jawaharal (1889–1964). India. Prime minister, 1947–1964.

Netanyahu, Benjamin (1949–). Israel. Prime minister, 1996–1999, 2009–; foreign minister, 2002–2003; deputy foreign minister, 1988–1991.

Nixon, Richard (1913–1994). United States. President, 1969–1974; vice president, 1953–1961.

Nkrumah, Kwame (1909–1972). Ghana. President, 1960–1966; prime minister, 1957–1960.

Novotný, Antonín (1904–1975). Czechoslovakia. President, 1957–1968; general secretary of the Communist Party, 1953–1968.

Pahlavi, Mohammad Reza, Shah (1919–1980). Iran. Shah, 1941–1979.

Peres, Shimon (1923–). Israel. President, 2007–; prime minister, 1977, 1984–1986, 1995–1996; vice prime minister, 2005; foreign minister, 1992–1995, 2001–2002.

Pol Pot (1928–1998). Cambodia. Dictator of Democratic Kampuchea, 1975–1979; general secretary of the Communist Party of Kampuchea, 1963–1979.

Pompidou, Georges (1911–1974). France. President, 1969–1974; premier, 1962–1968.

Putin, Vladimir (1952–). Russia/USSR. President, 2004–2008, 2012–; prime minister, 1999–2000, 2008–2012; KGB officer, 1975–1991.

Rabin, Yitzhak (1922–1995). Israel. Prime minister, 1974–1977, 1992–1995; defense minister, 1984–1990.

Reagan, Ronald (1911–2004). United States. President, 1981–1989.

Rhee, Syngman (1875–1965). South Korea. President, 1948–1960.

Roosevelt, Eleanor (1884–1962). United States. Chair of the UN Commission on Human Rights, 1946–1951; first lady, 1933–1945.

Roosevelt, Franklin Delano (1882–1945). United States. President, 1933–1945.

Sadat, Anwar (1918–1981). Egypt. President, 1970–1981; vice president, 1964–1966, 1969–1970.

Schmidt, Helmut (1918–). West Germany. Chancellor, 1974–1982.

Shevardnadze, Eduard (1928–). USSR and Georgia. Foreign minister of the USSR, 1985–1990, 1991; head of state of Georgia, 1992–2003.

Shultz, George (1920–). United States. Secretary of state, 1982–1989.

Sihanouk, Norodom (1922–2012). Cambodia. King, 1941–1955, 1993–2004; prime minister, 1945, 1950, 1952–1957.

Stalin, Joseph (1878–1953). USSR. General secretary of the Communist Party, 1922–1953.

Sukarno, Achmed (1901–1970). Indonesia. President, 1945–1967.

Taraki, Nur Muhammad (1917–1979). Afghanistan. President, 1978–1979.

Thant, U. (1909–1974). Burma. UN secretary general, 1961–1972.

Thatcher, Margaret (1925–). United Kingdom. Prime minister, 1979–1990.

Thiệu, Nguyễn Văn (1923–2001). South Vietnam. President, 1967–1975.

Tito, Josip Broz (1892–1980). Yugoslavia. President, 1953–1980; secretary general of Communist Party, 1939–1980; supreme commander of Yugoslav partisans, 1941–1945.

Trotsky, Leon (1879–1940). USSR. Commissar of foreign affairs and war, 1917–1924; anti-Stalinist opposition leader, 1926–1940.

Truman, Harry (1884–1972). United States. President, 1945–1953; vice president, 1945.

Ulbricht, Walter (1893–1973). East Germany. Chairman of the State Council of the GDR, 1960–1973; general secretary of the Socialist Unity Party, 1950–1971.

Vance, Cyrus (1917–2002). United States. Secretary of state, 1977–1980.

Wałęsa, Lech (1943–). Poland. President, 1990–1995; Solidarity union leader, 1980–2006.

Wilson, Woodrow (1856–1924). United States. President, 1913–1921.

Wojtyła, Karol Józef (Pope John Paul II) (1902–2005). Poland and Vatican City. Pope, 1978–2005.

Yeltsin, Boris (1931–2007). USSR and Russia. President of Russia, 1991–1999.

Zhdanov, A. A. (1896–1948). USSR. Communist Party official, 1917–1948; founder of Cominform, 1947.

Zhivkov, Todor (1911–1998). Bulgaria. President, 1971–1989; general secretary of the Communist Party, 1954–1989.

Zhōu Ēnlái (1898–1976). China. Premier and leading figure in the Chinese Communist Party, 1949–1976; foreign minister, 1949–1958.

BIBLIOGRAPHY

DOCUMENTARY ONLINE SOURCES

American Presidency Project. http://www.presidency.ucsb.edu/ws/.

"CIA Historical Collection Publications." Central Intelligence Agency. https://www
.cia.gov/library/publications/historical-collection-publications/index.html.

Cold War International History Project Digital Archive. http://wilsoncenter.org
/digital-archive.

"Declassified National Intelligence Estimates on the Soviet Union and International
Communism." Central Intelligence Agency. http://www.foia.cia.gov/collection
/declassified-national-intelligence-estimates-soviet-union-and-international
-communism.

EuroDocs: Online Sources for European History. http://eudocs.lib.byu.edu/index
.php/Main_Page.

Foreign Relations of the United States. http://history.state.gov/historicaldocuments.

German History in Documents and Images. http://germanhistorydocs.ghi-dc.org/.

German Propaganda Archive. http://www.calvin.edu/academic/cas/gpa/.

Great Britain. Foreign Office Records. National Archives. http://discovery.national
archives.gov.uk/SearchUI/Home/OnlineCollections.

Internet Modern History Sourcebook. http://www.fordham.edu/Halsall/mod/mods
book.asp.

National Security Archives. http://www.gwu.edu/~nsarchiv/.

"Presidential Oral History." University of Virginia Miller Center of Public Affairs.
http://millercenter.org/oralhistory/index.

"Revelations from the Russian Archives." Library of Congress. http://www.loc.gov
/exhibits/archives/.

United Nations Yearbook, 1946–. http://unyearbook.un.org/.

University of Minnesota Human Rights Library. http://www1.umn.edu/humanrts/.

Wilson Center Digital Archive. http://wilsoncenter.org/digital-archive.

Yale Law School Avalon Project: Documents in Law, History and Diplomacy. http://
avalon.law.yale.edu/.

OTHER WEBSITES

Cold War History Research Center. Corvinus, University of Budapest. http://www
.coldwar.hu/.

Dean Peter Krogh Foreign Affairs Digital Archives. Georgetown University Library.
http://www.library.georgetown.edu/krogh.

"National Cold War Exhibition." Royal Air Force Museum. 2012. http://www.national
coldwarexhibition.org/index.cfm.

Open Society Archive. Central European University, Budapest. http://www.osa
archivum.org/.

Parallel History Project on Cooperative Security. http://www.php.isn.ethz.ch/index
.cfm.

"Presidential Libraries." National Archives. http://www.archives.gov/presidential
-libraries/.

MEMOIRS

Garthoff, Raymond L. *A Journey Through the Cold War: A Memoir of Containment
and Coexistence*. Washington, DC: Brookings Institution Press, 2001.

Kennan, George F. *Memoirs*. 2 vols. Boston: Little, Brown, 1967–1972.

Sagdeev, Roald Z. *The Making of a Soviet Scientist: My Adventures in Nuclear Fusion
and Space from Stalin to Star Wars*. New York: Wiley, 1994.

FILMS

Cold War. 24-part TV series. Produced by Jeremy Isaacs. New York: CNN, 1998.

"March of Time." Newsreel series, 1937–1967. HBO Archives. https://www.hbo
archives.com/apps/searchlibrary/ctl/marchoftime.

Race for the Super Bomb. Directed by Thomas Ott. *PBS: The American Experience*.
Chicago: WGBH, 1999.

Red Files: Secrets of the Russian Archives Revealed. PBS/Abamedia, 1999.

The Wall: A World Divided. Directed by Eric Stange. PBS/Spy Pond Productions,
2010.

Walter Cronkite Remembers: The Cold War: Challenge and Crisis. Directed by Dale
Minor. New York: CBS Productions, 1997.

GENERAL HISTORIES

Barrass, Gordon S. *The Great Cold War: A Journey Through the Hall of Mirrors*. Stanford, CA: Stanford Security Studies/Stanford University Press, 2009.

Dunbabin, J. P. D. *The Cold War: The Great Powers and Their Allies*. 2nd ed. Harlow,
UK: Pearson Education, 2008.

Gaddis, John Lewis. *The Cold War: A New History*. New York: Penguin, 2005.

———. *We Now Know: Rethinking Cold War History.* Oxford: Clarendon, 1997.

Hanhimaki, Jussi M., and Odd Arne Westad. *The Cold War: A History in Documents and Eyewitness Accounts.* Oxford: Oxford University Press, 2003.

Harper, John Lamberton. *The Cold War.* Oxford: Oxford University Press, 2011.

Judge, Edward H., and John W. Langdon. *A Hard and Bitter Peace: A Global History of the Cold War.* Upper Saddle River, NJ: Prentice Hall, 1996.

LaFeber, Walter. *America, Russia, and the Cold War, 1945–1966.* New York: Wiley, 1967.

Leffler, Melvyn P., and Odd Arne Westad. *The Cambridge History of the Cold War.* 3 vols. Cambridge: Cambridge University Press, 2010.

Levering, Ralph B. *The Cold War: A Post–Cold War History.* 2nd ed. Arlington Heights, IL: Harlan Davidson, 2005.

Lightbody, Bradley. *The Cold War.* London: Routledge, 1999.

McCauley, Martin. *Russia, America, and the Cold War, 1949–1991.* London: Pearson/Longman, 2004.

McMahon, Robert J. *The Cold War: A Very Short Introduction.* Oxford: Oxford University Press, 2003.

Painter, David S. *The Cold War: An International History.* London: Routledge, 2002.

Smith, Joseph. *The Cold War.* 2nd ed. Oxford: Blackwell, 1998.

Ulam, Adam Bruno. *Understanding the Cold War: A Historian's Personal Reflections.* New Brunswick, NJ: Transaction, 2001.

Walker, Martin. *The Cold War: A History.* New York: Holt, 1994.

SPECIALIZED HISTORIES

Adomeit, Hannes. *Imperial Overstretch: Germany in Soviet Policy from Stalin to Gorbachev: An Analysis Based on New Archival Evidence, Memoirs, and Interviews.* Baden-Baden: Nomos Verlagsgesellschaft, 1998.

Aldrich, Richard J. *The Hidden Hand: Britain, America, and Cold War Secret Intelligence.* London: John Murray, 2001.

Andrew, Christopher M., and Vasili Mitrokhin. *The Sword and the Shield: The Mitrokhin Archive and the Secret History of the KGB.* New York: Basic Books, 1999.

———. *The World Was Going Our Way: The KGB and the Battle for the Third World.* New York: Basic Books, 2005.

Bacevich, Andrew J. *American Empire: The Realities and Consequences of U.S. Diplomacy.* Cambridge, MA: Harvard University Press, 2002.

Belmonte, Laura A. *Selling the American Way: U.S. Propaganda and the Cold War.* Philadelphia: University of Pennsylvania Press, 2008.

Bernhard, Nancy E. *US Television News and Cold War Propaganda, 1947–1960.* New York: Cambridge University Press, 1999.

Black, Jeremy. *War Since 1945.* London: Reaktion, 2004.

Borstelmann, Thomas. *The Cold War and the Color Line: American Race Relations in the Global Arena.* Cambridge, MA: Harvard University Press, 2001.

Brands, H. W. *The Devil We Knew: Americans and the Cold War.* New York: Oxford University Press, 1993.

Buchanan, Tom. *Europe's Troubled Peace, 1945–2000.* Malden, MA: Blackwell, 2006.

Burrows, William E. *By Any Means Necessary: America's Secret Air War in the Cold War.* New York: Farrar, Straus and Giroux, 2001.

Callanan, James. *Covert Action in the Cold War: US Policy, Intelligence, and CIA Operations.* London: I. B. Tauris, 2010.

Carroll, Mark. *Music and Ideology in Cold War Europe.* Cambridge: Cambridge University Press, 2003.

Caute, David. *The Dancer Defects: The Struggle for Cultural Supremacy During the Cold War.* Oxford: Oxford University Press, 2003.

Chilton, Paul A. *Security Metaphors: Cold War Discourse from Containment to Common House.* New York: P. Lang, 1996.

Coll, Steve. *Ghost Wars: The Secret History of the CIA, Afghanistan, and Bin Laden, from the Soviet Invasion to September 10, 2001.* New York: Penguin, 2004.

Craig, Campbell, and Fredrik Logevall. *America's Cold War: The Politics of Insecurity.* Cambridge, MA: Belknap Press of Harvard University Press, 2009.

Cronin, James E. *The World the Cold War Made: Order, Chaos and the Return of History.* New York: Routledge, 1996.

Dobson, Alan P. *US Economic Statecraft for Survival, 1933–1991: Of Sanctions, Embargoes, and Economic Warfare.* New York: Routledge, 2002.

Engel, Jeffrey A. *Cold War at 30,000 Feet: The Anglo-American Fight for Aviation Supremacy.* Cambridge, MA: Harvard University Press, 2007.

Enloe, Cynthia H. *The Morning After: Sexual Politics at the End of the Cold War.* Berkeley: University of California Press, 1993.

Evangelista, Matthew. *Unarmed Forces: The Transnational Movement to End the Cold War.* Ithaca, NY: Cornell University Press, 1999.

Evans, Tony. *US Hegemony and the Project of Universal Human Rights.* Basingstoke, UK: Macmillan, 1996.

Firth, Noel E., and James H. Noren. *Soviet Defense Spending: A History of CIA Estimates, 1950–1990.* College Station: Texas A&M University Press, 1998.

Friedman, Norman. *The Fifty-Year War: Conflict and Strategy in the Cold War.* Annapolis, MD: Naval Institute Press, 2000.

Gaddis, John Lewis. *George F. Kennan: An American Life.* New York: Penguin, 2011.

———. *The Long Peace: Inquiries into the History of the Cold War.* New York: Oxford University Press, 1987.

Gardner, Lloyd C. *Spheres of Influence: The Great Powers Partition Europe, from Munich to Yalta.* Chicago: I. R. Dee, 1993.

Gleason, Abbott. *Totalitarianism: The Inner History of the Cold War.* New York: Oxford University Press, 1995.

Glynn, Patrick. *Closing Pandora's Box: Arms Races, Arms Control, and the History of the Cold War.* New York: Basic Books, 1992.

Graham, Thomas, and Keith A. Hansen. *Spy Satellites: and Other Intelligence Technologies That Changed History.* Seattle: University of Washington Press, 2007.

Grandin, Greg. *The Last Colonial Massacre: Latin America in the Cold War.* Chicago: University of Chicago Press, 2004.

Greenwood, Sean. *Britain and the Cold War, 1945–1991.* New York: St. Martin's, 2000.

Haslam, Jonathan. *Russia's Cold War: From the October Revolution to the Fall of the Wall.* New Haven, CT: Yale University Press, 2011.

Herzog, Jonathan P. *The Spiritual-Industrial Complex: America's Religious Battle Against Communism in the Early Cold War.* New York: Oxford University Press, 2011.

Heymann, Charles. *The Politics of African Diplomacy and Decolonization: The African Experience in Cold War Diplomacy.* Accra, Ghana: Joycum, 2009.

Hinton, Harold C. *The People's Republic of China, 1949–1979: A Documentary Survey.* 5 vols. Wilmington, DE: Scholarly Resources, 1980.

Hoffman, David E. *The Dead Hand: The Untold Story of the Cold War Arms Race and Its Dangerous Legacy.* New York: Doubleday, 2009.

Inglis, Fred. *The Cruel Peace: Everyday Life in the Cold War.* New York: Basic Books, 1991.

Irwin, Ryan M. *Gordian Knot: Apartheid and the Unmaking of the Liberal World Order.* Oxford: Oxford University Press, 2012.

Johnson, David K. *The Lavender Scare: The Cold War Persecution of Gays and Lesbians in the Federal Government.* Chicago: University of Chicago Press, 2004.

Kalic, Sean N. *US Presidents and the Militarization of Space, 1946–1967.* College Station: Texas A&M University Press, 2012.

Kemper, Kurt Edward. *College Football and American Culture in the Cold War Era.* Urbana: University of Illinois Press, 2009.

Larson, Deborah Welch. *Anatomy of Mistrust: U.S.-Soviet Relations During the Cold War.* Ithaca, NY: Cornell University Press, 1997.

Laville, Helen. *Cold War Women: The International Activities of American Women's Organisations.* Manchester, UK: Manchester University Press, 2002.

Lebow, Richard Ned, and Janice Gross Stein. *We All Lost the Cold War.* Princeton, NJ: Princeton University Press, 1994.

Leebaert, Derek. *The Fifty-Year Wound: The True Price of America's Cold War Victory.* Boston: Little, Brown, 2002.

Lees, Lorraine M. *Keeping Tito Afloat: The United States, Yugoslavia, and the Cold War.* University Park: Pennsylvania State University Press, 1997.

Leffler, Melvyn P. *For the Soul of Mankind: The United States, the Soviet Union, and the Cold War.* New York: Hill and Wang, 2007.

Lindgren, David T. *Trust but Verify: Imagery Analysis in the Cold War.* Annapolis, MD: Naval Institute Press, 2000.

Little, Douglas. *American Orientalism: The United States and the Middle East Since 1945.* Chapel Hill: University of North Carolina Press, 2002.

Lucas, Scott. *Freedom's War: The American Crusade Against the Soviet Union.* New York: New York University Press, 1999.

MacQueen, Norrie. *The United Nations, Peace Operations and the Cold War.* New York: Pearson Longman, 2011.

Mandelbaum, Michael. *The Nuclear Question: The United States and Nuclear Weapons, 1946–1976.* Cambridge: Cambridge University Press, 1979.

Marte, Leonard F. *Political Cycles in International Relations: The Cold War and Africa, 1945–1990.* Amsterdam: VU University Press, 1994.

May, Elaine Tyler. *Homeward Bound: American Families in the Cold War Era.* New York: Basic Books, 1988.

McKnight, David. *Espionage and the Roots of the Cold War: The Conspiratorial Heritage.* London: Frank Cass, 2002.

McMahon, Robert J. *The Cold War on the Periphery: The United States, India, and Pakistan.* New York: Columbia University Press, 1994.

Miller, David. *The Cold War: A Military History.* New York: St. Martin's, 1999.

Motyl, Alexander J. *Imperial Ends: The Decay, Collapse, and Revival of Empires.* New York: Columbia University Press, 2001.

Murphy, David E., Sergei A. Kondrashev, and George Bailey. *Battleground Berlin: CIA vs. KGB in the Cold War.* New Haven, CT: Yale University Press, 1997.

Newton, Julie M. *Russia, France, and the Idea of Europe.* Basingstoke, UK: Palgrave Macmillan, 2003.

Oakes, Guy. *The Imaginary War: Civil Defense and American Cold War Culture.* New York: Oxford University Press, 1994.

Odom, William. *The Collapse of the Soviet Military.* New Haven, CT: Yale University Press, 1998.

Paterson, Thomas G. *On Every Front: The Making and Unmaking of the Cold War.* New York: Norton, 1992.

Peebles, Curtis. *Twilight Warriors: Covert Air Operations Against the USSR.* Annapolis, MD: Naval Institute Press, 2005.

Perkins, John H. *Geopolitics and the Green Revolution: Wheat, Genes, and the Cold War.* New York: Oxford University Press, 1997.

Reed, W. Craig. *Red November: Inside the Secret U.S.-Soviet Submarine War.* New York: William Morrow, 2010.

Roads to Space: An Oral History of the Soviet Space Program. Compiled by the Russian Scientific Research Center for Space Documentation. New York: Aviation Week Group, 1995.

Roberts, Geoffrey. *The Soviet Union in World Politics: Coexistence, Revolution, and Cold War, 1945–1991.* New York: Routledge, 1999.

Saunders, Frances Stonor. *The Cultural Cold War: The CIA and the World of Arts and Letters.* New York: New Press, 2000.

Schwoch, James. *Global TV: New Media and the Cold War, 1946–69.* Urbana: University of Illinois Press, 2009.

Sempa, Francis P. *Geopolitics: From the Cold War to the 21st Century.* New Brunswick, NJ: Transaction, 2002.

Shannon, Christopher. *A World Made Safe for Differences: Cold War Intellectuals and the Politics of Identity.* Lanham, MD: Rowman and Littlefield, 2001.

Shaw, Tony. *British Cinema and the Cold War: The State, Propaganda and Consensus.* London: I. B. Tauris, 2001.

Shenfield, Stephen. *The Nuclear Predicament: Explorations in Soviet Ideology*. London: Royal Institute of International Affairs, 1987.

Smyser, W. R. *From Yalta to Berlin: The Cold War Struggle over Germany*. New York: St. Martin's, 1999.

Stone, David. *Wars of the Cold War: Campaigns and Conflicts, 1945–1990*. London: Brassey's, 2003.

Thompson, Nicholas. *The Hawk and the Dove: Paul Nitze, George Kennan, and the History of the Cold War*. New York: Henry Holt, 2009.

Westad, Odd Arne. *The Global Cold War: Third World Interventions and the Making of Our Times*. Cambridge: Cambridge University Press, 2005.

Whitfield, Stephen J. *The Culture of the Cold War*. 2nd ed. Baltimore: Johns Hopkins University Press, 1996.

Wilford, Hugh. *The CIA, the British Left and the Cold War: Calling the Tune?* London: Frank Cass, 2003.

———. *The Mighty Wurlitzer: How the CIA Played America*. Cambridge, MA: Harvard University Press, 2008.

Winkler, David F. *Cold War at Sea: High-Seas Confrontation Between the United States and the Soviet Union*. Annapolis, MD: Naval Institute Press, 2000.

Wolfe, Audra J. *Competing with the Soviets: Science, Technology and the State in Cold War America*. Baltimore: Johns Hopkins University Press, 2013.

Young, John W. *France, the Cold War and the Western Alliance: French Foreign Policy and Postwar Europe*. Leicester: Leicester University Press, 1989.

Zaloga, Steve. *The Kremlin's Nuclear Sword: The Rise and Fall of Russia's Strategic Nuclear Forces, 1945–2000*. Washington, DC: Smithsonian Institution Press, 2002.

Zubok, V. M. *A Failed Empire: The Soviet Union in the Cold War from Stalin to Gorbachev*. Chapel Hill: University of North Carolina Press, 2007.

INDEX

ABM treaty (1972), 152–153, 209

Acheson, Dean, 62, 78

Adenauer, Konrad, 106–107, 109, 113, 137, 154

Afghan United Front, 284

Afghanistan
    Soviet invasion of, 188, 193–197, 195 (map), 197 (photo)
    UN role in, 264
    US aid to anti-Soviet forces in, 196, 204
    US invasion of, 284, 285
    withdrawal of Soviet troops from, 235, 264

Africa
    1970s borders of, 182 (map)
    Angola/Namibia Accords (1998), 268
    human rights issues in southern Africa, 143–144
    post–Cold War conditions in, 267–269
    US-Soviet rivalry in, 181–184, 204, 220–221, 249
    See also names of specific countries

African National Congress (ANC), 220, 221

Agreed Framework (1994), 266, 267

Al Qaeda, 263, 282–285

Albania, 68, 278

Algeria, 96, 101

Allende, Salvador, 167

Allied Control Council, 45, 46, 70

Amin, Hafizullah, 194

Amnesty International, 142, 176

Andropov, Yuri, 194, 205, 208–209, 211, 215–216, 230

Angola
    civil wars in, 181, 183, 267
    South Africa and, 220, 221, 268
    Soviet Union and, 183–235
    UN peacekeeping missions in, 264
    US and, 183

Antiballistic missile (ABM) programs, 151, 152, 157

Anticolonialism, 13, 35, 64, 77, 83, 96, 218

Anti-Comintern Pact (1937), 16

Apartheid, end of, 267–269

APEC (Asia-Pacific Economic Cooperation), 265

Apollo 8, 144

Arab League, 131, 134, 161

Arab states, 64, 104–105
    See also Egypt, Iraq, Jordan, Saudi Arabia, Syria

Arafat, Yasser, 263, 270, 271

Árbenz Guzmán, Jacobo, 95

Argentina, 43, 216–218, 217 (map)

Arkipov, Ivan, 219

Arms race. *See* Nuclear arms race

Aron, Raymond, 99

Asia
    decolonization and civil wars in, 64–68
    human rights issues in, 143–144
    post–Cold War conditions in, 265–266
    Potsdam agreements and, 47–48
    retreat of European imperialism in, 95–96
    US-Soviet rivalry in, 204, 218–220, 249
    World War II and, 30, 54
    See also names of specific countries

Assad, Hafez al-, 131, 166, 188

Association of Southeastern Asian Nations (ASEAN), 219, 265

Aswan Dam, 101

Atlantic Charter, 29–31, 34, 36, 42

Atomic age, 47–48
    See also Nuclear arms race; Nuclear weapons

Attlee, Clement, 45, 54–55, 77–78

Austria, 68, 75

Baghdad Pact, 108

Bahr, Egon, 153, 154

Baker, James, 252, 269

Baltic States, 20, 30, 37, 248
See also Estonia; Latvia; Lithuania
Bandung Conference (1955), 96, 97 (photo),
101, 218
Bangladesh, 163
Barak, Ehud, 271, 272
Basic Agreement (1972), 153, 167, 184
Basic Treaty (1972), 155
Batista, Fulgencio, 112
Bay of Pigs invasion, 112–113
Begin, Menachem, 188–190, 189, 190 (photo),
223–224
Ben Gurion, David, 102, 135
Benelux countries, 21, 106–107
Beneš, Eduard, 38
Berlin, 46, 91, 108, 110, 111–112, 112 (photo),
116, 234
Quadripartite Pact on (1971), 155, 159–168
See also West Berlin
Berlin Airlift (1948–1949), 70–72, 71 (photo)
Berlin Blockade (1948–1949), 70–72
Berlin Crisis, (1948) 70–73, (1958) 107–112,
(1961) 113
Berlin Wall
construction of, 112 (photo), 113
economic effect on West Berlin, 154
effect on Eastern Europe, 138
fall of, 240, 241 (photo), 280
as restraint on Superpowers, 114, 115
as symbol of Cold War, 113, 240
West Germany and, 137
Bevin, Ernest, 58
Bin Laden, Osama, 263, 282–284
Blum, Léon, 44
Bolshevik Revolution, 5–7, 10–12, 235
Bosnia, 276–278
Bosnian War, 276–278
Botha, Pieter Willem, 220
Brandenburg Gate, 112 (photo), 234
Brandt, Willy
assumes responsibility for Nazi war crimes,
247
Basic Treaty and, 155
Berlin Wall and, 113
Gromyko's meeting with, 141
Ostpolitik, 137–138, 153–156
US/Soviet relations and, 150
Bretton Woods Conference (1944), 39–40, 57,
90
Brezhnev, Leonid
in Africa, 183

Arab-Israeli conflict and, 132, 160, 161,
166, 167
arms limitation talks, 151–153
Basic Agreement with US, 153
Brandt's administration and, 153, 154, 155,
156
Carter's sanctions against USSR, 179–181
coup in Afghanistan, 194
defense of socialism, 138
détente and, 149, 174,199–200
Helsinki Accords and, 168–169
human rights, views on, 177, 179
invasion of Czechoslovakia, 139–140
noninterference principles of, 177
SALT II negotiations and, 185–189
Soviet-China relations, 159
Third World strategies, 159
Vietnam War and, 163–164
visit to US, 164–165, 165 (photo)
workers' strikes in Poland and, 199
Brezhnev doctrine, 140, 157, 204, 235–238, 243
Britain
Afghanistan and, 284
Berlin Airlift, 71–72
People's Republic of China and, 77–78
EEC membership, 107, 156, 167
Germany and, 14, 16, 17, 20, 21, 29, 31, 46,
57, 61, 68, 70, 109, 244
Falklands War, 216–218
in Grand Alliance, 27–34
Great Game with Russia, 1–2, 188
Greek Civil War and, 42
Hong Kong and, 77–78, 266
Middle East oil boycott and, 103–4, 134, 167
nuclear arms race, 107, 186
Polish unrest and, 199
Soviet Union and, 5, 14, 18, 19, 22, 29, 30,
32, 38–39, 44, 47, 58, 60, 61, 102
Suez crisis and, 101–104, 103 (map)
Summit Conferences. See Casablanca;
Cairo; Tehran; Yalta; Potsdam; Geneva;
Paris
in UN Security Council, 40
US and, 15, 17, 21–22, 29, 36, 39, 43, 47, 58,
60, 61, 62, 103–105, 113, 183, 199, 216, 218
withdrawal from colonies, 62, 64–65, 65
(map)
withdrawal of forces east of Suez, 136
World War I and, 6, 19
World War II and, 20, 21, 31–32, 33, 56
Brussels Pact (1948), 71–72

Brzezinski, Zbigniew, 178, 185
Budapest, 99 (photo)
Bulgaria, 38, 43, 47, 57, 62, 68
Burma, 95
Bush, George H. W., 236, 250, 252, 269
Bush, George W., 283
Bush (G. W.) doctrine, 284
Byrnes, James, 45, 56, 58, 60, 61

Cairo conferences (1943), 36–37
Cambodia, 158, 163, 205, 218–220, 235, 252, 264
Camp David talks, (1959) 109 (photo), 110, (1978) 189, 269, (2000) 271–272
Caribbean, 215 (map), 215–216
    See also Cuba; Grenada
Carson, Rachel, 262
Carter, Jimmy
    Camp David Accords and, 189
    diplomatic policies in Africa, 183–184
    Egyptian-Israeli peace treaty and, 188–190, 190 (photo)
    human rights policies of, 178–181
    Iran and, 190–191
    peacekeeping visit to North Korea, 266–267
    Soviet invasion of Afghanistan and, 193, 194–196
    strikes in Poland and, 199
    as US president, 178
Carter doctrine, 195–196
Casablanca Conference (1943), 32–33
Cassin, René, 144
Castro, Fidel, 112–113, 125, 184, 272–273
Ceaușescu, Nicolae, 241
Central America, 180, 205, 213–214, 215 (map), 249, 272–273
    See also El Salvador; Guatemala; Nicaragua
Central Intelligence Agency (CIA), 94, 95, 126, 196, 214, 283
Central Powers (World War I), 6–8
Chamberlain, Neville, 17
Chechnya, 263, 283
Chernenko, Konstantin, 205
Chernyaev, Anatoly, 231
Chiang Kai-shek, 37, 48, 64, 76–77, 78
China. *See* Nationalist China; People's Republic of China (PRC)
Churchill, Winston
    Atlantic Charter and 29–31
    at Casablanca Conference, 32–33
    on character of Hitler, 22

electoral defeat of, 45
in Grand Alliance, 27–34
Iron Curtain warning, 58
negotiations with Stalin, 38–39, 40
North African campaign of, 31–32
resistance to Nazi air offensive, 21
relations with Truman, 44–46
at Tehran Conference, 35–38
at Yalta Conference, 41 (photo), 42–43, 44
Clinton, Bill, 281–282
Cominform (Communist Information Bureau), 64, 70
Comintern (Communist International), 10, 15, 17, 34–35
Commission on Human Rights, UN (CHR), 67, 142–144
Committee for State Security (KGB), 94, 194
Common Market. *See* European Economic Community
Commonwealth of Independent States (CIS), 250, 252
Communism
    in Asia and Middle East, 64
    Bolshevik Revolution, 5–7
    collapse of in Eastern Europe, 274, 281
    Gorbachev's attempts to reform, 230
    in Southeast Asia, 164
    USSR control over, 100
    See also Cominform (Communist Information Bureau); Comintern; Lenin, Vladimir; Stalin, Joseph
Communist China. *See* People's Republic of China (PRC)
Communist International (Comintern). *See* Comintern
Communist Parties
    China, 78, 82, 157, 218
    East Germany, 138, 155
    Eastern Europe, 138
    South Africa, 220, 268
    Soviet Union), 2, 111, 116, 136, 140, 152, 160, 167, 194, 211, 226
    Vietnam, 260
    Western Europe, 91
    See also Comintern
Conference on Security and Cooperation in Europe (CSCE), 168–169, 178, 245, 246–247
Congo, 111, 113, 124, 264
Contact Group (Bosnia), 277, 278
Containment, 62, 79
Copenhagen standards (1993), 281

Council for Mutual Economic Assistance
    (Comecon, CMEA), 242
Council of Foreign Ministers (CFM), 46, 48
Cuba, 112–113, 183–184, 252, 260, 272
Cuban missile crisis, 113–115, 125
Cultural Revolution (China), 130, 156, 158
Czechoslovakia
    Charter 77, 177
    Communist coup (1948), 68
    establishment of diplomatic ties with West
        Germany, 155
    expulsion of ethnic Germans, 46
    Munich Agreement and, 17
    Nasser's arms deal with, 101
    Polish unrest and, 199
    Prague Spring reforms in, 139–141
    Soviet Union and, 17–18, 68, 139, 140–141
    US and, 140–141
    "Velvet Divorce" in, 262
    "Velvet Revolution" in, 241
    Warsaw Pact invasion of, 140–141
    withdrawal from Marshall Plan, 68

Daoud Kahn, Mohammad, 193
The Day After (television), 212
Dayton Peace Agreement, 277
D-Day Invasion, 37
De Gaulle, Charles. *See* Gaulle, Charles de
De Klerk, Frederik Willem, 267–268
Decree on Peace (1917), 6
Deng Xiaoping, 207, 218, 239, 253
Depression, global, 15, 16
    See also Great Depression
Détente, 149–150, 159, 169, 174–175, 199–200
Diệm, Ngô Đình, 97, 116, 125
Diện Biên Phu, 95, 96
Dobrynin, Anatoly, 152
Dollar Diplomacy, 273
Domino theory, 150, 169
    China and, 82
    Soviet Union and, 99
    United States and, 81, 97, 126
Dr. Zhivago (Pasternak), 92
Dubček, Alexander, 139, 140, 144
Du Bois, W. E. B., 99
Dulles, John Foster, 96, 97, 99, 243
Dumbarton Oaks Conference (1944), 40

East Germany
    Basic Treaty with West Germany, 155
    establishment of, 74 (map), 74–75
    exodus from, 239–241
    People's Republic of China and, 239, 253
    Polish unrest and, 199
    reunification and, 245–247
    Soviet Union and, 75, 108, 198, 243–244
    West Germany's refusal to recognize, 137,
        154
Eastern Europe
    cultural changes in, 138
    Helsinki Accords and, 169
    Iron Curtain and, 58, 91–93, 107, 115, 137
    Prague Spring and, 139–141
    transition of, 236–243, 251 (map)
    US "building bridges" policy and, 138
    USSR's collapse and, 260
    See also names of specific countries
Eden, Anthony, 35, 101, 102
Egypt
    Aswan Dam, 101
    Arab-Israeli conflict and, 131–134, 133
        (map), 135, 136, 159, 160, 165–168
    division of Palestine and, 64
    Khrushchev's courtship of, 95
    Suez Crisis, 100–105, 103 (map)
Egyptian-Israeli peace treaty (1979), 188–190,
    223
Eisenhower, Dwight David, 83, 91–92, 108, 109
    (photo), 110–111
El Salvador, 180, 206, 214, 252, 272
Elimination of All Forms of Racial Discrimina-
    tion, UN Resolution on (1965), 143
Emergency Committee (Soviet Union), 250, 253
Enigma code transmissions, 30
Environmental movement, 262
Eshkol, Levi, 132, 134–135
Espionage, 30, 94, 108, 110, 126
Estonia, 11, 19, 248
    See also Baltic States
Ethiopia, 16, 181, 184, 205, 235, 267
Euro, as first common currency, 280
Europe
    after Cold War, 274
    borders after World War I, 9 (map)
    division of, 62–64, 68–71, 69 (map)
    Helsinki Accords and, 169
    Iron Curtain and, 58, 91–93, 107, 115, 137
    Islamic militancy in, 263–264
    post–Cold War conditions in, 274
    post–World War II attempts to unify,
        106–107
    postwar growth and stability, 90

Europe *(continued)*
  World War II casualties and devastation
    in, 54
  See also Eastern Europe; *names of specific
    countries*
European Advisory Commission, 35, 46
European Coal and Steel Community (1951),
  106
European Community (EC). *See* European
  Economic Community
European Economic Community (EEC), 106–
  107, 123–124, 167–168, 276, 280–281
European Union (EU), 280–281
Europe-First strategy, 31–32

Falklands War (1982), 216–218, 217 (map)
Farouk (king of Egypt), 100
Federal Republic of Germany (FRG). *See* West
  Germany
Finland, 11, 19–20, 30, 47, 62, 68, 78, 98
Five-Year Plan, 14, 28
Ford, Gerald, 177
Foreign Affairs (magazine), 62
Foreign ministers' conferences, 35, 55, 56–57,
  68
Fourteen Points, 7, 8, 29
France
  Afghanistan and, 244
  Air France hijacking, 263–264
  Algeria and, 96
  division of Europe and, 140–141
  end of rule in Indochina, 95–96
  fall of (1940), 124–125
  Germany and, 8, 14, 15–16, 19, 68, 70, 73,
    244
  nuclear arms race and, 103, 115, 186
  People's Republic of China and, 78
  Polish unrest and, 199
  role in EEC, 106–107
  role in UN, 40
  Soviet Union and, 5, 6, 8, 12–13, 14, 16, 18,
    19, 21–23, 35, 42, 44, 68, 70, 109
  Suez crisis and, 101–104, 103 (map)
  US and, 20, 70, 103, 137, 157, 196, 199,
    284
  withdrawal from NATO command, 137
  in World War II, 19, 21
  Yalta agreements and, 42
Franco, Francisco
  Italy's support of, 16
Free Democratic Party (FDP), 153

French-Soviet Pact (1935), 16
Front for the National Liberation of Angola
  (FNLA), 183

Gandhi, Indira, 97 (photo), 162, 163
Gaulle, Charles de, 103, 109, 137, 140
GDR (German Democratic Republic). *See* East
  Germany
Gemayel, Bashir, 224
General Agreement on Tariffs and Trade
  (GATT), 90
Geneva Accords (1954), 95, 97
Geneva Convention (1949), 280
Geneva summit (1955), 107–108, (1985) 231,
  232 (photo)
Genoa Conference (1922), 13
German Democratic Republic (GDR). *See* East
  Germany
Germany
  aggression 1930s, 16, 17
  Anti-Comintern Pact (1937), 16
  division of, 73–75, 74 (map)
  Genoa Conference and, 13
  Helsinki Accords and, 168
  Locarno Treaties (1925), 14
  Nazi-Soviet Pact and, 19
  Nuremberg trials, 55–56
  post–Cold War conditions in, 262, 274
  post–World War I borders of, 9 (map)
  post–World War II governance of, 60–61,
    108–111
  Potsdam Agreement (1945) and, 46
  reunification of, 243–247
  Rome-Berlin Axis (1936), 16
  Soviet Union and, 13, 14, 15, 19, 31, 33
  Tehran Conference (1943) and, 36
  Versailles Treaty (1919) and, 10
  war crimes of, 43–44
  in World War I, 7, 8
  in World War II, 19, 21, 22, 37
  Yalta agreements and, 42
  See also East Germany; West Germany;
    Berlin; Berlin Airlift; Berlin Blockade;
    Berlin Wall
Glasnost, 230–231
Global culture
  advances in information technology,
    261–262
  antiwar movements, 129
  East-West competition and, 91
  1950s, 91–93

1960s youth revolts, 144
1980s peace movements, 205
in postwar Eastern Europe, 138
See also titles of films and books
Global warming, 262
Globalization, 261, 273
Gomułka, Władysław, 70, 98
Gorbachev, Mikhail
arms talks and, 231–234, 232 (photo), 236
on Brezhnev doctrine, 235–236
call to Sakharov, 233
coup in USSR and, 249–250
on East Germans' appeal for democracy, 240
election of, 225
farewell address, 253–254
glasnost policy of, 231
on Kosovo issue, 279
Nobel Peace Prize awarded to, 242
perestroika policy of, 230–231
as Soviet leader, 230–231, 242
at UN General Assembly, 235
visit to China, 239
Grand Alliance
about, 27
decisions on Germany, 45, 46
origins of, 28–33
postwar dissolution of, 54–55, 73
rivalries among partners in, 33–35, 37–40
war casualties, 43–44
See also Britain; Soviet Union; United States; Tehran Conference; Yalta Conference; Potsdam Conference
The Grand Illusion (film), 16
Great Britain. *See* Britain
Great Game, 1–2, 188
Greece, 42, 59 (map), 61, 62
Green Revolution, 123
Grenada, US invasion of, 214–216, 215 (map)
Gromyko, Andrei, 60, 141, 169, 230
Guatemala, 95, 180, 214, 272

Haig, Alexander, 212
Havel, Václav, 241
Helsinki Accords (1975)
decisions in favor of USSR, 175
human rights provisions of, 168–169, 177, 178, 181, 198
rights of sovereign states in, 245
Soviet violations of, 237
Heng Samrin, 219

Hitler, Adolf, 13, 31, 32–33
Ho Chi Minh, 79
Holbrooke, Richard, 277
Honecker, Erich, 155, 239–240
Hopkins, Harry, 29
Human rights
Carter and, 178–181
Gorbachev's proposals on, 233–234, 235–236
Helsinki Accords and, 168–169, 181, 198
humanitarian movements, 93, 141–144
Reagan's policies on, 212–213
Third World interpretation of, 96, 143, 144
UN defense of, 65–68
Hungarian Revolution, 98–100, 99 (photo), 102
Hungary
peace treaty after World War II, 62
Polish unrest and, 199
postwar communist control of, 68
Potsdam agreements and, 47
Red Army invasion of, 38
Revolution in, 98–99, 99 (photo), 100, 102
Soviet support of constitutional changes in, 238–241
transfer of Germans from, 46
US policy on transition of, 242–243
Yalta agreements and, 43
Husák, Gustáv, 241
Hussein, Saddam, 221–223, 246, 263, 270, 284
Hussein (king of Jordan), 132, 160, 161

Independence for Colonial Peoples, UN Declaration on (1960), 143
India, 62, 64–65, 65, 65 (map), 95, 162–163, 260
Indonesia, 95, 124
Indo-Pakistani War (1971), 162–163
Intercontinental Ballistic Missile (ICBM), 105
Intermediate-Range Nuclear Forces (INF), 212, 234
International Bank for Reconstruction and Development (later World Bank), 39
See also World Bank
International Conference on Human Rights (1968), 143–144
International Criminal Court, 264, 279
International Human Rights Year (1968), 143–144
International League for Human Rights, 177
International Monetary Fund (IMF), 39, 90, 273

Iran
    Bush doctrine and, 284
    defeat of pro-German government in, 30
    Khrushchev's courtship of, 95
    revolution in, 188, 190–193, 192 (photo)
    Soviet delay in withdrawal from, 59–60
    US coup in, 95
    US relations with, 179–180
Iran-Iraq War (1980–1988), 221–223, 264
Iraq, 101, 191, 284, 285
Iron Curtain, 58, 91–93, 107, 115, 137
Islam
    post–Cold War threats by militants, 263
Israel
    Arab-Israeli War (1967), 131–137, 133 (map)
    declaration of independence, 64
    Egyptian-Israeli peace treaty (1979),
        188–190
    establishment of, 66 (map)
    Israeli-Egyptian conflict (1967–1970),
        159–160
    Israeli-Palestinian conflict, 221, 223–224,
        269–272
    October War (1973), 165–168
    Oslo Accords (1993), 269–272
    peace treaty with Jordan (1994), 270
    role in Suez Crisis, 101, 102, 103 (map), 104
    support of Soviet Jewry campaign, 176–177
Italy
    fascist seizure of power in, 13
    invasion of Ethiopia, 16
    peace treaty with Allies (1947), 62
    postwar governance of, 61
    Potsdam agreements and, 46–47
    Rome-Berlin Axis, 16
    US aid to, 70
    US position on Afghanistan and, 196
    World War II and, 22

Jackson-Vanik Amendment, 167, 177
Japan
    aggression in 1930s, 15
    acquisition of German colonies after World
        War I, 10
    atomic bomb dropped on, 47–48
    China and, 16, 33, 77, 156, 265
    economic revival, 124, 229
    North Korea and, 265, 267
    Pearl Harbor attack by, 30
    Potsdam agreements and, 47
    revelation of war crimes by, 44

Soviet Union and, 19, 31, 45, 47, 48, 57, 77,
    231
    surrender of, 48
    United States and, 57, 76, 83, 94
    World War II and, 30, 31, 33
    Yalta agreements and, 42–43
Jaruzelski, Wojciech, 206–207, 238
Jews
    Brandt's acknowledgment of Nazi crimes
        against, 154
    establishment of Israel, 64, 66 (map)
    human rights protests, 176
    mass emigration from Poland, 136
    Nazi crimes against, 15, 22, 32
    post–Cold War emigration of, 274
    Soviet Union and, 136, 176, 274
Jiāng Zémín, 253
John Paul II (pope), 198, 237
Johnson, Lyndon B.
    Arab-Israeli War (1967) and, 132, 136–137
    Eastern Europe and, 138, 141,
    Soviet Union and, 134, 141
    Vietnam War, 126, 128, 129, 131, 163
Jordan
    Arab-Israeli War (1967) and, 131, 132
    British interests in, 101
    civil war in, 160
    division of Palestine and, 64
    peace treaty with Israel (1994), 271
    Syrian invasion of, 161–162

KAL 007 incident (1983), 209–211, 210 (map)
Kampuchea. *See* Cambodia
Karadžić, Radovan, 277
Karmal, Babrak, 194
Karzai, Hamid, 284
Kennan, George, 58–59, 62–63, 79
Kennedy, John Fitzgerald, 111, 115 (photo),
    115–116
Kennedy, Paul, 229
Keynes, John Maynard, 10, 39–40
Khmer Rouge regime, 219
Khomeini, Ruhollah, 191–193, 192 (photo)
Khrushchev, Nikita
    Berlin crisis, (1958) 108–110, 111, (1961) 113
    Cold War legacy of, 116
    criticisms of Stalin, 98
    Cuba and, 112, 113–114
    doctrine of peaceful coexistence, 98, 100,
        107–108, 125
    intervention in Hungary, 98, 99

Khrushchev thaw, 138
nuclear program, 105, 110
People's Republic of China and, 100, 110, 125
Poland and, 98
as Soviet leader, 92, 98, 111
Suez crisis and, 101, 102, 103
Third World policies, 95
United States and, 109 (photo), 110, 112, 113
Yugoslavia and, 99, 100
Kiesinger, Kurt-Georg, 138
Kim Il Sung, 79, 266
Kim Jong Il, 266
King, Martin Luther, 143
Kissinger, Henry
defense of US human rights policies, 175–176
diplomatic policies in Africa, 183
Eastern Europe proposals of, 242
Helsinki Accords and, 169
Indo-Pakistani War (1971) and, 162, 163
October War (1973) and, 165–167
role in détente, 149, 174
SALT talks and, 152
Vietnam War and, 163, 164
visit to China, 157–159, 162
Kohl, Helmut, 244, 245, 247, 250, 280
Korea, 57
See also North Korea; South Korea
Korean War, 78–84, 80 (map)
Kosovo, 278–280
Kosygin, Aleksei, 130, 132, 134, 136–137
Kosygin Reforms, 123–124
Krenz, Egon, 240
Kyoto Protocol (1997), 262

Laos, 111, 163
Latin America, 143–144, 260
See also Central America; South America
Latvia, 11, 19, 248
See also Baltic States
League of Arab States. See Arab League
League of Nations
anti-Bolshevik refugees and, 11
creation of, 8, 10
failure to resist fascist aggression, 16
Japanese invasion of Manchuria and, 15
as predecessor of UN, 40
Soviet attack on Finland and, 20
Lebanon, 189, 221, 223–225
Lend-Lease program, 21–22, 31–32, 33, 45

Lenin, Vladimir, 6–7, 10–11, 12 (photo), 13, 98
Libya, 61, 205
Lithuania, 11, 19, 248
See also Baltic States
Litvinov, Maxim, 19
Lloyd George, David, 7, 13
Locarno Treaties (1925), 16
London foreign ministers meeting (1947), 68
Lumumba, Patrice, 111, 113

Maastricht Treaty (1992), 280
MacArthur, Douglas, 81
Macmillan, Harold, 107
Madrid Conference on the Middle East (1991), 252, 269, 270, 272
Major, John, 250
Malta summit meetings (1990), 243, 244
Manchuria, 15, 16, 48, 57
Mandela, Nelson, 268
Manhattan Project, 34
Mao Zedong
establishment of PRC as communist power, 64, 75, 76–79
North Vietnam and, 130–131
role in Korean War, 81–82
Soviet Union and, 77, 100, 116, 125, 135, 140, 199
United States and, 77–79, 130–131, 156 (photo), 156–159
US-Soviet relations and, 150
World War II and, 30
Marshall, George, 62–63
Marshall Plan, 63–64, 73, 90, 106
Marxism, 6–7, 34, 75, 142
Mazowiecki, Tadeusz, 238
McNamara, Robert, 115 (photo), 128
Mein Kampf (Hitler), 15
Meir, Golda, 160, 161, 166
Middle East
Arab-Israeli War (1967), 131–137, 133 (map)
Egyptian-Israeli peace treaty (1979), 188–190, 223
Israeli-Egyptian conflict (1967–1970), 159–160
Israeli-Palestinian conflict, 269–272
Madrid Conference (1991), 269–270
October War (1973), 164–168
oil boycott against the West, (1956) 103–104, (1967) 134, (1973) 167
Oslo Accords (1993), 270–271

Middle East *(continued)*
  postwar decolonization in, 64–68, 95–96
  Suez Crisis, 100–105
  US-Soviet rivalry in, 221–225, 222 (map), 249
  See also names of specific countries
Mikołajczyk, Stanisław, 38
Milošević, Slobodan, 275, 278–279
Mitterrand, François, 207, 250, 280
Mladić, Ratko, 277
Mollet, Guy, 101, 102, 107
Molotov, Vyacheslav, 19, 45, 56, 63
Molotov-Ribbentrop Pact (1939). *See* Nazi-Soviet Pact
Moscow Conference of Foreign Ministers (1943), 35, 55, 56–57
Moscow Helsinki Watch Group, 177, 178–179
"Moscow Nights" (song), 93
Moscow Treaty (1970), 154
Mozambican National Resistance (RENAMO), 220
Mozambique, 220, 221
Mujahideen, 193, 197 (photo), 204
Munich Conference (1938), 3, 17, 18, 34, 41, 68, 72, 141
Muslims. *See* Islam
Mussolini, Benito, 19, 22, 33

Nagy, Imre, 98, 99
Namibia, 183, 206, 220, 268
Nasser, Gamal Abdel, 100–102, 104, 131–132, 134, 160
National Union for the Total Independence of Angola (UNITA), 183, 220
Nationalism, 262, 263
  Arab, 104, 191,
  in Eastern Europe, 2, 70, 237, 263–264
  economic, 39
  East German, 237
  in Japan, 15
  in Russia, 279
  in Soviet Union, 176, 229, 249
  US cautions against "suicidal," 249
  West German, 73, 244
Nationalist China, 76, 79, 81, 83, 100, 156, 157, 158, 159, 218, 265
NATO. *See* North Atlantic Treaty Organization
Nazi Germany. *See* Germany
Nazi war crimes. *See* Jews; Nuremberg trials
Nazi-Soviet Pact (1939), 19, 56, 248
Nehru, Jawaharal, 97 (photo)

Netanyahu, Benjamin, 271
Neutrality Acts (US), 16
New York Times, 236
Nicaragua, 180 (photo), 180, 205, 214, 216, 272
Nixon, Richard
  as architect of détente, 149–150
  arms limitation talks and, 151–153
  Brezhnev's visit to US and, 164–165, 165 (photo)
  human rights policies of, 176
  Indo-Pakistani War (1971) and, 162–163
  Middle East conflict and, 160–162, 163–165, 167
  as US president, 129, 157, 164, 177
  Vietnam War and, 129, 149, 151, 157, 163–164
  visit to China, 152, 156 (photo), 157–158
  visit to Soviet Union, 152–153
  Watergate, 165
Nixon doctrine, 159
Nonalignment, 94, 96, 100
Non-Proliferation Treaty (NPT). *See* Nuclear Non-Proliferation Treaty
Nontraditional agricultural exports (NTAEs), 273
Noriega, Manuel, 273
North Africa, 31–32, 33, 61, 95–96
  See also names of specific countries
North Atlantic Treaty Organization (NATO)
  Arab-Israeli War (1967) and, 135
  arms-limitation talks and, 205
  effect of Korean War on, 83
  peacekeeping role of, 278–279
  recognition of reunified Germany, 244, 245, 247
  role in Bosnian War, 276–279
  role in Falklands War, 218
  Soviet invasion of Czechoslovakia and, 137
  support for US War on Terror, 284
North Korea, 79–84, 80 (map), 260, 266–267, 284
North Vietnam, 125–131, 126 (map), 152, 158, 163–164
Novotný, Antonín, 139
NSC-68, 79
Nuclear arms race
  acceleration of, 105–106
  Britain as nuclear power, 107
  China as nuclear power, 115
  Cuban missile crisis and, 113–115, 125
  France as nuclear power, 103, 115

diminished West European confidence in
US protection, 125
end of, 249
escalation during Korean War, 83, 84
fear of nuclear confrontation, 211–212
fear of World War III, 53
first Soviet atomic bomb, 75–76
Geneva and Reykjavik talks, 231–234, 236
global nuclear disarmament movement,
106, 185, 205, 208 (photo)
India's entry into, 163
neutron bomb, 185
Non-Proliferation Treaty, 150–151, 246
North Korea's entry into, 266–267
Pakistan's entry into, 163
post–Cold War negotiations, 265
Reagan's expansion of, 205
SALT treaties, 151–152, 164, 185–187, 196
SDI proposal, 207–209
US-Soviet talks, 150–153
Nuclear Non-Proliferation Treaty (1968),
150–151, 246
Nuclear Test Ban Treaty (1963), 115
Nuclear weapons, 2, 34, 47–48, 57, 102, 185–186
Nuremberg trials, 55–56, 67, 264

OAS. *See* Organization of American States
October War (1973), 164–168, 188
Oil shortages, 103–104, 134, 167
On the Beach (Shute), 105
Open Skies proposal, 108
Operation Bagration, 37
Operation Enduring Freedom, 284
Operation Kavkaz, 160
Operation Musketeer, 102
Organization of American States (OAS), 65, 216
Organization of Security and Cooperation in
Europe (OSCE), 279
Oslo Accords (1993), 269–272
Ostpolitik, 153–156, 174–175

Pahlavi, Muhammad Reza, 95, 179–180, 190,
191
Pakistan, 64–65, 65 (map), 162–163, 282
Palestine
Arab-Israeli Wars and, 131–132, 134–135,
British withdrawal from, 62
division of, 66 (map)
refugee problem, 64, 134
Palestine Liberation Organization (PLO), 131,
206, 269–272

Palestinians
Arab League and, 131, 134
Egypt and, 132, 188
Egyptian-Israeli Peace Treaty (1979) and,
190
human rights issues (West Bank and Gaza),
143
Intifada, 269–271, 271–272
Israeli-Palestinian conflict, 221, 223–224,
269–272
in Jordan, 160–161
in Lebanon, 224
Oslo Accords, 270–271
Syria and, 131
violence and, 135, 190
USSR and, 225, 260
Paris summit (1960), 110–111
Pasternak, Boris, 92
People's Republic of Angola. *See* Angola
People's Republic of China (PRC)
in Africa, 267
Algeria and, 96
Bandung Conference (1955) and, 96
Cambodian conflict and, 219–220, 252
civil war in, 61, 64
as communist power, 75, 76–79, 253
Cultural Revolution, 130, 156, 158
domino theory of, 82
Egypt and, 101
Great Leap Forward, 125, 130, 156
Hong Kong, return of, 266
Iran-Iraq War, 223
Korean War, 83–84
militant Islamic opposition and, 263
North Korea and, 266, 267
North Vietnam and, 125, 130–131, 158, 164
nuclear arms race and, 115, 125, 186
Pakistan and, 162
Poland and, 207
post–Cold War economic development in,
265–266
post-Mao political changes in, 218, 229,
230
Soviet Union and, 77, 83, 96, 98, 125, 140,
150, 157, 158–159,165, 196, 199, 219,
252–253, 266, 283, 284, 292
Third World countries and, 96
Tiananmen Square massacre, 238 (photo),
239, 248
United Nations and, 40, 79, 81, 158, 159,
160, 283

People's Republic of China (PRC) *(continued)*
    United States and, 37, 57, 61, 76–77, 83, 152,
        156 (photo), 156–159, 181, 184, 188, 196,
        199, 205, 219, 266, 283, 284, 292
    US-Soviet relations and, 57, 150, 206,
        218–219
    Vietnam and, 219, 265
    Vietnam Wars and, 95, 124, 125,128–129,
        130–131, 164
    in World War II, 16, 30, 43
People's Republic of Kampuchea (PRK). *See*
    Cambodia
Perestroika, 230–231, 248
Poland
    China and, 207
    communist control of, 68, 197, 206
    French alliance system after World War I
        and, 16, 18
    Grand Alliance discussions over future
        borders and government, 34,36, 38, 42,
        43, 44–46
    resurrected after World War I, 8, 9 (map)
    Solidarność (Solidarity) in, 3, 198–199, 206,
        238, 239
    Soviet Union and, 11, 14, 16, 17, 18, 19, 21,
        30, 34, 35, 42, 44, 63, 75, 98, 238, 239,
        240, 248
    Soviet wartime atrocities in, 21, 34, 56, 197,
        242
    United States and, 61, 206, 242–243
    Warsaw Uprising (1944), 37–38
    West Germany and, 137, 154, 244, 246
    withdrawal from Marshall Plan, 63
    World War II and, 19–20, 21, 30, 32, 35
    See also Tehran; Yalta; Potsdam
Polish Committee of National Liberation
    (PCNL), 38, 42
Pompidou, Georges, 174
Popular Front, 15–19, 17
Potsdam Conference (1945), 45–47, 55
Prague coup (1948), 68
Prague Spring (1968), 139–141, 143
Putin, Vladimir, 283

Quadripartite Pact (1971), 155, 168

Rabin, Yitzhak, 270, 271
Radio Free Europe, 91
Rapacki plan, 108
Reagan, Ronald
    and Gorbachev, 231–236, 232 (photo)

human rights policies of, 212–213
    KAL 007 incident and, 211
    SDI proposal of, 207–209
    as US president, 199, 225
    US-Soviet relations and, 199, 205–206, 212
    visit to Beijing, 219
    visit to Moscow, 235
Reagan doctrine, 204–205
Red Army
    Battle of Stalingrad and, 32
    Grand Alliance support of, 29
    invasion of Manchuria, 48
    military successes of, 33
    Nazi invasion of Soviet Union and, 22, 23
    in Poland, 11, 35, 37–38
    revelation of war crimes by, 43–44
    victories in East Central and Southern
        Europe, 38
    See also Soviet Union
Red Scare, 11
Reed, John, 10
Republic of China. *See* Nationalist China
Republic of Korea (ROK). *See* South Korea
Reykjavik summit (1986), 232–233
Rhee, Syngman, 83
Rio Conference (1992), 262
Rio Pact (1947), 65
The Rise and Fall of the Great Powers (Paul
    Kennedy), 229
ROK (Republic of Korea). *See* South Korea
Romania
    communist coup (1945), 43
    French alliance system after World War I
        and, 16, 18
    Nazi-Soviet Pact and, 19
    peace treaty (1947), 62
    Polish unrest and, 199
    Soviet Union and, 21, 30, 38
    violence in transformation of (1989), 241
    Warsaw Pact ties severed, 135
    See also Yalta; Potsdam
Rome Statute (1998), 264
Rome-Berlin Axis (1936), 16
Roosevelt, Eleanor, 67
Roosevelt, Franklin Delano, 29–33, 39–40,
    44
Russia
    Bolshevik regime in, 10–12
    Bolshevik Revolution, 5–7
    Bosnian War and, 276–277
    formation of USSR, 13

Genoa Conference and, 13
Great Game with Britain, 1–2, 188
independence of, 248, 250–252
invasion of Chechnya, 263
Kosovo War and, 279
post–World War I borders of, 8–10, 9 (map)
in World War I, 3, 7
See also Soviet Union
Russian Revolution, 5–8
Rwanda, 264, 267

Sadat, Anwar, 166, 188–190, 189, 190 (photo)
Sakharov, Andrei, 178, 213, 233
SALT I Treaty, 151–152, 164
SALT II Treaty, 185–187, 196
Sandinistas, 180, 180 (photo), 214
Saudi Arabia, 104, 131, 181, 191, 222 (map), 263, 282
Schengen Agreement (1985), 280
Schmidt, Helmut, 175, 185, 207
Schultz, George, 209, 211, 213, 237
Schumacher, E. F., 262
September 11 terrorist attacks, 283–284
Serbia, 275–280
Sharansky, Natan, 233
Sharon, Ariel, 272
Shevardnadze, Eduard, 231, 248
Shute, Nevil, 105
Sihanouk, Norodom, 219
Silent Spring (Carson), 262
"Silent Spring," threat of, 123
Single European Act (1986), 280
Small is Beautiful (Schumacher), 262
Social Democratic Party (SDP), 153
Solidarność (Solidarity), 197–199, 206–207
Solzhenitsyn, Aleksandr, 205, 237
Somalia, 181, 184, 267
South Africa, 179, 183, 267–269
South America, 180, 214–218, 217 (map), 273
See also names of specific countries
South Korea, 79–84, 80 (map), 266
South Vietnam, 125–130, 126 (map), 174–175
Southeast Asia, 97, 124–131
See also names of specific countries
Southeast Asia Treaty Organization (SEATO), 97
Southwest Africa. *See* Namibia
Southwest Africa People's Organization (SWAPO), 220
Soviet Union
Afghanistan, invasion of, 193–197, 195 (map), 197 (photo)

in Africa, 181–184
arms limitation talks, 150–153, 231–234, 236
in Asia, 218–220
Basic Agreement with US, 153, 167
Berlin Crisis (1948), 71–72, (1958) 108–110, 111, (1961) 113
Berlin Wall, 113, 240
Brezhnev doctrine, 140, 167, 204, 235, 237, 243
Britain and, 14, 18, 58
Cambodian conflict and, 219–220
Central America and, 213–214
collapse of, 247–254, 251 (map), 250–251
collective security policies of, 17–18
Czechoslovakia and, 17–18, 68, 139, 140–141
Cuba and, 112–115, 161, 183, 184, 187, 197, 231, 252, 268, 272
Cuban Missile crisis, 113–115
détente, 149–150, 199–200
domino theory of, 82, 150, 169, 82
East Germany and, 243–244
Eastern Europe and, 234–235, 237–240, 242–243
economic contraction 1960s, 123, 124
economic contraction 1980s, 229
Egypt and, 95, 101, 102, 131–132, 135, 136, 160, 166, 189
Falklands War and, 218
Finland and, 11, 19, 20, 68, 98
Five Year Plan, 14, 28
formation of, 13
France and, 14, 15–16, 18, 81, 83, 137
German question and, 60–61, 68, 70, 73–75
German reunification and, 244–247
Germany and, 14, 15, 19, 21, 22–23
Grand Alliance, role in, 22, 28–30, 31–32, 35–38, 40–43, 45
Helsinki Accords and, 168–169, 175
human rights and, 67, 142–144, 235
Hungarian Revolution and, 99–100
Indo-Pakistani War (1971) and, 162–163
Iranian revolution and, 191–193
Iran crisis (1946) and, 59–60
Iran-Iraq War (1980–1988) and, 223
Israel and, 64, 136, 176, 252
KAL 007 incident, 209–211
Korean War and, 79, 81–83, 84
League of Nations and, 20
Lend-Lease program and, 33, 45

Marshall Plan and, 63–64
Middle East wars and, (1948) 64, (1956)
    101–103, (1967) 131–132, 135–136,
    (1967–1970) 160, (1973) 165–168, (1982)
    225
Nazi-Soviet Pact, 19
nonintervention principles of, 175–176,
    177, 235
North Vietnam and, 125, 130, 152, 163,
    164, 235
nuclear arms race and, 75–76, 105–106,
    185–189, 211–212, 225
Palestinians and, 260
People's Republic of China and, 77, 125,
    130, 158–159, 239
perestroika and glasnost, 230–231, 248
Poland and, 20, 21, 37–38, 42, 96, 198
purges, 14, 17, 18
South Africa and, 221
Spanish Civil War, intervention in, 17
Suez Crisis and, 101–103
Summit meetings. *See* Tehran; Yalta;
    Potsdam; Geneva; Camp David; Paris;
    Vienna; Vladivostok; Reyjkavik; Malta
Syria and, 131, 135, 136, 161, 166, 223, 224,
    225, 231
in Third World countries, 94–95, 159
Truman doctrine and, 62–63
United Nations and, 40
United States and, 15, 41 (photo), 54–55,
    58–59, 62–63, 109 (photo), 109–110,
    130, 132, 144, 149, 151–1543, 159, 160,
    161, 163–166, 165 (photo), 167, 168, 175,
    177–179, 181, 184, 185–187, 209, 211,
    229–230, 232 (photo) 234, 243, 244, 246,
    252, 253, 291
West Germany and, 73–74, 94, 141, 153,
    154, 155, 196
World War II and, 22, 32, 54
Yugoslavia and, 21, 38, 61, 70, 98
See also Russia; Lenin; Stalin; Khrushchev;
    Brezhnev; Andropov; Chernenko;
    Gorbachev; Yeltsin
Space programs, 144
Spain, 16, 17
Sputnik, 105
SS-20 missiles, 185, 187
Stalin, Joseph
    anti-West propaganda of, 91
    Churchill's percentage agreement and,
        38–38, 40

crimes denounced by Khrushchev, 98
dissolution of Comintern, 34–35
Five-Year Plan, 14, 28
historians' interpretations of intentions in
    Czechoslovakia, 17–18
influence on Mao, 77, 78
postwar diplomacy of, 55
purges of, 14, 17, 18
rebuff of US mediation offer during Finnish
    War, 20
response to Atlantic Charter, 30–32
response to nuclear attacks on Japan, 48
response to Roosevelt's Unconditional
    Surrender doctrine, 33
war crimes of, 21
"Star Wars." *See* Strategic Defense Initiative
    (SDI)
Stockholm Conference (1972), 262
Strategic Arms Limitation Treaties. *See* SALT I
    Treaty; SALT II Treaty
Strategic Arms Reduction Treaty (START),
    212, 232, 249
Strategic Defense Initiative (SDI), 207–209, 231,
    232, 233, 234
Suez Canal, 101–102
Suez Crisis, 100–105, 103 (map), 107
Superpowers, post-WWII. *See* Soviet Union;
    United States
Surface-to-Air missile (SAM), 160
Surveillance. *See* Espionage
Syria, 131–132, 135–136, 161, 165–168, 189

Taiwan. *See* Nationalist China
Taliban regime, 282–284
Technological innovations, 261–262
Tehran Conference (1943), 35–38, 55, 75
Ten Days That Shook the World (Reed), 10
Ten-Point program, 244
Tet offensive (1968), 129
Thant, U., 132
Thatcher, Margaret, 196, 207, 216, 218, 231, 247
Thiệu, Nguyễn Văn, 128–129
Things Fall Apart (Achebe), 92
Third Reich. *See* Germany
Third World countries
    human rights issues in, 143–144
    1960s economic structure of, 123, 124
    Reagan's anti-Soviet campaign and,
        204–206
    Superpower rivalry in, 93–98, 159
    Vietnam War and, 124–131

Tiananmen Square massacre, 238 (photo), 238, 248

The Tin Drum (Grass), 92

Tito, Josip Broz, 70, 98, 100, 262, 274

Tonkin Gulf Resolution (1964), 128

Treaty of Brest Litovsk (1918), 11

Treaty of Rapallo (1922), 13, 154

Treaty of Rome (1957), 107

Treaty of Versailles (1919), 10, 15, 16

Treaty on German Unity (1990), 246–247

Triple Entente, 5–6, 18

Trotsky, Leon, 11

Truman, Harry, 44–45, 54–55, 58, 64, 79

Truman Doctrine, 62–64

Turkey, 37, 43, 59 (map), 62, 114

"Two Thousand Words" (Vaculik), 139

U-2 Incident (1960), 108, 110

"Ugly American" stereotype, 95

Ukraine, 11, 43, 248, 249, 250, 251 (map), 252, 265

Ulbricht, Walter, 155

Union of Soviet Socialist Republics (USSR). *See* Soviet Union

United Nations (UN)
  anti-terrorist resolution, 283
  Arab-Israeli War (1967) and, 132
  Bandung Conference (1955) and, 96
  Bosnian War and, 276–277
  Commission on Atomic Energy, 57
  Commission on Human Rights, 67, 142–144
  Falklands War and, 216
  First Development Decade, 123
  founding of, 35, 40, 44, 45, 46
  humanitarian role of, 64, 65–68, 93, 267, 273
  International Atomic Energy Administration, 151
  Korean War and, 81–83
  peacekeeping role of, 188, 216, 264, 278
  Resolution 242, 134, 189
  Roosevelt's proposals for, 36
  seating of China, 77, 79, 158, 159, 160
  seating of East Germany, 155
  seating of West Germany, 155
  Stockholm Conference (1972), 262
  Suez Crisis and, 102, 104, 216
  United Nations Emergency Force, 132
  Universal Declaration of Human Rights (UDHR) (1948), 67–68, 96, 143–144, 189
  US Invasion of Grenada and, 216
  vetoes by permanent Security Council

members, 40, 43, 58, 81, 102, 216, 264, 283, 292

United Nations Emergency Force (UNEF), 132

United Nations Protection Force (UNPROFOR), 276

United States
  ABM treaty and, 152–153
  in Africa, 181–184, 183–184
  Algeria and, 96
  anticolonialism of, 35, 36, 62, 125
  anticommunism of, 94, 260
  Arab states and, 104–105
  Arab-Israeli War (1967) and, 132, 134, 135–137
  Argentina and, 43, 180, 216, 273
  arms talks, 150–153, 231–234, 232 (photo), 236
  Asia and, 218–220
  Basic Agreement with USSR, 153, 167
  Berlin Airlift, 71–72
  Berlin Crisis and, (1948) 70–73, (1958) 108–110, 111, (1961) 113
  Berlin Wall and, 113, 114, 116
  Bosnian War and, 276–278
  Britain and, 15, 17, 21–22, 29, 36, 39, 43, 47, 58, 60, 61, 62, 103–105, 113, 183, 199, 216, 218
  Bush doctrine, 284
  Cambodia and, 157, 160, 163, 205, 219–220, 235, 252
  Camp David talks (1959), 109 (photo), 110, (1978) 189, (2000) 271–272
  Carter doctrine, 195
  Central America and, 95, 205, 213–218, 215 (map), 249, 272–273
  Chile and, 165, 176, 179, 180, 212, 273
  Clinton's vision of global governance, 281–282
  Cuba and, 112, 115, 161, 180, 184, 187, 188, 214–216, 215 (map), 221, 252, 268, 272
  Cuban missile crisis, 113–115
  cultural propaganda, 91, 93
  in Depression era, 15, 16–17
  Dollar Diplomacy, 273
  domino theory of, 81, 97, 126, 150, 169
  Eastern Europe and, 32, 45, 58, 91, 93, 99, 138, 205, 237, 242–243, 260, 279
  Egypt and, 101, 102, 104, 134, 160, 161, 166, 189, 190
  Egyptian-Israeli conflict (1967–1970), 160–161

United States *(continued)*
  economic contraction 1960s, 123–124
  economic contraction 1980s, 229
  Eisenhower doctrine, 104
  end of Cold War and, 229–230
  espionage, 108, 110
  establishment of détente, 149–150
  expansion of ABM systems, 151, 152
  Falklands War and, 216
  foreign ministers' meetings, 35, 55, 56–57, 57–59, 68
  France and, 20, 70, 103, 109, 114, 137, 126, 157, 196, 199, 284
  German question and, 60–61
  global nuclear disarmament movement and, 106, 185, 205, 208 (photo)
  in Grand Alliance, 27–34
  Great Society, 126, 129
  Helsinki Accords and, 168–169, 175
  human rights movements and, 176, 177–178
  human rights policies, 67, 142–144, 175–176
  Hungarian Revolution and, 99–100
  India and, 162, 163, 283
  Indo-Pakistani War (1971) and, 162–163
  invasion of Grenada (1983), 215
  Iran and, 47, 57, 59–60, 95, 176, 179–180, 190–193, 222, 223, 233, 235, 284
  Iranian hostage crisis, 191–193
  Iran-Iraq War and, 222–223
  Iraq and, 223, 246, 248, 284
  isolationism of, 16–17
  Israel and, 64, 101, 104, 132, 134, 136–137, 160, 161, 165–167, 189, 196, 223, 270, 271, 272, 282
  KAL 007 incident, 211
  Kosovo War, 279–280
  Korean War, 81–84
  League of Nations and, 8, 29
  in Lebanon, 224–225
  Lend-Lease program, 21–22, 31–32, 33, 45
  Madrid Conference on the Middle East (1991), 269–270
  Marshall Plan, 63–64, 73, 90, 106
  in Middle East, 160–62, 164–168, 188, 221–225
  Middle East oil boycott and, 104, 134, 167
  Monroe Doctrine, 112
  Nationalist China and, 16–17, 33, 37, 42, 43, 57, 64, 76, 78, 79, 81, 83, 108, 157, 158, 218

NATO. *See* North Atlantic Treaty Organization
Nixon doctrine, 159
Neutrality Acts, 16
nonalignment and, 94, 96
North Atlantic Treaty Organization and, 72, 73, 81, 91–92, 96, 103, 106, 114, 116, 125, 136, 137, 167, 168, 185–187, 196, 204, 205, 207, 209, 213, 216, 232, 234, 244–245, 247, 276, 277, 278–280, 283, 284–285
North Korea and, 266–267
North Vietnam and, 125, 126, 127 (map), 128, 129, 152, 157, 163, 164, 205, 214, 220
nuclear arms race and, 75–76, 105–106, 150, 185–189, 211–212
nuclear attack on Japan, 47–48
October War (1973) and, 165, 165–168, 167
Operation Enduring Freedom, 284
Oslo Accords and, 269–272, 270
Pakistan and, 110, 150, 157, 162–163, 176, 196, 282, 284
"pactomania," 94
People's Republic of China and, 37, 57, 61, 76–77, 83, 152, 156 (photo), 156–159, 181, 184, 188, 196, 199, 205, 218–219, 266, 283, 284, 292
Poland and, 198–199, 206
post–World War II economic boom, 54
Reagan doctrine, 204
reunification of Germany and, 244, 247
rollback doctrine, 99, 243
Russia and, 250, 265, 267, 276–277, 277, 278, 279, 283, 284, 285
SALT talks and, 151–152, 186
South Africa and, 220–221
South America and, 65, 180, 216, 273
South Vietnam and, 97, 116, 124–125, 126, 127 (map), 128, 129
Soviet Union and, 15, 41 (photo), 54–55, 58–59, 62–63, 109 (photo), 109–110, 130, 132, 140–141, 144, 149, 151–154, 159, 160, 161, 163–166, 165 (photo), 167, 168, 175, 177–179, 181, 184, 185–187, 209, 211, 229–230, 232 (photo) 234, 243, 244, 246, 252, 253, 291
Suez Crisis and, 101–105
Summit meetings. *See* Tehran; Yalta; Potsdam; Geneva; Camp David; Paris; Vienna; Vladivostok; Reyjkavik; Malta

Syria and, 134
Taiwan and. *See* Nationalist China
targeted by Al Qaeda, 263, 282
in Third World countries, 93–98, 159
Treaty of Versailles (1919) and, 10
Truman doctrine, 62, 63, 64
U-2 reconnaissance flights, 110–111
United Nations and, 36, 40, 43, 60, 68, 79,
    81, 100, 102, 134, 142, 157, 158, 166, 188,
    216, 219, 283, 284
War on Terror, 283–285
World War I entry, 6
in World War II, 20, 22–23, 31,32, 33, 40,
    46–47
See also Vietnam War; Wilson; Roosevelt;
    Truman; Eisenhower; Kennedy; Johnson;
    Nixon; Carter; Reagan; Bush (G. H. W.);
    Clinton; Bush (G. W.)
Universal Declaration of Human Rights
    (UDHR), 67–68, 96, 143–144, 189
US Helsinki Watch Group, 178–179, 212–213
US Neutrality Acts, 16, 20
US War Powers Act, 279–280

Vance, Cyrus, 185
Vance-Owen Plan (1993), 276
"Velvet Divorce" in Czechoslovakia, 242
"Velvet Revolution" in Czechoslovakia, 241
Vienna meeting (1961), 112, 113
Viet Cong, 97, 126
Vietnam, 95–97, 205, 219, 235, 260
    See also North Vietnam; South Vietnam
Vietnam War, 124–131, 127 (map), 158,
    163–164, 164
V-E Day, 45, 48 (note), 73
V-J Day, 48
Vladivostok summit (1974), 186, 187
Voice of America, 91

Wałęsa, Lech, 198
Wallace, Henry, 59
War of Attrition (1967–1970), 160
War on Terror, 283–285
Warsaw Pact
    aid to North Vietnam, 130
    Eastern European withdrawal from,
        242
    Hungarian threat of withdrawal from, 98

invasion of Czechoslovakia, 139–141,
    140–141
military superiority of, 106
Romania severs ties with, 135
Washington Consensus, 273
Washington Naval Conference (1921–1922), 11
West Berlin, 70–72, 71 (photo), 74, 108,
    111–112, 154–155
West Germany
    Afghanistan and, 196
    Basic Treaty with East Germany, 155
    division of Europe and, 137–138
    economic conditions in, 153–154
    establishment of, 73–75, 74 (map)
    German reunification and, 244, 245–247
    Moscow Treaty and, 154
    oil boycott against, 134
    Ostpolitik, 153–156
    Polish unrest and, 199
    Soviet Union and, 73–74, 94, 141, 153, 154,
        155, 196
    takes part in war against Serbia, 279
    United States and, 72, 114, 153, 156, 185,
        186, 207, 244, 247
Western culture
    response to aftermath of WWI, 13
    response to Cold War, 92, 145, 205
Wilson, Woodrow, 7, 8, 29
Winter War (1939–40), 20
Wojtyła, Karol Józef. *See* John Paul II
Workers' Defense Committee (KOR), 198
World Bank, 90, 273
World Refugee Year (1959), 93
World Trade Organization (WTO), 266
World War I, 5–10
World War II, 19–23, 30, 39–40, 43–44, 48, 54
    See also Grand Alliance
World War III, fear of, 53

Yalta Conference (1945), 40–43, 44, 55, 77, 235
Yeltsin, Boris, 248, 250, 252, 278
Youth revolts of 1960s, 144
Yugoslavia, 38, 68, 70, 262, 264, 274–280, 275
    (map)

Zhdanov, A. A. [Andrei], 64
Zhōu Ēnlái, 78
Zimbabwe, 220

THE WORLD IN 2000

NUCLEAR WEAPONS OWNERSHIP STATES

NPT nuclear weapon states (China, France, Russia, UK, United States)

Non-NPT nuclear weapon states (India, North Korea, Pakistan)

Undeclared nuclear weapon states (Israel)

NATO nuclear weapons sharing states (Belgium, Germany, Netherlands, Italy, Turkey)

States formerly possesing nuclear weapons

Map 20. More than a decade after the end of the Cold War, the proliferation of nuclear weapons remained one of the world's major problems.